JAPANESE THEATER IN THE WORLD

Japanese Theater in the World

James R. Brandon
Andrew Gerstle
Goto Hajime
Gerhard Hackner
Hayashi Kazutoshi
Kishi Tetsuo
Laurence Kominz
Kusuhara-Saito Tomoko
Benito Ortolani
J. Thomas Rimer
Sakurai Hiroshi
Tanabe Saburosuke
Torigoe Bunzo
Günter Zobel
Gunhild Avitabile

Essays edited by Samuel Leiter

The Japan Foundation
Japan Society, Inc., New York
Museum Villa Stuck, Munich
In collaboration with the
Tsubouchi Memorial Theatre Museum,
Waseda University, Tokyo
1997

38/18617
2 LC

1-4-99

This catalogue is published in conjunction with the exhibition "Japanese Theater in the World" shown at the Japan Society, New York, from October 21, 1997, through February 1, 1998, and at the Museum Villa Stuck, Munich, Germany, from March 4 through May 24, 1998.

The exhibition in New York is co-organized by The Japan Foundation and Japan Society, Inc., in collaboration with the Tsubouchi Memorial Theatre Museum, Waseda University. At the Munich venue, it is co-organized by The Japan Foundation, Japan Society, Inc., and the Museum Villa Stuck, in collaboration with the Tsubouchi Memorial Theatre Museum, Waseda University.

This exhibition is supported in part by the Lila Acheson Wallace/Japan Society Fund, established at Community Funds, Inc. by the co-founder of Reader's Digest, The Ford Foundation, the National Endowment for the Arts, The Saison Foundation, Sony Corporation of America, and Friends of Japan Society Gallery. Air transportation is provided by Japan Airlines.

Managing editor: Erica Hamilton Weeder
Index: Kathleen M. Friello

Design/typography: Stefanie Krieg-Elliott
Computer imaging: Mark Green

Set in Weiss
Text paper: Diadem spezial gestrichen
Offset elementar chlorfrei
Printed and bound in Germany by the Benedict Press, Münsterschwarzach, in an edition of 3,000.

Exhibition design in New York: Art Clark
Installation in New York: Jeffrey Nemeth
Registration: Linda Powers

Cover and title-page illustration: "The Woman Without a Shadow," no. 1.33B; detail used on cover. Photo © Anne Kirchbach

NOTES TO THE READER:

Japanese names are printed in Japanese fashion with the family name first, except in the case of individuals who have chosen to adopt the Western system.

Citations in the essay endnotes refer to items listed in the relevant sections of the bibliography, to be found in the last part of the catalogue.

Suffixes of -ji and -dera (occasionally -dô, -in, and -an) indicate temple names. A long vowel in Japanese is indicated by a circumflex rather than a macron.

ERRATA

After all entries had been typeset, lender credit line corrections were received for section VIII (*shingeki*). The corrected lender credits are as follows:

No. 8.17. © Shochiku Co., Ltd.; in the collection of the Tsubouchi Memorial Theatre Museum, Waseda University

No. 8.25. © Bungaku-za; in the collection of the Tsubouchi Memorial Theatre Museum, Waseda University

No. 8.35. © Yume no Yûminsha (Noda • Map); in the collection of the Tsubouchi Memorial Theatre Museum, Waseda University

No. 8.42. © Shochiku Co., Ltd.; Matsumoto Kôshirô Office

No. 8.57. © Shochiku Co., Ltd.; Matsumoto Kôshirô Office

Also, the title of the play in the heading of no. 8.34 should be "Ninagawa Macbeth"; and the no. 8.44 photograph of the production of "Man of La Mancha" was taken in June 1995 at Aoyama Theater.

REPRODUCTION CREDITS

All photographs have been supplied by the owners of the works of art unless noted below. The name of a photographer whose work is displayed in the exhibition as an art object is cited in the relevant catalogue entry.

Julie Archer: no. 1.28
Shikosha Publishing Co., Ltd.: nos. 2/3.2, 3.43, 3.46, 3.47, 3.49, 3.50
Roman Szechther: nos. 1.10A-C, 1.21, 1.25, 1.26, 1.29, 1.30A-D, 3.8, 3.15, 3.21, 3.22, 3.23, 3.24, 3.39, 8.37, 9.11, 9,14B, 9,23A, 9.36/1, 9.36/9A, 9.36/10A, 9.37/1, 9.38/1
John Bigelow Taylor, The Newark Museum, Newark, NJ: no. 3.22A-B

CONTENTS

Catalogue Entries

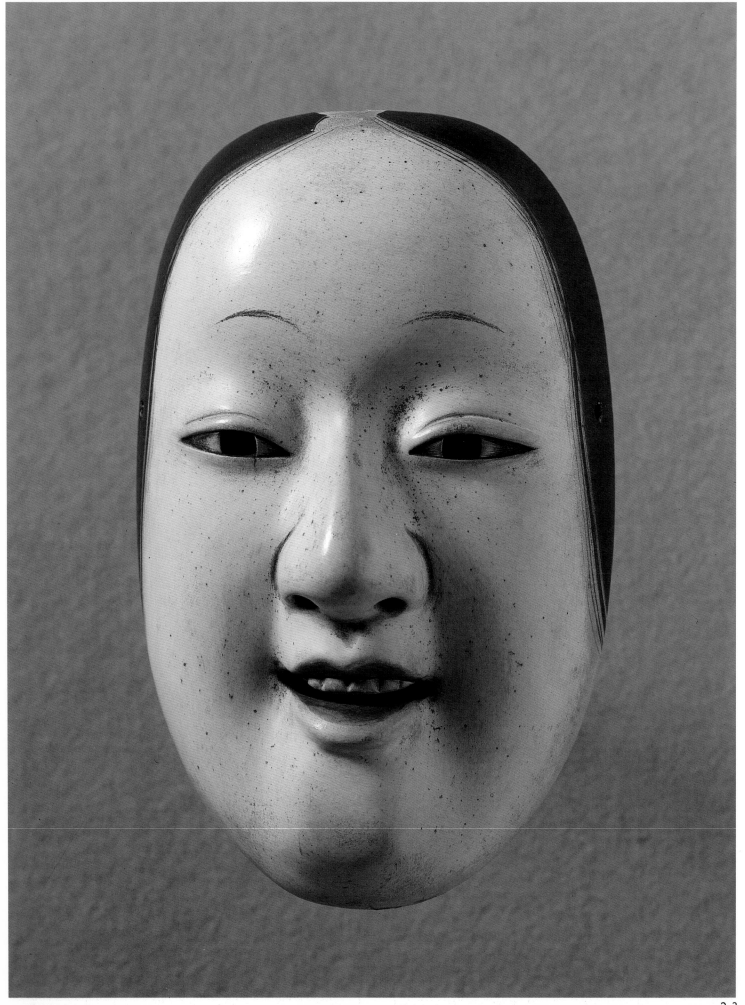

2.3

PLATE 1

INTRODUCTORY REMARKS AND ACKNOWLEDGMENTS

In 1993, when I first met with Benito Ortolani, our special advisor and author of two of the essays in this catalogue, to present to him my ambitious plans for an exhibition about Japanese theater, he closed our conversation with a famous Italian saying: *"Se sono rose, fioriranno"* (If these [what you are planting] are [in fact] roses, they will blossom). Now, four years later, the roses are blossoming. An exhibition with more then seven hundred objects can be put together, fulfilling a dream I dreamt when writing my thesis *The Masks of Bugaku: Profane Japanese Dance Masks of the Heian and Kamakura Periods* (1972).

For the first time, an exhibition covering the whole range of Japanese theater and its history is being presented to the public, not only of the United States, but also of the whole world. Never before has such an exhibition been presented, not even to the Japanese public. Therefore, this exhibition, in the enlarged spaces of the Japan Society in New York and also in the Museum Villa Stuck in Munich in 1988, can be called, without exaggeration, "the largest exhibition of the century to focus on Japanese theater"– as Professor Torigoe Bunzô, the Japanese chief curator, has formulated it in his foreword.

Japanese theater fulfills a unique role in world performing arts. It not only presents itself with a continuity of 1500 years of preserved theater forms, but also as a heaven for those creating avant-garde theater, which although being the most innovative of this second half of the 20th century, remains deeply rooted in Japan's past.

In this endless stream, theatrical forms have been created, preserved, and transmitted from generation to generation until our time. In other parts of the world, performance forms were extinguished and forgotten, and efforts had to be made to reconstruct them in modern times. When we are invited to a present-day representation of Greek and Roman theater, we are not watching a presentation transmitted over the generations, but rather a modern re-creation.

In Japan, generation after generation of actors, musicians, and dancers transmitted their knowledge to the next generation without significant interruption. The only major attempt at reconstructing a no longer existing theater form in our time has been that undertaken for *gigaku*, extinguished since early medieval times. This attempt has been made at several of the old Buddhist temples, such as the Tôdai-ji or the Taima-dera in Nara, where *gigaku* actually was performed during the time of its flourishing.

Japanese folk theater (*minzoku geinô;* section II) combines the ancient roots of Japan's indigenous pre-Buddhist performances with those of early Buddhism, as well as with shamanistic elements of Asia during the first millenium. Undoubtedly, such continental Asian influences can also be recognized in *bugaku*

and *gyôdô* (section III). Separated by sea from mainland Asia's tempestuous history, Japan was able to absorb and preserve traditions which have been totally lost on the mainland.

To preserve traditions, such as those referred to above, can lead to a petrified society in which the past suffocates the vigor of creativity in the present. In Japan, on the contrary, tradition often served as inspiration for new directions, as can be seen in today's avant-garde theater. Therefore, Japan can offer us, in addition to the above-mentioned forms, the theater of the medieval warrior class – *nô* and *kyôgen* – as well as the entertainment of the wealthy citizen class of the 17th century – *bunraku* and *kabuki* – or Western-style *shingeki*, which seeks to connect Japan with theater traditions of the West. Japanese theater has also had a significant impact on 20th-century Western theater and vice versa.

To present such a vast rainbow, I was aware that I would have to draw from many collections. It was one of the lucky circumstances of the project that the Tsubouchi Memorial Theatre Museum of Waseda University, Tokyo, Japan's only theater museum, approached me exactly at this time. Its director, Professor Torigoe Bunzô, became very enthusiastic about our plans and committed this project to us with full heart. Thus, the Tsubouchi Memorial Theatre Museum of Waseda University became our collaborating institution. When The Japan Foundation showed interest in our ideas and became our co-organizer, myriads of roses indeed began to flourish.

Most important in such a project is the team of scholars who bring abstract ideas to life. Each of these theater forms requires elaborate and intensive studies, and scholarly experts generally focus on only one subject. A most important part of our planning was dedicated to gathering a group of scholars of exceptional qualifications. Professor J. Thomas Rimer of the University of Pittsburgh, courageously took over the role of the American chief curator. His talent for coordinating and inspiring all of us served marvelously to bring such a show together. His great interest in modern theater in the East and West makes it possible for him to present to us Japan's theater in the world. Professor Günter Zobel of Waseda University, whom I have known for thirty years since we were classmates together in Rolf Badenhausen's famous lectures on theater history at Cologne University, has accompanied the project since its beginning with enthusiastic effort, and not without many personal sacrifices. Living in Japan for more than twenty years, he has become a well-respected expert on *minzoku geinô* and *nô* theater. One of the few scholars able to bridge the different fields is Professor Benito Ortolani of Brooklyn College/CUNY, whose *History of Japanese Theater* addresses the whole subject. Only the 1972 work of the late Johannes Barth, *Japans Schaukunst im Wandel der Zeiten,* can compete with Ortolani's studies. Therefore, I want to take this opportunity to thank Professor Ortolani for his involvement in our project.

When I was able to convince Professor Samuel Leiter, also of Brooklyn College/CUNY, the highly esteemed editor of the Asian Theatre Journal, to become editor of the essay section of the catalogue, I could be certain that his professional knowledge would create a unique compendium. Kathleen Friello offered her help in creating the index; she has done so with the same meticulous care she demonstrated when collaborating with us on other projects.

It became clear from the first meetings held in New York and Tokyo that it would be desirable for a Japanese and a Western expert to work together for each important section. The results are perfect examples of scholarly collaboration. Some of our essays were written as a common effort, others were written by the single curator considered to have the better knowledge of a certain aspect of the subject. Such collaboration would be desirable in many East-West projects. Once the team was formed, the two curators proceeded to select those objects that would make chosen aspects of their section's theater form visually accessible.

While Professor Rimer took over the explanation of the influence of Japanese theater on Western theater, Professor Kishi Tetsuo, well-known expert on Shakespeare and professor of English literature at Kyoto University, focused on Western-style theater (*shingeki*), which connects the Japanese with the Western theater community.

Günter Zobel collaborated with Professor Gotô Hajime of Waseda University, Tokyo, a pioneer in research on Japanese masks, especially those connected with Japanese folk theater (*minzoku geinô*) and *nô*. Nicola Liscutin adapted the essay on *minzoku geinô* for a Western audience. Professor Tanabe Saburosuke of Musashino Art University and Director of the Machida City Museum, Tokyo, who is an expert on the masks of *gigaku*, *bugaku*, and *gyôdô*, developed the complicated contents of section III. This required especially careful planning in order to visualize the complex connections with the Asian mainland. His expertise is reflected in his essay about lion dances and old rites of purification, both of which were taken over from the Asian mainland. As mentioned above, Benito Ortolani developed the essay on *gigaku* and *bugaku*, while I am responsible for the entries of that section. Günter Zobel and Gotô Hajime wrote about *nô* theater, while Laurence Kominz of Portland State University in Oregon, a professor and *kyôgen* actor, with his partner Hayashi Kazutoshi, a professor at Nagoya Women's University, provided a brilliant analysis of this comical Japanese theater form. Professor Andrew Gerstle, Chairman of the Japan Research Centre at the University of London, brought the reality of the unreal *bunraku* puppet theater to life, in a common effort with Sakurai Hiroshi, a curator at the National Theater of Japan, Tokyo. Professor Torigoe created a most splendid essay on *kabuki*, which illuminates the incredible treasures of *kabuki* from the Tsubouchi Memorial Theatre Museum. Professor James Brandon of the University of Hawaii/Manoa, translated and adapted his essay for a Western audience.

One of the most difficult parts of the project is the kaleidoscope of contemporary avant-garde theater. For the Western public, the myriad directions, philosophies, and groupings are difficult to understand, although they show in astonishing ways the whole spectrum of Japan's theatrical past. Professor Kusuhara-Saitô Tomoko, Tokyo, has undertaken the task of increasing our understanding of the actual flux of Japanese avant-garde theater. Gerhard Hackner, of the University of Tsukuba, has laid out in front of us a description of the magnificent art of *butô* dance, an art which has caused such a sensation in the West.

Thus, the goal of this exhibition is to demonstrate the thousand-fold aspects of the diversity and relationships of Japanese theater. It is, therefore, most desirable that such an exhibition is accessible not only to the public in the United States. From the beginning, we explored the possibility of presenting it in another country, and were delighted and grateful when Jo-Anne Birnie Danzker, Director of the Museum Villa Stuck in Munich, decided to become our partner. With her commitment, the show has become a reality.

Most important for the project has been the commitment of The Japan Foundation. Except for a small group of loans provided by Western collections, all objects in the exhibition come from Japan. The Japan Foundation's Exhibition Division, directed by Ogo Hayato, negotiated the loans, collected them, and brought them to New York. Its advice on many subjects was valuable for us, and the enthusiasm of the collaborators assigned to the project, especially Ms. Koyama Naomi, was impressive. We thank her as well as Ms. Takatori Mana with all our hearts. Our thoughts accompanied them on their numerous trips all over Japan to collect the items. We also would like to express our gratitude to The Japan Foundation for its support of our efforts to present a symposium on Japanese theater in conjunction with the exhibition. The symposium was organized by Ruri Kawashima, Director of Japan Society's U.S.-Japan Department, and Katharina Belting, Program Officer in that department.

Many organizations and individuals have helped us in the preparation process. Their names are listed in a sequence to this acknowledgment. My special thanks, however, goes to the collaborators of the Tsubouchi Memorial Theatre Museum: first to Torigoe Bunzo, its Director, then to Matsuyama Kaoru, Shimane Shigeru, and Takayama Shigeru.

The collaboration with the Museum Villa Stuck has always been very professional and pleasant. I would like to thank Jo-Anne Birnie Danzker, Director of the Museum and her team, especially Susanne Baumann, exhibition coordinator, and Daniela Goldmann, public programs coordinator, for their support and effort in solving the numerous complications which arise in such an ambitious tour. I am delighted that, together, we have been able to present this exhibition to a European public.

My staff members have worked over the years with energy and enthusiasm to help me put this project together. During the planning stage, my staff included Elizabeth Rogers, now Director of the Jacques Marchais Museum of Tibetan Art on Staten Island, and Miyuki Dellarso and Akiko Chiba Mereu, my Administrative Assistants until Sawako Takemura took over that position in 1997. The highly complex subject was taken good care of in the hands of my long-term collaborator Erica Hamilton Weeder, Curator of Education and Editor of the Japan Society Gallery. The complicated duties of a registrar and difficult administrative requirements of such an exhibition were handled by Linda Powers, Registrar and Administrator of Japan Society Gallery. Morihiro Satô of Kyoto helped us with the Japanese loan list in its early stages, while Miwa Suwada entered the project in its final stage. I wish to express my warmest thanks to all of them.

The installation of such a show requires special imagination. Art Clark, who has designed the environments for our exhibitions with excellence many times in the past, has done so again. Jeffrey Nemeth, Director of Building Services at the Japan Society, built up and carefully supervised the complex installation.

The very special nature of the objects required expert help. Nobuko Kajitani, a conservator in the Textile Department at The Metropolitan Museum of Art, New York, immediately accepted the role of special advisor for textile matters. She was assisted by Mie Ishii, who installed the many textile objects with professional knowledge and care, as part of a Mellon Grant from The Metropolitan Museum of Art. I would like to take this opportunity to thank Philippe de Montebello, Director of The Metropolitan Museum of Art, for permitting Ms. Kajitani and Ms. Ishii to work with us. Yûko Fukatsu also helped. I want to express my gratitude, too, to Sondra Castile, Associate Conservator, Asian Art Conservation, The Metropolitan Museum of Art, who, for many years, has been our special conservatorial consultant and a member of our Advisory Committee on Care and Handling. She helped us with all problems related to Japanese paintings and prints.

My gratitude goes also to Christie's New York for its help in identifying all the *kabuki* theater prints in section VII.

Stefanie Krieg-Elliott designed the magnificent catalogue in an extremely short period of time and Mark Green scanned all black-and-white images for it. Meg Crane, of Ponzi & Weill, Inc., New York, designed all labels and panels for the exhibition installation. Her special commitment to the Japan Society Gallery cannot be praised enough.

The exhibition has been made possible because of generous support received, in part, from: the Lila Acheson Wallace/ Japan Society Fund, established at Community Funds, Inc. by the co-founder of Reader's Digest, The Ford Foundation, the National Endowment for the Arts, The Saison Foundation, Sony Corporation of America, and Friends of Japan Society Gallery. Air transportation is provided by Japan Airlines.

Last but not least, I would like to thank Nishikawa Kyôtarô and Roger Goepper, my long-time mentors, for all their help and encouragement.

This exhibition is the twentieth and final show I have had the honor of preparing for the Japan Society Gallery of the Japan Society, one of the finest institutions in the United States for presenting Japanese art and culture. In the eight years I have been responsible for the Gallery, it has been my aim to help promote understanding between Japan and the United States of America. I want to express my special gratitude to, and admiration for, my scholarly colleagues and the members of the Art Advisory Committee, especially its chairman Richard Lanier. They have supported me with all their professional knowledge, making it possible for me to fulfill my commitment.

Gunhild Avitabile
Director
Japan Society Gallery

We thank all these institutions and individuals in Japan and the West for their generous help and advice.

IN JAPAN:
Asakura Chikako, Idemitsu Museum; Atelier Hinode, especially Sakurai Kumiko, Tokyo; Hakusan Shrine, Kuzemura; Hokimoto Hideyo, Matsushita Museum; Honda Mitsuhiro; Inoue Yûichi, Nagoya Kyôgen Kyôdô sha; Itô Shizuo, Shôchiku Costume Co., Ltd.; Japan Actors' Association, Tokyo; Kabukiza Theater, Tokyo; Kadoya Mitsuaki, Oni-no Yakata; Kamitsukasa Nobekuni, Tamukeyama Hachiman Shrine, Nara; Don Kenny; Kitamura Yû, Yûki-za; Seiwa Chôji, Kurokawa Nô Denshû-kan; Matsumoto Kôshirô Office; Matsuura Sawai, Osaka Municipal Museum; Miya Hiromi, Tokugawa Reimeikai Foundation, Tokyo; Miyajima Shinichi, Chief Curator, Nara National Museum; Nagasaki Iwao, Curator, textile section, Tokyo National Museum; Nakagawa Fumihisa, National Diet Library; National Theater of Japan; Nedachi Kensuke, Senior Specialist for Cultural Properties, Agency for Cultural Affairs, Government of Japan; Omodaka Co, Ltd; Process Shizai Co., Ltd.; Masahiro Ii, Director, and Saitô Nozomu, Curator, Hikone Castle Museum; Sengoku Tsuruyoshi, Tokyo Metropolitan Museum of Modern Japanese Literature; Shibuya Masato and Eguchi Tadahiro, Yamagata Prefecture; Shimizu Eiseki, Jôshin-ji; Shimizu Yôichi, The Japan Foundation, Tokyo; Shôchiku Co., Ltd.; Takatsu Kôichi; Takenô Masahiro, Imperial Household Agency; The Nippon Foundation; The Shôyô Kyôkai Foundation; Ueda Shinji, Takarazuka Revue Company; Ueda Takashi, Director, Japan Cultural Institute, Cologne; Washizuka Hiromitsu, Deputy Director-General of Tokyo National Museum; Yamamoto Tsutomu, Curator, sculpture section, Tokyo National Museum; National Bunraku Theater; Yoshioka Sachio and his workshop.

IN THE WEST:
Christie's New York, especially Toshi Hara; Dr. Alfons Dufey and Dr. Erwin Arnold, Bayerische Staatsbibliothek, Munich; David Farneth, The Kurt Weill Foundation for Music, New York; Victor Harris, Senior Keeper, The British Museum, London; Anne Kierstein, Starnberg; Dag Kronlund, Curator, Swedish National

Museum, Stockholm; Riff La Roche, Dance Butter Tokio, Berlin; Max Reinhard Archiv, Vienna; Dr. Hedwig Müller, Curator, Theatermuseeum des Institutes für Theater, Film- und Fernsehwissenschaften, Universität zu Köln, Cologne; Dr. Claudius Müller, Curator, Staatliche Museen zu Berlin, Museum für Völkerkunde, Berlin; Sara O'Connor, Milwaukee Repertory Theater, Milwaukee; Ono Mari, Music from Japan, New York; Jacques Pimpaneau, Director, Musée Kwok On, Paris; Valrae Reynolds, Curator, The Newark Museum, Newark; Kerstin von Riegen, Bayerischer Staatsoper, Abteilung Maske und Kostüm, Munich; Dr. Adele Schlombs, Director, and Dr. Heike Kotzenberg, Curator, Museum für Ostasiatische Kunst, Cologne; Robert Tuggle, Archives of the Metropolitan Opera, New York; Dr. Johannes Wieninger, Curator, Österreichisches Museum für Angewandte Kunst, Vienna; Prof. Dr. Willibald Veit, Staatliche Museen zu Berlin, Museum für Ostasiatische Kunst, Berlin; Dr. Erdmut Wizisla, Berthold Brecht Archiv, Berlin; Dr. Bettina Zorn, Curator, Österreichisches Museum für Völkerkunde, Vienna.

FOREWORDS

The Japan Foundation is profoundly pleased that, with the cooperation of the Tsubouchi Memorial Theatre Museum, Waseda University, the "Japanese Theater in the World" exhibition is to be held in New York and Munich. This exhibition, prepared from a scholarly perspective, provides a comprehensive introduction to Japanese theater today.

The exhibition is among the commemorative events planned in celebration of the 90th anniversary of the Japan Society. At the time of its founding in 1907, international understanding of and knowledge about Japan were very limited, but from the outset, the Japan Society worked actively to promote diverse and unrestricted U.S.-Japanese exchange, conducting a wide variety of programs in fields ranging from politics and economics to culture.

Over the past ninety years international exchange between Japan and other countries has expanded dramatically in quality and quantity. The Japan Society has always been a pivotal presence in U.S.-Japanese exchange. Through the countless persons it has sent to Japan and brought to the United States, as well as various projects it has conducted, strong and deep bonds of friendship have been established between the two countries. The Japan Foundation has been deeply indebted to the Japan Society, since its own founding in 1972, for its assistance in laying the groundwork for Foundation activities in the United States. Over the years, we have carried out many projects jointly.

Co-sponsorship of this major exhibition is particularly meaningful for us at The Japan Foundation, not only as an event commemorating the Japan Society's 90th anniversary, but also as a landmark attempt to present, from various angles, in the context of the whole world, the full spectrum of Japanese theater from ancient to contemporary times. The planning of the exhibit was done through the collaboration of fourteen curators from Japan, the United States, and Europe.

After going on display at the Japan Society, the exhibition will be sent to the Museum Villa Stuck in Munich. It is my hope that at both sites the more than 700 items included will vividly project, transcending the centuries they represent, the rich spectrum of the Japanese theater.

I would like to take this opportunity to express our sincere appreciation to the Tsubouchi Memorial Theatre Museum, Waseda University, for its enormous cooperation in making this exhibition possible. We are also deeply grateful for the generosity of the many individuals and organizations who have provided valuable items from their collections for the exhibition, and to those whose assistance and support helped make the exhibition a reality.

Asao Shinichiro
President
The Japan Foundation

The Japan Society is both pleased and excited to bring to the American public this exhibition of "Japanese Theater in the World." It is the second major exhibition in our 90th anniversary year and the first since the expansion and renovation of our headquarters building has been fully completed. It is the largest exhibit ever attempted by the Japan Society Gallery and involves all other Society departments. Thus, there are live performances during the exhibition, related film offerings, lectures, and workshops. We believe this is the first time ever that such an exhibition on the full sweep of Japanese theater, with attendant activities, has been attempted in the United States.

The influence of Japanese woodblock prints, ceramics, textiles, and other objects on Western art has long been acknowledged. Conversely, the Western forms have insinuated themselves into the Japanese cultural milieu. The interaction in the theatrical world has not been well documented to this point. We are most grateful for the major support we received from our co-organizer, The Japan Foundation, and its President, Asao Shinichiro, and for the collaboration of the Tsubouchi Memorial Theatre Museum of Waseda University and Torigoe Bunzô, Director of the museum and Chief Curator in Japan for the exhibition. These institutions, along with the Japan Society, and our Gallery Director, Dr. Gunhild Avitabile, have conceptualized and realized this project, one that Dr. Avitabile first envisioned while in the midst of her doctoral research. In bringing together this exhibition, she has also been aided and assisted by the exhibition's Chief Curator in the West, Professor J. Thomas Rimer of the University of Pittsburgh, and thirteen additional curators from Japan, the United States, and Europe.

The cooperation we have received from the Tsubouchi Memorial Theatre Museum, from which the core of objects shown are drawn, has been exceptional, as has been the help from so many others who have provided the objects, advice, and assistance which have made the exhibit possible.

From New York, the exhibition will travel to the Museum Villa Stuck in Munich, where it will be the first major Japanese exhibition in that city in many years. We are very grateful to Jo-Anne Birnie Danzker, Director of the Museum Villa Stuck, and to Siegfried Hummel, Minister of Culture for the City of Munich.

We at the Japan Society are proud of our ninety years of explaining Japan to the United States, showing the interaction between our two cultures, and considering the possibilities for the future. This opportunity to trace Japanese theater from its earliest inception to the present, and to demonstrate its impact upon the world is a challenge. Prior to the renovation of our building, such an exhibition would have been only a dream. Today, with greatly expanded possibilities for gallery space, state of the art climate control, and vastly improved lighting, we are stretching our wings as never before and moving in new and unexplored directions. We are confident that all who see this exhibition will come away with a greater appreciation for the Japanese theater and the linkages that bind us all.

Michael I. Sovern
Chairman
Japan Society

William Clark, Jr.
President
Japan Society

Documents about Japanese performing arts first appeared in Japan in 612 AD. Because of their own ancient tradition of Greek classical theater, people in the West might think that Japan is only a developing country in terms of its performing arts. If one considers the initial date of the history of performing arts, it would be reasonable to think so; however, the history of these arts in Japan is unique.

Even as we approach the 21st century, the performing arts in Japan continue to adapt, and we Japanese continue to appreciate those forms which came into the country from China in 612. Many new forms have also been inspired by Western culture.

Once the Japanese government reopened Japan's ports at the beginning of the Meiji Period (1868), our performing arts frequently were seen abroad. In recent times, especially, not only *nô*, *kabuki*, and *bunraku*, but also newer forms have been appreciated all over the world. It is fitting, therefore, that "Japanese Theater in the World" introduces the West to the many aspects of Japan's performing arts and to their transformations – from ancient times until the present day.

It is my hope that this exhibition will increase the understanding in the West of these arts and of Japanese culture. My museum, the Tsubouchi Memorial Theatre Museum of Waseda University, has already presented exhibitions of Japanese performing arts in Europe and Australia. This exhibition at the Japan Society, on the 90th anniversary of that institution, provides a wonderful opportunity to collaborate with the Japan Society in presenting the first comprehensive exhibition in the United States that examines the role of Japanese theater in the world. I feel confident about this exhibition, with Dr. Avitabile as Director of the Japan Society Gallery, and believe that it will stand as the final and largest exhibition of the century to focus on Japanese theater.

Torigoe Bunzô
Director
Tsubouchi Memorial Theatre Museum
Waseda University

Museums, the theoretician James Clifford wrote in his landmark book *The Predicament of Culture: Twentieth Century Ethnography, Literature and Art*, are historical-cultural theaters of memory[1]. But, he asked, whose memory and for what purposes?

The exhibition, "Japanese Theater in the World", presents costumes, masks, instruments and object d'art as tangible memory, as witnesses of an unbroken artistic tradition extending over many centuries and several religious transformations. It will be presented in Germany in a highly eccentric historical-cultural theater of memory, in a museum situated in the nineteenth century villa of the Munich painter, sculptor and furniture designer Franz von Stuck. The artist, who decorated the villa that now bears his name, was a gifted designer of spectacular settings for his own life and work. Referring to this element in Stuck's art, Werner Hager writes: "Such a preoccupation with self-dramatization and visual display is scarcely surprising in a native of Bavaria, for the people of this region still take an old-fashioned delight in theatrical show and flummery . . . This has to do with the idea of the world as a stage, where each person must play his or her allotted part until the final curtain falls."[2]

Theater has been a recurrent theme in the program of the Museum Villa Stuck. Exhibitions such as "Max Beckmann World-Theater" (1993), "Gianni Versace – Theater of Fashion" (1992) as well as the 1997 exhibition featuring the work of Robert Wilson, the internationally renowned opera and theater director, are the more obvious, direct expressions of this discourse. In numerous other exhibitions in our museum, however, the relationship between theater, dance and the visual arts has been a constant, and central, issue. The desire, so strong in nineteenth and twentieth century Western culture, to shatter artificial barriers between the arts, the desire to integrate art and everyday life, found much of its inspiration in non-European cultures, especially Japanese. In our 1995 exhibition devoted to the turn-of-the-century dancer Loie Fuller, we documented the impact of the Japanese dancer Sada Yacco on artists such as Rodin and on dancers such as Isadora Duncan with her performances at the Paris World Fair in 1900.

It is a great privilege for the Museum Villa Stuck to be able to continue this dialogue on the relationship between the theater and the visual arts, between Japanese and European cultural traditions, by hosting this exhibition, initiated and organized by the Japan Society Gallery Inc. in New York under the direction of Gunhild Avitabile.

I would like to take this opportunity to express our deep gratitude to the numerous private and public lenders in Japan, who so generously agreed to release their superb and most precious objects for a period of nearly six months thereby enabling us to present this first ever comprehensive overview of Japanese theatrical traditions to European audiences. Special mention should be made of our colleagues at Waseda University, especially Professor Bunzo Torigoe, who agreed to part with the major part of their collection for such a long period, and to individuals such as Professor Günter Zobel, who facilitated negotiations with the lenders in Japan and agreed to act as guest curator for the exhibition in Munich.

We are deeply indebted to The Japan Foundation in Japan, who generously supported this exhibition tour, and to its officers in Germany, director Takashi Ueda, and Heinz-Dieter Reese, who supported us at every stage of the planning with support and advice.

The cooperation of several European institutions also enabled us to include a number of additional works for the Munich venue. I wish to thank the individuals who made this possible: Victor Harris, from the Department of Japanese Antiquities at the British Museum, London; Wolfgang Till, the director of the Munich City Museum; Peter Jonas, the artistic director of the Bavarian State Opera; and Dr Erwin Arnold from the Bavarian State Library.

This exhibition, a long-standing dream of Gunhild Avitabile, would not have been possible without her passion and commitment, an enduring source of motivation to all those involved. I would like to express my deepest appreciation to her and to her team at the Japan Society Gallery for their tireless efforts, without which it would have been impossible to present these works in Europe.

Numerous individuals and organizations have supported the project in Munich, not only the exhibition but also the public program and symposium which accom-panied it. Among those who provided invaluable support are Shin'ichiro Asao, President of The Japan Foundation, Tokyo, Ambassador Haruhiko Shibuya of the Japanese Embassy in Bonn, Professor Peter Pörtner, Director of the Japan Centre of the Ludwig Maximilians University Munich, Professor Stanca Scholz-Cionca in Berlin, who together with Professor Hans-Peter Bayerdörfer from the Institut for Theater Research at the Ludwig Maximilian University in Munich, organized a symposium in conjunction with the exhibition; Petra Keidel, Department of Culture, City of Munich; and last, but not least, Daniela Goldmann, who undertook the task of organiz-ing the public events program which accompanied the exhibition. In this regard I would like to express my appreciation to the numerous institutions, both state and municipal, which co-organized the public programs in Munich.

We are deeply honoured that the exhibition, events pro-gramme and symposium Japanese Theater in the World is being presented in Munich under the patronage of the Japa-nese Consulate-General in Munich. I would like to express my gratitude to the Consul-General Yoshinori Katori and his predecessor Ryuichi Tanabe, First Consul Toshihiko Mochizuki and Vice-Consul Ichiro Shimogaite for their extraordinary personal commitment and their assistance and advice in every aspect of the organization of these events. I sincerely believe that, as a result, Munich's cultural life, its "memory," will be greatly enriched.

Jo-Anne Birnie Danzker
Director
Museum Villa Stuck, Munich

1. James Clifford, The Predicament of Culture: Twentieth Century Ethnography, Literature and Art (Cambridge: Harvard University Press, 1988), p.229.
2. Werner Hager, Zur Villa Stuck, in: Dr. Jochen Poetter. (Ed.) Villa Stuck. Franz von Stuck 1863-1928, München 1984, p. 40.

Lenders to the Exhibition

Aitani Yoshiko, Kyoto
Andô Gisaku, Saitama Prefecture
Aoki Shinji, Tokyo
Archives of the Metropolitan Opera, New York
Asakura Setsu, Tokyo
Asubesuto-kan, Hijikata Tatsumi Memorial Archives, Tokyo
Gunhild Avitabile, New York
The Ayervais Collection, New York

Bayerische Staatsoper, Munich
Bayerische Staatsbibliothek, Munich
The British Museum, London
Bunraku Kyôkai, Osaka

Dai-san Erotica, Tokyo
Dairakudakan, Tokyo
Dance Butter Tokio, Berlin
Dumb Type, Kyoto

Engeki Jikkenshitsu Ban'yu Inryoku, Tokyo
Engeki Kikaku Group The Gazira, Tokyo

Fûren Dance, Tokyo

Gakushûin University, Japanese Language and Literature Center, Tokyo
Gekidan 300, Tokyo
Gekidan Seinendan, Tokyo
Andrew Gerstle, London
Gotô Hajime, Tokyo
Colin Graham, St. Louis, Missouri

Hakusan Shrine, Kuzemura, Gifu Prefecture
Hayachine Dake Kagura Hozonkai, Iwate Prefecture
Hikone Castle Museum, Shiga Prefecture
Hillman Library, The University of Pittsburgh, Pittsburgh, Pennsylvania

Ichikawa Danjûrô
Idemitsu Museum of Arts, Tokyo
Ikeda Masao, Shizuoka Prefecture
Thomas Immoos, Tokyo
Isokawa Shizuo, Gifu Prefecture
Itô Hiroko, Tokyo

Japan Society, Inc., New York
Jitensha Kinqureat, Tokyo
Jôshin-ji, Tokyo

Kamonegi Shot, Tokyo
Kenny & Ogawa Kyogen Players, Tokyo
Kunaicho (Imperial Household Agency), Tokyo
Kuro-tento (The Black Tent), Tokyo
Kurokawa Nô Denshû-kan, Yamagata Prefecture

Kurt Weill Foundation for Music, New York
Kusuhara Tomoko, Tokyo

Matsumoto Kôshirô Office, Tokyo
Matsushita Art Museum, Kagoshima Prefecture
Milwaukee Repertory Theater, Milwaukee, Wisconsin
Mabou Mines, New York
Munakata Kuniyoshi, Shizuoka Prefecture
Staatliche Museen zu Berlin, Museum für Ostasiatische Kunst, Berlin
The Museum of Modern Art, New York
Music from Japan, New York

Nagoya Kyôgen Kyôdo sha, Aichi Prefecture
Nakajima Hideo, Tokyo
Nakamura Ganjirô
Namerikawa Gorô, Tochigi Prefecture
Narita-san Shinshô-ji, Chiba Prefecture
National Bunraku Theater, Osaka
National Diet Library, Tokyo
National Museum for Ethnology, Osaka
National Theater, Tokyo
The Newark Museum, Newark, New Jersey
Nichiei Scientific Film Production, Tokyo
Nishihashi Takeshi, Niigata Prefecture
Nito-sha, Tokyo
Noda Map, Tokyo
Nôgaku Shiryô Center, Tokyo
NOISE, Tokyo

Barbra Okada, New York
Oni-no Yakata, Iwate Prefecture
Ôno Kazuo Dance Research Center, Yokohama
Opera Theatre of Saint Louis, St. Louis, Missouri
Osaka College of Music, Department of Folk Music, Osaka
Osaka Municipal Museum, Osaka
Ôta Shôgo, Tokyo
Ôtsuka Ryôji, Shizuoka Prefecture

Pappa Tarafumara, Tokyo
Philadelphia Museum of Art, Philadelphia, Pennsylvania

J. Thomas Rimer, Pittsburgh, Pennsylvania
Rinkôgun, Tokyo
John Roslevich Jr., St. Louis, Missouri

Sakurai Hiroshi, Tokyo
Jonah Salz, Shiga Prefecture
Sankai Juku, Tokyo
Sasame Hiroyuki, The Modern Theatrical Posters Collection Project
Hans Schavernoch, Vienna

Uta Schreck, Tokyo
SCOT, Tokyo
Barbara Sellers, Davis, California
Shôchiku Co., Ltd., Tokyo
Shôchiku Costume Co., Ltd., Tokyo
Shibuya Masato and Eguchi Tadahiro, Nagai, Yamagata Prefecture
Shigeyama Akira, Kyoto
Shigeyama Sengorô, Kyoto
Shigeyama Sensaku, Kyoto
Shimoda Seiji, Tokyo
Shinjuku Ryôzanpaku, Tokyo
Shintennô-ji Hômotsukan, Osaka
Shizuoka University, Shizuoka Prefecture
Helmut Steinhauser, Kyoto
Swedish National Theater, Stockholm

Takarazuka Revue Company, Hyôgo Prefecture
Takatsu Kôichi, Kanagawa Prefecture
Takemoto Miwadayû, Kyoto
Tamukeyama Hachiman Shrine, Nara
Tanabe Saburôsuke, Tokyo
Theater of Yûgen, San Francisco, California
Theaterwissenschaftliche Sammlung der Universität Köln, Cologne
Third Stage, Tokyo
Tôdai-ji, Nara
Tôhô Co., Tokyo
Tokugawa Art Museum, Nagoya
Tokyo Metropolitan Museum of Modern Japanese Literature, Tokyo
Tokyo National Museum, Tokyo
Tomoe Shizune & Hakutôbô
Torigoe Bunzô, Tokyo
Toyama City
Tsubouchi Memorial Theatre Museum, Waseda University, Tokyo
Tsutsumi Harue, Tokyo

Waseda University Library, Tokyo

Yamaguchi Kan'non, Saitama Prefecture
Yamaguchi Nô Costume Research Center (Sato Yoshihiko Memorial Yamaguchi Nô Costume Research Center), Shiga Prefecture
Yoshida Chiaki, Tokyo
Yoshida Minojirô, Osaka
Yûki-za, Tokyo

Zenchiku Jûrô, Tokyo
Günter Zobel, Yamagata City

PLATE 2

2./3.6

2.45D

3.24

9/33/2

FROM SHAMANISM TO *BUTO*:
Continuity and Innovation in Japanese Theater History

Benito Ortolani

The "Japanese Theater in the World" exhibit provides the most comprehensive, copiously illustrated exhibit ever shown in the West of the multifaceted accomplishments of the Japanese theater over a period of fifteen centuries. An event of this nature would have been unthinkable at the end of World War II. Even in the late 1950s, in spite of the rising tide of interest in Japan and a few performances abroad of *nô* and *kabuki*, only a handful of Western specialists and artists in search of new cultural frontiers were aware of the variety and extraordinary richness of the Japanese theatrical heritage.[1] The fact that, today, an extensive documentation of the complexity of Japan's theater history is offered to the public right across the street from the United Nations headquarters, testifies to a substantially improved international awareness of and esteem for the cultural importance and world-wide impact of the Japanese theatrical arts. This abundant documentation is focused on the relation of Japanese theatrical arts to the rest of the world. It stresses their vital importance as a link in the chain of international cross-fertilization and cultural interdependence.[2] Japan is an insular country that depended for her artistic development on foreign imports and yet, through the centuries, experienced periods of strict isolationism. The major forms of Japanese performance, however, far from resembling stagnant, dead-end extensions of imported crafts, developed into original arts that mirrored highly creative periods in Japanese cultural history. Eventually, they became powerful sources of inspiration for playwrights, stage and film directors, actors, and puppeteers around the globe. In our days, this tradition has become an important catalyst in international efforts toward the creation of performance styles for the third millennium.

Japan's spectacular growth into a first-rate technological and financial power is certainly one of the best known events of recent history. The time has come to offer a special opportunity to become aware of Japan's complex, varied, original, and enduring theater tradition.

This introductory essay does not seek to provide an overview/summary of the specific Japanese performing arts illustrated in the exhibition. The bounteous written, pictorial, and audiovisual documentation provided capably fulfills that function. The following, on the contrary, introduces the visitor to certain results—some of them controversial—of the ongoing research concerning imported and indigenous factors that shaped the birth and influenced the development and aesthetic continuity of Japanese theatrical genres over a period of some fifteen centuries.

While the essays that follow occasionally present concrete examples of the impact the Japanese theater has had on the modern Western theater, I wish here to propose the Japanese theater as an international treasure belonging to the mainstream of world culture, alongside the leading Asian and Western traditions. I will consider its beginnings as part of the worldwide phenomenon of shamanism, its later evolution as one of the finest theatrical expressions of the great Asian traditions of Buddhism and Confucianism, and, beginning with the 17th century, as a manifestation of the process of secularization that has peaked in today's Westernized and internationalized culture.

PRIMORDIAL COMMUNITIES AND SHAMANIC POSSESSION

In recent decades, a flurry of anthropological research into ancient and contemporary shamanism throughout the world has coincided with a rising interest among theater scholars concerned with popular entertainment and performance. These interests have sometimes overshadowed the traditionally dominant approach based on dramaturgical values. For example, Japanese theater critics have passionately discussed the notion of engekisei (theatricality) as opposed to bungakusei (literary value). In the West, theater scholars have insisted on the importance of origins, and have investigated periods rich in performance traditions but poor in, or even totally deprived of, literary dramatic masterpieces. Mixed results have followed, including a controversial theory proposing shamanism as the root of all world theatrical traditions.[3] In addition, certain avant-garde experiments have attempted to recycle the ancient fascination with shamanic trance.

More convincingly, insights gained from research into worldwide shamanism by students of folk religion, anthropology, and theater were applied by Japanese and Western scholars to the interpretation of the beginnings of Japan's performing arts. They have led, as well, to the discovery of the continuing influence of shamanistic lore—such as ancient trance techniques and conjurations of haunting ghosts—on the dramatic structure, performance styles, music, costumes, makeup, and masks of theatrical forms from kagura to the post-shingeki avant-garde.[4]

It is generally admitted that—before and concomitant to the development of the "official" performances anchored in Shinto and Buddhist traditions—shamanic ecstasy was widely practiced in Japan. It does not seem possible to establish the approximate date of its first introduction, nor is its route to Japan known, although a powerful Korean influence is often entertained because of the geographical closeness of Korea and the strong presence of shamanism there. A native origin cannot be excluded since, according to Mircea Eliade, "ecstasy (trance, losing one's soul, losing consciousness) seems to form an integral part of the human condition, just like anxiety, dream, imagination, etc. . . . [Ecstasy] is a primordial phenomenon in the sense that it coexists with human nature. Only the religious interpretation given to ecstasy and the techniques designed to prepare it or facilitate it are historically conditioned."[5]

Many specialists nowadays acknowledge at least some connection between the first written, performance-related records of ancient Japan and the widespread network of shamanistic beliefs and practices that still survive in folk religions among such far-flung cultures as North and South American Indians and Eskimos, and the people of Northern and Central Asia, Mongolia, Manchuria, and, especially, Korea. The world of ancient kagura can be better understood when, at the least, it admits a link to trance dances by miko, the mostly female shamans of Japan. The myth of the goddess Ame no Uzume's ecstatic and erotic dance, narrated in great detail in the oldest indigenous written sources of Japanese history (Kojiki and Nihongi, 8th century AD), is traditionally considered to be the beginning of Japan's performing arts, and is often referred to as the first known kagura. It centers on Ame no Uzume's trance dance, performed to the rhythm of her feet stamping on a small hollow surface, and welcomed by a roaring audience. Many scholars agree that the author was probably projecting into mythical timelessness his experience of a contemporary (6th to 8th century AD) kagura ritual. Stage decorations and props still used in kagura are minutely described in these old texts and confirm the primordial connection between shamanism and kagura.[6]

Shamanism in Japan never coalesced into any set of clearly defined beliefs nor was it strictly institutionalized as an independent religion.[7] It penetrated deeply into official rituals and popular religious practices of both Shinto and several sects of Buddhism. The syncretistic talent of the Japanese was successfully at work in this area from the very beginnings, gradually adapting the basic activity of the shaman to the requirements of rituals pertaining to the official religions; that is, the Shinto kannushi (priests) and Buddhist monks, who tended to the needs of the faithful throughout the Japanese islands, were entrusted with performing rituals based on contacting the "other dimension," conjuring, exorcizing, praying for the appeasement of souls (tama) of the departed, and so on.

As in other Asian countries, so also in Japan did shamanic trance techniques become elements of the performing arts. Japanese shamans seem to have adopted a form of ecstasy appropriate for a powerful public performance and for providing a solid dramatic structure for future genres.

On the other hand, when the shamans of, say, the Siberian tradition practice trance, they lose consciousness of their surroundings while their souls leave the temporarily lifeless body and travel into the "other dimension," where the powers to be contacted reside. The most important part of their "theatrical performance" before the community begins after the shaman's spirit reenters the body and regains the usual state of consciousness. It often consists of a narration of the just experienced mythical trip, which is projected in the form of stylized mime onto a stage, where the supernatural messages to the community are made public. In most common continental shamanic traditions, therefore, the supernatural powers do not leave the "other dimension" where they are believed to reside. It is the shaman's spirit that travels to the faraway, mysterious area of the encounter.

Japanese shamans, however, adopted a form of trance in which the encounter with the *kami* happens in the presence of the community. The *miko* or shamaness, entering a state of trance, loses her individual consciousness when the visiting *kami* (deity, supernatural power) takes possession of her soul as a result of techniques such as dancing, rhythmic stamping, singing, and so forth. These techniques become an extremely important part of the process that conjures the *kami*. Messages to the community are communicated directly by the possessing *kami* via the mouth of the possessed *miko*. The encounter of shamaness/*kami* happens, therefore, in the middle of theatrically suggestive, sometimes erotic or comical actions. When angry, vengeful powers are involved, it may occur during terrifying high points of the rhythmic dances that contribute to the trance-inducing techniques. The very word *kagura* expresses the phenomenon of possession, since it probably derives from a euphonic contraction of terms (*kam*[*u*]+*kura*) indicating the "seat of the *kami*."

The centuries-long resistance in many Japanese theatrical arts to performing without a fan, even when the fan is more a nuisance than a functional prop, seems to have its source here. This resistance may be traced to the widespread belief that the precise "abode of the *kami*" during possession is the *torimono*, that is, the object held in the miko's hand, such as a branch of the *sakaki* tree or a spear, which was later substituted for by the omnipresent fan. The great reverence toward such sacred "held-in-the-hand" objects would have exerted a mighty psychological pressure, transmitted from generation to generation, creating a definite reluctance to performing without the important prop. This would be true even when the primitive meaning had vanished from the consciousness of performers whose dances were no longer related to trance.

One of the controversial explanations of the multilayered myth described in the ancient sources goes as follows: the prototypical shamaness Ame no Uzume performs her techniques of ecstasy before a community in distress because of the solar eclipse. Her purpose is to conjure back the sun (identified with the *kami* Amaterasu, the progenitor of the Japanese), luring her out of her concealment through the trance. Uzume dances and stamps her feet and performs a ritualistic stripping naked of her body, which is accompanied by the boisterous laughter of the audience. Her techniques of conjuration leading to ecstasy become successful when she loses her consciousness and the *kami* leaves her abode to take possession of the shamaness's soul. Once Amaterasu is out of the cave, the light and the warmth of the sun are given back to the world. Since the stripping happens in the trance state, it is actually the sun goddess herself who shows to the audience, through the manifested genitals of the possessed *miko*, the symbols of the once again uncovered generative powers of the sun.

In the ancient narration of Uzume's trance scholars also have noticed connections with different, not necessarily shamanistic, rituals practiced—on the occasion of solar eclipses—in Assam, Burma, South China, and among certain populations of southeast Asia. A talent for syncretism, which would become a pattern in most later Japanese performing arts, seems to have

been at work from the very beginning. The scholar is therefore confronted with complex layers of influences that must be sorted out. In Uzume's myth the influence of worldwide practices of white magic also should be considered; it may help to explain the erotic nature of the shaman's dance. White magic believes in the power of forcing the gods to grant wishes through rituals consisting in actions that symbolize an anticipated granting of the desired favors. During Uzume's ecstatic dance the revelation of the genitals would symbolize the anticipated granting of the renewed manifestation to the world of the sun's vital generative powers, while the audience's ritual laughter would anticipate joy at the wish's being granted.[8]

The recurring discussion about the relationship of primitive *kagura* to popular entertainments (*geinô*) has helped scholars to establish the following structure of shamanistic performance as one of the factors of continuity in Japanese performing arts: conjuration, leading to a visit of a being (or beings) from the other dimension, leading to entertainment for the visitor(s) and the assembled community. This formula became standard for a variety of *kagura*, and is to be found, with some adaptations, in *nô* plays, in the very origins of *kabuki*, and even in traces that can be identified in certain examples of *shingeki* and post-*shingeki*.

Because a *kagura* invites the gods to come from their residence (*tokoyo no kuni* or the land of eternity) and preside over the celebrations, it is understandable why the primitive Japanese would have followed the performance of shamanic techniques of conjuring the *kami* with special entertainments in honor of the illustrious visitors. In some cases, the performances related to trance induction did not change substantially through the centuries, often preserving the ancient ritual with stubborn conservativism; in other instances, when their purpose faded away, they simply ceased to be performed.

The final section, on the contrary, dedicated to the entertainment of the divine guest, occasionally kept pace with changing contemporary tastes, as it still may do today. Through the centuries it offered popular spectacles such as *nô* and *kabuki*, and, in more recent times, even included Western music. In other cases, the entertainments froze in a form having little relation to the original ceremony. This explains the confusing variety of today's *kagura* spread throughout Japan: some present strictly shamanistic ancient rituals to which have been added entertainments that might reflect influences imbibed by local talent from touring performers of *nô*, *kyôgen*, *kabuki*, and the like; these entertainments were eventually crystallized in a manner suggesting some level of corruption from the original model. Other *kagura* may have dropped the ritual beginning section, and may consist of any one of many traditional or modern popular entertainments, thus becoming a kind of performance potpourri during local festivals.[9]

When the *kami* were conjured to visit the community during the innumerable *kagura* festivals throughout Japan, it was common to seek favors from them for the *tama* of dead or living individuals, or to provide protection from dangerous inhabitants of the other dimension. Important elements in

Japan's major performing arts developed during the celebration of numerous rituals concerned with *tama*, a concept often translated as "spirit" or "soul," but that might better be described as the vital force–shared by *kami* and humans alike–that controls one's physical well-being. According to the early Shintoistic way of thinking, it is the quantity of *tama* that determines the difference between man and the divine *kami*, between the great leader and the common man. A weakened *tama* can lead to disease and, eventually, death, which consists in the separation of the individual *tama* from the body. The powerful *tama* belonging to a great warrior killed in battle or to a powerful leader who died in anger was believed to turn into a vengeful ghost (*onryô*) and to cause endless misery to the living.

In Shinto belief, the separated *tama* must be appeased after death through appropriate ceremonies, without which it cannot finally be reunited with the comprehensive *tama* of the "common ancestor," where individual existence finds final rest. In the popular religiosity that developed out of the syncretistic fusion of Buddhism with Shinto, the same belief provides a practical basis to widespread Buddhist ceremonies for the repose of the souls of the departed. Buddhist temples were as busy as Shinto shrines with exorcisms based on the common (shamanistic) belief that the mysterious and often menacing other dimension is populated by the ghosts of innumerable departed that have not achieved salvation (whose meaning varies among the different sects) and that the prayers of the living are needed to enter that realm (again, a concept varying from sect to sect, and ranging from Amida's paradise to an enlightened liberation from the cycle of reincarnation).

It is no wonder that officers of the main Japanese religions have been busy for centuries performing rituals geared to the increase and invigoration of *tama* for the living, to the pacification of *tama* for the deceased, and to the exorcism of angry ghosts. *Tama* of powerful heroes, emperors, or other leaders required the special attention of the clergy and usually solemn and powerful rituals of appeasement to avoid national calamities. Temples and shrines were built for the appeasement of those powers. A few years ago a controversial and successful Japanese book proposed that the Hôryû-ji, the most venerable Buddhist temple of Nara, was built to placate the angry *tama* of the Prince Regent Shôtoku (the great patron of the introduction of Buddhist culture into Japan at the end of the 6th century); this suggests how deeply recent studies of the impact of shamanism on early Japanese culture may have influenced previously reluctant Japanese intellectuals.[10]

Contemporary scholarship has detected a lasting influence on Japan's performing arts of elements originally belonging to *tama*-related ceremonies, not only in *kagura*, but also in the fundamental structure of *nô* plays, especially those representing the appearance and appeasement of ghosts; in *kabuki*, from the first dances of Okuni; and in the content of numerous plays of every period down to the present day.

The shamanic structure of *kagura* may easily be discovered in the *nô*. Typical *nô* plays feature the apparition of *kami* or dangerous ghosts, in which the secondary actor, the *waki*, verifies many features of the shamanic conjurer. The *waki*, often impersonating the role of a monk or a *kannushi* (Buddhist and Shinto priests usually functioned in religious services as professional conjurers), travels to the place of the trance and meets there the soon-to-be-revealed visitor from the "other dimension," who appears first in disguise and then in his/her supernatural reality.

According to some scholars the accompanying music of the *nô* flute and the strange utterances of the chorus (*kakegoe*) were both in some form also part of the conjuration ritual. The *kakegoe* have been explained not only according to their present musical function, but also as remnants of invocation/conjuration calls to the *kami*.

The resulting appearance of the conjured inhabitant of the "other" dimension in the *nô* is made more dramatic through an important development. What had been the double role of the shamaness in primitive *kagura*—first as herself in possession-inducing ritual techniques and then as the possessed channel for the visitor from the "other dimension"–is now clearly split between two actors. The theatrical performance is now centered, not on the conjurer, the *waki*, who in *nô* is the secondary actor, but on the visitor, impersonated by the masked *shite* or main performer, who plays the double role of the disguised apparition and then the fully revealed conjured *kami* or inhabitant of the other dimension.[11]

Scholars also have found that the earliest *kabuki* performances adapted a shamanistic dramatic formula similar to that used by the *nô*. At the end of the 16th century, when *kabuki*'s acknowledged founder, the presumed *miko* Okuni, presented her fabulously successful, popularized religious dances, called *nembutsu odori*,[12] she demonstrated her masterful sense of how to please the emerging merchant culture and bored samurai alike: as a *miko* collecting funds for the repairs of a temple she introduced charming trance techniques to conjure not an illustrious hero of the classical past, as in the *nô*, but a pop celebrity, Nagoya Sanza, her alleged samurai lover, recently killed in a brawl. Here again, as in *nô*, the focus is on the visitor from the "other dimension." Now, however, the conjured pop star enters the stage from the audience, and vivifies a sentimental soap-opera scene in which Sanza, in erotic remembrances, relishes his newly lost happy times of lovemaking with Okuni. In *nô*, he would have been a samurai recalling his heroic exploits before his death. The added detail that Okuni may have reserved the role of Sanza for herself added the spice of transsexuality to the performance. This notion would be overused in the sexually provocative performances of early *kabuki* types (*onna kabuki* or "women's kabuki," *yûjo kabuki* or "prostitute kabuki," and *wakashu kabuki* or "youth kabuki"), but it eventually gave birth to *kabuki*'s famed, sophisticated world of the *onnagata* or male actor of female roles.[13]

Important traces of the shamanistic formula recently have been disclosed in *kabuki* plays of the Genroku period (1688-1703), where superheroes are represented as capable of incredible, divine deeds, such as effortlessly and single-handedly defeating a large number of armed enemies. Their deeds are possible because they have been possessed by a powerful *kami*, thus making them *hitokami* (man-gods). The still visible remnant of this tradition in the *aragoto* or "rough business" style is evident when one scrutinizes the details of the *hitokami*'s costume, which even today maintains the original magic paraphernalia used by ancient shamans, while neglecting the gear typical of the ordinary warrior. Moreover, the numerous later adaptations of famous *nô* plays for *kabuki* carried over into the latter world the shamanic formula and the highly dramatic phenomena of conjuration, exorcisms, possession, angry ghosts, and so on.

In modern drama and performance–notwithstanding the sweeping Western influence following the reopening of the country at the beginning of the Meiji era (1868-1912)–the deeply rooted shamanistic tradition continued to provide a bottomless resource of inspiration, from Mishima Yukio's modern *nô* plays to the haunting atmosphere of *butô*.

COURT ARISTOCRACY, BUGAKU, AND THE BUDDHIST FASHION

Shamanic practices penetrated all strata of primitive Japanese society, including the first rulers of the clans and, among them, the Yamato chiefs who were to form the basis of the still reigning imperial dynasty. While some village *kagura* (*sato kagura*) in remote mountain areas maintained–in a few cases, to the present time–a primitive and popular form of possession, the imperial court *kagura* (*mikagura*) at the main shrines of Shinto worship transformed those irregular and nonsophisticated rituals into well regulated, elegant ceremonies. This process led to a significant loss of the mysterious, primordial atmosphere, while stately and refined Shinto rituals soon ossified in the form of symbolic actions characterized by a solemn, simple, and sophisticated beauty.

The formation of a new aristocratic sense of beauty reflected in fresh performance genres was decisively influenced by the recently imported Buddhism and Confucian learning, and, in general, by Chinese culture. Scholars of Japanese art and literary aesthetics have dedicated volumes to the study of such subtle aristocratic feelings, expressed in antiquity by terms like *mono no aware* (elegance, pathos). Later, in the Japanese middle ages, this developed into *yûgen* (elegance, grace, sublime beauty) and *ushin* (gentleness, elegance) and, more recently, *wabi* (restrained, quite beauty) and *sabi* (elegant simplicity).[14] Such beauty belonged to a world almost totally different from the rather rough, illogical, and confused shamanistic encounters with the "other dimension." However, it also bore, from the beginning, the goal of a breaking through to awareness of an "other dimension." This was conceived in a more sophisticated way under the influence of the classical Buddhist holy books, and was expressed now in the esoteric terms of harmony with the universe, a feeling of cosmic unity, and–during the late middle-ages formation of the *nô*–in the language of then prevalent Zen and Ji Buddhist speculation about enlightenment.

In the realm of the performing arts, the process for the creation of such encounters was initiated with the introduction of Buddhist-inspired processional performances of *gigaku*.[15] *Gagaku* music and *bugaku* dances soon followed and became fashionable among the court nobility, eventually gaining the imperial court's favor and being established there as the official ceremonial entertainment.

The introduction and ensuing success of Buddhist/Chinese entertainments in temples, at court, and eventually in nearly all places of celebration and worship, meant a sweeping change that, like the first shamanistic wave, would become one of the permanent elements of continuity in Japanese theater traditions.

This meant the inception of a so-far unknown degree of refined splendor in entertainment. In place of the predominantly undyed, whitish hemp garnments worn by the primitive Japanese, and still predominant in Shinto ritual, brightly dyed silks and beautifully crafted, colored masks now brightened the processions/performances of *gigaku*, and later the solemn, sometimes gracious, sometimes imposing, but always highly professional *bugaku* dances. The new *gagaku* orchestral music resulting from a union of complex instruments differed distinctly from the haunting call of the lonely flute or the stamping of a dancing *miko* disrobing in trance to conjure the spirits and entertain an agrarian community. Performance was no longer related to a shamanic concern with ghosts, but aimed rather at suggesting the evolution of the universe in the limitless, cyclical flow of time. The irregular movements of the possessed shaman were no longer recognizable in the forceful, symmetrical movements of *bugaku* dances. These were performed by professional members of the court household, using imported, exotic, colorful costumes and sophisticated masks, all harmonized in an effort to produce a magical atmosphere reflecting the harmony of the celestial spheres, and of celebrating the vast, solemn force that gives birth to all cosmic and earthly movement.

Besides the stately elegance of the dances, costumes, stage, and props, *bugaku* contributed to the creation of a very important structural element of the Japanese performing arts, the tripartite *jo-ha-kyû*, usually translated as beginning, middle, and end, or exposition, development, and climax. This tripartite musical movement was actually meant to be interpreted in terms of a prelude in tempo rubato, a development of orchestral music, and a final "allegro" movement as a finale. The structure became standard in all Japanese performing arts. *Jo-ha-kyû* eventually determined the number and type of plays performed in each *nô* program, dictated the dramatic structure of each *nô* play and dramaturgical unit, and influenced the music and the rhythms of the acting itself. The same structure is to be found in the text, music, and performance of *kabuki* and *bunraku*, and in the traditional dances of *nihon buyô*. It is as pervasive as is, in the Western tradition, the Aristotelian structure of beginning, middle, and end, and can be found even in many of today's intentionally anti-Aristotelian avant-garde experiments.

5.33

PLATE 4

Westerners have admired *bugaku* dances and have also been intrigued by *gagaku* music. Although their occasional performances abroad were not met with the same enthusiasm accorded to the *nô*, they nevertheless earned a mixture of admiration and curiosity from critics and audiences alike.

Traditional discussions of *bugaku* by historians emphasized its unique preservation of music, dances, masks, and costumes from over a thousand years ago and derived from many ancient countries of origin. Recently, however, the emphasis has shifted to reclaiming for the first centuries of *bugaku* activity qualities of flexibility and creativity in the adaptation/assimilation of native *kagura* elements in certain dances. This was before the almost total hardening of the genre as an imperial court and imperial shrine ceremony. Moreover, even in recent times, new *gagaku* music has been composed and some ancient compositions newly adapted by *gagaku* masters who have altered a tradition previously believed untouchable.

It is sometimes not possible to establish either the degree of fidelity to the originals, or whether certain compositions or dances are actually later modifications or additions to the repertory. There is no doubt, however, that the core of the experience today transports us into the refined world of the golden ages of the imperial court and aristocracy (*kuge*, preceding the military aristocracy of the samurai). It represents in Japanese theater history the splendor of Nara through the Kyoto of the Heian period (approximately the 10th and 11th centuries), and becomes the mirror of the court transformation under the influence, assimilation, and Japanization of a very high world culture rooted in Hinduism and its offspring, Buddhism and Confucianism.

SAMURAI CULTURE, THE *NO*, AND THE WAY TO THE SUBLIME

A new type of beauty, expressing the ideal of samurai society, emerged from the decadence of the court aristocracy. It was not the product of a relentless striving for formal perfection by the established professionals at the imperial court but was achieved by newcomers, the vital *sarugaku* performers. They used their extraordinary skills to breach the gap between their low social status, as outcastes forced to live in the outcaste villages (*sanjo*), by becoming part of the staff of famous temples and shrines. They thus eventually were regarded by the citizens as respectable members of the clergy.[16] They were constantly in contact at the places of worship with rituals for appeasing the *tama* of the dead, or with the conjurations, exorcisms, and other more or less shamanism-related ceremonies that were daily requested by thousands of the faithful and that provided one of the clergy's most lucrative sources of revenue. Their skill as entertainers was in demand during the major popular festivals at shrines and temples, from Kyoto to the nation's small villages.

It was to one such festival that the most powerful man in Japan, the shôgun Ashikaga Yoshimitsu (1358-1408), then not yet in his twenties, went in order to see a group of Yamato *sarugaku* actors about which he had heard wonders. He was mightily impressed by the extraordinary skills of the main performer Kan'ami, and fell in love with his young son, Zeami. The Lord of Japan ordered father and son with their troupe to court and became the mighty patron of an art that was then developing into the *nô*. This explains how the beautiful youngster Zeami, one of the most talented theater personalities in world history, assimilated both the refinements of the shôgun's court and the healthy vigor of the developing provinces. He learnt to apply to the art a unique synthesis of popular appeal and samurai discipline, court refinement and the Buddhist way to enlightenment. The result was a gift to the world of a profound stage beauty that would last beyond his life to become a symbol of Japanese artistry.

Japan's traditional lifestyle and arts in general share the concept of the *michi* (the way), according to which the status of each individual is conceived as a challenge to strive relentlessly for the perfection of a state of life; i.e., as a samurai, or, in the arts, as a master of the tea ceremony. The way of the samurai (*bushidô*), or the way of tea (*sadô*), are among formulations of that conception. The outcaste youngster Zeami, while sharing the favors and meals of the young shôgun, had the opportunity to live close to the best minds and best artists of the time. Yoshimitsu, the ruler who, in Japanese history, best exemplifies the idea of a "Renaissance man," was fond of having such individuals around in his sumptuous court.

Zeami therefore also became conversant with the religious masters of Buddhist sects (Yoshimitsu favored Zen) that established enlightenment as the supreme lifetime goal to strive toward, according to the rigid rules of that sect's "way." In such Buddhist tenets and in the praxis of the monks who spent their lives striving for enlightenment, Zeami found inspiration to draw up fundamental life-rules demanding total dedication to the rigorous, relentless training required by the "way" of the *nô*. He outlined for the first time in the East the conditions necessary for a "vocation" allowing the artist to be admitted into the "way" of the professional *nô* performer. This included the almost monastic discipline required for the young aspiring actor to progress and to learn from the Master the secrets of the school, the signs that reveal to the Master the degrees of proficiency achieved by his disciples, and the Master's final mysterious achievement. The supreme degree is a new encounter with the "other dimension," now conceived not as a possession by a mysterious *kami* or a ghost, but, in Buddhist terms, as a glimpse into the final unity with Permanence behind illusion, with the force that keeps together all things, the Buddha-nature of the universe, that also unites performer and audience in an ineffable experience.

Recent translations of and commentaries on Zeami's treatises in Western languages have made available to a larger number of non-Japanese readers than ever a better understanding of the theories of the *nô*.[17] The fundamental notions of *monomane* (mimesis, imitation), *hana* (the flower or the efficacy of performance), *yûgen* (elegance, grace), *kokoro* (the heart, or the unifying principle), *rojaku* (the unique beauty of the essential), *mushin* (beyond *yûgen*, a transcendent, sublime, intuitive beauty), and others, have been reexamined in the context of the religious-aesthetic atmosphere of sophisticated speculation about the nature of peak experiences of artists and their audiences. Zeami's theoretical work has come to be better understood in the light of the sometimes abstruse, but always intriguing, theoretical work of his son-in-law, Komparu Zenchiku, who is still too little known in the West.

Zeami found in Zenchiku the profound theoretician of the Buddhist dimension in the artist's creativity. His speculations go beyond the nô, and, for the non-initiated in the complex history of Buddhist texts and their commentators, are difficult to follow. Only lately have English translations of a number of his writings become available, as have comprehensive studies providing an erudite background to the world that Zeami shared.[18] Such research supports scholarship attempting to shed light on the notion of unexplainable, ineffable Sublimity (myôkafû, the mode of the mysterious flower). Zeami set this as the supreme degree of achievement of the great master in terms similar to those used in the sacred texts related to the ultimate Buddhist experience of enlightenment. In the Kyûi, the treatise in which Zeami traces the various ranks of the nô performer, the myôkafû is indicated by a kôan (Zen riddle) that suggests the impossibility of rational description. Perfect acting technique, the fruit of a lifetime's relentless training and total, religious dedication, eventually leads the superbly talented Master to a commanding performance where the performer is taken over by a superior force, in trancelike enhancement of consciousness (mushin, which also indicates a superior intuitive beauty). The possession by, and epiphany of, something ineffable, are no longer the shamanistic encounter with an individual kami or ghost. Nor do they happen strictly in terms of the religious enlightenment (satori) strived after by Zen and other Buddhist sects. They are conceived rather as marvellous moments of grace, fleeting like everything in the theater, but memorable; the Master becomes for the audience a vehicle through which to experience the Permanence of the one, all-pervading Buddha-nature beyond the distracting multiplicity of surfaces, as in a temporary aesthetic enlightenment. The performing Master might or might not be conscious of the "miracle" of the Presence operating as he feels carried by and at one with an unknown force which operates in his performance, unifying actor and audience. We could talk in Western psychological terms of peak experiences, in Christian terms of contemplation in action, or of a quasimystical experience of the Supreme Being. Aspects of God's infinite beauty are miraculously revealed through the Master, who has been transformed by lifelong training into an instrument/vessel capable of divine revelation.

Because of such spiritual dimensions of depth, the nô has probably attracted more admirers among Western artists and scholars than has any other form of Japanese theater. Western pilgrims to the Orient in search of inspiration were fascinated by something they could not explain and that they could hardly experience through the limitations of realism: even today, relentless training with a quasi-religious striving for formal beauty can still effect the miracle of "the mode of the mysterious flower" in the nô, as well as in other styles of performance.

Western admirers of the 19th and 20th centuries were thrilled and surprised to find that the deep treasures of nô performance were still preserved. Few foreigners, however, were aware that one of the main factors responsible for the preservation of and, in general, the conservativism of the established forms of Japan's performing arts over the centuries was the iemoto system.

Although it already had been applied in some form to bugaku and other post-Heian period arts, the iemoto system reached its maturity in the performing arts at the time of the nô's formation. During the Edo period (1600-1868), it became a general organizational pattern for all the arts. No subsequent modernization or Westernization could ever really undo this system, which has been present de facto in practically all theatrical organizations associated with shimpa, shingeki, post-shingeki, and butô. (It does not, however, exist in bunraku.) The iemoto system undoubtedly played a decisive role among the main forces responsible for the continuity and stubborn preservation of the patterns discovered by the great masters.

In one form or another, with or without using his technical name, the iemoto is the head or "foundation of the house," who is in charge of preserving and transmitting the art in its purity, without breaking the tradition of excellence and fidelity to the rules that ensure continuity. His responsibility extends primarily to the professionals of the family and, especially, to the individual, usually the current iemoto's oldest son, who is designated to succeed him. The treatises of Zeami's secret tradition, for instance, were written for only his designated successor. In the Edo period, when a large number of people, including merchants, farmers, nobles, samurai, and priests, became disciples of nô masters and practiced nô chanting and dance, it was the iemoto's task to make sure that, even among amateurs, the tenets and characteristics of the school would not be changed or forgotten. The powers of a nô iemoto have been traditionally decisive in the casting of roles, in choosing performance texts, in determining the correct interpretation of traditional movements, and in deciding which costumes, masks, and props are to be used. Since the introduction of printing, he has held the copyright for the publication of the school's nô textbooks. In a word, he rules like an absolute king within the school, revered and served by people who depend on his decisions for the possibility of their developing a professional career.

This type of organization tends to reappear in every new group of artists that come together under the leadership of a strong individual. The history of classical and modern Japanese theater arts provides plenty of examples of this organization, which has an enormous influence in resisting change once the genre, or a particular school within the genre, is established. The iemoto system is thus one of the most powerful elements of conservativism in Japan's performing arts. Because of the iemoto system it is easier, in a certain sense, to form a totally new genre, as happened in butô, than modify an established genre of performance like the nô, which is protected from change by the vigilant care of school heads. Butô, the last important addition to the list of Japan's theatrical genres, fell rather quickly under iemoto control. One example is the group founded by Hijikata Tatsumi, who exerted an incredibly tight

7.131

PLATE 5

control over his followers, obliging them to live in a cult-like atmosphere and even in their personal life to be totally obedient to his whims.[19]

BIG CITIES, MIDDLE CLASS TASTE, AND THE AMBIGUOUS REFINEMENT OF THE "FLOATING WORLD"

In the late 16th century and throughout the 17th, following the age of civil war (sengoku jidai), the rise of a special kind of middle class in enormous cities like Edo, Osaka, and Kyoto provided the environment for a fresh theatrical creation that was to fascinate the West and become a new symbol of the Japanese theater: kabuki.

In kabuki a totally worldly, melodramatic, eyefilling, colorful, spectacular synthesis was achieved by a new brand of artists, who were as crowd-pleasing as the popular acrobats and magicians on the riverbanks, and as dedicated to their art as nô and kyôgen actors. They also were as devoted to pleasing the wealthy, business-minded middle class as were the most refined brothel entertainers. They had no scruples about dramatizing any ancient story of the aristocratic or samurai past, the lurid scandals occurring the day before in the nearby pleasure quarters, or terrifying stories of ghosts and vengeance. They also were adept at adapting nô plays by dressing them up according to the new, quasi-bourgeois tastes. With legendary elegance, they impersonated the most famous beauties of the red-light districts, ultimately even dictating to them the latest fashions in clothes and behavior. While imaginatively adapting the ideals, costumes, and typical behavior of aristocrats and samurai for the delectation of the townspeople, they also created a wide range of middle-class heroes, from an exaggerated samurai/hitokami dressed in shamanistic paraphernalia who defeats rows of enemies in a stylized battle, to a realistic "chivalrous commoner" (otokodate) who roams the teahouses, apparently for pleasure, but in reality searching for a precious heirloom, to the "prostitute with a golden heart" ready to make any sacrifice for her endangered lover.

The list can go on, but the point is that kabuki actors created a spectacular potpourri that perpetuated the popular shamanic element (one famous actor was even venerated by his fans as the incarnation of a kami). They kept alive, in their way, the Shinto and Buddhist sense of elegance and the quest for the perfection of newly developed techniques, achieving extraordinary results and immense popularity, and, ultimately, producing an art that can still impress, move, and inspire Japanese and foreign spectators.

Although kabuki is considered as one of Japan's most "indigenous" arts—being born out of totally native circumstances and reaching its zenith during a time the nation was isolated from the rest of the world and seemingly having no non-Japanese input—recent research has pointed to the possibility of Christian missionary influence. The first kabuki dances coincide with performances of plays produced by Jesuit missionaries during the so-called Christian epoch, at the end of the 16th and the beginning of the 17th centuries. During this formative period, kabuki was particularly susceptible to influences, and eager to use exotic foreign experiences and ornamentations. The prostitutes that performed onna kabuki were keen on attracting attention with anything new, fashionable, and exotic. They used such adornments as a crucifix hanging at the bosom, or stage decor including an imported tiger skin laid over a high chair, or costuming such as the baggy long pants worn by contemporary Portuguese visitors.[20]

Some scholars have objected that Jesuit dramatic activity was limited to the faraway islands of Kyûshû and did not influence the big cities where kabuki developed. Recent research, however, has established that Jesuit missionaries in Kyoto as well as in Kyûshû showed the same eagerness to use the theater as a means of propaganda and education as they had in their European schools.[21] The Jesuits—known for their practice of adapting to a local culture in order to gain the confidence and the esteem of the native population—became familiar with nô and kyôgen, and adopted those modes and other popular dances to present their message-laden plays.

Although it is almost impossible to prove with certainty that early kabuki made any attempt to imitate foreign models, it does seem possible that kabuki probably would have evolved in a different way had it not had some contact with the dramaturgy of Christian plays and the solemn processions and ceremonies introduced by the Jesuits in which large crowds, including distinguished Japanese guests, participated. It is important to remember that the Jesuits introduced into Japan the production of what Westerners would consider "regular" plays in several acts; that model might have lingered in the memory of the actors when a few decades later, in 1664, they introduced the earliest kabuki versions of multiact plays (tsuzuki kyôgen).

The heavy and colorful kabuki makeup called kumadori, used for aragoto-style heroes and villains and for supernatural characters, might also have looked different had there not been previous models used for the painted-face roles (l'ien pu) of Chinese opera. Moreover, China's dramatic masterpieces, especially those of the Yuan period (1280-1368), which abound in melodramatic situations, are thought by some to be echoed in kabuki plays.

CATCHING UP WITH THE WEST AND FINDING THE ROOTS AGAIN

The first contact with Western visitors in the 16th century had offered, for a few, a brief experience with Western dramaturgy. Soon, this was practically wiped out by the official suppression of Christianity and the strict policy of isolating the country from most foreign contact. That first period of contact with the West could not bring to the Japanese theater the kind of deep change initiated by the second wave of contact, which still continues. Modernization and Westernization took their immovable place in Japan's performing arts alongside the persisting shamanic influence of village kagura, the aristocratic elegance of court bugaku, the pursuit in samurai society of the highest experience of the sublime flower (myôkafû) in the nô, and the spectacular showmanship of the kabuki actor as an expression of Edo-period townspeople society.

When the second wave of official contact with the West hit Japan in the mid-19th century, an unstoppable process of catching up followed. Eventually, this was highly successful as far as financial and technological modernization/Westernization are concerned. In the performing arts, however, the path to critical approval and international recognition of the new Western-influenced forms of *shimpa* and *shingeki* was difficult and strewn with obstacles.

Shortly after the reopening of the country, the traditional performing arts went through a severe crisis because the nation was in turmoil, and the innovations sweeping Japan were not creatively applied to the stage for a long time. With the Meiji Restoration (1868), the *nô* lost the powerful protection of the shogunate and seemed headed for quasi-oblivion, while *kabuki* held on to its monopoly of popular appeal and was not seriously challenged by the availability of new, Westernized theatrical entertainments.

In the first few decades after the Meiji Restoration, insurmountable barriers of language, know-how, and cost made it impossible for foreign theater companies to visit Japan. Only twenty years into Meiji, however, the discrediting of Edo era ways and the desire to fight the crumbling old political system introduced into the Japanese theater a previously almost unknown element, which, under the shogunate, had been banned by strict censorship. *Shimpa* (lit., "new school") was born in 1888 as an openly political theater, conceived as a weapon aimed at the conservative powers, and belonging to the impatient young political activists known as *sôshi*. *Shimpa* was responsible for the first stirrings of Westernized productions in Japan. Its contributions included the introduction of contemporary political events (banned under the shogunate), the return of women to the playing of female roles (also previously banned), and the adoption of what was then considered realism.

It took until 1894 before a small number of Japanese experienced the performance of a foreign opera, and a much longer time was needed before professional foreign actors performed Shakespeare in Japan. And when Kawakami Otojirô, the founder of *shimpa* and introducer of realism into Japan, tired of his lack of recognition by the Japanese public, he tried his luck abroad in 1899 with a tour to Honolulu, San Francisco, Chicago, and Paris. However, he had to fake an expertise in *kabuki* and rely on his wife, Sada Yacco, a trained geisha, building on her experience as a classical entertainer/dancer to garner unexpected success with European audiences as, ironically, the introducer of traditional Japanese performing arts abroad![22]

The introduction of Western influence—which embraced dramatic content, dramatic structure, performance style, set design, lighting, theater architecture, seating arrangements, and every other aspect of the multifaceted theater organization from advertising to ticket sales—eventually brought Japan into the contemporary international theater world. The new Westernized theater was there to stay, in the form of *shingeki*, opera, musicals, revues, and other Western forms. These were more or less assimilated as the theatrical counterpart of a way of life that had become part of the international community, and included the new, commonly held beliefs based on the hopes held out by science, the temptations of social utopias in the form of Marxist propaganda (many *shingeki* people were firm believers), the art for art's sake movement, and so on. The *shingeki* world increasingly reflected the multiplicity of ideological and political positions in the Western world. It seemed committed to obliviating the pillars of Japanese tradition, thereby opening the door to absorption within an international common denominator.

The excitement of the shamanic possession of the village festivals was gone, *bugaku's* aristocratic beauty seemed irretrievably lost, and *nô's* relentless striving for perfection and its sense of the "way" toward a profound encounter at the end of the journey had given way to a pseudo-realistic approximation of a not-yet personally experienced way of life. The spectacular power of the *kabuki* superstar was too often substituted for by middle-class *shingeki* actors who performed poorly digested Western plays.[23]

The history of *shingeki*, with its few major, longlasting companies and its hundreds of continuously forming and dissolving groups, is a mirror of the imported ideologies and aesthetic positions that dominated the field. Of these, the dominant ones were, on the one hand, the openly political and predominantly Marxist and, on the other, the apolitical/artistic. The often contradictory multiplicity of approaches to the primary task of rejuvenating and—largely through realism—modernizing the new theater had to contend with *shingeki's* limited appeal to the average paying spectator, its lack of funds, adequate rehearsal, performance spaces, and—because of the financial hardships involved—scarcity of good actors.

Although *shingeki* eventually gave to Japan several outstanding playwrights of international caliber, such as Mishima Yukio and Abe Kôbô, as well as a few memorable productions, it was the cinema and then the post-*shingeki* avant-garde and *butô* dance that once more spoke a language of intensity, and that fused experience of the West with a revitalized appreciation of the *nô* and *kabuki* heritage, paradoxically rediscovered through international interest in a tradition that had been almost forgotten by thoroughly Westernized, creative, and gifted young generations of theater people. For them, Westernization was a fait accompli. They had grown up with it, and had studied modern Western ideas more than old Japanese ones. Discovery of *nô* and *kabuki* was almost as new, surprising, and shocking to them as it is for Western performers who travel to Japan and enter those worlds that still occupy a space in Japan's modern cultural mentality as half-ossified museum pieces. In the 1950s, the borrowing by film directors Kurosawa Akira, Mizoguchi Kenji, or Ozu Yasujirô of powerful imagery, sounds, and visual intensity, and even shamanic effects from rediscovered native performing arts, stunned the world when transferred to cinematic art.

The post-*shingeki* movement of the 1960s and 1970s—while sharing the demons of the European and American search for a new identity in the aftermath of post World War II spiritual confusion—gave birth to a vital rediscovery and reelaboration of the traditional performing arts, not in their specific techniques, but in their spirit of total dedication. The founders of *butô* also found in their dark, iconoclastic revolution of dance principles a new, almost desperate discipline, achieving stunning results that mesmerized the international dance world. The circle seemed completed, once again mainly by artists outside the traditional performing arts. These were artists that had been trained in Western techniques, but who had discovered among Western admirers of the Japanese tradition an impulse, a curiosity to return to native sources and to find there inspiration, discipline, and spiritual power that would ultimately lead to international recognition and success for their original accomplishments.

1. Miner (1958), 214: "Relatively unknown until recent times, *kabuki* and *nô* and even the Japanese film seem suddenly to have become a source of fertile inspiration for writers and producers." Typically, however, this authoritative book makes no mention of other dramatic genres besides *nô* and *kabuki*.

2. See the following essays in this volume, especially "Japanese Theater in the World" by J. Thomas Rimer.

3. See Kirby (1975).

4. See the following essays and a bibliography on the subject in Ortolani (1995), 332-335.

5. See Eliade (1961), 142-186.

6. A summary of the ideas concerning the shamanic nature of Uzume's god-possession (*kamugakari* or, now commonly, *kamigakari*) can be found in Philippi (1969), 83-86.

7. Hori (1983), 181.

8. Exposure of the genitals in order to exert magic powers in driving away evil spirits was practiced among the Ainu in Japan, and in other populations, to entertain and impart vigor. See Matsumura (1954-58) III, 91-107.

9. Hoff (1978), 141, proposes a description of present-day *kagura* as "an environment for performance" and "a system which has produced various performance types during its long lifetime." See also Thornbury (1997) for updated information about today's *kagura* performances and an extensive bibliography on the subject.

10. See Umehara ([1972] 1981).

11. Ortolani (1984),166-190, also provides a bibliography of Japanese scholarly research on the subject.

12. *Nembutsu odori* was a dance during which an invocation to Buddha was continuously repeated. See the connection between *nembutsu* and the pacification of spirits of the dead in Hori (1983), 117-139.

13. An English translation/commentary of the text of this *nembutsu odori* is to be found in Webber (1982), 93-99. According to that text, Okuni is presented as the incarnation in disguise of the *kami* of Izumo who came to visit in order to appease the soul of Sanza.

14. See the definitions of these concepts and the change in the nuances of aesthetic meaning in Hisamatsu (1963), 103-112.

15. The first master of *gigaku*, Mimashi, arrived from the kingdom of Kudara in 612, when Chinese music had already reached the Japanese court.

16. See the description of this planned effort of acquiring social respectability in Gotô (1975), 574, and Ortolani (1984), 171-173.

17. See especially Rimer and Yamazaki (1984), and the translations/commentaries of *Kyûi*, *Kakyô*, and *Kyakuraika*, by Nearman (1978, 1970, and 1982).

18. While Thornhill (1993) focuses on Zenchiku's Buddhistic background, Pinnington (1994) stresses the Shintoistic aspects in Zenchiku's writings.

19. See the Ph.D. dissertation by Kurihara (1996), especially chapter 4, dedicated to the training, and chapter 5, about the cult of Hijikata. Kurihara also handles the excesses of the eccentric founder of *butô*, which went well beyond the routine authority of an *iemoto*.

20. See Ortolani (1964), where the Western ornaments are illustrated.

21. Leims (1990), represents the most important research in this field.

22. The actual name of the lady who accompanied her husband, Kawakami Otojirô, on tour was Kawakami Sadayakko (sometimes spelled Sadayacco). Her geisha name in Japan had been Sada Yakko (or Yacco), which was the name she chose for her tours abroad and which was used by the press and in the programs. See Savarese (1992), 243-254.

23. One of the severest critics of *shingeki* but also one of its most valiant promoters was Fukuda Tsuneari, who translated Shakespeare's plays into modern Japanese. His perspectives on *shingeki* history and the genre's problems may be found in his many volumes of essays and commentaries. See Fukuda (1966) and Ortolani (1971), 463-499.

1.34

PLATE 6

1.9 A

1.9 C

1.9 D

1.9 F

I. JAPANESE THEATER IN THE WORLD

J. Thomas Rimer

Theater, related as it is to the human response to the universe on every level, may well be less confined by geographical or national boundaries than many other forms of art. Skill and conviction on the part of performers, as well as a natural curiosity on the part of at least some audiences, allow for the transcendence of many barriers. This is certainly true in the case of Japan, whose geography, at least until the coming of convenient air travel in the postwar period, placed it at a daunting remove from the continent of Asia as well as from Europe and the United States. Nevertheless, the influences of Japanese theater have become increasingly profound on diverse stages around the world.

In early periods, from the beginning of Japanese civilization until the Middle Ages, it was the Japanese theater which received diverse influences from the continent of Asia. In our time, the wheel has come full circle: Japanese theater, classical and contemporary alike, has become a notable influence on the work of adventuresome theater practitioners around the world, from Paris and New York to Beijing.

It is true, of course, that the earliest contacts with China and Korea, which constituted virtually the entire civilized world as perceived by the Japanese in those early centuries, were sporadic. Travel was difficult at best, and periodic internal political dislocations within China made consistent patterns of travel and influence difficult to maintain. While written sources are scarce, it seems clear, for example, that many of the theatrical ceremonies practiced at the court during the T'ang dynasty (618-907) were known to the Japanese. They thereby influenced the proto-theatrical ceremonies and enter-tainments created during the period in which Nara served as the early capital (740-786), and also had an impact in the Heian period (790-1190) as well, when the court in Kyoto set the patterns. From the descriptions of the elegant court dances and other ceremonies recorded in such 11th-century literary works as *Genji Monogatari* (Tale of Genji, c. 1025) and *Makura no Sôshi* (The Pillow Book of Sei Shônagon, c. 1010), it is appar-ent that continental influences were warmly welcomed. The sections of this catalogue dedicated to the early forms of Japanese theater make these influences and inspirations clear.

The fall of the T'ang Dynasty cut off possibilities of travel for Japanese and Chinese alike and, after the final successful repulsion in 1281 of the Mongols who, having conquered China, attempted to invade Japan, further developments of the Japanese theater were largely confined within her national borders.

From the 1500s on, however, the coming of the West brought an increasingly complex set of relationships between Japanese theater and the theater of the European world. The United

States, too, had her place in this multilayered exchange, but this relationship was not to achieve any lasting significance until the postwar years. For 400 years, from roughly 1550 to 1950, it was the European/Japanese dialogue which did most to enlarge the vision of both sides as to the nature and potential significance of the theater.

The coming of the great Catholic missionary St. Francis Xavier (1506-1552) to southernmost Japan in 1549 brought the first systematic confrontation of sophisticated Europeans with Japanese culture. Curious and often enthusiastic about the Japanese arts, these early European visitors left written accounts that are often surprisingly observant. And while it is true that those first European spectators of the Japanese theater unconsciously maintained a sense of the innate superiority of their own traditions, they were nevertheless able to record what they experienced with discrimination. One of the first references to the Japanese theater occurs in the writings of the Portuguese missionary Luis Frois (1532-1597). Concerning the *nô*, for example, he remarks as follows.

> In our theaters the masks cover the chin starting from the beard downward; the Japanese ones are so small that an actor who appears in a woman's role has his beard always protruding from below.

> Among us polyphonic music is sonorous and pleasant; since all sing together in one single voice in falsetto, Japanese music is the most horrible imaginable. Among us the music of the gentry usually sounds more pleasant than that of the commoners; the music of the Japanese gentry is unendurable for us, while that of their sailors is pleasant.[1]

So successful were these missionary efforts that a leading Jesuit father, aided by a Christian feudal lord (daimyô) of Kyûshû, in southern Japan, sent a delegation of four young Japanese boys (aged 12 or 13) to the courts of Philip II of Spain and Pope Gregory XIII. The mission left Japan in 1582 and returned in 1590. The young men and their entourage had a tremendous effect on those who saw them in Spain and Italy. In particular, they were given a spectacular reception in Venice, where they witnessed a number of theatrical and musical events. They went on to Padua, then Vicenza, where a plaque shows them in attendance at the famous Teatro Olimpico, the great Palladian structure that was so influential in the development of European theater.[2]

The visit of this group created both a lively sympathy and a considerable curiosity about the Japanese arts and culture among Europeans. Had events not turned so precipitously against the Christians in the early 1600s, exchanges, including cultural exchanges, would surely have begun. By the end of the 1630s, however, the country was closed off, Christianity prohibited, and foreign influences severely curbed. This first period of flowering, however, did leave traces in a series of dramas written by Jesuit playwrights during the next two centuries. Widely performed at Jesuit schools in Europe, usually in Latin, these dramas used music, dancing, drama, even fencing, in order to exalt the Christian ideals shown by the Japanese,

often those who accepted martyrdom for their belief in Jesus. Some of the plays, indeed, had happy endings. Accounts suggest that the plays drew on Western, rather than on Japanese dramaturgical principles, but these dramas, widely performed, helped keep the subject of Japan and Japanese culture alive for 200 years.[3]

The closing of Japan again reduced to a minimum both the opportunity for Westerners to learn about the traditional Japanese performing arts or for the Japanese to learn about the developments of the post-Renaissance tradition in Europe. True, there did remain a Dutch outpost in Nagasaki, but the writings left by these merchants and others do not indicate that they were able to witness any theatrical performances. It was in 1853 with the opening of Japan by the American Commodore Perry, that significant contacts were renewed with the Western world. And, as in 1585, the Japanese caused a sensation wherever they went. The poet Walt Whitman, observing the first Japanese delegation to the United States in 1860, one of the first official visits by the Japanese abroad after a period of more than 200 years, wrote with enthusiasm and wonderment of these new people who seemed exotic strangers stepping into the Western world.

> Over the Western sea, hither from Niphon come,
> Courteous, the swart-cheek'd two-sworded envoys,
> Leaning back in their open barouches, bare-headed,
>   impassive,
> Ride to-day through Manhattan.[4]

From this time onwards, the complexity and richness of the connections between East and West grew ever greater. China, too, would develop brief but important connections with modern Japanese theater in the years prior to World War I, but in the period from the 1880s to World War II, the European-Japanese link remained the most important.[5]

With Japan now opened to commerce, education, even missionary activity again, more and more visitors flooded into the country in the 1870s and afterwards. Generally speaking, the Americans then living in Japan remained for business or other practical interests, and there were relatively few persons of culture among them, with the obvious exception of the writer Lafcadio Hearn, who wrote widely on Japanese life and culture with such skill that much of his work remains evocative even today.

Some Americans, however, made real contributions, sometimes even involuntarily. For example, in the confusions of post-restoration politics, such classical forms as the *nô* theater, which had been patronized for several centuries by the now discredited shogunate, had difficulty in finding subsidies needed to sustain their troupes. A group of actors assembled for a special performance prepared for General Ulysses S. Grant, who toured Japan in 1879, so impressed this unlikely aesthete that his praises eventually led to timely government assistance.

European theater groups also made trips to Japan and provided entertainment both for the foreign population and for those Japanese who wished to attend. Interest in Shakespeare was apparently high among both groups from the first contact, but, according to the British scholar Basil Hall Chamberlain, resident in Japan in the late 19th century, opera (a form which, after all, comes closest to Japan's conception of "total theater") found little immediate sympathy:

> Oh! The effect upon the Japanese audience! When once they had recovered from the first shock of surprise, they were seized with a wild fit of hilarity at the high notes of the prima donna, who was really not at all bad. The people laughed at the absurdities of European singing till their sides shook, and the tears rolled down their cheeks; and they stuffed their sleeves into their mouths, as we might our pocket-handkerchiefs, in the vain endeavor to contain themselves.[6]

In this case, of course, increased familiarity by no means came to breed contempt; tickets for performances of opera, particularly as sung by Western troupes at wildly inflated prices, remain one of the most highly sought-out luxuries in contemporary Japanese life.

If Westerners visiting Japan were fascinated by Japanese theater, visits by Japanese artists to the Western world during the period brought even greater excitement to European and American audiences. Those visiting Japan were, on the whole, not specialists of drama, music, or dance, and the observations, however sincerely offered, remained those of interested amateurs. By the time that Japanese performers came to the United States and Europe, however, audiences, critics, and theater practitioners were increasingly prepared to greet them. Then too, as Kishi Tetsuo writes in his essay on the modern theater of Japan, the influences of Western spoken drama were being felt in Japan itself.

There are doubtless two reasons for this initial enthusiasm for Japanese theater in the West. In the first place, the artistic side of Japan had become widely known through the export of traditional woodblock prints, which had caught the eye of such diverse artists as Whistler, Degas, Manet, and Van Gogh. Their enthusiasm in turn validated the Japanese sense of space, color, and line, all of which can be said to show a certain consonance with the use of color, space, and movement in the classical Japanese theater.

Secondly, Japan soon found its representation in Western works written for the European and American stages. Such works as Gilbert and Sullivan's *The Mikado*, written in 1885, and *The Geisha* of Sidney Jones, a "Japanese musical play" written in 1896, became enduringly popular not only in English-speaking countries but in France, Germany, Austria, and elsewhere, where they were regularly performed down to the time of World War II. In these productions, and dozens like them, Japan was, of course, "represented" on stage by foreign performers, virtually none of whom had any first hand experience of the culture at all, so that during this period the Japanese themselves seemed denied the possibilities of any direct self-expression. With the extraordinary visit to America and Europe, in 1889 and 1900, of the troupe of Kawakami Otojirô (1864-1911) and his wife Kawakami Sadayakko (1872-1946), known in the West as Sada Yacco, Sadayacco, or Sadayakko (used hereafter), however, all that was to change.

By the 1880s, Japanese artists and intellectuals had become increasingly interested in the Western theater. *Kabuki*, the popular theater of the Tokugawa period, now seemed unwieldy as a vehicle for the expression of current concerns, particularly in the political realm. Among those who first attempted political drama during this period was the actor and theater entrepreneur Kawakami Otojirô; after a number of professional vicissitudes, he decided to recoup some of his losses by embarking on an American and European tour. Gathering up a little band of eighteen performers, all male (as was still the custom), as well as his wife, Sadayakko, an elegant former geisha, he headed first for the United States, where the group began performing on the West Coast before moving on to Chicago, Boston, and New York. According to some accounts, Sadayakko herself had not intended to perform but was drafted to take part when one of the female impersonators fell ill.[7] The troupe staged a number of short plays based (some Japanese spectators considered them debased) on *kabuki* and other traditional texts. Met at first with indifferent success, the group began to find enthusiastic audiences in Boston and was tremendously successful in New York, so much so that the Japanese consul invited the group to perform in Washington for President McKinley and other distinguished guests. Some accounts posit a meeting between Kawakami and that great figure in the British theater, Sir Henry Irving himself, who was performing in New York with Ellen Terry. The encounter supposedly spurred Kawakami on to create his own adaption into Japanese of Shakespeare's *The Merchant of Venice*.

Buoyed by these successes the group moved on to London, where they performed, among other places, at Buckingham Palace for the Prince of Wales. By this time, it was clear that the reason for the extraordinary success of the troupe was because of the performances of Sadayakko. Without training in acting for the theater, she used her dancing skills and winsome personality to create a stage persona that overwhelmed contemporary audiences.

Sadayakko and the troupe scored their most extraordinary success in Paris, where they began performing in July of 1900 for the World Exposition. Part of her achievement, undoubtedly, came from Sadayakko's encounter with the American dancer Loïe Fuller (1862-1928), herself something of an anomaly. Fuller, born in Fullersburg, Illinois, began as an actress in vaudeville but eventually turned herself into a dancer who, by manipulating lights and wearing flowing, diaphanous robes, created a whole new visual vocabulary. By the end of the century, she was the toast of Paris. She had a theater in which to present innovative works at the World Exposition. When she heard about Sadayakko's performances, she went to see for herself and invited the troupe to perform. The reviews were extraordinary. Sadayakko was compared to Duse and other great actresses of the period, and her praises were sung by many of the greatest artists and intellectuals of the day, among them Rodin, Gide, and Antoine, whose Théâtre Libre did so much to bring contemporary drama to France. Once the Paris performances were concluded, Fuller organized a contract for the troupe that took them to find equal success in Brussels, Berlin, Leipzig, Rome, Milan, Venice, Vienna, Moscow, and elsewhere. Such diverse European artists as Hugo von Hofmannsthal and Vsevolod Meyerhold fell under her sway. Isadora Duncan, another great dancer of the period, was so entranced by what she saw that she followed Sadayakko to Berlin in order to observe additional performances. The young Picasso did a drawing of Sadayakko. One account suggests that Puccini consulted her during her visit to Italy concerning details of Japanese life that found their way into his 1904 *Madama Butterfly*, which was to succeed *Iris*, Mascagni's once-popular opera of 1898, much loved by Caruso, as the representative "Japanese" musical work. The triumph was, apparently, total.

Cultural reflections and counter-reflections, however, reveal shadows as well as light, and this first encounter had its detractors as well. For many Japanese, observing this first attempt at an East-West theatrical dialogue, popular and merely sensational dramas such as *The Geisha and the Knight*—the greatest success of the troupe—seemed vulgar and hardly worthy of Japan's greatest traditions. Americans and Europeans, however, were watching the troupe through their own eyes, and with their own predilections. For them, Kawakami's troupe brought something more authentically Japanese than had ever been available to them before, and they took away with them both a sense of respect and a larger curiosity for Japanese theater. Kawakami, on his side, gained much as well. He brought back to Japan a passion for Shakespeare, whose works began to be used, and indeed still continue to be employed, as a means to fuel the development of modern and avant-garde theater in Japan. Sadayakko's performances increased the possibilities for actresses to perform on the stage, at least in Tokyo, and, indeed, Sadayakko in later years founded the first school for professional actresses in Japan.

Concerning the reception of Japanese theater in Europe during this period, however, one point in particular should be noted. Each Western theater artist observing Kawakami's repertory tended to view these productions in terms of his or her Western artistic specialty. For dancers such as Duncan and Fuller, Sadayakko was a dancer; for others, she appeared an actress. Playwrights tended to react to these productions as though they were basically spoken drama, rather than, as was apparently the case, theatrical creations which included mime and possibly some modest acrobatics in order to represent, however modestly, the kind of "total theater" possible in *nô* and *kabuki*. Thus at this time the Japanese ideal was most often awkwardly cast into pre-existing European and American artistic forms. Some drew on this material for operas, some for ballets, some for spoken dramas. The kind of synthesis posited by the great Japanese traditions would long continue to elude Western artists. True, after his encounter with Sadayakko, Meyerhold made a translation from German into Russian of

one act of a well-known scene from *kabuki* and *bunraku*, "Terakoya" ("The Village School," part of *Sugawara Denju Tenarai Kagami* [Sugawara and the Secrets of Calligraphy]), and Max Reinhardt incorporated in a few of his Berlin productions certain techniques (including the *hanamichi* runway, brought to New York for his 1912 production of *Sumurun*) from Japanese stagecraft suggested to him by his gifted designer Emil Orlik, who had lived in Japan for two years at the beginning of the century. The revolving stage was an even earlier technological import from Japan, being introduced in Munich in 1896. Perhaps the most consistent response to Japanese theater was that maintained by the Soviet film maker Sergei Eisenstein, whose excited response to a visit of a *kabuki* troupe to Moscow and Leningrad in 1928 inspired him, by his own account, to create "symphonic images" in his films.

Many distinguished writers found inspiration in the texts of Japanese theater, insofar as they could learn about them through translation. In Ireland, for example, William Butler Yeats, wearying of the kind of realistic theater prevalent in his period, began to compose a series of *nô*-inspired dramas, beginning with *At the Hawk's Well*, first staged in 1916. The plays often deal with Irish mythology, just as *nô* often deals with similar subjects from Japan's past. Yeats came to the Japanese example through a remarkable series of coincidences. Ezra Pound, the young American poet, had been asked to revise the unpublished translations of *nô*, made some years before by Ernest Fenollosa, the American enthusiast for Japanese culture who had lived in Japan for more than a decade at the end of the 19th century. He showed them in turn to Yeats, who, now reinforced in his wish to create a truly poetic style of drama, began to fashion his text, but without any precise idea of how such a play might be realized on the stage. An encounter with Michio Ito, a young Japanese dancer who came to Europe to study with the Swiss Emil Jacques Dalcroze, founder of eurhythmics, permitted the first production. Ito, incidentally, went on to earn fame as a choreographer in New York and Hollywood; his reputation dimmed only because of the atmosphere in the United States during World War II.[8]

Others were drawn to *kabuki*. The poet John Masefield, a disciple of Yeats and eventually poet-laureate of England, became friends in about 1910 with Laurence Binyon, one of the great early scholars of Asian art, who worked at the British Museum. Encouraged by Binyon's enthusiasm, Masefield, who, like Yeats, was also trying out his abilities as a dramatist, decided to adapt the 18th-century drama of the 47 loyal samurai (*Kanadehon Chûshingura* [Chûshingura: The Treasury of Loyal Retainers]) for the contemporary stage: "I had known the story of the Ronin for many years," Masefield wrote, and his adaption, entitled *The Faithful*, was first presented in 1914 by the Birmingham Repertory Theater, and had subsequent, and successful, productions in London and New York.[9] Masefield's play has its modest attractions, but it is fascinating to note that he found himself compelled to add lengthy and specific psychological justifications for the actions of his characters. In the original, Asano, as the lord of his fief, must be avenged; no questions are asked, at least in the text itself. In Masefield's version, revenge is possible because the lord has initially been

1.33

PLATE 7

shown to the audience as a good and kind man. The shift of vision shows how far apart the two worlds still remained.

As translations improved, Western visions of the nature and accomplishments of the Japanese theater broadened. In this regard, no one made a greater contribution during this period than Arthur Waley, whose elegant recreations, found in his *The Nô Plays of Japan*, first published in 1921, and still widely read and admired, showed for the first time the deeper beauty of the texts he chose to render into English. Waley's collection was soon translated in turn into German. In 1930, Bertolt Brecht, fascinated by what he considered a dramatic structure capable of use as a means of moral persuasion, wrote with composer Kurt Weill *Der Jasager* (The Yes-Sayer), an opera for schools that, although relatively simple to perform musically and dramatically, remains, after *The Threepenny Opera*, one of their most mordant and lively works. Although the Buddhist piety of the original text (the *nô* play *Kantan*) is here replaced with Communist dialectics, Brecht's use of the *nô* structure, and Weill's and his understanding that music as well as text were required in order to create a more powerful resonance, were altogether successful.

All of these writers learned about Japan from a distance. Indeed, Arthur Waley never left London. However, one of the greatest dramatists and poets of the prewar period (although his reputation has not fully carried into the English-speaking world), Paul Claudel, makes use of Japan in his work with an authority denied to the others, since he served as the French ambassador to Japan from 1921 to 1927. Long fascinated by Japanese art and aesthetics since a trip to Japan early in the century, Claudel wrote famous essays on *nô*, *bunraku*, and *kabuki*,[10] and used many of the insights he gained from watching such performances in his own dramatic works, perhaps nowhere more notably than in his mammoth epic drama *Le Soulier de Satin* (The Satin Slipper), most of which he wrote while living in Tokyo. An enormously long and difficult play to stage, Claudel's intransigent masterpiece gained world renown when Jean-Louis Barrault, himself long an admirer of classical Japanese theater, staged and restaged it in the postwar period.

The play is divided into four "Days," a vast structure that itself recalls a lengthy *kabuki* play, and is set in the 1600s. In the Fourth Day, there is a particularly striking exchange between Don Rodrigo, the protagonist, and his Japanese colleague, the artist Daibutsu. Their conversation reveals Claudel's sharp and ironic understanding of the political implications of those first encounters between Europe and Japan.

The Japanese: Was it with cannon-balls that you reckoned to show your sympathy?
Don Rodrigo: One uses what one has, and I have never been free with flowers or fondling. You were too well-off in your little dry hole in the middle of the ocean, in your little tight-shut garden taking your tea in little sips out of little cups. It worries me to see people well off; it's immoral; I itched to butt into the middle of your ceremonial.

The Japanese: Whether you liked it or not you had to spend some time with us learning repose and stability.[11]

In the period prior to World War II, it was perhaps Claudel most of all who, through his long residency in Japan and his attraction to traditional Japanese culture (and, perhaps, despite his militant Catholic sympathies), managed to absorb the traditions of the Japanese theater and best bend them to his own creative use.

The coming of World War II broke the active connections between Europe, the United States, and Japan, and they were not to be renewed until the late 1950s. Once renewed, the sense of contact, and of a shared theatrical vocabulary, grew enormously. Perhaps the main change that occurred involved the emergence of the United States, both as an influence on Japanese theater, and as a conduit through which Japanese ideas reached Europe and elsewhere. In the years prior to World War II, the main axis had been between Japan and Europe. That was now to change. Some have attributed the upsurge of American interest in Japan, and thus in Japanese culture and the arts, to the Allied Occupation of Japan, when a multitude of American soldiers and civilians lived all over the country, many for protracted periods. Most, as it turned out, came away with a continuing fascination for the country. Several of the best postwar books on Japanese theater, in fact, were written by Americans who had served in the armed forces during the Occupation.

Perhaps the first crucial event in the postwar period that helped to develop this nascent American interest in Japanese theater was the initial tour of kabuki to the United States in 1960.[12] In this gesture of cultural reconciliation, the Japanese promoters were initially nervous that, despite the fact that the greatest actors of the generation were to appear, this classical theater would be misunderstood and found to be merely stilted or feudalistic. They need not have worried.

The American audience was ready for the *kabuki*. Every seat was sold and the troupe could easily have played another month. The reviews were almost entirely enthusiastic and upon those occasions when they were not, respectful. And the same people kept coming again and again: Garbo was one, another was Anne Bancroft, another was Irene Worth. There were others too, not famous, but faces one would recognize in the intermissions or after the performances, someone who had been there before. The audience was intelligent and completely receptive. After the first performance of *Dôjô-ji* the applause thundered as it never does at the Kabuki-za. Utaemon stood in front of the curtain, almost bewildered; then he stepped forward, smiled, and took bow after bow.[13]

This postwar American fascination with Japanese theater, once ignited, has continued ever since.

Now, for the first time, Western musicians became actively interested in the Japanese example. A number of composers, among them Lou Harrison and Harry Partch, attempted to make use of Japanese elements in their own work. The most notable among these experiments was *Curlew River*, composed by the great British composer Benjamin Britten in 1964. While on a trip to Japan in 1956, Britten was so drawn into the world of *nô* that he had his librettist William Plomer recast the play *Sumidagawa* (The River Sumida) as a medieval Christian legend. The opera retains some of the characteristics of the *nô* (the protagonist is masked; all performers are male), but he replaced the original Japanese choral passages, redolent of Buddhist music, with Gregorian chant, used with brilliance to underscore the heartbreaking discovery by a madwoman of the grave of her dead child.

Interest in Japanese theater has also found its way into more popular forms of theater. Stephen Sondheim's *Pacific Overtures*, for example, uses Japanese theatrical devices and certain Japanese musical motifs in creating a sometimes comic, sometimes somber retelling of how America came to Japan in the 19th century. This theater work, since its first New York production in 1976, has gone on, particularly in Great Britain, to receive productions that have firmly established it as a modern masterpiece of musical theater.

The world of dance also now became involved with Japan. Perhaps the first work of substance to be produced in the United States was the ballet "Bugaku," choreographed in 1962 by George Balanchine. In his attempt to recast his vision of the ancient court dances of Japan into a contemporary work, Balanchine was much aided by his choice of a musical score by the brilliant young Mayuzumi Toshirô, who recast the sounds and rhythms of these ancient musical forms for modern symphonic instruments. Mayuzumi went on to write other influential scores, including his music for the Maurice Béjart ballet of 1986 entitled "*Kabuki*," produced with the Tokyo Ballet, Japan's best-known company. Béjart, then based in Belgium, had long been a central figure in postwar European dance, and it was on that basis that he was chosen to work with the Tokyo Ballet, which early on had received Soviet training but now sought European expertise as well. Mayuzumi, who also composed the opera *Kinkakuji* (The Golden Pavilion) in 1976 for Berlin (revived by the New York City Center in 1995), along with Miki Minoru, who wrote the highly successful opera *Jôruri* for the St. Louis Opera Theater in 1985, often mix both Japanese and Western instruments together in their scores, producing a sound that continues to hold its appeal for Western audiences. Virtually unknown in Western performing circles before World War II, Japanese theater music is now becoming at least somewhat familiar in Western opera and dance circles.

It is perhaps not surprising that Mayuzumi chose a novel of Mishima Yukio as the basis for his opera, for the appearance of this writer, who may be said to have dominated Western perceptions of Japanese literature during the entire postwar period, was himself active as a playwright. The series of one-act modern *nô* plays he wrote, beginning in 1950, combined the elegance and ritualistic qualities of that tradition with fresh and piercing erotic and psychological insights. The plays have gone on to a variety of productions throughout Europe and America, often in Donald Keene's beautiful English trans-

lations. Mishima's other plays, superficially less exotic and more resolutely Western in form, have been slower to achieve translations and productions, but his *Sado Kôshaku Fujin* (Madame de Sade) of 1965, again thanks to an eloquent translation into English by Donald Keene, came to the attention of the Swedish director Ingmar Bergman, whose brilliant production of the play by the Royal Dramatic Theater of Stockholm has been seen on two recent occasions in New York.

Other widely-translated postwar writers, among them Abe Kôbô and Endo Shûsaku, have also had their dramatic works staged abroad. Abe's *Tomodachi* (Friends), a chilling, macabre rejection of traditional Japanese family "togetherness," written in 1967, has intrigued audiences, and a recent dramatization of Endo's *Chinmoku* (Silence), his gripping 1966 novel dealing with the apostasy of a Christian priest in Japan living in hiding during the Christian proscriptions of the 17th century, has been a recent success in both Japan and the United States. Regional theaters, in particular the Milwaukee Repertory Company, have been particularly active in promoting these kinds of cultural experiments, which have helped to construct a base for a greater appreciation of modern Japanese theater.

Perhaps most significant in creating a mutual vocabulary of understanding is that more and more Japanese artists and performers have been working directly in the West. The actor Oida Katsuhiro (known as Yoshi Oida outside of Japan), for example, has been an important performer in the company of the British director Peter Brook, who, like the French director Ariane Mnouchkine and American directors such as Robert Wilson, Lee Breuer, Anne Bogart, Julie Taymor, and Peter Sellars, continues to take a profound interest in the techniques of the classical Japanese theater. Oida, seen in such celebrated productions of Brook's as *The Conference of the Birds* in 1975 and *The Mahabharata* of 1985, has brought the rigor of traditional Japanese theater training to his colleagues in the company, thereby contributing to the ongoing experiments of Brook.[14]

Among Japanese directors active in Europe and the United States, Suzuki Tadashi, with his powerful techniques of acting that require a virtual remaking of the actors' bodies, combined with his own search for texts that speak universally, has created projects such as *The Trojan Women* (loosely based on the original of Euripides), first presented in 1974 and revised often since. Suzuki's productions have helped redefine the nature of contemporary international avant-garde theater. Ninagawa Yukio, like Suzuki active in the politicized avant-garde theater in his earlier years, has created for himself a powerful reputation in the West as well as in Japan through his productions of such classics as *Macbeth*, *The Tempest*, and *Medea*.

Theater designers, too, such as Asakura Setsu, despite busy careers in Japan, have been asked to create stage environments all over the world. Asakura, who often uses sophisticated electronic and lighting effects, has done work ranging from intimate stage areas, such as her work in St. Louis for *Jôruri*, to large-scale assignments, such as her settings for Munich and Nagoya productions of the Richard Strauss opera *Die Frau ohne Schatten* (The Woman without a Shadow) in 1993.

Such opportunities give these complex cultural connections a natural chance to expand even further. This production of the Strauss opera was staged by one of the most highly regarded contemporary *kabuki* actors, Ichikawa Ennosuke III. While in Germany, Ennosuke took the occasion to attend performances of Wagner's Ring Cycle at the Bayreuth Festival. Much taken with the celebrated stage settings for this production by the Austrian designer Hans Schavernoch, Ennosuke in turn invited the Austrian designer to do the settings for his 1992 so-called "super *kabuki*" production of *Satomi Hakkenden* (Satomi and the Eight Dogs), adapted from the celebrated 19th-century Japanese novel of the same name by Takizawa Bakin (1767-1848).

What thus began as mutually remote glimpses from both Japan and the West of geographically and culturally differing theatrical traditions has turned into a virtual flood of mutually supportive activity. The differences in those traditions, once considered a liability, now constitute points of intense stimulation. Japanese theater is certainly with us in today's world. And who knows where it will now take us, and in doing so, thereby continue to transform itself yet again?

1. Quoted in Eppstein (1993), 148. This article provides a useful summary of the shifting attitudes of Europeans from the 16th down to the 20th century.

2. A lively fictional account of this journey can be found in the novel *The Samurai* by Endô Shûsaku (1984).

3. A good deal of fascinating research on this intriguing topic has been undertaken by Professor Margaret Dietrich and Father Thomas Immoos, but much of their work has not yet been published. See, though, Immoos (1963). A more recent English-language account of these plays is Takenaka Masahiro (1995), which also includes translations by Charles Burnett of two important examples of these dramatic texts.

4. Whitman (1982), 383.

5. Young Chinese intellectuals, studying in Tokyo in the early years of the 20th century prior to Sun Yat-sen's revolution of 1911, were inspired by successful Japanese experiments in creating a modern spoken drama. They formed a group they called the Spring Wind Society and began to translate and perform plays in colloquial Chinese, with the help of their Japanese colleagues. This subject is one of great interest but is as yet to be fully explored by any scholar writing in English. There are a few pages on the subject in Dolby (1976).

6. Chamberlain (1890), 446.

7. Details concerning the trip and the performances vary considerably. Among the more reliable English-language sources is the article by Chiba (1992). See also the thoughtful essay by Salz (1993). For a detailed account of the French sections of the tour, see Kei (1986).

8. The story of how Yeats wrote his play has often been told, and the details are truly fascinating. Among the best of these accounts are those of Sekine and Murray (1990), and Caldwell (1977)

9. Masefield does not state precisely how he came to know the play, which was not then available in an accurate translation. Doubtless he used the somewhat bowdlerized English account by Dickins (1880), which enjoyed considerable popularity in England and America.

10. Translations of some of these essays can be found in Claudel (1972).

11. These lines come from the translation of the play by O'Connor (1937).

12. Actually, a company calling itself a *kabuki* troupe had toured America in 1955. This was the so-called "Azuma Kabuki," a group of geisha and male dancers who performed traditional dances in *kabuki* style. Among the dancers was the present *kabuki* star, Nakamura Tomijûrô V, whose mother was the troupe leader.

13. These and other delightful and insightful comments by Donald Richie on this tour are found in the "Postscript" section of the book of translations by Richie and Watanabe (1963).

1.11

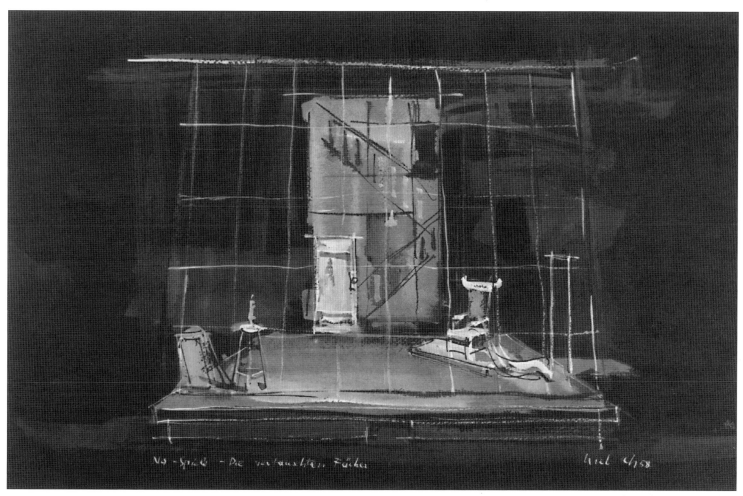

No-Spiele – Die vertauschten Fächer   Kiel 4/58

1.16 A

No Spiele – Die hundertste Nacht   Kiel 4/58

1.16 B

PLATE 8

1.27

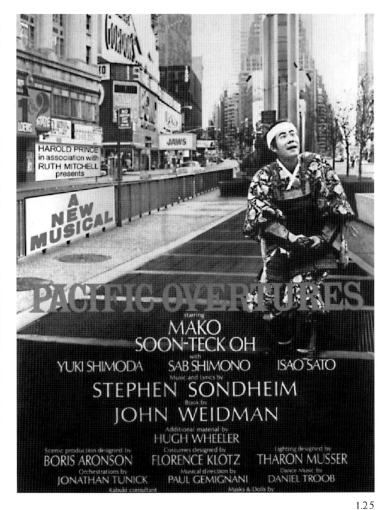

1.25

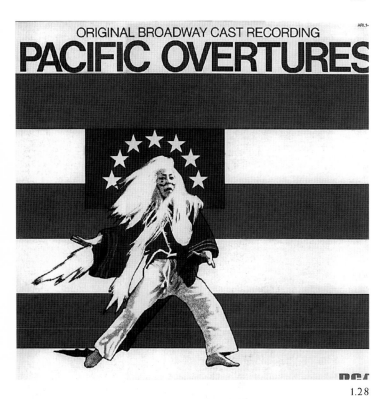

1.28

1.26

PLATE 9

1.30 A

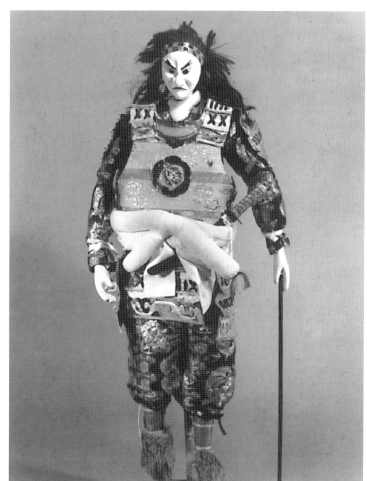

1.30 B

1.30 C

1.30 D

PLATE 10

2.17/2.18

PLATE 11

2.30

2.31C

2.9

II. Ancient Roots in Rural Traditions: *Kagura* and *Minzoku Geinô*

Günter Zobel and Gotô Hajime

Essentials of the Japanese Folk Performing Arts

Minzoku geinô, Japan's folk performing arts, possess strong local colors and are therefore also called *kyôdo geinô* (local performing arts). They emerged naturally from the daily and religious life of the people in ancient times and continued to be an integral part in the calendar of rural communities. Japanese folk performing arts are characterized by a particular combination of elements that have been preserved since primitive times and various elements that have been added and developed over the ages. If we examine what is old and what is new in *minzoku geinô*, we may gain significant insight into the general history of traditional performing arts in Japan. Indeed, one could say that *minzoku geinô* is a kind of kaleidoscope of all the traditional Japanese performing arts.

Minzoku geinô did not arise simply for the purpose of entertainment, but developed within the context of religious rituals, such as annual and seasonal festivals. Japanese folk performing arts share this fundamental principle with various folk arts around the world, and it is exactly this continuous and intimate relation to religious festivals which helped to secure the survival of *minzoku geinô* until the present day.

Many of the performing arts of the early centuries (i.e., after the introduction of Buddhism to Japan in the 6th century AD), including *gigaku*, *bugaku*, *gyôdô*, and *sangaku*, were imported from the Asian continent and then "Japanized." The preexisting, indigenous folk performing arts played a crucial role in this process of acculturation. For they provided the matrix within which these foreign arts were adopted, changed, and eventually incorporated as parts of the native tradition. Likewise, *nô*, *kyôgen*, *bunraku*, and *kabuki*, the theater arts of the feudal era (late 12th century to 1868), have their roots in the folk performing arts. *Minzoku geinô* has often (and unjustly) been regarded as primitive or simple. However, we need to acknowledge its apparent significance and value as the birthplace of those arts that are considered representative of classical Japanese theater.

Enriched by a long and complex history, *minzoku geinô* continues to be performed today in various forms. Because of space limitations, only representative forms will be introduced here, namely *kagura*, *dengaku*, *sarugaku*, and *furyû* dances. These four types form the basis for all *minzoku geinô* performances; likewise, they are related to the forms of later Japanese theater.

Kagura

Kagura has the longest documented history; moreover, it contains a fair number of elements which have survived from ancient times. As *kagura* was performed and enjoyed both by the aristocracy as well as the common people, it may well be called an art of the entire Japanese population.

Kagura, literally "entertainment for the Shinto deities (*kami*)," can best be described as a type of mask-dance-drama. Local and imperial myths provide the narrative material that is acted out in mimetic dances and dramatic scenes by performers wearing masks. These parts are framed by rituals with a strong shamanistic element: the space of the festival is purified, and a deity is then invoked, asked to reveal its will or, at the end of the performances, to give the community its blessing before it is sent back to its realm. Generally speaking, *kagura* aims at pacifying the deities, keeping the gods, as it were, in good spirits, and thereby at renewing or re-confirming the bond between a community and its deities.

Kagura, through its very long history, developed into various types and was dispersed throughout the country. The classification devised by the eminent *minzoku geinô* scholar Honda Yasuji for *kagura* of "miscellaneous contents" is now the most commonly accepted one. According to it, *kagura* is divided into imperial court *kagura* (*mikagura*) and local or "village" *kagura* (*sato kagura*). The imperial form of *kagura* was developed by the court aristocracy, whereas local *kagura* was shaped at the Shinto shrines of the countryside. Although these two kinds of *kagura* once shared the same origin, the differences of the surroundings in which they developed engendered variations and divergences in their contents. The changes that took place in local *kagura* were greater than those occurring in imperial court *kagura*.

Local *kagura* is now subdivided into the following four styles: *miko kagura*, *Ise kagura*, *Izumo kagura*, and *shishi kagura*. Miko kagura is performed by a *miko* (female shaman), who is possessed by a *kami* (Shinto deity) in a sacred, ritual dance. The highlight of the ritual occurs when the *miko* transmits the words of the *kami* to the people. *Miko kagura*, as explained later, became an influential factor in the development of both *nô* and *kabuki*.

Ise kagura was developed by the Ise Kotai Jingu, the Inner Shrine of the imperial Shinto sanctuary in Ise. Here, the *kami* is invoked in a ritual utilizing the steam of boiling water. This form of *kagura* is therefore also known as *yudate kagura*. While Shinto priests recite incantatory prayers to call forth the *kami*, a huge kettle is placed at the site of the festival and water is boiled. Branches of the sacred *sakaki* tree are dipped into the hot water, then waved over those present in order to purify the space and the participants of the festival. One of the central performances following this ritual enacts the famous solar eclipse myth of the goddesses Amaterasu and Ame no Uzume, recounted in Benito Ortolani's essay at the beginning of this catalogue. The wild dance of the *miko* Ame no Uzume before the Rock Cave throws the other deities into fits of laughter which, in turn, so provokes Amaterasu's curiosity that she emerges from her hiding place. While Uzume, the mythical *miko*, is said to have bared her breasts and other private parts in her dancing, thereby inciting roaring laughter from the gods, modern spectators may find their curiosity disappointed by the rather solemn performance.

Izumo kagura is said to have originated at the Sada Shrine in Izumo Province. In this case, the initial invocation of the *kami* is carried out through sacred dances in which the performers hold in their hands tree branches or other objects used as a kind of "conductor" to attract the divine. These *torimono* (hand-props; lit., an object to seize something) were believed to contain magic power that could be utilized to exorcize evil spirits and, by extension, to secure happiness and a prolongation of human life.

At a later stage, performances of a more entertaining character, which took the rich material of the Izumo myths as their source, were added to the ritual dances. *Izumo kagura* spread throughout Japan in this form. *Izumo kagura* performances are particularly famous for their masks and dramatic style. Especially entertaining, for instance, are those pieces which represent the ancient myth of how the god Susano-o fought and subdued the giant, eight-headed snake which menaced the province. Susano-o subsequently became the ruler of the province. Other dances depict the various brave deeds of his son and successor, Okuni-nushi, who came to be revered as a cultural hero.

In *shishi kagura*, the device used both to invoke a *kami* and to transmit its magic power is a lion (*shishi*) mask. As "conductor" for the divine, it thus has a similar function to the handprops used by the dancers in *Izumo kagura*. The two forms of *kagura* differ, however, in so far as in *shishi kagura*, the lion mask itself is regarded as *kami*. A distinguishing feature of *shishi kagura* is, moreover, that the *kami* does not remain in one fixed place during the festival. Instead, the "lion deity," represented by two or more dancers, tours the villages or houses of one area, thus driving out evil spirits and bringing happiness to the community. The lion masks and costumes as well as the dances strongly suggest continental influences on this type of *kagura*. Like *Ise kagura* or *Izumo kagura*, *shishi kagura* includes entertaining performances. It is in these parts of *kagura* that masks are most commonly used.

The broad classification of *kagura* into these four types is based on the form and content of *kagura* as it is today performed around Japan. We cannot be explicit about its content at the time of its birth. The entertaining, dramatic parts, in particular, changed considerably in the course of history. It seems, for instance, that masks were not used in *kagura* of the earliest period. As no records exist of ancient local *kagura* performances, it is difficult to say what *kagura* was like at the time. There do exist, however, some records describing imperial *mikagura*. Because *mikagura* played a central role in the ceremonies and rituals of the imperial court, its form was, to a certain extent, fixed and preserved. For this reason, *mikagura* can be regarded as the most authentic old form of *kagura*.

In ancient times, imperial court *kagura* usually was performed during festivals. Judging from historical records, such festivals had the following basic structure: at the beginning and the end of a festival, ritual cleansing of the site and its participants was carried out. The festival proper commenced with Shinto priests invoking the *kami* to the purified space of the festival. Shrines were not necessarily thought to be the place where a *kami* resided permanently, but more often were regarded as a temporary abode. For the purpose of the festival, the *kami* had, of course, to be "present" and it was, therefore, the primal necessity to invite the deity to descend. Food offerings were then made and the people's wishes transmitted to the deity. These sacred rituals were essential to any festival. After the ritual, *kagura*, which can also be seen as an expression of the deity's will, was performed.

At the imperial court, Shinto priests conducted the rituals, while members of the palace guard (*konoe kanjin*) seem to have been in charge of the *kagura*. It appears that, before imperial court *kagura* developed, special persons, such as *miko* or *kanbe* (female or male shamans), would perform *kagura*. The *kami* would possess the dancing *miko* or the *kanbe* who would then transmit the words of the *kami*. Alternatively, the *kami* was invoked with objects of magic power, such as the branch of the *sakaki* tree, a bow, a stick, or holy *shide*-paper. The deity would then reveal its power, exorcize evil spirits, and grant happiness. Such magic objects were called *kandakara* (treasure offerings) or *torimono* (handprops). Besides invoking the *kami* by using hot water (so that, as mentioned earlier, the deity's will could be heard and one would be purified), there were also methods such as fortune-telling (*uranai*) or ritual fights (*shôbu*), through which the will of the *kami* was expressed.

Arts such as dances, music, and songs were employed both to heighten the effect of the representation of a deity, and to signal the transmission of a *kami's* will. *Kagura* is, thus, a combination of religious acts and artistic performances. One may even say that *kagura* consists of religious acts expressed, at least partly, in artistic performances.

As we have seen, the purpose of *kagura* was to express the will of the gods. But *kagura* had another important function: it was an act of showing one's obedience, as can be demonstrated with the example of imperial court *kagura*. There, the *torimono* dance was followed by the *karakami* dance. *Karakami* refers to deities of Korean or Chinese origin. This *karakami* dance within imperial court *kagura* was performed by the office of the so-called *ninjo*. It seems that the *karakami* dance was incorporated into *kagura* after the Hata family (of Korean origin), who served as imperial palace guards (*konoe kanjin*), inherited the special function of *ninjo*. It was the Hata family's duty to protect the emperor and his court; this duty even extended to the tutelary deity of the Hata, which was called a *karakami*. Thus on the palace grounds there was a *karakami* shrine, which was to protect the imperial family and court and its tutelary deities. Furthermore, every time the Hata performed the *karakami* dance, both the family and their tutelary deity acknowledged their duty of protecting the court and expressed obedience to the *tennô* (emperor). To put it differently, the very act of performing the *karakami* dance can be understood as a gesture of submission. *Matsuri* (festival), therefore, implied obedience or submission. The word *matsuri* is said to derive from the word *matsurau*, which means "to obey" or "to yield to." The word *mairu* (to visit a shrine or temple) appears to be related to the expression *maitta* (I have surrendered). In turn, this implies a feeling of submission to and obedience toward a great power or the object of one's worship.

The formal part of the festival comes to an end with the *kagura* performances. The festival is concluded by a ritual called *naorai*. The term *naorai* means "to return to everyday life," from which the festival has a separate existence. In *naorai*, a purification dance is performed, sacred sake is shared, and the festival is declared to have reached its conclusion. A banquet takes place after this final ritual. This is an occasion for amusement and the performance of various arts. Originally, the term *kagura* referred only to those performances during the festival which were regarded as an expression of the deities' will and also had the function of showing the participants' obedience. Later, however, the performances at the banquet also came to be called *kagura*. These entertainments consisted mainly of performing arts popular at the time in that particular region, but as such local popular arts were gradually incorporated into the repertory, *kagura* was much enriched and became a performing art with a great number of variations. Another important influence on the *kagura* repertory was the festival sponsors, such as, for example, aristocrats, warrior families, or commoners, whose tastes and expectations shaped its form and content. The last, but not least, changes in *kagura* were those inflicted by the influences of various religious groups, such as the Shugendô sect of the Yamabushi or the esoteric Buddhist sects (*mikkyô*) and their thought/belief systems.

Dengaku

Dengaku, literally "field dances," developed in agricultural communities and has a long history as a folk performing art. It is still performed in many regions of Japan and is, like *kagura*, representative of *minzoku geinô*.

Dengaku was performed in rural areas to pray to the god of the rice fields (*ta no kami*) for fertility. Although it seems to have been a popularly performed folk art since ancient times, it is not clear when it first appeared. Characteristic choreographic features of *dengaku* dances are jumping and stomping movements. *Binsasara* (a rhythm instrument made of bamboo), *tsuzumi* (small hand-drum), *taiko* (drum), *fue* (flute), and *kane* (gong) provide the musical accompaniment to *dengaku*. Musical instruments such as the *binsasara* suggest a relation to Chinese traditions, but the link between *dengaku* dance and its possible Chinese origin is unclear. *Binsasara* are made of strips of bamboo or wood which are put on two parallel strings, thus forming something like an over-sized necklace; they are used for *dengaku* performances at shrines, whereas *surisara*, which consists of two bamboo sticks, of which one is serrated, are used for performances in rural areas.

The *dengaku* dances, with their movements of jumping and stomping performed to the accompaniment of mainly percussion instruments, appear to resemble certain dances for pacifying the souls of the dead and for exorcising malevolent spirits. It was believed in ancient times that infertility was caused by invisible evil spirits. Driving these spirits out or purifying them by *dengaku* was seen as a shortcut to fertility. The *dengaku* performed at *ekijin-okuri* (rites for sending off the gods of disease) and at *go-ryô-e* (rites of appeasing the *ekijin* and the restless souls of the deceased) appear to have had the same meaning. Like-wise, the power of benevolent spirits, particularly of the god of the rice field, was awakened and called forth by stomping the ground. Choreographic features with a similar function can be found in *nô* and *kabuki*, and it is most likely for them to have derived from *dengaku*.

Dengaku was especially popular from the latter half of the 10th century to the 12th century. During this transitional period the aristocracy finally lost its political power to the samurai, the warlords. Wars between the various political factions swept over much of Japan during the 12th century, causing destruction, chaos, and the death of many civilians as well. It was believed that the spirits of those who were killed in wars could cause natural disasters, famine, and epidemics.

Such folk religious elements were fairly prominent in *dengaku*; at the same time, the very attractive rhythms of the dances made *dengaku* highly entertaining as well. In addition to the dances, a number of other entertaining art forms, mostly acrobatic, were incorporated into *dengaku*. These elements were originally part of the *sangaku* arts, described below, which were imported from China. In the middle ages, other dramatic contents, such as the so-called *dengaku no nô*, were added to *dengaku*. *Dengaku no nô*, in turn, adopted *sarugaku no nô*. It is for this reason that nowadays, within *dengaku*, both the *dengaku* dance and the old *sarugaku no nô* can be jointly found.

SARUGAKU

Whereas *kagura* and *dengaku* are considered to be ancient native arts, *sarugaku* is based on art forms imported from China, which were then combined with indigenous arts and, as mentioned earlier, Japanized. *Sarugaku* is the precursor of both *nô* and *kyôgen* and, therefore, cannot be excluded from any discussion of the development of Japanese traditional performing arts. It also deserves serious attention as a *minzoku geinô* that persists today in every region.

The imported *sangaku* consisted of acrobatics, conjuring, and humorous imitations. *Sangaku* developed in the hands of the common people and was, therefore, of a popular and entertaining nature. The main emphasis was laid on acrobatics and conjuring; humorous imitation was of secondary importance. On the other hand, humorous imitation became the dominant element in *sarugaku*, to which various miscellaneous accomplishments were added over a long period. Among these miscellaneous arts were, for instance, storytelling accombanied by *biwa* (an early type of lute), puppet shows (*karagei*), or sacred dances that were characterized by their fast pace. It is fair to assume that the humorous art of *monomane* (imitation, mimicry) already existed in Japan before *sangaku* was imported from China. Likewise, arts that used people existed in ancient times.

Sarugaku was an art with a remarkable variety of contents and styles that became the bases for later performing arts. For instance, imitation should be considered a prototype of *nô* and *kyôgen*, while *karagei* and the storytelling art of the *biwa hoshi* (Buddhist priests who recited stories to the accompaniment of the *biwa*) form the origins of *ningyô jôruri* (the puppet theater, now called *bunraku*) and *heikyoku* (the medieval Heike epic sung to the *biwa*). Shaped, performed, and loved by the common people, these arts can truly be called folk performing arts, and as such are of great value.

As mentioned, in the development of *sarugaku* from *sangaku* the emphasis gradually shifted away from acrobatics and conjuring to the humorous mimetic arts. Among these one could find, for instance: (1) Dramatic sketches of a comical nature. They depicted, such things as the amazement of a country bumpkin when he comes to the capital for the first time and is stupefied by the luxurious life of the aristocrats and the city's splendor. (2) Comic imitations of a monkey's (*saru*) act. (3) Parody of those priests (*senzumanzai bôshi*) who used to visit every village at New Year and offer congratulatory songs. (4) The mimicking of sexual intercourse.

It seems that the power of dialogue and movements was of central importance in these sketches.

Sarugaku emerged during the Kamakura period (12th to 14th centuries) and gradually developed into various types. One type of *sarugaku*, in particular, should be mentioned here, as it provided an essential base for the development of *nô*. This *sarugaku* (presumably of the late Kamakura period) was played in two versions: in the first, a *kami* represented by means of a mask as Okina (an old man with a happy face and laughing expression) appeared and performed an auspicious dance which was meant to prolong human life and happiness; in the other, the deity was presented as Kishin (a demon god, with a fierce facial expression), who would expel evil and thereby bring happiness to the people. Giving the deity a concrete representation and making it appear before the audience was a new practice. It had existed neither in the early *sarugaku* nor in any of the other indigenous performing arts. Moreover, the role of the *kami* was not performed by a Shinto priest serving it, but by the so-called *sarugaku* artist who would represent the figure of a "*kami* in disguise," because his main occupation was imitation. This "disguise" was achieved by wearing a mask, a device that was new to *sarugaku* as well. Models for such masks often were commoners' faces or their folkloristic types as they existed in the imagination of the Japanese people.

Sarugaku in its *sangaku* form was, as mentioned earlier, originally imported from China. It was not only performed at shrine festivals, but also on the occasion of Buddhist ceremonies in temples. It seems, for example, that *sarugaku* became a common element of temple events like the *shujo-e* (New Year's prayers for the welfare of the state). Because temples were

2.45A

PLATE 12

places with a pronounced Chinese atmosphere, Chinese narratives came to be included in *sarugaku no nô*. The influential role of Buddhist temples also became apparent in the fast-paced dances, such as *jushi*, or in the magic religious ceremonies. The *shujoe* event was performed in the manner of exorcistic rites from China. This exorcistic element shared by Chinese rites and *shujoe*, in turn, came to be connected to *sarugaku*. Thus there are numerous cases in the *shujoe* events, which are still conducted in most regions of Japan, where *sarugaku*, *jushi*, and *tsuina-e* (exorcistic rites) are performed together.

Sarugaku consisted fundamentally of imitation, literary works, legends,and other narrative materials used as sources for the sketches. The dramatic contents gradually expanded and eventually came to include the aforementioned plays about *kami* and ghosts who took human form. In these plays, masks were used. Although these masks seem to be modeled after human faces, they do not represent human beings. For that reason, they show expressions that are different from those of "real" persons. Two good examples of such masks are the expressionless mask (*muhyôjô*) and the mask representing absent-mindedness (*hôshin*).

These changes in the content of *sarugaku* affected the central importance humor had been been given in *sarugaku*. Of course, the tradition of humor did not wholly disappear. Instead, two completely different *sarugaku* arts were born: one of a serious content which used masks as a significant feature, and another with humorous content that made for less use of masks. The former developed into *nô*, and the latter became *kyôgen*. *Nô* and *kyôgen* are representative of classical Japanese drama and have become highly regarded theater arts; but both have their roots in the folk performing art of *sarugaku* which developed within shrine festivals and temple events. In a similar manner, *heikyoku* and *ningyô jôruri*, from which *bunraku* developed, are closely related to *sarugaku* and its history.

THE *FURYU* DANCES

Like the performing arts depicted on the previous pages, *furyû* dances form an essential part of *minzoku geinô*. And, like *kagura*, *dengaku*, or *sarugaku*, *furyû* dances have taken various forms and have a long history, even though most of the dances performed today became popular only as recently as the 17th century.

It appears that *furyû* dances always gained popularity in times of dramatic social and political changes. Thus the first *furyû* craze took place during the 12th and 13th centuries, when the political hegemony of the imperial court and its aristocracy collapsed and was seized by the samurai class. This period was characterized by wars, famines, epidemics, and natural disasters, all of which were interpreted as clear signs that the Last Age of the Buddhist Law (*mappô*) had arrived. Likewise, it was during these centuries, that the relatively new Amidist sects of Buddhism gained great popularity and, subsequently, found themselves in bitter and often violent competition with the established, hitherto politically highly influential, Tendai and Shingon sects.

The popularity of *furyû* soared again in the 14th century, when the imperial family split into the rival Southern and Northern dynasties, and Japan had two emperors, a *shôgun*, and several contenders for his office.

The third *furyû* vogue came during the second half of the 16th century, when the three warlords, Oda Nobunaga, Toyotomi Hideyoshi, and Tokugawa Ieyasu, were fighting endless battles to reunite Japan which had, in the course of almost 130 years of unrest, disorder, and warfare, become divided into many feudal fiefdoms. This third peak of *furyû* popularity coincided with the beginning of what is regarded as Japan's premodern age (*kinsei*), at the turn of the 17th century.

Thus *furyû* dances tended to thrive against a background in which Japanese society experienced the threat of disorder and social upheaval, if not the complete destruction of social order and values, and when the people came to have a sudden, keen sense of the fleetingness of human life.

Furyû dances have two essential elements. One derives from the original meaning of "*furyû*," which refers to brightness, gaudy expressions, and the enjoyment of worldly pleasures. The decorative costumes and props used in the dances are an excellent reflection of this meaning of "*furyû*." The word is also used when costumed dancers perform in large numbers, as in *bon odori* (*obon* festival dancing); it also implies wearing especially luxurious kimono, such as those found in *bon odori*.

Kabuki, which is representative of the premodern Japanese drama, appears to have had its origins in such *furyû* dances. In its early stages, *kabuki* consisted mainly of alluring dances that were performed by beautiful young women or boys. This clearly shows the nature of *furyû* dances. Okuni, believed to be a *miko*-cum-dancer from Izumo province, is said to have been the first performer of *kabuki* dance. Her performances in Kyoto around the turn of the 17th century soon became famous, drawing enormous crowds. Okuni and her performances often became the subject of the genre paintings of the time; they sometimes show her dressed as a man, with a gaudy costume, a long sword in her hand, and a cross hanging over her breast. Such images reveal the characteristics of *furyû* very well.

Likewise, the well-known Gion Festival of the Yasaka Shrine in Kyoto, with its splendid float procession, is a good example of *furyû*. Ever since the beginnings of the festival, the citizens of Kyoto appear to have vied with each other in making the decoration of their quarters' floats ever more elaborate and splendid. Many are decorated with superb goblins, and others have elaborate constructions attached to their roofs, such as an over-sized sword. Similar processions exist in the city of Hitachi; there, puppets are mounted on enormous floats (*dashi*) and puppet plays are shown.

Furyû dances are performed to songs and accompanied by musical instruments, such as drums and flutes. The rhythms are brisk and the pace of the dances often vigorous, thus giving the festival its special lively atmosphere. It is said that the Japanese love festivals. The *furyû* dance is the climax of a festival and excellently expresses the feelings of the people.

The other element that shapes a *furyû* dance is its relation to the belief in spirits. One of the dances, which is linked to *bon odori*, is the *nembutsu odori*. The name derives from chanting the *nembutsu* (invocation of Amida Buddha, with the hope of rebirth in his Pure Land paradise) and its accompanying dance. The characteristic feature of this dance lies, as does *dengaku* choreography, in jumping and stomping movements to appease the spirits. It is usually performed to the loud music of drums, bells, and flutes, which seem to aim at assisting exorcism. Both *furyû* and *dengaku* dances are, in this sense, ritualistic dances which aim at driving away epidemics and pacifying the spirits of the deceased. *Dengaku*, therefore, is often performed in concert with *furyû*.

Besides the genre paintings of *Okuni kabuki* described earlier, there also exist some pictures depicting her in a black bamboo hat and dark-colored costume, striking a small gong hung from her neck. In other words, such pictures show Okuni chanting a *nembutsu* song and consoling the spirits of the deceased. Representations such as this underline the fact that all *furyû* dances contain the element of a belief in spirits. The combination of these two elements—gorgeous dances and gaudy costumes, on the one side, and belief in the spirits of the departed, on the other—was clearly expressed in the famous Hokokusai (festival of the Hokoku Shrine in Kyoto, early 17th century), of which a fantastic set of genre paintings survives. This festival was supposedly performed on the death anniversary of the warlord Toyotomi Hideyoshi, in order to offer prayers for the repose of his soul. Never before and never again did the capital witness such splendid *furyû* dances, which lasted for almost a week.

The reason for the popularity even today of *furyû* dances, which are performed everywhere in Japan during the *obon* festival in August, lies in the cheerful mood of the colorful group dances, though they are performed to appease the spirits of the dead. This belief is rooted deeply in the minds of ordinary people.

CHARACTERISTICS OF JAPANESE FOLK PERFORMING ARTS

In this essay, we have selected from the miscellaneous genres of *minzoku geinô* only their representative forms—*kagura*, *dengaku*, *sarugaku*, and *furyû* dances—to consider certain general aspects of Japanese folk performing arts. Although we have looked only at a few examples, it should be clear that they are characterized by a broad popular appeal and close link to folk beliefs. These elements have ensured the survival and continued popularity of most *minzoku geinô* forms to the present day.

Another characteristic of *minzoku geinô* is their great variety. The span of their formation is indeed long and, if we examine this process, we can understand the history of all Japanese performing arts. *Minzoku geinô* are thought to have provided the basis for the development of *nô*, *kyôgen*, *bunraku*, and *kabuki*, Japan's most artistic and classical theaters. This point cannot be overemphasized, if one wants to learn about the history of Japanese theater. In the *minzoku geinô* section of this exhibition, the representative folk performing arts are introduced with the purpose of encouraging such an understanding.

2.24 B

PLATE 13

2.45C

2.45F

2.45D

2.45E

PLATE 14

2.22

2.16

2.14

2.50

PLATE 15

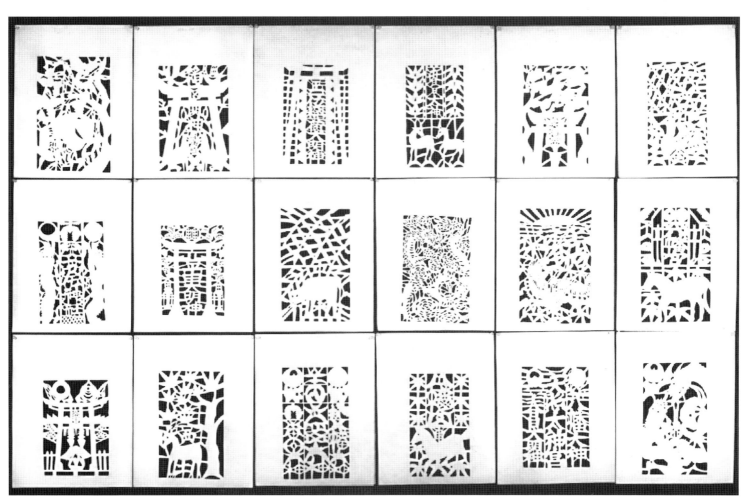

2.55

PLATE 16

2.21A

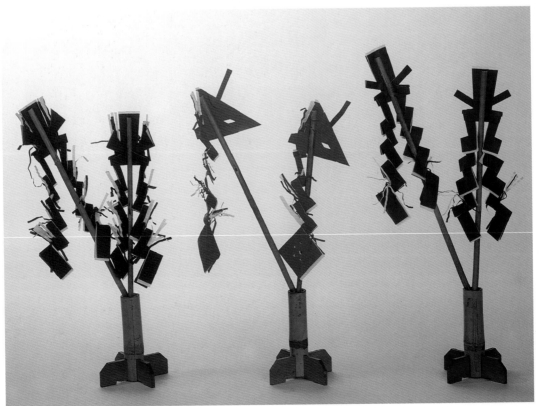

2.12 A-F

PLATE 17

四方拝田庫男
田行変力士示
行事古代田楽
座
明治二十三年庚寅秋日宮
本七十有
六年如来

2.28

PLATE 18

2.7

PLATE 19

2/3.1

2/3.7

2.49

2.46

PLATE 20

3.42

PLATE 21

III. To Court and shrine from the world: *Gigaku* and *Bugaku*

Benito Ortolani

The Last Eastward Frontier

In the 6th and 7th centuries AD, when the Roman Empire had disintegrated and Constantinople had consolidated her function as New Rome in Southeastern Europe and Asia Minor, a number of traveling entertainers from the Mediterranean basin joined the many artists from all over Asia who were attracted to the busy capitals of the Chinese empire, the greatest power in the East. Lo-yang and, especially, Chang-an, the booming metropolises of the T'ang Dynasty (618-907), became extraordinary points of encounter, where artists from the most varied traditions competed to win both popular and court favor. From Chang-an, the eastward-traveling performers reached the kingdoms located approximately in the area of modern Korea. From there they landed on the Japanese islands, the last frontier before the formidable barrier of the North Pacific Ocean.

Starting in the early seventh century, Japan's rapidly developing Yamato court became intent on imitating the splendor of the Chinese model. This involved a process of importing and assimilating, not only Buddhism and Chinese culture, but sophisticated mainland music, dances, and ceremonies, as well. These developments reached a peak in the Nara (646-710) and Heian (710-1185) periods. While almost every trace of the performing arts of Europe and Asia during those centuries was eventually wiped out in their native countries by political upheavals and changing fashions, a good deal managed to remain in Japan, which continues to preserve priceless documentation of artifacts and performances from what originally were non-Japanese theatrical traditions. Japan's task of being the custodian of significant ancient theatrical treasures was fulfilled with particular efficacy in the case of *gigaku* and *bugaku*.

Apart from certain difficult-to-identify remnants assimilated by other genres, *gigaku* is generally considered to have been extinct since the 14th century. Nevertheless, it left behind an astonishing group of artifacts. Over 250 *gigaku* masks are preserved in Nara's Shôsô-in treasure house, the Tokyo National Museum, and other museums, temples, and collections. Many are dated with certainty from before the mid-8th century, but were probably created even earlier. Such a number and variety of authentic masks is extraordinary among the ancient performing arts, many of which left only a small number of pictures of their theatrical masks, if that.

Bugaku, on the contrary, with its accompanying *gagaku* music, is still alive and regularly performed at the Japanese imperial court and major shrines. It continues to perform the fascinating rhythms of ancient music and dances that preserve many characteristics of their originals, imported from the continent twelve centuries ago.

Gigaku's Ties to Continental Mythology

Written documentation about the introduction of continental music and dance during the Asuka period (552-646) is sparse. The first Japanese record explicitly mentioning *gigaku* reports that, in 562, an envoy from the Yamato court brought back from Korea unspecified objects (presumably head masks, colorful costumes, and musical instruments) used in performances never before seen in the Japanese islands. The envoy was certainly unaware that those paraphernalia belonged to a performing art that was the carrier of a variety of influences

which would reach the end of their long eastward journey in Japan after traveling half-way round the world. Among those influences may have been the classical and Hellenistic theatres of Greece, the comedy of Rome, and the arts of the Near East, India, Southeast Asia, pre-T'ang China, and Korea.

Although scholars have never pinned down precise origins of the *gigaku* masks, or even been able satisfactorily to trace their passage—presumably from the Mediterranean basin via the Silk Road to the Far East—it is at least obvious that a number of the masks represent types and were used for the performance of myths. These myths were neither Chinese nor Korean, and must be traced back to traditions as distant as those of Asia Minor, if not all the way to the European continent. Scholars have discerned in the head masks of *gigaku* the carving art of the Scythians, an ancient people of Southeast Europe and Asia Minor. They also have argued for the connection of *gigaku* head masks and characters with Greek and Roman models. It was the achievement of Niizeki Ryôzô, a Japanese comparatist and scholar of Western classical drama, to elaborate on possible similarities and connections with the Dionysian myths and to provide documentation of striking similarities between Greek and *gigaku* head masks. He hypothesizes that the only known *gigaku* text—the episode of Kuron seducing the women of Wu—is the transferral of a Greek legend into Buddhist mythology. Hera and Iris would be the models for the women of Wu, the satyrs would have inspired the two Kurons, and Herakles would be the model for the savior Buddhist guardian god Rikishi. "The possibility of a long arch stretching from the Near East to Japan—traveled by nomadic populations who combined the western art of carving masks with Indian mythology and Buddhist faith—remains as intriguing and fascinating as the surprising presence of Greek modeling of a pillar in the Hôryû-ji temple in Nara, or the discovery in Japan of the winged horse, possibly a Pegasus motif, in decorative patterns contemporary to *gigaku*." [1]

GIGAKU MODERNIZES COURT ENTERTAINMENT

In 612, half a century after the first *gigaku* accoutrements reached Japan from Korea, the first *gigaku* performer-teacher, Mimashi, arrived in Japan. [2] During that half century, over the strong opposition of the conservative faction and under the leadership of the progressive faction, the Yamato court experienced a period of intensive assimilation of Chinese culture. The arrival of a *gigaku* master was therefore welcomed by the progressive, policy-making court majority. Mimashi was bringing the live experience of a new art that perfectly matched the vision of a Japanese culture being "modernized" according to sophisticated continental models. Prince Regent Shôtoku, the most powerful and enlightened reformist leader, was happy to become a patron of the new art and to entrust Mimashi with the mission of establishing a school for the training of indigenous professional *gigaku* performers. Soon after, while Nara, the new capital, was being planned and built according to the model of the Chinese imperial city, a new era in performance began. The accurately carved and finely laquered *gigaku* masks provided a touch of previously unknown sophistication, while elegant, colorful costumes replaced the colorless attire of the

dancers of local traditions, and foreign rhythms increased the appeal of the more elaborately developed foreign mythology. Within a few years, *gigaku* was flourishing at court and in the main places of worship, also becoming part of the recently established Buddhist liturgy, notwithstanding the lack of any relationship, in origins or content, between Buddhism and many of the musical compositions, dances, pantomimes, costumes, and masks. Sometimes, these elements even reflected doctrines and mentalities opposed to Buddhist fundamentals. Part of the answer as to why certain *gigaku* pieces were interpreted (probably erroneously) in terms of the Japanized Buddhist pantheon lies in *gigaku*'s having been imported and promoted as part of a cultural revolution that gave a central position to Buddhism. Moreover, *gigaku* performances were de facto connected with Buddhist ceremonials during the same festivals and on the same grounds. [3]

Gigaku was the most successful performing art between the end of the 7th and the beginning of the 10th century, a time that saw the birth of Japan's early masterpieces of architecture, sculpture, and literature in Nara and Kyoto, the two major centers of classical Japanese civilization. Its decline, however, set in during the 9th century, when *bugaku* took over as the official court entertainment.

GIGAKU IN PERFORMANCE

The *gigaku* masks have been used as a clue to discovering its content and performance style, which still remain sketchy. As far as written documents are concerned, the golden age of *gigaku* has transmitted only a few catalogues of masks, props, and musical instruments; no description of contents has survived. The source used by all scholars attempting to reconstruct performances is found in a book from 1223, the *Kyôkunshô* (Selections for Instruction and Admonition), written by Tachibana Narisue a couple of centuries after the court *gigaku* had ceased being performed. This source's testimony is weakened by the fact that, when it was written, the performances called *gigaku* had decayed and become similar to *gyôdô*, a processional ritual consisting primarily of carrying a Buddha statue around to the accompaniment of Buddhist monks chanting prayers.

The titles of programs and the catalogues of masks from *gigaku*'s golden age indicate that it probably consisted of a series of "numbers," such as dances, pantomimes, and solemn processions, performed with beautiful, impressive masks painted in strong colors, vividly dyed exotic costumes, and accompanied by imported music of which we know nothing for sure. According to tradition, *gigaku*'s remnants were assimilated into *komagaku*, now part of *gagaku* court music, comprising compositions from the ancient Korean kingdoms of the period. [4] There is no clear record left, older than the *Kyôkunshô*, about any special place(s) or stage(s) where court *gigaku* was performed. If we accept that late source as our guide, we must conclude that *gigaku* was performed only outdoors, within the grounds surrounding either the imperial palace or major temples and shrines.

The Testimony of the *Kyokunsho*

The performance of *gigaku* described in the *Kyôkunshô* began with a solemn procession led by Chidô, wearing a red head mask with a wide mouth, very long nose, bulging eyes, black eyebrows, and whiskers. With a spear in his hand and accompanied by two assistants, he had the task of purifying the path from evil influences. Further, an exorcizing function was fulfilled by the lion (*shishi*) that followed, manned by two performers, with a brightly painted, large mask covering the head. The mask had a movable jaw maneuvered by the movements of the head. The *shishi* was accompanied by three children (*shishiko*), with smiling, friendly, large-eared masks. Baldachin bearers and numerous musicians with seven-holed Chinese flutes, drums, and cymbals followed. The procession was followed by the performance of a series of "numbers," probably dances by such characters as Kuregimi (possibly a gentleman from Kure; i.e, the province of Wu, around Nanking), Kongô (a popular Buddist god), Karura (the snake-eating bird-god venerated in India and Southeast Asia), and Baramon (a member of the Brahman caste from India). The most dramatic part of the show followed, a piece describing the exploits of (perhaps) two Konron (or Kuron) who seduce and make love to (perhaps) five women (*kure otome*). The Buddhist deities Kongô and Rikishi take revenge by tearing off the Konrons' phalli and swinging them around in a victory dance. The interpretation of the text remains vague and leaves unsolved many problems regarding the origin and meaning of the dance/pantomime. Scholars, at any rate, have noticed some kind of parallel to the processions of the *phallophoroi* (phallus-carriers) in the Greek *komos*, usually interpreted as the seed of Attic comedy.

The Main Types of *Gigaku* Masks

Scholars distinguish fourteen basic types of *gigaku* masks:
(1) Karura: the Indian bird that eats snakes. The mask shows bird-like features with a pronounced beak, slightly open because it holds a pearl. The upper part of the eyes and the forehead look human, but the ears resemble a bat's. The dominant colors are usually green for the beak and painted feathers on the cheeks, and red for the crest on top of the head. Gold and black are used in some cases.
(2) Shishi: the "lion" mask, which is probably the most commonly used in various "lion" dances, including *kagura*, *gyôdô*, *gigaku*, *bugaku*, *nô*, and *kabuki*, and many popular festivals. The Shishi masks in all such cases, however, barely resemble a lion. The ears are very small, similar to those of a cat. One of the most important characteristics is the movable lower jaw.
(3) Kure Otome is the only female *gigaku* mask. The mask of a young woman, it corresponds to the *koomote* of the *nô*. Rather realistic in appearance, it is usually painted white, with hues of red on the cheeks and earlobes. The lips are bright red and the hair black.
(4) and (5) Kongô and Rikishi, the two Buddhist guardian gods. They look very much alike, with the difference that Rikishi always has a beard. They appear powerful, terrible to demons but friendly to man. The face is often reddish or brown with black teeth and black hair.

(6) Kuron (Konron): a dark-complexioned man from the South Seas ("K'un-lun"), he represents the villain, the non-Buddhist, the "alien." His expression sometimes stresses demonic/beastly traits, enhanced by the bat-like ears.
(7) Suikoô: the "drunken king from the Western land," whose major characteristic is often a very long, phallic nose. The expression is usually dignified and a beard is often present. An ornate, tailored head covering, which differs among the specimens, gives the mask a regal dignity.
(8) Suikojû: the king's followers, six or eight of them, with phallic noses and long ears like those seen in Buddhist sculptures.
(9) Taikofu: the aged father of the Taiko children, smiling in his wisdom, with a long but not phallic nose, "planted" beard and eyebrows, and long ears.
(10) and (11) Taikoji and Shishiko: masks for children, worn by assistants to the major figures. They present round, smiling faces and long ears, and are often painted white with red lips, white teeth, and green/blue eyes.
(12) Baramon: an older man, smiling, with a phallic nose and without "planted" hair. The face is painted in red tones, the teeth are painted white or silver, the lips are bright red, and the eyes are blue/green.
(13) Kuregimi: another regal type, usually interpreted as the noble man from Wu. He is young, occasionally presenting a slightly phallic nose and long ears, but always noble looking, with a face painted in green or ultramarine, and having white or silver teeth and purple-red lips.
(14) Chidô: a strong, vigorous man, with a pronounced phallic nose, sometimes smiling, sometimes almost without expression.

Gigaku's Influence

Because of its disappearance as an independent genre centuries ago, it is extremely difficult to establish with any precision how much of the primitive *gigaku* actually survived in other arts and, even less, how deep its influence was on the development of *bugaku*, *nô*, and Japan's performing arts in general. During its development, *gigaku* was probably more intermingled with and influenced by *gigaku* than is usually acknowledged. The same might be said of the assimilation into *bugaku* of *gigaku*'s dances and music.[6] It seems probable that the lessons learned from the *gigaku* masks had a strong influence on the creation of the *nô* mask masterpieces, either directly or through the continuing use of the *gyôdô* masks in Buddhist ceremonials, and/or through intermediate mask types that recently were studied and catalogued by Gotô Hajime.[7]

Bugaku Introduced to Japan

Soon after the introduction of *gigaku*, other kinds of music and dance of various origin were imported. These eventually constituted the repertory of *gagaku* music and *bugaku* dances.[8] They include the already mentioned *komagaku* imported from Korea, which is believed to have assimilated certain elements of *gigaku*, when it was toppled by *bugaku* from its place as the major court entertainment.[9] The music of T'ang (*tôgaku*) China, music from South Asia (*rinyûgaku*), music from India (*tenjikugaku*), and others, together with dance-pantomimes bearing the same

PLATE 22

names as today's *gagaku* music and *bugaku* dances, are already mentioned in documents of the 7th century.

Gigaku and *bugaku*, therefore, from their very beginnings, shared the characteristic of being conglomerates of different dances, pantomimes, and music originated in, or at least influenced by, some of the main world cultures of antiquity. Both had in common the fact of having found their way into the Japanese islands from a variety of lands and civilizations at a time when the still young Japanese court was evolving into an important center of world-class artistic creativity. Both contained secular entertainments that, in some cases, became an integral part of official Buddhist temple rituals, and were adapted to Buddhist meanings.

HISTORY OF *BUGAKU*

In the early years of *bugaku*'s introduction into Japan and, until the 11th century, of its adapatation to the taste of the Japanese court, *bugaku* artists enjoyed and used a creative freedom in sharp contrast with the conservative tendency of preservation that set in after the 11th century. As with *gigaku* before, *bugaku* was at first a lively, theatrical, creative art of the court avant-garde. However, the increasingly formalistic tendency that developed froze *bugaku* into the slow-paced, highly solemn dances still performed today.

In the bleak years of civil war that accompanied the decadence of the old aristocracy and the rise to power of the samurai elite, groups of *gagaku/bugaku* performers left the imperial court and found a sounder economic base at several major temples and shrines. They also migrated to outside the capital, Kyoto, establishing still-living traditions, especially at the Shitennô-ji temple in Osaka and the Kasuga shrine in Nara.

By the 15th century, *bugaku* had become a kind of secret tradition that had lost most of the financial support of an impoverished and politically weakened imperial court, unable to maintain the glorious traditions of previous centuries.

The reorganization and revival of court *bugaku* happened after 1870, amidst the atmosphere of the Meiji Restoration (1868), as part of the post-shogunate effort to revive the ancient prestige and functions of the emperor. Court *bugaku* was reorganized at the imperial palace in Tokyo under the Gagaku Kyôku (now called Gakubu, or Music Department), which is in charge of providing performances in honor of distinguished state guests and at stated yearly festivities. As a result, there are three categories of groups performing *bugaku* nowadays: (1) the Imperial Household Music Department, which cultivates *bugaku* as a court ceremony; (2) a few major temples and shrines, which use *bugaku* as part of religious celebrations; and (3), amateur groups, which cultivate *bugaku* out of interest and love for the form.[10]

MASKS OF *BUGAKU*

Bugaku masks are smaller than *gigaku* masks and generally cover only the face. A few of the older masks, closer to *gigaku*, also cover the sides of the head. Some present the feature of a separate chin, tied to the upper face with strings. In general, *bugaku* masks represent in a relatively realistic fashion the features of individuals from the countries of origin of the dances, birds and other animals, and gods from Chinese and Indian mythologies. The long noses, as in *gigaku*, are evidently exaggerated, probably reflecting the profound impression that the big noses of Western people had on Oriental artists.

Masks belonging to the category of *zômen* are basically white silk or paper rectangles with highly stylized features painted in black. The others are built in paulownia wood, sometimes coated several times with hemp cloth and sometimes laquered. The old specimens show the small holes where the head and beard hair was inserted.

The impact on the stage of the great variety of *bugaku* masks was enhanced by the imported costumes, which brought to a height the process of change, initiated by *gigaku*, in the color patterns worn by most performers. The ancient, fundamentally white garments were preserved for the few *bugaku* dances, like *Sonokoma*, of Japanese origin and adapted from *kagura*. They also were used for costumes developed from the white uniforms of the *konoe* imperial guards. Otherwise, and for most cases, the brightly colored silk robes of the new court fashion dominated the stage.[11]

CONTENT OF THE DANCES

Bugaku dances can be divided into four major groups according to their contents.
(1) Military dances, or *bu no mai*, are characterized by broad and strong movements; slow paced, highly stylized sword or spear fights; and dancers costumed as ancient warriors. A typical example is *Bairo*.
(2) "Literary" or court dances, called *bun no mai*, representing the majority of the pieces, are related to court life and the values of peaceful culture. For example, *Shundeika* (Flowers in the Spring Garden) represents four courtiers dancing under the cherry blossoms.
(3) Children's dances, or *warawamai*, are performed by elaborately costumed children, as in *Karyôbin*, where four young boys in female attire gracefully dance carrying copper cymbals and wearing feathered gear.
(4) Female dances, or *onnamai*, were originally performed in the Heian period by women. Nowadays, they are performed by men masked as women, displaying a touch of feminine grace otherwise unknown in *bugaku*.
(5) "Running dances," or *hashirimono*, are characterized by once quick, now highly stylized, dance movements that describe "barbarian" hunters chasing snakes and symbolically eating the killed prey, as in *Genjôraku*.[12]

BUGAKU'S AUDIENCE

Bugaku, in general, has never been a "popular" art, and its audiences have always been limited. Traditionally, the *bugaku* of the Imperial Household was not open to the public. After World War II, selected performances inside the imperial

Palace in Tokyo were made available to a limited number of visitors. *Bugaku* may also be seen by the general public attending festivals where the performances are presented as religious rituals. They are given on permanent outdoor stages, within the grounds of about twelve major temples and shrines. Large crowds come and go during the performances. Amateur groups, on the contrary, perform for small audiences of aficionados; they are active in several cities, and are helped in their recruitment by courses given in many universities as part of the instruction in Japanese music history. Since the early sixties, a few courses in *gagaku/bugaku* also have been given, albeit sporadically, at a few American universities, with the guidance of invited Japanese instructors.[13]

BUGAKU ABROAD

The first visit of the imperial *bugaku* troupe to the United States was in 1959. Other visits by different groups (including enthusiastic amateurs) to Europe and America followed. They have always had a positive, and sometimes enthusiastic, reception by critics and limited audiences. Two memorable visits were to the U.S.A., one in 1978, by the group based at the Shitennô-ji temple, and another in 1997. The latter offered *bugaku bôe*, an ancient mixture of *shômyô* chant and *bugaku* dance, performed by a group of Buddhist monks, musicians, and dancers from the Tendai Chants Research Society and the Tsukiji Hongan-ji Gagaku Kai.[14]

Although *gagaku* music and *bugaku* dance did not have as wide an impact as the *nô* on the creativity of Western composers and performers, a number of Western musicians and dancers were fascinated and inspired by them. *Bugaku* inspired several experimental dances/plays, among which the piece *Hikari*, created in the late 1970s by avant-garde composer/author Karlheinz Stockhausen, was received coldly by the *gagaku* world, which was offended by the gratuitous mixing of nudity and *bugaku* costumes. Probably the best and most famous contemporary uses of *bugaku* methods by a contemporary Japanese theater artist are to be found in some of Suzuki Tadashi's inspired and highly technical creations, which were well received in the West. In the Western ballet world, the most famous creation might well be the ballet "Bugaku" by George Balanchine, music by Mayuzumi Toshirô, that was premiered by the New York City Ballet in 1963, and remained in the company repertory for decades.

CREATIVITY AND CONSERVATISM IN BUGAKU

Today's *bugaku* dance and *gagaku* music, as preserved at the imperial court and in major shrines, is quintessentially conservative and well known for its fidelity to ancient models. Scholars, however, recently have stressed the fact that, even during the centuries of greatest formalism and conservativism, there has been a moderate input of originality and creativity by the official musicians and dancers, and the repertory has been enriched with new pieces and adaptations of older classics.

Considerable alteration of the imported materials certainly did happen during the centuries of introduction and Japanization, and there must have been other transformations during the centuries-long, occasionally tempestuous transmission of the tradition. Still, *gagaku* and *bugaku* present an extraordinary, unique experience of substantially unchanged traits that echo, in ancient rhythms and forceful movements, the perception of and conformity to the limitless, solemn force giving birth to all movements of the earth and cosmos. *Bugaku* can still be a celebration of the way human behavior conforms to such universal order and to the rhythms of this supreme force.[15]

1. Ortolani (1990), 36. See Niizeki (1964), 13, 15, and the photographs at the beginning of that volume's illustration section.

2. The *Nihongi* reports: "Mimashi, a person of Kudara, arrived as an immigrant. He is said to have studied in Wu [China] and learned *gigaku*. He was given permanent residence in Sakurai, where he gathered youths and taught them *gigaku*." (Araki 1964, 36).

3. A similar symbiosis of Buddhist ceremonies with imported non-related dance and music happened later, as well, in the case of *bugaku bôe*, a fusion of *shômyô* (Buddhist ritual chants) and *bugaku* dances. It was used in solemn Buddhist ceremonies starting from about the mid-9th century, but fell into a quasi-total oblivion in modern Japan (Nelson 1997, 1). A contemporary example of such an impressive ceremony was presented on May 15 and 16, 1997, in New York, at the Japan Society's Lila Acheson Wallace Auditorium, by the Tendai Chants Research Society and the Tsukiji Hongan-ji Gagaku Kai.

4. See Harich-Schneider (1973), 51, and Tanabe (1936), 481.

5. Kleinschmidt (1966), 44-108.

6. Harich-Schneider, 51-52.

7. Gotô (1965).

8. See the introductory essay of this volume, p. 15, for considerations of the spiritual background of *gagaku* and *bugaku*. Also Gabbert (Avitabile) (1972), 5-47.

9. Harich-Schneider, 51-52.

10. See Wolz (1981), 115.

11. Gabbert (Avitabile), p. 48ff.

12. Gabbert (Avitabile), p. 6-31.

13. See Togi Suenobu, "Gagaku and Bugaku", in Susilo (1981), 23-24, and Wolz, 115-124.

14. See Nelson (1997), and endnote 3, above.

15. Ortolani (1995), 51.

Trajectory from the Asian Continent: Chidô, Shishi, Gyôdô

Tanabe Saburosuke
Translated by Shirai Hiro

Leading the Way: The Role of Chido, Ômai, and Shishi

At the beginning of the 8th century, the *Nihon Shoki*, one of the six ancient histories of Japan, recorded the well-known mythological tale of the grandson of the sun goddess Amaterasu, named Ningi no Mikoto, who descended from heaven to earth. Sarutahiko no Mikoto, who met the gods on earth, led the way for the young god. Sarutahiko no Mikoto is portrayed as tall, with a long nose, a red face, and eyes like mirrors. Although he appears in conjunction with gods related to the shrine at Ise in the event recounted here, he is otherwise not mentioned in the *Nihon Shoki*.

Shaku Nihongi, the annotated edition of the *Nihon Shoki*, reports that a mask of Ômai (lit., "King's Dance") was modeled after the face of this god. In later times, various other records mention a red mask with a large or long nose called Hanataka ("High Nose"). This type of mask was generally used by a man who walked in front of a portable shrine in a religious procession (*gyôdô*). Additionally, he stamped the ground on which the shrine was to be placed in order to drive away the bad spirits there. The mask and its wearer's exorcistic function was reminiscent of *gigaku's* Chidô mask and activities when he led a procession before pantomimic scenes were performed. (See chapter IV, part 2, "*Gigaku and Bugaku*.")

Gigaku had come to Japan, together with Buddhism, in the 7th century, and over the years was performed at major temples. Chidô, as well as the other figures of *gigaku*, appeared dressed in costumes which recalled their origins in Western China. It is possible to hypothesize that portrayals of the Shinto god Sarutahiko no Mikoto reveal elements related to exotic-looking foreigners.

Together with Chidô, a group of lions (*shishi*) led the procession of *gigaku* dancers to the stage. Over time, the role of Chidô gradually changed from that of an independent, exorcistic character to a lion master, who held the beasts by their bridles. He is portrayed in this role, holding a whip and bridle, in the *Shinzei Kogaku-zu* (Shinzei's Illustrations of Ancient Music), a 12th-century scroll of ink drawings of theatrical representations.

As early as 780, the inventory of the Nara-based temple Saidai-ji lists a pair of red and black Chidô examples. After the 12th century, red and blue (or black) lion grooms appear in Buddhist ceremonies at various major temples.[1]

Pictorial evidence of Chidô-like figures with lion dancers are pictured on the *Nenjû Gyôji-emaki* (Yearly Events Illustrated Scrolls), a set of handscrolls depicting annual events of the late Heian period (794-1192). As shown on scroll nine, a man with a long-nosed mask, bird helmet (*tori kabuto*), and long dress, who is accompanied by two lions, marches in front of a portable shrine in Kyoto's Gion Festival. Another scene, on scroll twelve, depicts the special, Shintoistic Inari Festival, with a horseman leading the procession. He wears a long robe and headgear of the *eboshi* type, with a white veil over his face, and a long-nosed mask hanging in front of his chest. In those days, this part of the procession was called *shishimai* (lion dances) and *ômai*.

If one considers this historical evidence, *ômai* seems to have resulted from combining elements of the indigenous Shinto god Sarutahiko no Mikoto with those of Chidô, introduced from the Asian continent.

Shishimai, so popular in Japan, had also come from the continent, as part of *gigaku*. Since ancient times, the lion (actually, an imaginary, pug-faced idea of one), with its fierce character and imposing appearance, had been admired as a divine symbol of power and authority. Today confined to Africa and the northwestern part of Southeast Asia, lions once were at home in a vast area stretching from Pakistan to Greece. In China, lions appear as guardians of the imperial tombs because they are considered, along with dragons, to be sacred animals. Since the time Buddhism was introduced into China, a pair of lions has been represented, as guardians, seated to the right and left of Buddha's throne.

We believe that *gigaku*, described in the previous essay, is a descendent of Chinese dance and music, as can be seen on a container of Buddhist relics found in Kucha in Sinkiang, China. A procession of dancers, with the leader wearing an animal mask, is portrayed moving around energetically.

Proof of the existence of *shishimai* in Central Asia was found in Turfan. A small clay figurine, dating from the T'ang dynasty (618-907), shows two men under a fur-like costume with a lion mask. The image on the relic casket suggests that this type of lion dancer was substituted for the animal dancer at the beginning of the procession.

When Buddhism entered Japan, the figure of the lion was introduced as well, as can be seen in the decoration of the Tamamushi Shrine (first half of the 7th century) and on the murals of Hôryû-ji (around 700). A mask of Chidô, but not one of Shishi, has been preserved with 7th-century *gigaku* masks from the Hôryû-ji, and is now preserved at the Hôryû-ji Pavilion of the Tokyo National Museum. These masks are believed to have been carved by Japanese artists and not to have been imported from the continent. Nevertheless, masks of the Shishiko ("Lion's young attendants") type confirm that *shishimai* belonged to the repertoire of masks required for a *gigaku* performance. The previously mentioned *Shinzei Kogaku-zu* scroll gives us proof: every lion is accompanied by a couple of children known as Shishiko. Finally, the inscription on one of the Hôryû-ji masks of these children, used at the *shôryô-e* ceremony for Shôtoku-taishi's spirit at that temple, indicates that such a mask was also known as Haeharai ("Fanning Away Flies").

In Buddhist processions, two children accompanying each Shishi and two grooms (thought to be transformations of Chidô) form a group. In Shinto processions, we do not find such a grouping; instead, Ômai accompanies Shishi. A typical example was performed until recently on the occasion of the Tôdai-ji Chinju Hachiman Tegai-e, a festival in honor of the Shinto god Hachiman. The remaining appurtenances are preserved at the Tamukeyama Shrine.

Depending on the scale of the procession, the number of Shishi varies from one to several. We know from a procession at the Gion Festival of 1172 that three portable shrines, which had been made earlier, and seven Shishi heads, made later, were each carried by two men. Nowadays, it is a general practice throughout the country at various shrines to have three Shishi, each operated by one man. This might come from a different tradition. Since he was introduced from the continent, the popularity of Shishi, with his special powers for destroying evil, has swept throughout Japan.

SACRED FIGURES IN THE SERVICE OF BUDDHA

In the first half of the Heian period, all the different theatrical and musical forms were recognized, as were the Buddhist services. In the middle of the Heian period, Japanese court aristocrats became deeply involved in building numerous temples and shrines. Memorial services were organized when they were completed. Some large temples held their own special services, such as the Shari-e, the festival to honor Buddha's relics, or the Raigô-e, commemorating the descent of the Buddha and his attendants, as previously mentioned.

A typical example from 1083 took place at the Hosho-ji in Kyoto, which was later destroyed by fire. The *bugaku* dances performed were *Enbu*, *Shishi*, *Bosatsu* (Bodhisattva), *Karyôbin* (Heavenly Bird), and *Kochô* (Butterfly). A second set started with *Ama*, a dance paired with *Ni-no-mai*, then *Manzairaku*, *Sanju*, *Taiheiraku*, *Sogoko*, *Dakyugaku*, *Ryôô*, *Chikyû*, *Kitoku*, and *Ringa*. While the first set of dances, especially *Enbu*, was completely compatible with the process of a Buddhist service, the second part of the program put a visible emphasis on entertainment. The first part was called *kuyômai* or *hoemai*, dances performed as a sacrifice to Buddha. The second part was regular *bugaku*. As *bugaku* is described in the "Gigaku and Bugaku" essay, we will examine here only the first group of dances.

The initial part of the performance began with *Enbu*, a dance which does not require masks, but which is related through its exorcistic content to Chidô and Ômai. Next, the Shishi led the officiating priests to the meeting place and performed the act of welcoming on a stage. Needless to say, this type of Shishi is clearly related to the Shishi of *gigaku*, as well as to *shishimai*. This welcome was followed by the rite of offering performed via *Bosatsu* and the *Karyôbin* and *Kochô* dances, which are children's numbers. Finally, a grand procession was performed by the Shishi and the other participants.

The *Bosatsu* dance originally required a mask. A theory connects this *Bosatsu* piece with the *Bosatsu* of today's *bugaku*, as well as with a *Bosatsu* dance introduced with *rinyûgaku*, music that came from India or Southeast Asia in the 7th-8th centuries. It may also be related to the *Bosatsu* that was well known in T'ang China. Several Shishi participated, each accompanied by four attendants; i.e., two grooms and two Shishiko, with two kinds of masks.

The grooms are definitely transformations of Chidô from *gigaku*, although the description of the masks connected with the 1083 event does not mention big noses or red or black faces. Their mouths are described as either shut or wide open. The Shishiko correspond exactly to *gigaku* Shishiko and were called Haeharai.

Another aspect of visualizing faith is worth mentioning. Depending on the type of service, those who carried the palanquin of the officiating priest, as well as those around him protecting Buddhist law, were dressed as Jûniten, Hachibushô, or Nijûhachibushi, all Buddhist guardian gods.

Several temples held such events. Hôryû-ji should be mentioned first. Shitennô-ji in Osaka also performed them on the occasion of the Shôryô-e Festival. Especially beautiful masks were produced for the Shari-e, formerly held by the Kyôogokoku-ji in Kyoto, as well as for the Nifutsu-Hime Shrine. These masks are now preserved at the Tokyo National Museum.

The most elaborate event with people disguised as this type of sacred being was the Kuyô-e for the Head of the Great Buddha, held in 861, and described in the *Tôdai-ji Yôroku* (Records of Todai-ji). The priest Eun, who had just returned from China, was in charge of the occasion. As T'ang China was deeply admired during this time, he might have been inspired to give a special cosmopolitan flavor to the event. A huge stage decorated with trees was erected in front of the Great Buddha. The figures making their appearance on stage were disguised as Fugen Bosatsu, the Bodhisattva of Wisdom, who rode on an elephant; Tamonten, one of the Guardian Deities of the Four Directions, who was accompanied by fourteen demons; Kichijôten, a goddess who bestows wealth, who appeared with twenty *tennyo* (female heavenly beings); and, finally, Daijizaiten (based on the Hindu god Shiva), who was surrounded by sixty *tennin* (celestial beings). We do not know what these individuals actually did on the stage, but we can imagine that the total picture was splendid.

3.54 A

3.54 G

PLATE 23

As mentioned, the presentation of such figures disguised as sacred beings became formalized by the mid-Heian period. During this period, the Pure Land sect organized performances in which the descent of Amida Buddha (Amida Raigô) from his Western Paradise was presented to encourage belief in Pure Land Buddhism. This type of Buddhist service, called Mukaeko and Raigô-e, was held after the Kamakura period (1192-1333) and is performed today at the Taima-dera and Joshin-ji temples in Tokyo. The finest masks used in such ceremonies are preserved at the Jôdo-ji in Hyôgo prefecture.

Unrelated to the previously mentioned theatrical forms, disguised figures were also used in another import from the continent. T'ang folk customs were introduced in the Nara period (710-794) in the form of the *tsuina-e* ("expelling of demons"). This took place at large temples as a kind of religious service and was called Oni-oi or Oni-hashiri after the Heian period. The ceremony that was held at the Saien-dô is still performed at the Hôryû-ji.

All examples described had their origins on the Asian continent, especially in China before or during the T'ang dynasty.

Some left fairly dramatic traces, as happened in *gigaku*. All of them came to Japan with Buddhism and were modified according to Buddhist needs. When these theatrical forms entered Japan, many of the secular elements were removed so that the forms could better be used to promote Buddhism. In a similar manner, baroque Jesuit theater disseminated and popularized information about Roman Catholicism. Theatrical elements described in this essay were transmitted to, and are reflected in, performing arts such as *sangaku*, *sarugaku*, and *kyôgen*, described in later chapters of this catalogue.

1. [Editor's endnote] Such ceremonies, generally called *gyôdô*, actually refer to three different types of masked procession. One, possibly originating in India, involves priests walking around the temple or principle image of worship, as they chant sutras; an extant example is seen at the Hana (Flower) Festival at Nara's Yakushi-ji temple. Another *gyôdô* procession around the temple is part of a *kuyô*, or service for the dead. The third, mentioned below, is intended as a reenactment of Amida's descent to welcome a dying believer to the Pure Land. Many of the masks described in this essay were worn in *gyôdô*.

3.14

PLATE 24

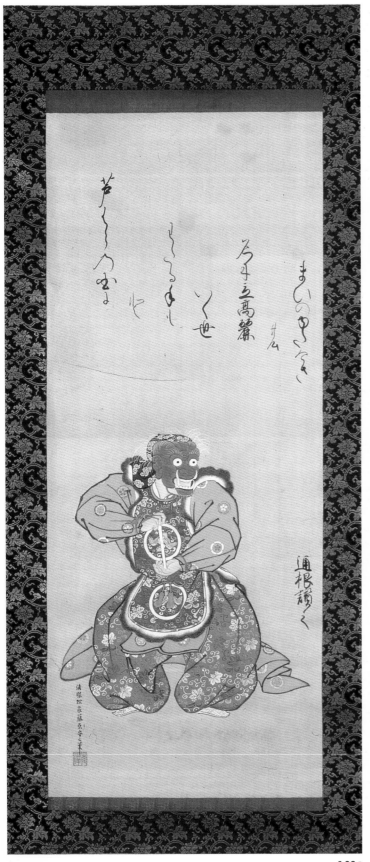

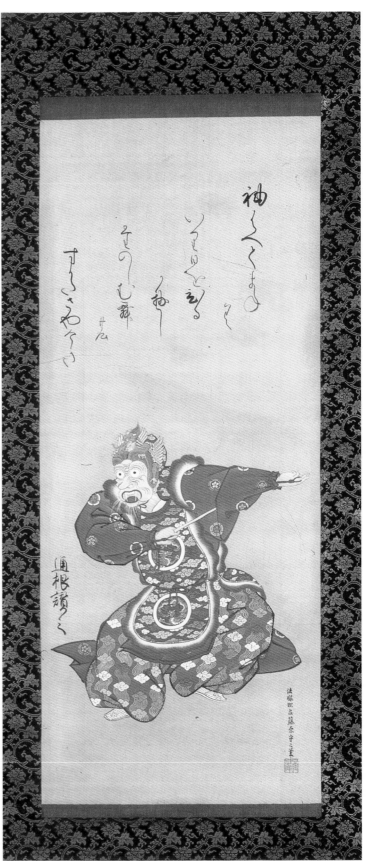

3.22 B

3.22 A

PLATE 25

3.48

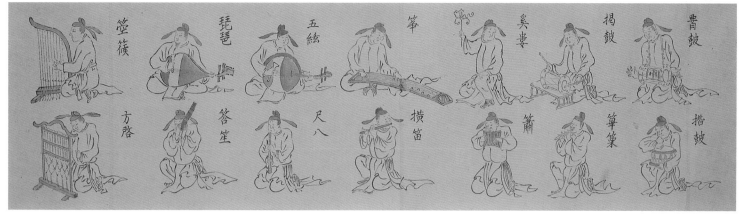

筝篌　琵琶　五絃　筝　吳妻　揭皷　齊皷

方瞽　答笙　尺八　横笛　簫　笙簧　楷皷

3.6

Plate 26

3.44

3.37

3.38

3.53

PLATE 27

3.35

PLATE 28

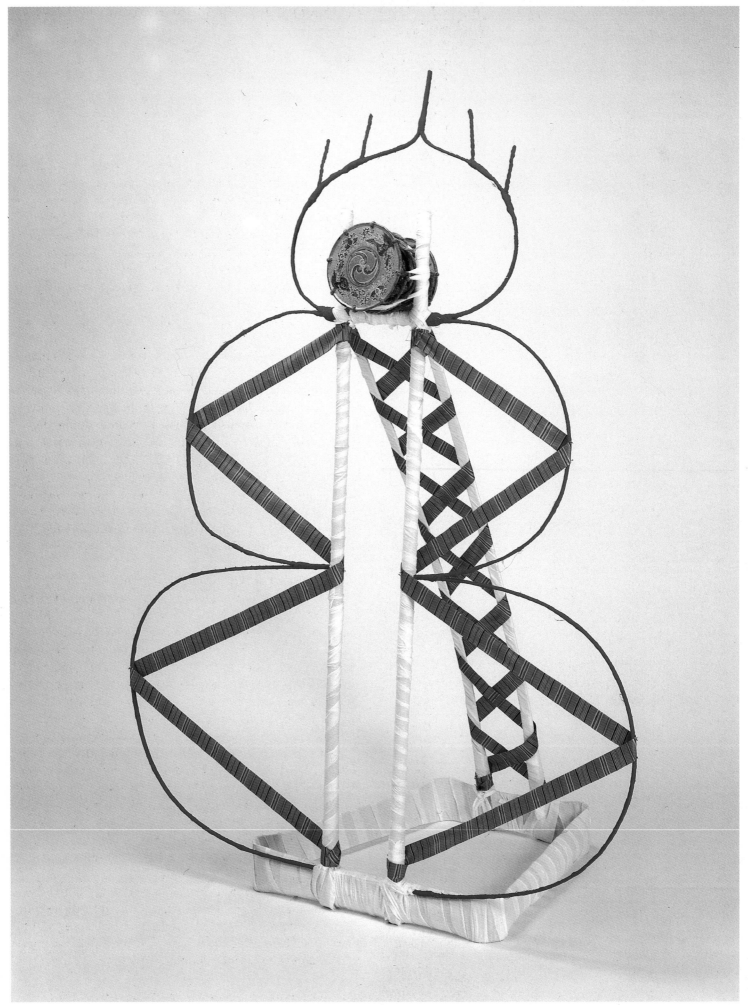

PLATE 29

4.17

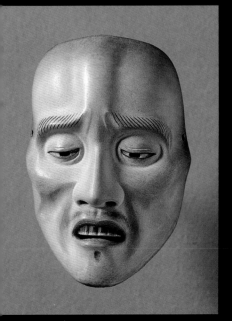

4.18

4.19

IV. SNOW IN A SILVER BOWL: *Nô* Theater

Günter Zobel and Gotô Hajime
Translated by Arthur Birnbaum

HISTORY AND DEVELOPMENT

"*Nô* is a demanding drama form, perhaps even the most spiritual among all the numerous other forms that cultured peoples use for their entertainment. Without doubt, it is the most sublime, intense and extensive. It challenges one's sensibility and intellect in equal degrees."[1] This art, which is now over 500 years old and which is referred to in terms similar to the above by many experts on world theater, would not have been possible, had the groundwork not been laid by previously developed dance and lyrical art forms. Yet it took two outstanding creative geniuses, favored by great fortune, to create its near perfect form, which is revered even today. Kan'ami Kiyotsugu (1333-1384) and his son Zeami Motokiyo (1363-1443) combined *sarugaku*, one of the larger and more widely-spread ritual forms of popular theater (see the essay, "Ancient Roots: *Kagura* and *Minzoku Geinô*"), with the dramaturgy of a highly artistic and sophisticated visual art. In so doing, they gave *nô* a strong literary basis built on traditional Chinese and Japanese poetry. The great moment in history which was to see Kan'ami and his twelve-year-old son placed under the patronal protection of the shôgun, Ashikaga Yoshimitsu, thus opening up the possibility of giving free and artistic expression to their ideas, is described by Benito Ortolani in the opening essay of this volume.

While only a few fragments of the *nô* dramas written by Kan'ami have been handed down, Zeami created his own large repertoire. As many as ninety can be attributed to him. Moreover, in a series of writings on aesthetics he discussed the theoretical basis of the acting and dramaturgy of *nô*. However, Kan'ami's contribution to the dramaturgical development of *nô* was considerable. By partially incorporating the once popular rhythmic dance called *kusemai* as an element of tension in the form of a recitative between the chorus and the principal actor, who sometimes also dances, he laid down a dramaturgical cornerstone on which the first part of the *nô* play was to build, leading into the dramatic development of the play. For this is the point in the play where the audience is enlightened as to the content and meaning, the intellectual and religious background of the drama. At this juncture, they experience what Zeami was later to refer to as the "opening-up of ears" (*kaimon*). This concept contains the double meaning of the acoustic as it is inherent in *nô*: hearing and understanding the words, on the one hand, and experiencing and feeling the musical and rhythmic sound on the other. Both of these elements are simultaneously picked up by the ear of the listener, and their harmonizing effect is intended to captivate him at this point and rivet him for the duration of the play.

Even though the two *sarugaku no nô* artists were accorded unlimited patronage by the most powerful and richest man in the country, the shôgun, this by no means meant that they were guaranteed lasting success. Yoshimitsu was, in a sense, only a person in the audience whose taste they catered to and who was enthralled by their performances. But they also needed to capture as large an audience as possible for the new art form; otherwise, lasting success would elude them. This is why Zeami was preoccupied with the idea of creating a type of nô that could be appreciated by both the upper class (kijin) and the masses (shûjin). And here we also find the reason why he strove to balance out mutually contradictory elements for the sake of artistic expression. Kan'ami had already associated the idea of the flower (hana) of a performance with his goal of direct aesthetic participation by the audience. In several writings, all containing the word hana in their title, Zeami went on to develop his theory of the flower that allows a relationship to be built with the audience. For Zeami the terms "flower," "surprisingly new" (mezurashii), and "enticing" (omoshiroi) stem from the same roots: in order for the audience to be drawn into the experience as a whole, the peaceful flow of visual beauty must be interrupted by a moment of surprise that captures their attention and rekindles their interest. The limits of this visual art are defined by the aesthetic concept of yûgen (yûgenbi, or "yûgen beauty"), which, in essence, means beauty and elegance, refinement and gracefulness. This was the ideal of the court nobility and the warrior class. Moreover, the concept of yûgen extended to the metaphysical boundaries of the "mysterious, profound beauty of cosmic truth" or included a "peaceful feeling of Weltschmerz." [2]

The style of acting and staging chosen by Zeami reflected his own special attitude to imitation (monomane): there was no question of nô drama being confused with common or garden variety realism or being a shoddy naturalistic portrayal of reality. The depiction of life had to be sublimated to the level of exemplary fundamental traits and then reproduced as molded symbols. Whereas the actor identifies deep down completely with his role and the mask helps him to lay aside his own personality (honi), permitting him to take over completely the character he is portraying, the gamut of his movements is reduced to a minimum of intimations and these movements are abstractions of the symbolic essence contained in gestures. His overall stage appearance also conjures up a different meaning, one of a transcendant aesthetic world, often elevated to the level of a fairy tale by the magnificent costumes. Here we see the way in which nô symbolizes and idealizes, for "through what you see, you only get an indication of what really should be there." [3]

Over a long period of time this traditional Japanese performing art adopted a stylized form of its own. A nô drama contains many so-called kata, patterns of gestures and movements conveying exemplary and abstracted meanings, which are combined together and may reappear in other plays in the same form, although not necessarily in the same context. This is why a photo or a drawing of a single dance position, in itself, is not sufficient to tell you which play it is from. These kata are compiled for each play in katazuke, lists containing the patterns of gestures, steps, and dance movements, and are then handed down to the next generation. The advantage of this is

that a nô play which has not been performed for a long time can be revived without major difficulty by following these katazuke. What is generally understood by the word kata is, for example, the gesture with which the impression of weeping is created: the actor raises one or both palms slowly until they are level with his eyes and, at the same time, lowers his masked face slightly. This abstract kata, which nowadays is called shiori, emerged only in the Edo period (1603-1868), at a time when nô was being stylized and formalized.

In Zeami's day, nô would seem to have been more strikingly realistic, for we now know with certainty that, at that time, the actor still showed sorrow by wiping both eyes with his sleeve. Ultimately, the stylized form, rather than the concrete gesture, was accepted as the more refined means of expression and was passed on to succeeding generations in as beautiful and perfect a form as possible. Even to this day, it is still considered to be the most important goal of a performance to captivate the audience by means of the charm of consummate dancing and expressive recitatives, which are near perfect in form, and not through the storyline, no matter how exciting the protagonist's history may be. For this reason, dramatic themes which could be expressed in beautiful and elevated dance forms always have been preferred. The concept of "beauty" was itself subject to the changing times. Initially, it referred principally to the way in which young women and children were portrayed in a fine, enchanting, and refined manner. Beauty was then found in the portrayal of older people. In their world of loneliness and grief was planted the nô aesthetic ideal, which transformed it into a place of peaceful and touching beauty.

Nô Dramas and Repertoire

Those plays still surviving today—which number more than 240 and of which approximately 130 are performed regularly— are customarily divided into five categories. They are best known under the headings of: "deities, men, women, mad persons, demons" (shin, nan, nyo, kyô, ki) and are arranged in a fixed sequence from the First to the Fifth Plays, which is a simpler term used to describe them. Each of these terms underlines the importance of the role of the shite ("doer") or principal actor, who usually wears a mask. In addition to these, there are a few other frequently used terms: First Plays are labeled waki nô (subsidiary or secondary nô) or kami nô (god nô), and kiri nô (fast-ending nô or conclusion nô) is applied to Fifth Plays. A certain ritual unity is in evidence in the appearance of Shinto-istic gods in the prologue, which deals with the ordination of Okina, the old man who brings blessings, and without whom a festive and complete nô program is unthinkable.

It is not until the Second Plays that we reach the realm of earthly matters, those pertaining to mortal men. The predominant theme in the Second Plays is suggested by the name for them, shura mono or shura nô. The subject in question is that of the warrior who, as a result of tragic death in battle or after having celebrated a great victory later in eternity is, in accordance with Buddhist belief, locked in the struggle for his soul: shura dô, or the shura "way," one of the six life cycles man has to endure. The majority of plays in this group are named after heroes, and the central dance section contains a scene depicting the life-and-death struggle of the hero. Unlike the supporting actor (*waki*), the principal actor (*shite*) can also take on female roles. This fact is reflected in the common term used for Third Plays of *katsura* (or *kazura*) mono, "wig plays." These dramas, of which there are thirty-eight and which are to a certain extent very lyrical, introduce tender love themes.

The following group, Fourth Plays, cannot be classified as easily, since it contains plays with varied themes. They are commonly described nowadays by subdividing them into approximately five categories, comprising some of the categories put forward by previous *nô* experts:
(1) *kyôran mono*, *kyôjo*, or *kurui mono* are plays centered around people who have gone mad.
(2) *yukyô mono* and *yugaku mono* are plays containing music, a large drum, and dancing; i.e., cheerful performances.
(3) *shûnen mono* and *onryô mono* are plays with somber themes relating to spirits. The soul of the deceased is trapped in his past life on earth through mourning and torment (*shûnen* or *shûshin*), or is still aroused by interminable wrath and an insatiable thirst for revenge (*onryô*).
(4) *ninjô mono* are plays which are intended to arouse human sympathy (*ninjô*) because of the particularly harsh stroke of fate encountered by the protagonist.
(5) *genzai mono* ("in-the-present plays") are so-called "historical dramas" about the world of the warrior. They reflect the world the way it is at any given moment, so the principal actor does not wear a mask.

The Fifth Plays (*kiri mono*), named after the type of dancing performed in them, are generally classified under the broader label of *kichiku*, since figures from the realm of demons, good and evil spirits, and goblins appear in them.

In *nô*, the elements of text, music, dance, and performance are all subordinate to the principle of *jo-ha-kyû*, which is taken from *gagaku* music (see "*Gigaku* and *Bugaku*" in the essay "Court, Shrine, and Temple"). *Jo* describes the slow, formal beginning, the exposition. *Ha* refers to the increasingly rapid development of the theme and its "execution" or the increase in dramatic tension, and as such may be compared to a movement of a sonata. Since this is the longest section, it is further divided into three parts before reaching the *kyû*, the external intensification, final climax, and rapid end.

A formal, festive *nô* program (*shiki nô*) is arranged along the lines of this principle, with one *nô* play from each of the five categories representing the elements from *jo* to *kyû*. The Second to the Fourth Plays provide the great span of variations necessary for three parts of *ha*. The principle of *jo-ha-kyû* is applied to almost all elements of *nô* drama; for example, to the distance that the performer has to cover when he steps from behind the curtain (*agemaku*) on to the stage bridgeway (*hashigakari*) and, accompanied by music, moves on to the *kyû* part of the passageway leading to the main stage. Each individual *nô* play is also more or less built along these lines: *jo* represents the part when the maskless *waki*, who mostly plays

a traveling monk or official, enters, and says his name and where he is headed. Once he has stated that he has reached his destination, he comes to rest downstage right in front of the *waki* pillar, which is named after him. When the *shite* enters, the *ha* part begins: he describes himself by performing different types of songs. The chorus intervenes at the *kuse*, a point in the play first introduced by Kan'ami. There then ensues a dialogue between the *waki* and *shite*, ending with the revelation of the true nature of the *shite*'s character. The *kyû* section, following an intermission for the principal actor to change, contains a song by the *waki* while he waits, the appearance of the *shite* in his true form, his dance, yet another dialogue with the *waki*, and the finale (*kiri*).

No new member of a *nô* audience can fail to notice how considerable the length of this variably termed dance section can be. It demands the utmost in patience from a Western audience. Since the latter are used to a cause and effect story line, they do not immediately understand the overall meaning and the dramatic significance of the *nô* dance, which often appears to them to be a special part of the performance. Only repeated vewing of *nô* dances, which are often performed separately as interludes, and intensive study of them can help one to understand the theoretical descriptions and explanations.

Basically, all *nô* dramas can be divided into two categories according to their dramaturgical form: one-act and two-act plays. The former account nowadays only for approximately a third of the entire repertoire, whereas over 160 two-act plays have been recorded. As previously described, the majority of present-day *nô* plays, therefore, are influenced by the form that the later transformation and revelation takes once the *shite* appears for the first time in a hidden form, as described previously. Moreover, since Zeami's time, the prototype of a *nô* drama has been seen as the *mugen nô*, which accounts for most of the two-act *nô* dramas. In these plays the *shite* does not appear as a real person, but rather in the form of a ghost or an apparition. A deity, a demon, the ghost of a dead person, the spirit of a flower, plant, or animal temporarily assumes the form of a human being and appears to the traveling priest. He tells the priest of his earlier and true existence, with the aim of getting him to pray for the release of his soul. Before he departs, he lets the priest know that he is not a mortal being. In the second part, he appears in his past or true form, and reveals himself, before disappearing forever, in a dance before his partner, who is praying for him. This type of "dream world *nô*" (*mugen nô*) is the opposite of *genzai nô*, in that the latter takes place only in the world of the living, either historical or contemporary, depending on when the story takes place. It is therefore characterized as "*nô* of the present moment." It is said that *genzai nô* are older in form than *mugen nô*. However, one must not forget that the latter were performed, as has already been mentioned, during Zeami's lifetime. The best way nowadays to enter into this world of deities and spirits is to experience simple theater, as in the *sarugaku* and *dengaku* scenes in the masked dance dramas of *kagura*, which are devoted to Japanese mythology and which are kept alive throughout the whole country in popular festivals (see the essay "Ancient Roots: *Kagura* and *Minzoku Geinô*"). This is probably the simplest method, since people who can become thoroughly involved in a Japanese festival (*matsuri*) invariably find it difficult to resist the charm of *nô*.

A good example of this unspoilt synthesis is the *nô* of the farmers of Kurokawa in Yamagata Prefecture, which has become internationally famous. Here we can see *matsuri* and theater still united, as conceived by folklorist Yanagita Kunio, in the form of a festival and ceremony to the gods.[4] For here the gods still appear on ground that has been consecrated, here the appearance of the spirits of mythical heroes is still accompanied by shamanistic-sounding drums in the night, while the heavenly sound of the flute is heard and, beyond the gates, a snow storm rages.

The latest research shows striking similarities between the *shinji* (festivals of the gods), which form the framework of *nô* dramas, and the death rites of the Ainu, who once lived as close as the mountains of Tôhoku. This is also a reminder of another great popular custom, which can be easily compared with *nô*. The appearance of ghosts is no longer felt to be strange if one has already experienced the intensity with which the dead in Japan are remembered by their families. To this end, cities such as Tokyo are almost half emptied at *obon* in order to allow as many as possible to appear before the altar of their ancestors in their parents' houses.

Carl Niessen, a Cologne drama expert, has discussed how the dramaturgical basis of interviews with ghosts in *nô* corresponds to the tales of the dead from the hereafter, as found in the Pali Canon of early Buddhism.[5] The plots of these ghostlike stories are different from the sources and contents of the *nô* dramas, but the form the dialogue takes in the interviews at the heart of each episode shows clear similarities with the dramaturgical basis of the *nô*. Moreover, in a rare case of concurrence with *nô*, it cannot be denied that these figures from the "Peta Vatthu," which were transmitted orally and then written down in South India in the 5th century after Buddha's death, were so-called "revenants," characters resurrected from the realm of the dead. By calling upon Buddha, the traveler who meets them, once again in most cases a monk, can eventually extricate them from the unresolved situation in which they have become involved through committing culpable acts during their lives on earth. In addition, he can cause their souls to be reincarnated on a higher level. So much for the clear parallels to the function of the *shite* and *waki*. Finally, however, Niessen had to admit that by far the most important dramaturgical element was still missing, namely that of dance, which has had such a formative influence on *nô*. His assumption that this dance emerged from Shinto's worship of the land and that it synthesizes *nô* drama on a higher level with the "festival" (*sairei*) is perfectly correct.

NÔ ACTORS AND PERFORMANCE

Masks are worn in *nô* drama only by the *shite* and the accompanying actors, called *tsure*. Like the chorus, which generally has eight members, they come from the same *nô* school. The names of the five traditional schools are Kanze, Hôshô,

Komparu, Kongô, and Kita. A public performance usually takes place after only one rehearsal. It takes the form of a staged arrangement between the *shite*, the *waki*, who has been invited and engaged for this performance, and the *tsure*. In addition, there are the instrumentalists, who are always necessary: someone on the flute, the shoulder drum, the hip drum, and, for some plays, the free-standing stick drum. The actor in the interlude, who bridges the two halves of the *nô* play and also sometimes appears in a supporting role, is taken from one of the two *kyôgen* schools.

Mention already has been made at several junctures of the *shite* and his promordial significance, in the role of main character, for the dramatic development of the play. Kan'ami and Zeami were themselves making a living from their acting when they wrote the first of their masterpieces of poetic drama. The intensity of every action and the meaning of every event seems to have been tailored to the *shite*. Thus the *waki*, who usually appears in front of him without a mask, cannot be seen as an "opposite number," but rather a "supporting actor," as his name suggests. The term *waki* could easily be translated as "side actor" when one thinks of his position at the side of the stage in front of the pillar named after him. Here is where he remains for most of the play, welcoming the *shite*, asking him questions, providing him with a reason and time to hide his true identity, and to explain, present, and reveal himself. The few instances of dialogue or even of dispute (*rongi*) are followed by long scenes of contemplative, lyrical reflections on the part of the *shite*. In this, he is supported by the chorus, which not only describes events in space and time objectively or, like the chorus in Greek tragedy, comments on the situation, but also slips into the role of the principal actor and, speaking in the first person, takes over the *shite*'s part, especially in the dance sequence.

The view that all the parts of *nô* mentioned here can simply fall under the term "dance" needs to be continually questioned. The original idea associated with the Japanese word *mai* is that of one person—two or three at most—dancing in peaceful, rotating, and circular movements. The opposite would be an *odori*, a dance for groups or couples, which is less stringently uniform and which has varied gestures and lively steps. The main aesthetic difference between this and Western dance is to be found in the extreme "earthiness" of Japanese dancing. If one closely examines all forms of lively, traditional dance, it is possible to see a line connecting the point of gravity around the hips with the ground. This line gives the impression that the body is shorter and in permanent contact with the earth, as if it is continuously checking to see that the earth is still there.

Earlier commentators on *nô* went so far as to say that the purpose of these plays was to produce "solo performances by the principal actor"; if not, they were atypical. If one considers the great detail and possible variations in terms of masks and costumes with which the *shite* is equipped, not to mention the possibility that only he, as the principal actor, can express himself on stage by means of gestures and dancing, then it becomes clear how underdeveloped the role of the *waki* is, as

4.34 A

4.35

PLATE 30

seen from the viewpoint of visual theater. And yet the *waki's* appearance on this stage, special also for its form, is of a strange, inductive, dramaturgical nature. At the beginning of the play, his entrance via the bridgeway (*hashigakari*) denotes the "Way and Path" of the wanderer; in point of fact, his route. The *waki* has reached his destination when he has kneeled on one knee in front of his pillar; in *nô*, kneeling on one knee signifies resting in a seated position. Without a mask and clad in the simple colors of a bonze or court official's costume, he is in full view of the audience. This is different from the *shite*, who enters after the *waki* and meets him at stage right on the same line of vision. The *waki*, in effect, has been "waiting" for him. As a representative of the dramatic present, the *waki* has taken up his position based on a line of vision joining himself with the audience.

It is easy to draw, on a plan of the *nô* stage, a straight line which starts from the *waki's* seat and crosses to the middle of the striped *agemaku* curtain at the end of the *hashigakari*. This passageway did not find its final, present-day position on stage left until the end of the 15th century. However, the angle at which the bridge turns off from the stage and its length are still subjects for debate. One should not underestimate how important the dramaturgical construction of this real perspective is for the transcending nature of the *shite's* appearance. Otherwise, his attire would lead the audience to expect a purely fairy tale or illusionistic character. It is not until the *waki* observes and interviews the *shite* that the human aspect of the episode related to the life and fate of the hero can be comprehended paradigmatically and symbolically.

In addition, the role of the *waki* as an intermediary is particularly strong, as is very clear in "dream world *nô*" (*mugen nô*), which probably causes the audience to feel that its powers of imagination have been overtaxed. The role of the *waki* contains, of course, more possibilities for a bolder, dramatic challenge and confrontation with the *shite*. It is no surprise, therefore, that, after Zeami, plays called *geki nô* (drama *nô*) were written in which the *waki* was assigned a more important and dramatically active role than in the traditional dance-based *nô* (*furyû nô*). Kanze Kojirô Nobumitsu (1435-1516) created *genzai nô* along these lines for no lesser reason than that he himself acted as a *waki*. Plays with more than one character, such as *Ataka*, *Funa Benkei*, and *Momijigari*, were easily adapted by *kabuki* and work successfully even today. In *nô*, however, the play could be acted only by the *shite* and *waki*.

If servants or companions (*tsure*) are required by the text, they appear on stage as *shitezure* or *wakizure*. Characters accompanying the *shite* can also wear masks, but some do not speak a word. Where the text of the play requires it, a local person can appear before the *shite* or *waki*. In this case, the roles are played by *kyôgen kata*, actors from the *kyôgen* schools.

Another special feature is the appearance of children, *kokata*. Boys with high, still thin voices embody, above all, characters of high social status such as emperors or popular heroes, like Yoshitsune. Out of respect for these high-ranking and honored persons, the customary requirement of nobility and dignity is supplemented by a portrayal of the person in question in as abstract and symbolic a fashion as possible. In order to avoid all too realistic characteristics, which could suggest a love affair, among other things, the childlike figure is the representation par excellence of all human emotions without showing emotions. This is yet another example of how important it is to understand the essentially transitory experience of the *nô* performance, the point at which contradictions collapse and cancel one another out, an aesthetic "coincidence of opposites," which is conjured up by the term *yûgen*. Mention has already been made of the fact that the sadness and loneliness of old age were used as theatrical techniques in *nô* and that, despite splendid brocade costumes reminiscent of past courtly taste, the image of sublime harmony and beauty was able to be conveyed. If a *nô* performance accomplishes this, "a white bird with a flower in its beak flies through the room" or "a silver bowl, filled with snow" is proffered, to quote two Zen *koan*-like paraphrases used by Zeami to describe *yûgen* as it unfolds.

NO MASKS

In actual fact, the *nô* performance has already begun when the *shite* holds the mask up in front of himself in the mirror room (*kagami no ma*) behind the *agemaku* and the mask is tied to his face. As his title implies, he is the "doer," the leader of the play, since his "skill" (*nô*) largely determines whether the performance is a success or not. There is no actual director in *nô*, but the mask, which the *shite* himself has chosen weeks in advance of the performance, fulfills this function in suggesting how the role should be enacted. Through the rich fund of masks handed down to them, the individual schools have a definite store of role patterns in their repertoire. This used to find expression in a strong preference for a particular type of mask; for example, those for young women. On seeing their first *nô* play, people from the West are mesmerized by the masks. That the *shite* stays on the *hashigakari* briefly while turned toward the audience seems intended to catch the latter's attention, allowing it to recognize the mask. At this moment, the actor is bent forward slightly, but is in such a position that the mask, held upright on his slightly raised head, comes to rest on a clear vertical line with the tips of the actor's feet, if one imagines this line extended to the stage. Moreover, when the *shite*, in the second half of the play, dances the *hataraki* ("work") section, with its powerful stamping and jumping movements, the raging spirit or demon he embodies (usually holding a magic wand in his right hand) rises up on his tiptoes for a brief moment in order to bring out even more clearly the symbiosis between the threatening traits of his mask and his stiffened gestures.

The careful observer is quick to realize that the traditional size of the *nô* mask is somewhat smaller than the face of the actor. In this way, his cheeks and chin can be partly seen under the mask, which, most important of all, is aligned over his eyes. However, it does not take long before the audience becomes accustomed to this feeling of confusion, intended to prevent them from thinking that they are looking at the face of a puppet. Instead, they can practice looking for the nuances in the expressions of the mask as reflected in the movements of the actor. Nô players use the term *kumoraseru*, "clouding over," to describe the way in which the mask leans forward and its eyes come closer together as they fall under the shadow cast by the forehead, a movement which often creates a sad expression. In contrast, the raising of the mask into a warm light is called *terasu*, "illumination." Nô is not the only traditional dramatic art to use the mask, but there is no other dramatic form which has endowed the mask with so much dramatic meaning and has tried over time to improve and capitalize on its possibilities for dramatic expression. It was during the time of Kan'ami and Zeami that the *sarugaku* mask play developed from being a demonstration for the masses at ritual festivals to being an aesthetically refined, esoteric performance.

Recent research has seen in Yoshimitsu's patronage of Chinese art and religion a good reason to look to China for elements of *nô* that developed under his aegis. Masks reminiscent of examples of the later types of *nô* masks, particularly because of their flat, half mask-like forms, have been found among the masks of the *nuotanshi*, mask plays from the region of Tongren in the Province of Guizhou.[6] It is assumed that these plays flourished in China at the same time as Zeami's plays in Japan. Irrespective of the question as to what extent *nô* was influenced by Yoshimitsu's enthusiasm for China and his lively trade with this same country, it is undoubtedly the case that the sublimation of the power of expression to faces full of the utmost aesthetic and dramatic intensity is the major achievement in art history accomplished by Japanese contemporaries.

The origins of the mask in the *sarugaku* faces of demons, spirits, and deities were never quite forgotten, but in the wake of the refinement of the means at the disposal of the theater, different demands were placed on the mask's expressive potential for newly developed roles. Most importantly, masks with genuinely human expressions had to be created. Moreover, those masks that, a priori, bore a particular expression were supplemented by masks with what was called *chûkan hyôjô*, "medium" or "middle" expression."[7] A mask of this sort not only expresses a clearly defined emotion, such as joy, anger, or mourning, but can be used to mirror a variety of feelings. Nor did this mean a return to a complete lack of expressiveness (*muhyôjô*). After all, masks such as these, which were used earlier for purely ritual purposes, had progressed to the artistically much more complex *chûkan hyôjô* expression. It has been confirmed that, when *nô* was first developing, it was not yet customary to use masks for female roles. What we consider today to be the perfect example of a *nô* mask, the beautiful depiction of a young woman, goes back to the later period of its development and is evidence of the increasingly independent development of the art of mask carving and of its continual movement toward a graphic and decorative genre.

The book which the Japanese themselves claim first drew their attention to the beauty and significance of the classical *nô* mask is Friedrich Perzynski's *Japanese Masks, Nô and Kyôgen* (1925). On its publication, serious research began in Japan into the collections of masks available at that time and their history. Perzynski's and subsequent descriptions of masks focus on the "Ten and Six Masters" of the so-called *honmen*, the "original masks." These 131 masks are recorded in the oldest cataloguing document, which, in fact, dates back to 1721, but has been preserved in a copy from 1770. This is a written document, in which, on orders of the shôgun, all masks owned by *nô* schools and families had to be listed. In 1771, a further list followed which included the masks owned by provincial rulers, daimyô, and the shôgun himself, thereby producing a grand total of 162 *nô* masks. In addition, there were some smaller lists drawn up by *nô* dynasties, which, all told, formed the quite unreliable basis for a retrospective on the art of carving *nô* masks and its beginnings, around which legends often have been woven. The basis is unreliable since the view that these "original masks" all originate from great masters going back, in part, to mythical times, must be questioned. By that time, in fact, it had become customary for the *nô* schools to guard the famous masks of their forefathers as family treasure and not show them. Coveted masks were secretly copied when, for example, they had to be given as presents to the rulers, who liked being flattered in this way as patrons of *nô*.

As early as the mid-15th century there were professional carving schools which, as with *nô* actors, were represented by certain families. Depending on the skill of the carver, who was allowed only a brief glimpse of the mask and who then had to work on it from memory, there emerged more or less exact copies (*utsushi*) or individual creations containing new elements. But new types of masks as such were not created, the existing ones being enough for the *nô* repertoire as it became established during the Edo period. Nowadays, the total number of types is put at approximately 260 and, in line with the *nô* plays, they are divided into five parallel categories. Since those days, mask carvers have had their work cut out supplying *nô* actors with continually recarved copies of the old patterns, to which they can contribute, at the very most, minimal personal touches.

NO COSTUMES AND DÉCOR

Flanked by the chorus and the musicians, who are at right angles to one another, the single figures of the *waki* and *shite*, accompanied periodically by one or more *tsure*, fill the spartan, limited stage. The effect of the mask is supplemented decisively by that of the costume. An essential part of the experience of *nô* theater is the brocade splendor of the spirits and deities as they appear. By choosing his mask carefully, the principal actor puts a lot of thought into the interpretation of the character he is playing and, by carefully selecting his costume for its color and pattern, he avails himself of a means of external expression which virtually makes up for the otherwise nonexistent scenery. In addition, the volume of the costume, in contrast to which the mask often appears miniscule, dominates as the preeminent visual effect. The text books (*utaibon*) of each school describe at the beginning of every play the *shite*'s mask, wig, and costume. However, the actor can still add his own nuances to the role by carefully choosing one of a wide selection of costumes appropriate for the standing, rank, and personal integrity of the character. It was not until the

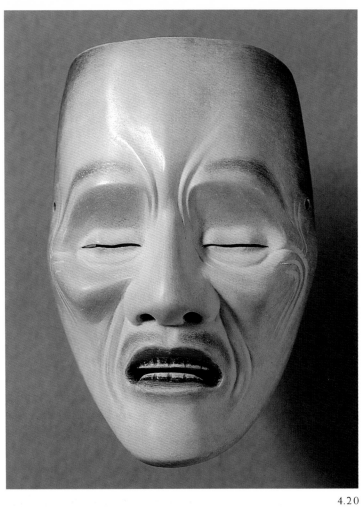

4.20

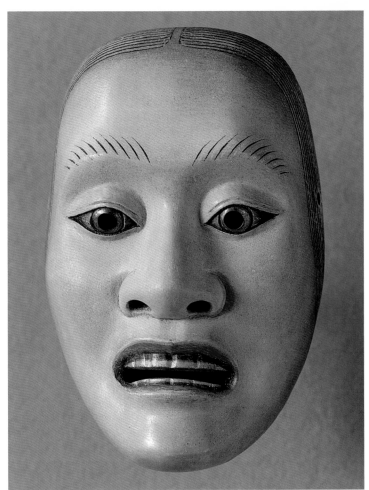

4.21

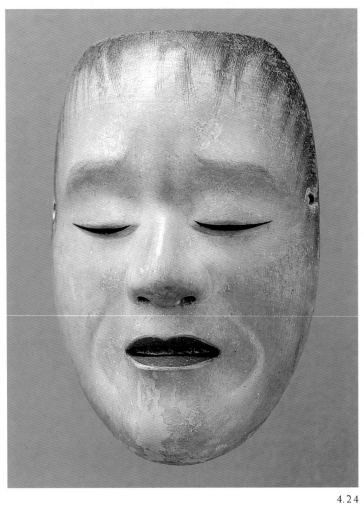

4.24

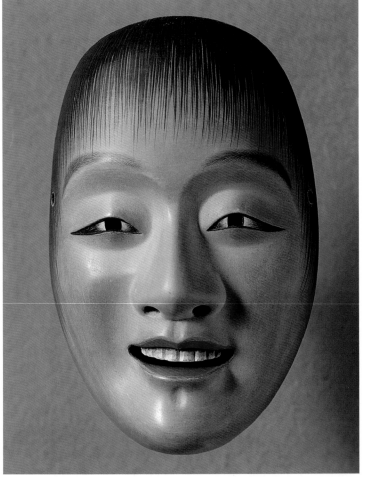

4.25

PLATE 31

Edo period, though, that costumes reached the heights of splendor. It is presumed that the earliest plays used much simpler and more discrete costumes. Zeami's dislike of the gold and silver brocade patterns on Chinese costumes, which his lord and patron Yoshimitsu so admired, is well known. It took the expectations of someone like Toyotomi Hideyoshi and the baroque attitudes to art shared by the Momoyama generation (1573-1600) to raise standards to the level of exaggerated courtly grandeur. There then followed under Tokugawa rule a trend toward stylized costumes that standardized the character of each role. These had to obey the aesthetic rule of absolute beauty (yôshikibi) in each portrayal—even that of poverty and misery—and someone of nobler origins had to be suitably distinguished by means of colors and designs.

With the exception of special annual public performances for the masses (kanjin nô), nô theater and its dancing served almost exclusively as a form of entertainment for the nobility and warrior castes of the upper classes at court, a form of entertainment in which they themselves liked to participate. Over a period of more than 200 years, the taste of these refined people, brought up to follow a strict etiquette, was able to steer this drama—viewed as their national, religious, literary, and musical heritage—in the proper direction. This applied not so much to the cornerstones of this art form, as represented by the text, masks, and musical accompaniment, but rather to the tempo and style of the performance, which are also primarily determined by the embellishment and decorative quality of the costumes. A thoroughly researched monograph has been written on the subject of variety in the cosmos of costumes still in existence today. It examines in detail their material, production, colors, emblems, and patterns.[7]

The twenty basic types of nô costume, which, in accordance with the older bugaku tradition, is called shôzoku and not, as in kabuki, ishô, is generally classified according to two sleeve forms. The shorter and narrow sleeves are called kosode, and its representational form, the garb made of Chinese brocade for female characters, is called karaori. The broad long sleeves, ôsode, form an integral part of the apparel worn, above all, by the transformed shite (nochijite) after the intermission for the costume change. They are responsible for some unusual costume movements in nô dances. In addition to the fan, which is held in different ways during various kata, the flapping of the long sleeve appears as a visual high point in an extensive dance sequence. No matter whether it is a fan or a weapon that is being held, or the katalpa, a magic wand drawn against an exorcist (as in Dôjô-ji), it is accompanied by wild circling of the outstretched left arm around its own axis, like the fluttering of a wing, while performing the hataraki dance section with its swift steps and intense footwork. As far as possible, the full length of the seam which runs along the bottom of the broad sleeve is wrapped around the forearm and the upper arm from the inside outwards (sode okake) or from the outside inwards (sode omaki). Through this dynamic flapping movement, the typical wrapped sleeve effect is produced, being unfolded somewhat later during the following steps. Occasionally, both sleeves are wrapped outwards or inwards. Sometimes a bunched-up sleeve like this is held above the head of the actor for some moments, in a manner similar to the impressive gesture of blessing which occurs as part of the New Year's festival of Okina and is reminiscent of the ritual invoking of the gods and goddesses.

A large number of the forty or so First Plays currently in the repertoire close with the appearance and dance of a tennyo, the "woman of heaven" or angel, who wears the tengan, the "crown of heaven," on her head. At its center shines the fiery orb made of bright metal as the emblem of Amaterasu, the Sun Goddess and progenitrix of all Shinto descendents. In many cases, a tsure then dances the tennyo mai, the dance of the woman of heaven, as a reminder of the dance performed by Ame no Uzume to lure the goddess from the Rock Cave. It is easy to see where the richly decorative crown of heaven, in its nô function as the kaburimono (headdress), most likely came from. To this day it can still be seen throughout the country in the miko mai, the festive dance of shrine maidens. In the rural sato kagura (see the essay "Ancient Roots: Kagura and Minzoku Geinô") of the most varied regions of Japan, this crown reappears as the headdress worn by all Daughters of Heaven, who descend from Amaterasu, and is worn in conjunction with the appropriate kagura mask.

In the nô dramas of the remaining categories, the tengan is used to provide an emblem on the shite's head and thus make clear the symbolism of the role he is portraying. It is possible to use flowers and birds, small or large animals, even a dragon. These ringan, hoops around the headdress, rest atop the mask and are both decorative, yet clear in form, often forming a true, baroque partnership with the resplendently patterned silk costumes. However, when seen in unison with the entire role, they represent and underline the fairy tale and mystical nature of the character, which points toward a different world.

Often, once the chorus and the orchestra have been long since seated and before the play has, in fact, begun, scenic units are brought onto the stage by one or two stagehands. Placed at various spots on the area enclosed by the four pillars, but sometimes—if rarely—on the hashigakari, these units serve various functions during the course of the play. They can illustrate points in the text which refer to time and geography, nature and architecture. Some are raised platforms to be acted or danced on. Others are enclosed spaces for costume changes. In a large number of nô plays, these tsukurimono, or "functional pieces," are often placed between the two front pillars of the stage. Generally these pieces are made out of bamboo sticks wrapped in white cloth. Attached at them at some point may be real objects, given prominence as a type of "décor." Mostly, these tsukurimono at the front edge of the stage are not integrated into the storyline or the dancing. Unlike a backdrop, which marks the background on the proscenium stage, the actors and their movements are seen behind the scenic units by the audience. This means that, in the majority of plays, the audience joins in the mood and, when the nochijite performs the final dance behind the allegorical scenery, it experiences an eminently visual climax.

At the beginning of *Yôkihi*, a Third Play, a *tsukurimono* the size of a man is brought in via the *hashigakari* and set in front of the musicians. This is a square, roofed, framework created by a pole at each of the four corners of a small platform, draped on all four sides. The transparent roof is adorned with temple or shrine ornaments. This vertical box-shaped *tsukurimono* represents the Paradise Palace of the Emperor's deceased loved one, Yôkihi (Yang Kuei-fei), in the "Eternal Kingdom." After the entrance of the *waki*, in this case a magician sent by the T'ang Emperor Gen-sô (Hsüan-tsung or Minghuang), two stagehands unhook the cloth drape from the four corner posts, let it drop to the ground, roll it up, and carry it away. Meanwhile, Yôhiki, the *shite*, can be seen in the open frame sitting under the roof of the Palace of Heaven. She is dressed in a magnificent costume and is wearing a *waka* or *zô-onna* mask and the *tengan*, the crown of heaven.

The story begins when the magician is handed a memento in the form of a golden miniature of a bird of paradise, a gift intended for the emperor. This play abandons the conventional *hashigakari* entrance of the *shite*, through the raising of the *agemaku*'s two bamboo poles, in favor of revealing the character when the *tsukurimono*'s cloth drape is lowered by the stage assistants, thus permitting an unimpaired view of the entire proceedings. This alternate method of disclosing the *shite* contains an incomparably more potent element of surprise: the sudden exposure of the character, hidden behind drapes from the very beginning.

Nô plays in which the *shite* has a costume change between parts one and two make use of this kind of framework; the principal actor disappears behind the draped *tsukurimono* at the end of the first part and, during the interlude, is changed by his dressers and given a different mask. He reappears before the *waki* and the audience as the *nochijite*, the true form of the main character, by means of the removal of the drape or by his stepping back out of the box. In *Dôjô-ji*, the bell in which the *shite* is hidden is lifted by a rope and pulley. There is no element of décor in *nô* theater that adds so much richness to the dramatic structure of the plays as does this type of *tsukurimono*, which serves both as a place of revelation and for making a mask and costume change. Basically it is a set piece, in the sense that once it is placed on the stage, it replaces a part of the stage setting or gives the impression of having been moved. Thus, the *hashigakari* is not always required for the *shite*'s first entrance or for his *nakairi*, "going inside," and his reappearance; even the mirror room with its curtained partition is replaced. The drape of the *tsukurimono*, in particular, gains its true importance in the staging of the play: the audience is accorded immediate visual access to characters already on stage and not merely given a clear view of them as they slowly enter, as when they come on to the *hashigakari* through the striped curtain. At any rate, this form of onstage revelation must be taken into account when talking about the curtain in Japanese theater.

In addition to the aesthetically resplendent elements in its costumes, which were determined by the audience's taste during the Edo period, it can undoubtedly be said that *nô* drama has its own, truly theatrical means. It is by no means a drama form to be merely read aloud or studied, nor simply a spoken art form set to music. To appreciate it in the context of world theater requires, however, the indispensible ability to look carefully, the getting-to-know-through-seeing (*kengaku*), which, we are sure, an exhibition can also help to impart.

1. Hagemann (1921), 187.

2. Ortolani (1990), 1637.

3. Nobori (1954), 4.

4. See Yanagita (1975).

5. Niessen (1958), 847 ff.

6. Gotô and Hirota (1991), 4 ff.

7. See Gellner (1990).

4.1

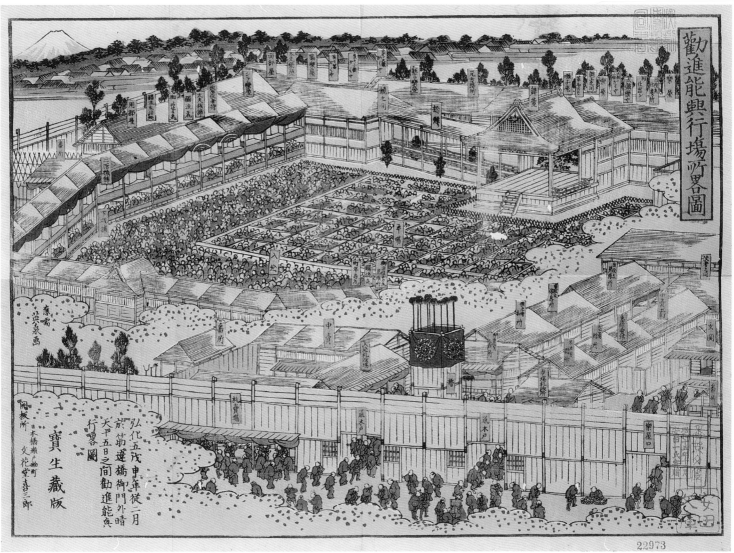

4.5

4.8 A–D

PLATE 32

4.61

4.63 A, B

PLATE 33

4.37 B

PLATE 35

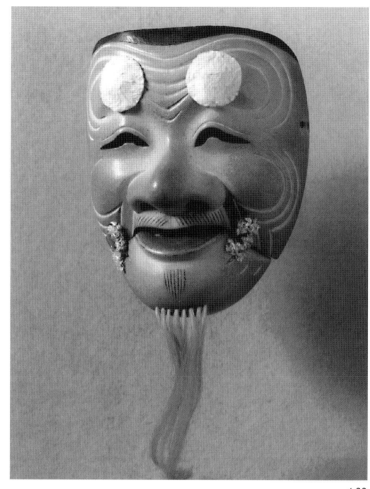

4.22

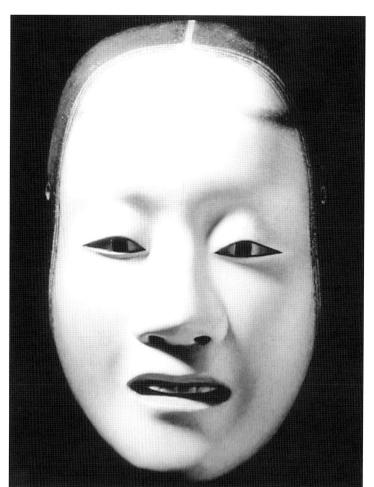

4.23

4.26

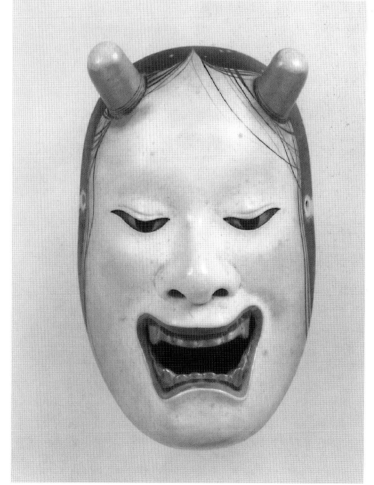

4.29

PLATE 36

4.38B

4.36B

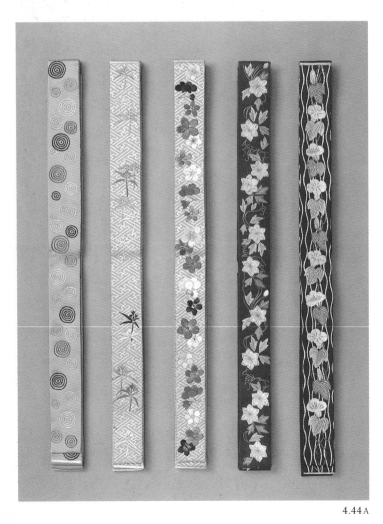

4.44A

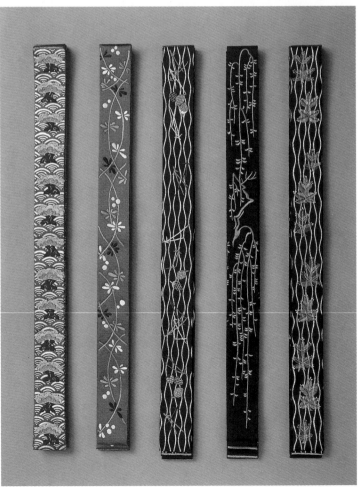

4.44B

PLATE 37

4.39

PLATE 38

4.85

4.31

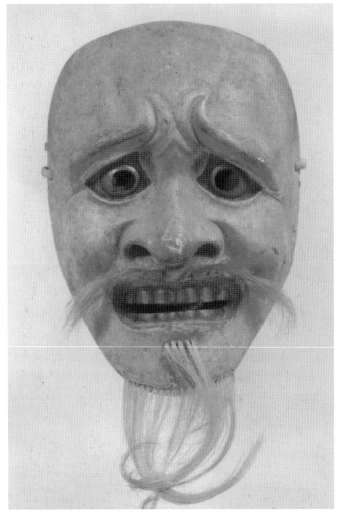

4.27

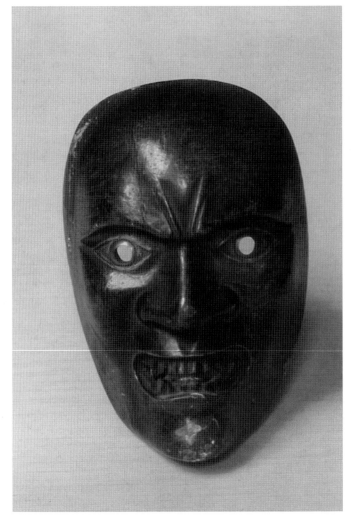

4.84

PLATE 39

4.28

4.30

4.87

4.86

PLATE 40

PLATE 41

5.22 A–G

V. Satire, Parody, and Joyous Laughter: *Kyôgen*

Hayashi Kazutoshi and Laurence Kominz

What Is *Kyogen*?

A shyster, pretending to be a sculptor, impersonates a Buddhist statue to trick a rich country bumpkin out of his money; two mischevous servants manage to drink their master's sake while he is out, even though he tied them up to prevent it; a warlord cavorts about, imitating the trained monkey that only a few moments before he intended to kill. This is the world of *kyôgen*, a world which turns traditional Japanese society upside down and often stretches the consequences to absurd extremes.

Kyôgen is Japan's classical comic theater. Japan's oldest dialogue drama, *kyôgen* plays have been performed since the 1300s as interludes to the intense, lyrical, danced *nô* plays. Today *kyôgen* is more popular than ever before and all-*kyôgen* shows often include original new plays and experimental dramas.

Until the 1600s *kyôgen* was performed without complete texts. Actors, trained in portraying different character types in certain stock situations, performed extemporaneously following partial scripts and plot outlines, much like the commedia dell' arte performers of Renaissance Europe. Play titles, diary records, and the few surviving partial scripts from the 15th and 16th centuries show us that *kyôgen* plays derived from many sources: folk tales, comic sections of religious tales, parodies of religious teaching, and fictional exaggerations of actual daily occurences.[1] Origins of *kyôgen* performance techniques include popular songs and dances, recitations by wandering minstrels, festival performances, and elements from the *nô* drama.

Complete play texts and critical theory for *kyôgen* appeared comparatively late in its development. In the 1620s, Okura Toraakira set down a collection of scripts used by his troupe, and, in *Waranbe Gusa* (Grass of Laughter), he elaborated fundamental aesthetics and acting techniques. Toraakira's literary activity came in response to the new Tokugawa government's restriction of *kyôgen* performance to just three licensed schools (the Okura, Izumi, and now defunct Sagi schools). These, along with the five schools of *nô*, were to perform primarily for the ruling warrior class for the duration of the Edo period (1600-1868).

Today, *kyôgen* plays are performed to best advantage on *nô* stages, but they are readily adaptable to any clean, open performance space. As in *nô*, stage sets are not used and properties are kept to a minimum, with the fan used to represent all sorts of implements, from sake bottles to saws to sliding doors. While the *kyôgen* actor's basic posture, movement, and vocal production are related to *nô*, their effect is strikingly different. The voice of the *kyôgen* actor rings out as clear as a bell, each syllable reaching even the farthest in the audience, and frequent variations in tempo and constant modulations of pitch make even monologues amusing to listen to. *Kyôgen* scripts reflect the Japanese fascination with onomatopoeia. Physical gestures such as drinking, opening doors, and wrestling, are all accompanied by imaginative onomatopoetic vocalization. Physical movement in *kyôgen*, while as precisely controlled as

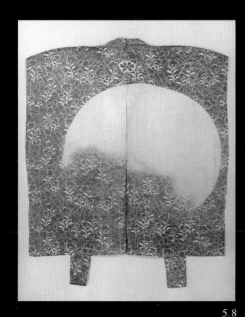

in *nô* plays, is more mimetic than symbolic, and is broad, exaggerated, and easy to read. The overall tempo of *kyôgen* plays is much brisker than *nô* plays, and contemporary audiences understand almost everything said on stage. The accessibility of *kyôgen* performance to Japanese people today is one reason for the "*kyôgen* boom" that is currently underway.

Masks are used when *kyôgen* actors play supernatural characters or animals. The roles of elderly men and women usually require masks in *kyôgen* as they do in *nô*, but while the women of *nô* are paragons of beauty and all require masks, for the commoner housewives of *kyôgen* the actor's masculine face in a *binan* turban is just right. *Kyôgen* actors also use masks to disguise themselves when engaging in acts of deception, a use for masks that never occurs in *nô*.

Even to a casual observer it is apparent that the *kyôgen* masks depicting demons, ghosts, and gods are strikingly different from corresponding *nô* masks. *Kyôgen* masks are grotesques or caricatures, sometimes intentionally crude in execution. They are much closer to their folk art origins than are the lofty and ethereal *nô* masks. The faces of *nô* masks often have a "middle expression" that can change subtly when moved by the actor, but most *kyôgen* masks have strong, set expressions. They are clearly laughing, angry, befuddled, leering, or sometimes just plain silly looking. In the world of *kyôgen*, the thunder god (see no. 5.39), for example, is much more amusing than awesome and the mask works along with the actor and the text to decrease the distance between god and man.

Kyôgen costumes are much simpler than those of *nô*, and, like the plays themselves, many costumes convey rural settings, seasonal variety, and a celebration of the activities and objects of daily life. Of all the costumes, *kataginu* vests epitomize the aesthetic values of *kyôgen*. Quite a few *kataginu* are on display in this exhibition and they are characterized by very striking patterns and designs. Examples include the "array of toys motif" with its bold depiction of tops, pin wheels, *tengu* demon masks, and wheeled-fish pull toys, and the "array of insects," worn by evil characters, with the large praying mantis at the center, surrounded by a moth, a bee, and a grasshopper. For an original modern *kyôgen* we find a *kataginu* decorated with space ships. The boldness of these designs is found in few other performing arts costumes.

This aesthetic is, of course, far different from the refined beauty of the *nô* drama, epitomized by the quality of *yûgen*.[2] *Kyôgen* partakes of none of the refined rusticity or elegant loneliness embodied in the aesthetic terms, *wabi* and *sabi*.[3] There is no *shibumi* in *kyôgen*—no restraint or subdued monochromality in costume designs. Clearly *kyôgen*'s aesthetic is something of a different order. It is an aesthetic of boldness and originality, redolent with the spirit of daily life. It is a Japanese aesthetic that has received too little attention in the past, but should not be dismissed in discussions of the history of Japanese art and design. Bold and unique costumes are central to *kyôgen*'s character and impact as a stage art.

MEDIEVAL JAPANESE HUMANISTIC VALUES: PARODY AND SOCIAL SATIRE

The two ideologies that dominated medieval Japan were *bushidô* ("way of the warrior"), a body of law and custom that governed the ruling elite and dictated the nature of its rule over the whole country, and Pure Land Buddhism. According to *bushidô*, a samurai should readily sacrifice his own life and the lives of his family members if so required by the dictates of honor or duty. While medieval Buddhism held that all sentient beings partake of Buddha Nature, it placed no value on daily human affairs. Believers were advised to forsake the mundane world as they would "flee a burning house."

The *kyôgen* repertory stands as the medieval era's humanistic counter-ideology to the harsh, formal social values intended to govern life in premodern Japan. In *kyôgen*, human life is sacred. Although in a few plays bad men set out with murderous intent, human beings are never killed in *kyôgen*, nor is there any suicide. While hierarchy dominated the social and political power relationships of the feudal age, *kyôgen* plays ridicule elite characters and elevate the low. Conflicts between unequal rivals invariably end with a victory for the party who is socially inferior. This levelling extends up to the realm of the gods and down to animals. Human weaknesses are emphasized in gods and noble human sentiments attributed to the animals.

We do not know who thought up medieval *kyôgen* plays, but the *kyôgen* masters were akin to the medieval Western parodists described by Mikhail Bakhtin, for whom "everything was, without exception, comic. Laughter was as universal as seriousness: it was directed at the whole world, at history, at ideology."[4] Parody is at the center of much *kyôgen* humor. It brings together the lofty and the low, the great and the insignificant, the wise and the stupid.[5] By bringing the lofty close to the audience, "valorizing distance"[6] is eliminated, and elite or exalted figures are turned into comic characters. The *kyôgen* masterpiece *Utsubozaru* (The Monkey Quiver) brings a feudal lord, a monkey, and a monkey trainer (a social outcast) into intimate contact. The feudal lord initially intends to kill the monkey, but is surprisingly moved by the trainer's grief and in the end is so delighted by the monkey's antics that he capers about imitating it, giving all of his possessions as gifts to the monkey (see no. 5.38). The haughty samurai discovers humanity in an animal and an outcaste, and so discovers a hidden humanity in himself that he had not known before.

Parodic laughter in *kyôgen* is "ambivalent laughter, burning away all that is stilted and stiff, but in no way destroying the heroic core of an image."[7] The thunder god in *kyôgen* is a hypochondriac who howls more loudly than a child while undergoing painful acupuncture treatment (see no. 5.39). Everyone in the audience has suffered such ministrations, so the thunder god becomes, in a way, "one of us." He remains the powerful thunder god nonetheless, able to guarantee 800 years of seasonable rains as payment to the doctor for his cure.

One of the best parody plays, *Hige Yagura* (The Fortified Beard), is wonderfully entertaining thanks to its movement

5.38

5.39

5.40

PLATE 42

from the rational world to a world of absurd burlesque. It begins with a husband and wife arguing over his long beard. It is his only pride, but she wants it off—it is smelly, gets in his food, and tickles her. The couple exit separately, each vowing to prevail. He reenters with his beard protected by a miniature castle supported on his shoulders, complete with gate and tower. She returns with her women friends, all dressed like samurai ready for battle. Instead of swords and halberds they carry over-sized scissors, tweezers, clippers, and other barbers' implements. In a sung and danced parody of a military siege, the women break through the castle gate and clip and pull out the beard. Not only is military campaigning rendered absurd, but a wife, typically weaker than her husband, proves the more powerful warrior.

Classical parody requires the simultaneous presence of two texts, and the best example of formal parody in *kyôgen* is *Tsûen* (Tsûen, the Tea Priest), a take-off on the *nô* play *Yorimasa*. The *nô* play presents the ghost of Minamoto Yorimasa, who tells of his defeat in battle and subsequent *seppuku* (ritual suicide) in the town of Uji. The hero of the *kyôgen* play is the ghost of the tea master Tsûen, who, on the occasion of a memorial service commemorating the Uji Bridge, was obliged to make tea for travelers. He was so worn out by making tea that he died. The story of Tsûen's tea-making is a direct parody of the story of the Battle of Uji in the *nô* play, and the character's lines in the *kyôgen* play poke fun at the originals. The mock-heroic *kyôgen* play uses the chorus, instrumentalists, and solemn dance of *nô* to portray the exhausted tea master.

Satire is more critical of the objects of humor than parody. There are relatively few *kyôgen* plays in which social satire seems to be the main theme, but one example is *Konomi Arasoi* (The Battle of Fruits and Nuts), in which a chestnut and a tangerine quarrel over the right to hold cherry viewing parties on a certain mountain. They lead their clans to war and a parodied samurai battle ensues (see no. 5.40), but before either side emerges victorious, a strong wind blows both armies away. This play clearly satirizes the ruling samurai class, depicting samurai honor as no more than petty pride and pique, and the samurai penchant for violent solutions as needless and self-destructive. Time and history will "blow away" self-important samurai bullies just as the wind disperses the self-important fruits and nuts in the play.

Shûron (A Religious Dispute) satirizes Buddhist sectarian strife. Its protagonists are a Pure Land priest and a Lotus Sect priest, each proclaiming the efficacy of the teachings of his sect. Each proudly explains the sutras and dogma of his sect, but both presentations are so formulaic that neither seems convincing. In the end, the priests compete with each other in danced recitations of religious formulas, one chanting "Hail Amida Buddha!" as he dances, the other "Hail the Lotus Sutra!" The priests become so engrossed in their repetitive movements and chants that soon, without noticing it, each is chanting the mantra of his rival. When they realize what they have done the priests laugh and conclude that the Pure Land and the Lotus Sutra are manifestations of the same truth and the play ends with a harmonious dance. It is clear that in this *kyôgen* the

playwright's message is embodied in the experience of the two priests: mindless religious disputation is stupid—the teachings of the Buddha are, in fact, all one.

In 1579, Oda Nobunaga, then the most powerful warlord in Japan, summoned leaders of the same two sects to Azuchi Castle in his capital near Lake Biwa to argue the merits of their doctrines. The event is known as "The Azuchi Disputation."[8] Despite the fact that Nobunaga declared the Pure Land priests the victors, weaknesses were discovered in their arguments, and, in the end, the officials refereeing the dispute resorted to force in their suppression of the Lotus Sect advocates. It is unclear whether or not the *kyôgen* play draws directly on this incident, but the play does reflect a medieval society in which it was common knowledge that these two Buddhist sects hated each other as much as did proverbial dogs and monkeys.

In general, *kyôgen*, along with the *nô*, was supported by those in power. *Konomi Arasoi* and *Shûron* are among the very few that criticize social structures and elites, but there are quite a few that direct ridiculing laughter at the social phenomena of daily life. *Sado Gitsune* (The Sado Fox) ridicules an official who accepts a bribe, popular homosexual practices are the target of laughter in *Fumi Ninai* (Two to Deliver One Letter) and *Yao* (A Sinner with References), fake sculptors of Buddhist images are satirized in *Busshi* (The Fake Sculptor) and *Rokujizô* (The Six Statues), mountain wizards are portrayed as violent and high handed in almost all the plays featuring them, and priests are depicted as worldly and depraved in *Haratatezu* (Priest Angerless Honesty), *Naki Ama* (The Crying Nun), and in several other plays.

A Celebration of Rural Japanese Life

Kyôgen plays depict the life of the commoner classes in the medieval period. Some are set in medieval towns and cities, others in the countryside. *Kirokuda* (The Half-Delivered Gift) provides a special glimpse of rural life. A master orders his servant, Tarô Kaja, to lead six oxen laden with charcoal and six ladened with firewood from the depths of Tamba province to the capital at Kyoto. To Kyoto residents in medieval times the very word "Tamba" conveyed an image of the far-off countryside. On the Tamba-Kyoto border there is a pass called "Old Slope" (Oinosaka). Apparently the people of Kyoto had the impression that once you crossed this pass you were almost certain to be attacked by hordes of demons and ghosts. A well-known folk tale told of a powerful demon living in Oeyama on the Tamba-Tango border, but some ancient accounts indicate that Osoyama near the Old Slope Pass was the original Oeyama of the demon tale. Kirokuda begins in the depths of Tamba, a place that must have epitomized a distant rural setting for medieval viewers.

Firewood and charcoal were the fuel of medieval Japan, and both indispensable items came from deep in the mountains. These two items also symbolize rural life. The servant is to take his caravan to his master's uncle in Kyoto, but on the way he encounters a blizzard. The play depicts him traveling on his way, struggling to herd twelve head of oxen over the pass.

The snow on the road over the pass makes the going very difficult. There is a tea stall on the pass and Tarô Kaja takes a well-deserved rest, but the stall is out of the hot sake he has been longing for. Desperate, he drinks up the sake his master had him take along as a present to his uncle. In an expansive mood after his sake, Tarô Kaja gives the six ox-loads of firewood to the owner of the tea house. The life and struggles of Tarô Kaja depicted here are rich in the aura of rural life. There is a poignancy in the image of Tarô Kaja trudging along the snowy road, which brings to mind the landscapes of Hiroshige.

Mizu Kake Muko (The Water Throwing Son-in-Law), *Kitsune Zuka* (The Fox Mound), *Naruko* (Bird Clappers), and *Taue* (The Rice Planting Ceremony) have rural settings, as do many other plays. *Mizu Kake Muko* portrays a mud-flinging fight between a man and his father-in-law, each seeking to divert water from an irrigation channel into his own rice field. In *Kitsune Zuka* and *Naruko* a master orders his servant to take noisemakers into the fields to scare away flocks of birds. In *Taue*, as the name suggests, we see young maidens planting rice fields. The life-rhythms and scenery in these plays feel true to the life of rural, medieval Japan.

Kuri Yaki (Roasting Chestnuts) and *Nawa Nae* (Rope Twisting) afford close-up glimpses of certain aspects of life in rural families. As their titles suggest, they depict Tarô Kaja roasting chestnuts over the coals of an open hearth and braiding rope in an earth-floored room, each activity mimed in a realistic manner and conveying to the viewer scenes from rural life. *Kyôgen* costumes, too, depict almost every aspect of rural life, from beautiful country scenes, to products of the harvest, to the insects that can make rural life so unpleasant.

LAUGHTER AND FARCE: FROM MEDIEVAL TIMES TO THE PRESENT

The passion of hearts in love, the devastation of love betrayed, the sadness of parting from those we love, the bitterness and pain of losing a child . . . the joys and sorrows of human existence are the literary and dramatic themes that have been repeated since ancient times, and because of the universality of these themes, works that address them have entered classical traditions. But laughter is rarely so universal, and classical comedic works are relatively rare. Laughter is usually occasional and spontaneous. Spontaneous laughter comes from witty responses to specific situations, often unconscious reactions to very special and ephemeral moments. This sort of laughter, of course, changes as times change. Last year's joke may no longer be funny this year, and when we try to recreate the "big laugh" at last night's party, it comes out sounding stale and unamusing.

But *kyôgen's* comic plays have a 600-year heritage. In *kyôgen's* long history, the plays' themes and the way in which laughter is inspired have been passed down as classical traditions and have been constantly refined. When contemporary audiences watch *kyôgen* plays from the Muromachi era (the 1400s) they often laugh uproariously. And this is not the vulgar laughter

inspired by scatological humor; it is refined laughter, suitable to accompany the lofty *nô* drama. It differs from what we usually think of as the laughter of the stage. With its tradition of continual performance from medieval times until today, *kyôgen* teaches us about the nature of uplifting laughter. This is one of the most valuable gifts that *kyôgen* has to offer today.

Farce is epitomized by the dramatic sketches of medieval France. They were short, frivolous, comic pieces often performed as interludes between acts of religious plays. In this they greatly resemble *kyôgen* plays, and the two forms are often compared. Iizawa Tadasu recently wrote a new *kyôgen* play, *Susugigawa* (Laundry River), basing it on the French farce *The Washing Bucket*, demonstrating the affinity of the two forms.

Most European farces center on humorous incidents taking place in life in the towns, and most concern wives' illicit love affairs or priests lusting after women. This subject matter is quite different from most *kyôgen*. Only one *kyôgen* play, *Okosako*, concerns a wife's illicit love affair, and even it only hints indirectly at the affair in the closing lines.

On the theme of licentiousness, several *kyôgen* plays reflect the medieval predeliction for homosexual relations with young boys, but very few concern heterosexual erotic relationships. Two that do are considered masterpieces—*Hanago* (Visiting Hanago) and *Dontarô* (Dontarô's Method for Handling Women). The former shows an unhappily married man who tricks his wife in order to visit his mistress, while the hero of the latter is a man who manages to keep both a wife and a mistress on good terms with each other. But neither of these plays contain any action that could be considered a love scene. Pleasant times spent with one's mistress are described indirectly through dialogue and song. *Mizu Kumi* (Drawing Water)—in the Okura School version—depicts the illicit, yet innocent, carnal love between a temple maid and a temple acolyte. Two plays, *Kanaoka* (Kanaoka, the Love Crazed Painter) and *Makura Monogurui* (Grandfather in Love), are sympathetic portraits of foolish men driven to the brink of insanity by hopeless infatuations. Nevertheless, plays on the subject of love are very few in a performable repertory of 200 plays, and the relative unimportance of sexual dalliance and betrayal in *kyôgen* sets it apart from medieval European farce.

CONTRASTS WITH *NO* AND *KABUKI*

While *kyôgen* plays are performed in "*kyôgen* only" shows, the traditional format is to perform them between *nô* plays in a program featuring several *nô* and one or more *kyôgen* plays. It is probably an over-simplification to refer to kyôgen as "comedy" and *nô* as "tragedy," but it is a fact that the two theater forms contain many contrasting elements. The *nô* is a form of dance drama that employs an aristocratic aesthetic doctrine epitomized by *yûgen* in order to express human beings' deepest emotions and loftiest sentiments. In contrast, *kyôgen* is dialogue drama that seeks out the humor in people's daily lives in order to entertain with mirth. The contrast is seen in costumes as well. *Nô* costumes are made of silk and performers wear white *tabi* on their feet, while *kyôgen* actors wear costumes made of flax and yellow or brown *tabi*.

The fact that *kabuki* plays in the Edo period were called *kabuki kyôgen* is testimony to the importance of *kyôgen's* impact on the development of *kabuki*. *Kabuki* began as dance-centered performance and only when it incorporated *kyôgen* was *kabuki* able to evolve into real drama. Many *kyôgen* plays were subsumed in their entirety into *kabuki* scripts and *kabuki* actors learned much about the art of dramatic performance by studying the *kyôgen* actor's craft. This being said, it is equally important to recognize that the two are entirely different genres, and it would be a mistake to think that they resemble each other very closely. For example, love scenes, called *nureba*, are an important part of *kabuki*, and the women in them are performed by actors called *onnagata* for whom the depiction of feminine eroticism is at the very core of their dramatic art. As has been mentioned, there is nothing at all like this in *kyôgen*.

Early in the Edo period, Okura Toraakira, the head of the Okura School of *kyôgen*, wrote in his treatise *Waranbe Gusa* that the *kabuki* humor of his day was "confused, vulgar, and formless. *Kabuki* actors get their audiences to laugh by telling rambling anecdotes, twisting their faces and goggling their eyes and mouths, and by engaging in abnormal antics."[9] These words express the pride of a leading *kyôgen* master in the vocal and physical expressivity of his art. While they lack objectivity, it cannot be denied that there is some truth in them. They are strong words of caution to fellow *kyôgen* actors, warning them not to imitate *kabuki* humor. And these words convey a fundamental difference between *kyôgen* and *kabuki*, for *kyôgen* was obliged to remain uplifting comedy, suitable for performance on the same program and on the same stage as *nô* plays. In the Edo period, *kyôgen* was required to control its content and aesthetic expression, and it required a firm body of performance values and techniques. Fortunately, these were provided in a timely fashion from within the *kyôgen* world. The result was the formalization of *kyôgen* theater into the art that we see today, and its preservation as a classical dramatic genre that epitomizes the humor inherent in human social interaction.

KYOGEN IN THE WORLD AND EXPERIMENTAL *KYOGEN*

Because all that is required for a full program of *kyôgen* plays is two or three actors and a bare stage, *kyôgen* is the least costly Japanese theater to send abroad. Since World War II Japanese *kyôgen* masters have traveled to all five continents, and in the last decade it seems that every year several *kyôgen* troupes embark on foreign tours. Everywhere *kyôgen* has visited, it has been received with joyful laughter. Foreign actors and drama teachers have journeyed to Japan to study with master performers and today several non-Japanese professional troupes and a few foreign universities present *kyôgen* plays in English on a regular basis.

After World War II, leading *kyôgen* families in Japan sought to broaden their audience base by performing in high schools and junior high schools and by writing and staging experimental *kyôgen* plays, sometimes in collaboration with actors from other theater genres, such as *kabuki*, *shingeki* (modern drama), and the Takarazuka all-female revues. Original experimental productions have retold Japanese folk stories and legends, brought Shakespeare's comedy and Beckett's black humor into the world of *kyôgen*, and relocated traditional *kyôgen* plots abroad or even on distant planets.[10] The success of these experiments and the enthusiastic response to English-language *kyôgen*, from school productions to the professional stage, are a testimony to the universal appeal of *kyôgen's* themes and performance style.

1. Matsumoto (1970), 2122.

2. *Yûgen* has been described by terms such as "elegance," "grace," and "mysterious beauty."

3. *Wabi* means "restrained/quiet beauty" with overtones of loneliness. *Sabi* means "elegant simplicity." Both terms suggest rusticity and subtle, subdued shadings of color.

4. Bakhtin (1984b), 84.

5. Bakhtin (1984a), 123.

6. Bakhtin (1981), 21.

7. Bakhtin (1984a), 133.

8. Tsuji (1983), 122-160.

9. Okura (1973), 682.

10. A few examples of many original and experimental *kyôgen* plays include *Hikoichi Banashi*, a Takechi Tetsuji-produced dramatization of a Kumamoto folk tale; *Komachi*, a parody of the paragon poetess, and *Falstaff* by Nomura Mansaku; Beckett's *Act Without Words I* and *Rockabye* by the NOHO Theater Group; two versions of Yeats's *The Cat in the Moon*, by Don Kenny and Dan Furst; a *Busu* set in New York by Mishima; Shigeyama Sennojô's *Hontô ni Busu no Busu* (A Truly Ugly *Busu*) set on a planet without women in a distant galaxy; and the combined Nomura Mansaku/Shigeyama Sensaku troupe's *Yabu no Naka*, a *kyôgen* version of *Rashômon*.

5.18 A-E

5.21 A-C

PLATE 44

5.23A-C

PLATE 46

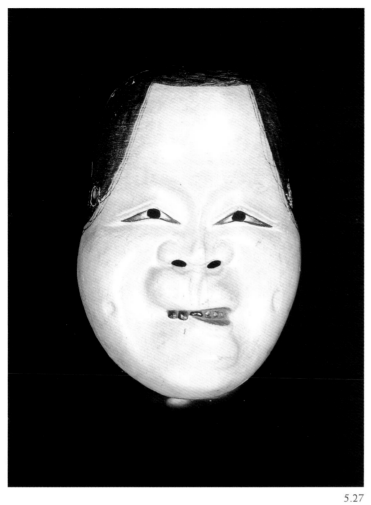

5.27

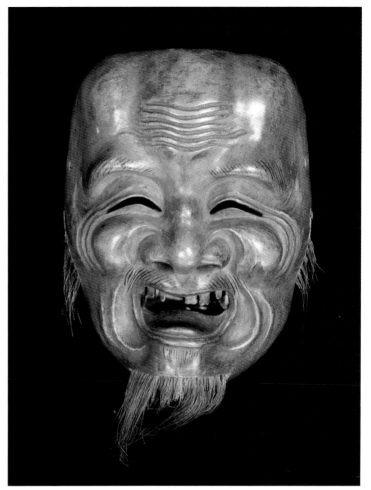

5.35

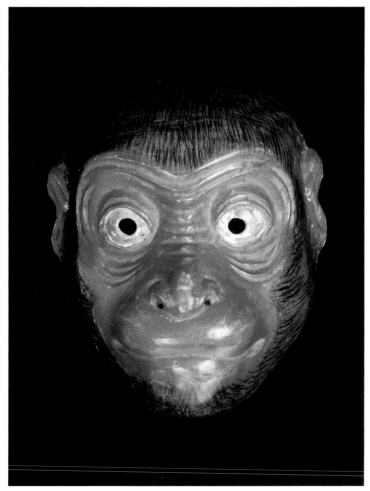

5.32

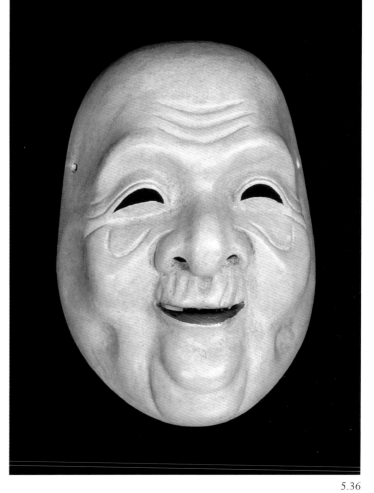

5.36

PLATE 47

6.17

PLATE 48

6.20A

6.23C

6.23A

VI. Margins between the Real and Unreal: *Bunraku*

Andrew Gerstle and Sakurai Hiroshi

Audiences around the world have enthusiastically received the *bunraku* puppet theater [1] over the last thirty years as it has toured the globe gaining recognition as the most sophisticated living puppet theater tradition. *Bunraku* is unusual in the world of puppet drama because from its beginnings in the early 17th century it was aimed at urban adult audiences and competed commercially with the *kabuki* theater of human actors. *Bunraku's* mecca is Japan's traditional merchant capital Osaka, where it developed and matured from the late 17th to the end of the 18th century. Puppet playhouses were also found in the theater districts of the cities of Kyoto and Edo (Tokyo), as well as smaller castle towns. These urban, professional puppet theater troupes were, however, part of a vast network of chanters, shamisen players, and puppeteers who performed throughout Japan in villages and smaller cities until the early 20th century. The level of national participation—patrons, semi-professional performers, amateur chanters, and musicians—was remarkable. Along with the array of activities associated with its sister *kabuki*, which also flourished both in the cities and countryside, it formed the base of popular Japanese culture until well into this century.

The tradition produced over 1000 plays, most of which filled a complete day of performance, and all of which were published in full, authorized editions complete with chanter's notation at the time of first staging. Many of these plays also sit at the core of *kabuki's* current repertoire and because of their availability in print (in contrast to *kabuki* plays, which were not published in full until this century) were the primary source for *kabuki* playwrights throughout the Tokugawa (1600-1868) and early Meiji (1868-1912) periods.

Bunraku's roots lie in the heroic epic-storytelling tradition based on the civil wars and sagas of the medieval period, particularly as reflected in the *Heike Monogatari* (Tale of Heike) and its spin-offs. As a consequence, from early on, the central figure in the puppet theater is the chanter, who usually voices all of the roles, accompanied by a shamisen player. Puppets, originally held by one man, increasingly became more complex from the 1730s and, from the mid-18th century, the main roles were worked by three puppeteers. The master takes the puppet's right hand with his own right hand and works the head and facial features with his left hand, which is inserted through the back of the kimono. The assistant puppeteer, usually a disciple of the master, works the left hand with his own right hand. The youngest works the feet. The technical skill of these three produces the powerful, realistic, yet magical effect which fascinates audiences. Roland Barthes evocatively described it: "Bunraku does not aim at 'animating' an inanimate object as to make a piece of the body, a scrap of man, 'alive,' while retaining its vocation as a 'part'; it is not the simulation of the body that it seeks but, so to speak, its sensuous abstraction."[2]

The famous puppet head maker Tenguya Kyûkichi (Tengu Kyû, d. 1943 at 86, mentioned by the novelist Tanizaki Jun'ichirô in *Some Prefer Nettles*, 1929), several of whose works are on display in the exhibition, was interviewed by the writer Uno Chiyo in the 1940s. She became fascinated by the puppets and sought the old puppet maker out. His words on his craft give us some insight into the art:

Three days out of the month I go to the family shrine to pray. . . . As I'm making my puppets, I feel as if I'm praying to the gods. Don't you see, where my skill stops–here it doesn't go any further–that's where you'll find the gods. Yes, they're just beyond human understanding. . . .

Before I start to carve a puppet I have it all clear in my mind how that puppet ought to look. But there's always one part I just can't get no matter how I try–yes, there's always something missing, and it's in that part, that missing part, where the gods reside.

What's difficult about carving a *jôruri* puppet is first of all making one that'll come to life on the stage, and second of all making one that'll be in keeping with the story of the play. Puppet makers have to keep these two facts in mind. . . .

They say that when you're fixing to carve a young girl puppet you should make your heart like a young girl's–all meek and mild. But when you're to carve a samurai you should pull yourself up proud and proper. Now it'll sometimes happen that when I set out fully intending to carve a manly looking fellow like a samurai, by some accident I end up with a puppet that looks downright mean. This is the mystery. . . .

When I'm to carve Yuranosuke [the star role of *Kanadehon Chûshingura* (Chûshingura: The Treasury of Loyal Retainers)] I try to imagine what he must have felt. There he was a masterless samurai, yet he was bent on slaying the man who wronged his lord. While I'm thinking on it I start to carve, and while I carve I think about which way I ought to cut to bring out the face I want.

In a puppet play they'll sometimes use a different puppet head for the same character, depending on the scene. The play featuring the warrior Kumagai [featured in the exhibition, from the play, "Kumagai Jinya" ("Kumagai's Battle Camp," originally part of *Ichinotani Futaba Gunki* [Chronicle of the Battles of Ichinotani]), for instance. The Kumagai head they use in the second act won't do at all for the third. In the third act his face has got to be full of the sorrow he feels as he trudges back to camp after slaying the handsome young Atsumori [in fact he has sacrificed his own son to save Atsumori]. A Yuranosuke puppet looks a good deal like the third act Kumagai, and that's why the same head is used for each character. But I suppose Kumagai looks more courageous. He's a bit fierce, truth be told. You see, in the puppet theater there are two types of chief retainers. There are the Great Retainers and there are the Yuranosuke Retainers. In the old days, those who were puppet connoisseurs would tell you which type they wanted when they placed an order.[3]

Tengu Kyû's words give us a sense of the spiritual elements that infuse puppet theater. The origins of both mask and puppet drama are in religious ritual; the convention is that the god or spirit enters the puppet and it comes alive. This is true for the Ebisu and Sanbasô puppets, which feature so importantly in rural religious festivals. In the *bunraku* ritual of "putting in a spirit (*tamashii*)" for a new puppet head (occasionally performed today), the puppet performs a dance manipulated by the three puppeteers to the point of physical exhaustion; their physical state allows the spirit to enter.

The core of every *bunraku* performance is a scene where a character meets a tragic death, often by his or her own hand, sacrificing himself for love or a higher cause. In the Buddhist tradition, if one dies a violent or untimely death, it is thought that the spirit will roam about and perhaps cause havoc to those left behind. The pacifying of such an angry spirit (*onryô*) is the convention that underlies both *nô* and *bunraku*. The reenactment of its heroic tale calms the spirit, who enters the puppet on stage. This is true for historical figures and would have been even more realistic for the audiences of love-suicide plays, which were often performed within weeks of the actual incidents. In Buddhism it is also thought that even those who die in peace will not pass on to the next world until after forty-nine days. The first audience for *Sonezaki Shinjû* (Love Suicides at Sonezaki), which was performed within a few weeks after the incident in 1703, would certainly have believed that the souls of Ohatsu and Tokubei were actually on the stage. The fates of characters seem to be led by the three, shadow-like puppeteers, but we also have a sense that the puppeteers are being led by the spirit of the character, who grows more forceful as the drama reaches its climax.

For the playwright this concept of infusing the puppet with a spirit was, of course, important as well. Chikamatsu Monzaemon (1653-1725) emphasized that the words must have the power to give life to the puppets:

Jôruri differs from other forms of fiction in that, since it is primarily concerned with puppets, the words must all be living and full of action. Because *jôruri* is performed in theaters that operate in close competition with those of *kabuki*, which is the art of living actors, the author must impart to lifeless wooden puppets a variety of emotions, and attempt in this way to capture the interest of the audience.[4]

Hozumi Ikan, the Confucian scholar who recorded these famous words of Chikamatsu, acknowledged the power of his words in the same book.

He was a warm and upright man who even at seventy was full of youthful vigor. Everyone who met him was struck by his depth of heart. He read with a clear mind a myriad of books, and in his plays mixed skilfully the language of the sages and popular songs. At the touch of his brush even ordinary words gain the power to take our breath away.[5]

Chikamatsu further elaborated his views on writing for the puppet theater in a famous passage:

Someone said, "People nowadays will not accept plays unless they are realistic and well-reasoned out. There are many things in the old stories which people will not now tolerate. It is thus that such people as *kabuki* actors are considered skilful to the degree that their acting resembles reality. . . . People will not stand for childish nonsense as they did in the past." I answered, "Your view seems plausible, but it is a theory which does not take into account the real methods of art. Art is something which lies in the slender margin between the real and the unreal. . . . It is unreal, and yet it is not unreal; it is real, and yet it is not real. Entertainment lies between the two."[6]

Chikamatsu and the other playwrights of the tradition, however, were not independent souls writing when their spirits so moved them. They were employed by a troupe initially as apprentices to senior, experienced writers; eventually they learned to write for particular performers, to meet regular deadlines, and to produce commercially successful works. Chikamatsu wrote primarily for chanters such as Takemoto Gidayû (1651-1714), who set the text to music for voice. After the development of three-man puppets from about 1734, however, playwrights like Namiki Sôsuke (also known as Senryû, 1695-1751, author of "Kumagai Jinya") wrote within a team of playwrights for both chanters and puppeteers, such as the famous Yoshida Bunzaburô (d. 1760), who is credited with the great advances of three-man puppetry. From the 1760s, *bunraku* shows a further development with the rise of the authority of shamisen musicians (such as Tsuruzawa Bunzô, d. 1807) who came to usurp from the chanters the role of composing music for new plays.[7] Playwrights such as Chikamatsu Hanji (1725-1783), therefore, wrote for all three elements of *bunraku*. Play production, throughout *bunraku's* history, has definitely been a collaborative effort.

Performance as well is collaborative. The chanter, in full view to the right of the stage takes all the voice roles including narration; he is accompanied by the shamisen player, whose role at first seems subordinate. These two give life to the movement of the puppets on stage. The recently deceased shamisen player Tsuruzawa Jûzô left us some important insights into the role of the shamisen (also samisen):

Learning to play the samisen is one thing, but learning to accompany a *tayû* (chanter) is quite another matter. . . . As I grew older, I realized that the hardest thing is to learn when not to play, when not to interfere with the narration, and exactly how to strike a single note to suit exactly the mood or emotion the *tayû* has established, to fit the scene or specific character at that particular point in the play. A young musician learns the notes and the beat and where his playing fits in with the *tayû's* words, but the most important thing is feeling, and that can only be learned in maturity.[8]

Jûzô also gives us a magnificent glimpse of the traditional training regime. He began at the age of twelve in 1911:

Nowadays people ask about the hardships of my early training. At the time, I didn't think a thing about it—life was that way then and young people were used to discipline, punishment, and grueling training. I used to get up early to get to my teacher's house for a lesson at six every morning. Samisen players prided themselves on living without heat, not even a tiny charcoal brazier, and on winter mornings it was a cold wait until my teacher was ready for me. I used to rub my numb fingers together inside the sleeves of my kimono or tuck them in the bends of my knees as I sat waiting. . . . And what lessons they were! My teacher would play a passage, maybe fifteen minutes long, just once. I was then expected to play along with him. Next I was made to play the passage solo. My teacher would sit there scowling at me, scolding, sometimes hitting me in the face. Knowing the punishment that lay in store, I learned quickly to listen very, very carefully, straining every fibre in my body to absorb everything I possibly could with eyes, ears, and mind. Oh, it was good training all right, in observation and memorizing, and since the next day's lesson was a new passage, I had to learn fast.[9]

For Jûzô, whose father had been a chanter, his whole life revolved around *bunraku*, and this continues to be true today for all members of the troupe.

Most *bunraku* plays were originally composed to fill a full day of theater beginning in the morning and ending at dusk. Takemoto Gidayû, the founder of the tradition whose name *gidayû* now means *bunraku* music, laid out his ideas on what a five-act (each act with two to four scenes) play should consist of in a preface to a collection of plays published in 1687.[10] Act one, he says, has the mood of "love"; act two is "*shura*," warriors and battles; act three is "pathos," tragedy; act four is the "travel song" (*michiyuki*), where the melody is most important; finally, act five ends "auspiciously." This structure for a day of theater is generally modeled on the orchestration of a day of *nô* drama. Essentially the pattern is to begin at the court or seat of government of the historical time of the play. During act one there is a crisis that causes the ordered world to fall into chaos. The conflict continues in act two, and in act three the heroic self-sacrifice of a character turns the wheel of fortune toward the good forces who manage to restore order to the world. Plays often begin and end at the same place, following a Buddhistic circle of movement in which the tragedy in act three is the climax of the whole play. Chikamatsu's *Kokusenya Kassen* (The Battles of Coxinga) (1715) is considered the classical model of this form.[11]

Chikamatsu also wrote shorter, essentially one-act plays (with three scenes) on contemporary topics and ordinary townspeople, perhaps inspired by *kabuki*, for which he had been writing during the 1690s. *Sonezaki Shinjû*, first performed in 1703 to great success, led to the development of this genre, known as *sewamono*; the five-act plays then became known as

6.43

PLATE 49

jidaimono, or period plays. Donald Keene has translated ten of these domestic works in *Major Plays of Chikamatsu*.

The development of puppet technology after Chikamatsu's passing, from the 1730s onward, led to the golden age of *bunraku's* popularity when, at least in Osaka and Kyoto, it eclipsed *kabuki* for a period from about 1740 to 1760, during which the most famous *bunraku* (and *kabuki*) plays were first performed: *Yoshitsune Sembon Zakura* (Yoshitsune and the Thousand Cherry Trees) (1746);[12] *Sugawara Denju Tenarai Kagami* (Sugawara and the Secrets of Calligraphy) (1747);[13] *Kanadehon Chûshingura* (Chûshingura: The Treasury of Loyal Retainers) (1948);[14] and *Ichinotani Futaba Gunki* (Chronicle of the Battles of Ichinotani) (1751).[15] These were written by a team of three playwrights led by Namiki Sôsuke (Senryû).

"Kumagai Jinya," the third act of *Ichinotani Futaba Gunki*, is one of the most popular pieces in both *bunraku* and *kabuki*. The story is based on the *nô* play *Atsumori*, the source of which is the *Heike Monogatari* (Tale of Heike). Zeami, the famous playwright and theorist of *nô*, wrote that the playwright should stick as close as possible to the original seed of the story, even using language from the earlier text. *Bunraku* contrasts with *nô* in this regard. In both *kabuki* and *bunraku*, the idea is that one sets the story into a *sekai* ("world"), an historical context or setting, around certain texts and historical characters. The writer draws on these figures from the tale, but he must innovate (*shukô*) by creating a new twist to the source, usually shifting the focus to a lesser known or fictitious figure. In the original *Heike Monogatari* version of the 12th-century incident, the seasoned Genji warrior Kumagai slays the sixteen-year-old Heike courtier Atsumori. Kumagai is old enough to be Atsumori's father and regrets having to kill the young man, about the same age as his own son. Kumagai, then, after the wars ended, became a priest and prayed for Atsumori and the other Heike warriors' souls. The *nô* play focuses on the encounter of Atsumori's spirit with the priest Kumagai. Atsumori has his chance for revenge but forgives the man, who now prays for him.

Namiki Sôsuke in 1751 took this story and shifted the focus to Kumagai, who is asked obliquely by the Genji commander General Yoshitsune to sacrifice his own son in place of Atsumori, supposedly of imperial lineage. The climax of the play is the scene in act three when Kumagai must present the head to Yoshitsune for inspection in front of his own wife Sagami and the mother of Atsumori, Lady Fuji. Kumagai had disgraced himself sixteen years earlier in an affair with Sagami, who was in service to Lady Fuji. He and Sagami were pardoned by Lady Fuji, who allowed the pair to flee and get married. Kumagai is, therefore, a relatively low and ordinary figure, who was disgraced while in service to the Heike side, an inconsequential player in the civil war between the Heike and the Genji. From the beginning of the act, Kumagai has had to act as if he actually killed Atsumori, relating the death to a distraught Lady Fuji, and then maintaining the fiction even after the inspection in front of Sagami, who is devastated to learn that her husband has killed their only child. Kumagai is a magnificent role because the actor or puppeteer, chanter,

and shamisen player must present the character at two levels and somehow express the pain that lies just beneath the surface. His strong, even gruff expression must also suggest the agony that has crushed his soul and made him take the decision to become a priest and set off on an eternal pilgrimage. Unlike most Western tragedies, the tragic heroes and heroines of *bunraku* plays are almost always relatively ordinary folk, commoners not in high positions of power: orphans, courtesans, low level samurai, disgraced samurai, and widows. In the context of Tokugawa society, where self-sacrifice was the essence of the samurai cult of heroic honor, one can argue that the tragedy of these ordinary, relatively "weak" individuals is not just showing the less powerful to be slaves to loyalty but rather is a forceful demanding of the right to high virtue. It is fascinating that it was the popular *bunraku* theater which created such a powerful tradition of heroic honor during the Edo period.

During the 1750s the playwrights Namiki Sôsuke and Takeda Izumo II (1691-1756) died, and then in the early 1760s famous performers also passed away, leaving the theaters weakened in their creativity and vitality. Osaka *kabuki* had recovered its dominant position (partially by taking the *bunraku* plays into its repertoire) and the two great rival Osaka puppet theaters Toyotake and Takemoto suffered financial collapse in 1765 and 1767 respectively, and ceased to be solely puppet theaters. Plays continued to be written and performed, and the success in 1771 of *Imoseyama Onna Teikin* (Mt. Imo and Mt. Se: An Exemplary Tale of Womanly Virtue) ushered in the final period of significant playwriting, primarily by Chikamatsu Hanji and Suga Sensuke (ca. 1767-1791).[16] After 1800, however, few new plays were written for the puppets. Though nearly all *bunraku* plays were composed and first performed in Osaka, Edo was host to a brief period of puppet playwriting from the 1760s to 1790, during which about fifty plays were written by Edo writers such as Hiraga Gennai (1728-1779) and Utei Enba (1743-1822) for local theaters. This efflorescence was largely due to the patronage of Mitsui Jirôemon (1747-1799), the director of Edo's famous Mitsui house (ancestor of the modern Mitsui corporation), who was an avid *jôruri* fan. He was no ordinary patron, being a playwright himself under the name Ki no Jôtarô. With his death, however, the brief period of Edo *bunraku* playwriting ends, though performance continued to flourish, growing in popularity during the following century.

Some histories of *bunraku* give the impression that, after the collapse of the Toyotake and Takemoto theaters in Osaka, the puppet theater ceased to be popular and, further, that after 1800 it was no longer creative. To be sure, the finances of large theaters solely for puppet drama became difficult. There was, however, a proliferation of small theaters often set up on shrine or temple grounds, and the actual number of performers in the main cities increased dramatically from the 1760s. Moreover, amateur activity, which had been popular throughout the 18th century in Osaka, Kyoto, and Edo, spread to the smaller cities throughout the country. After 1800, when *bunraku* became a truly national tradition, creativity flourished in performance rather than in the writing of new texts.

Chanters, musicians, and puppeteers again and again sought, and achieved, new ways and means of interpreting the many plays of the repertoire. Shamisen players developed a code of notation that enabled increasingly complex composition.[17] Chanters' names came to be used for the distinctive styles and melodies they created for passages and scenes. The creativity ushered in a second "golden age" of performance from the 1880s until the 1920s. The general image of *bunraku* in decline from the late 1700s is not entirely accurate. Significant decline does set in when modern entertainments, such as movies, radio, and phonographs, begin to compete for talent and audiences. Today, the government does give support primarily through the Osaka National Bunraku Theater (Kokuritsu Bunraku Gekijô), founded in 1984. This home of the sole remaining troupe has as its raison d'être the training of new generations of performers.

From at least the late 17th century, amateur activities have been integral to the life of *bunraku*. Such patrons in the 17th century initially convinced the chanters to include the code of notation in the published texts to provide them with practice texts for lessons. This love of participation is not unique to *bunraku*. *Nô*, and to a lesser extent *kabuki*, were dependent on revenue from giving lessons to patrons in dance or music. *Gidayû* chanting and, later, *gidayû* shamisen became a wide-spread hobby from the mid-18th century. By the late 18th century we begin to have writings about the popularity of amateur *gidayû*, such as the 1786 book *Kishin Shirôto Jôruri Hyôbanki* (Amateur *Jôruri* Critiques) published in Osaka, Kyoto, and Edo. This is a remarkable document because it is a criticism of public performances of amateurs at temples or shrines (*kishin*), which means that audiences paid to see these performances and that the proceeds went to support the temple or shrine.[18]

Though *bunraku* is essentially an entirely male troupe and has been from its beginnings, a separate tradition of "women's *gidayû*" (*onna gidayû* or *musume gidayû*) flourished from the second half of the 18th century.[19] These women were primarily teachers of *gidayû* but would also perform in the small variety theaters (*yose*) in the large cities. Officially women were not permitted to perform in public, but this blanket restriction was not always enforced. The 1820s and 1830s saw a tremendous boom in "women's *gidayû*" until the crackdown on public morals in the Tempô reforms of 1841. Their popularity re-emerged after a relaxation of the restrictions. In the Meiji period, when such restrictions were abolished, "women's *gidayû*" entered its golden age of popularity, particularly in Tokyo, where it was all the rage for young university men to form fan clubs to support their favorites. Several famous writers, such as Natsume Sôseki, Masaoka Shiki, Takahama Kyoshi, Nagai Kafû, Nakae Chômin, and Shiga Naoya, are known to have gone through periods of adulation for these women who seem to have produced a strongly erotic effect on young hearts. The best of these women were able to make a good living from their performances of what has to be considered a relatively difficult art. They were the first Japanese female stage stars of the modern era. A much larger group of women made a living as teachers of the art. Women also

performed in rural troupes in Awaji and Shikoku and this continues to be true today. The level of popularity of *gidayû* and *bunraku* until World War II throughout Japan is certainly remarkable considering its rapid decline in the postwar era. Tsuruzawa Jûzô once told Andrew Gerstle of his experience in the immediate postwar years when he had left Japan to support his children by teaching *gidayû* chanting and shamisen to Japanese immigrants who had settled in Washington, California, and Hawaii. Tsuruzawa was able to support his children through university by teaching *gidayû* to Japanese-Americans who had come from rural Japan, many from the prefectures of Wakayama and Hiroshima. *Gidayû* (and other traditional arts) were an integral part of prewar Japanese life.

One measure of the popularity was the number of magazines devoted to "things *bunraku*." *Gidayû Zasshi*, begun in Tokyo in 1893, and *Jôruri Zasshi*, founded in Osaka in 1899, are the most prominent examples of several magazines devoted to the *bunraku* world, particularly amateur activities.[20] An element of these amateur activities, distinct from other traditional arts, is its competitive nature: amateurs tended to perform in well-organized tournaments and compete for prizes. The magazines report all of this in great detail, complete with photographs of the winners and a list of their "best" pieces. This competitive edge, as noted above, is evident even from the 18th century. *Bunraku* is different from both *nô* and *kabuki*, which hold to the ideals of the *iemoto* system where there is a master of a school or house and transmission is from father to son. In the *iemoto* ("family") system open competition is anathema. *Bunraku*, from its origins in the Takemoto-za under the influence of Takemoto Gidayû, has relied on open competition, not father to son lineage, among both professionals and amateurs. In this it is, even today, more severe than the other traditional arts. At its best moments, such as the first quarter of this century, it has tremendous depth and power because of its competitive, merit ethic, but when social or outside factors alter, it does not have the strength or will of the *iemoto* system structure to maintain itself. Sons are not dependent on it for their livelihood, nor do they feel responsible to maintain the "family" tradition.

Bunraku's influence outside of Japan has been most notable, not in the puppet theater, but in the theater of living actors. Its impact on non-puppet indigenous forms, such as *kabuki*, is demonstrated both in scripts and acting styles, while in the West the use of *bunraku*-like puppets is often included in productions otherwise dominated by players of flesh and blood. The most notable of Western theater artists employing *bunraku* techniques is avant-garde master Lee Breuer. In some productions, such as *Prelude to Death in Venice* (1979), Breuer has included *bunraku*-influenced puppets fashioned as Western characters. In the epic-scaled *The Warrior Ant* (1988), he used an actual *bunraku* puppet to play his samurai hero, with Westernized adaptations for other roles; moreover, three authentic Japanese puppeteers were part of the extensive cast. Breuer's recent *Wendy and Peter* (1997), an acclaimed adaptation of *Peter Pan*, continued to reveal *bunraku*'s important place in his work. Similarly, if not so overtly, influenced, has been Julie Taymor, who also mingles puppets (*bunraku*-style and others) and live actors in her remarkable creations. And Canada's cutting-edge director, Robert LePage, made striking use of *bunraku*-like puppets in his renowned *The Seven Streams of the River Ota*, which toured to Brooklyn in 1996.

Today, *bunraku* receives government assistance through the National Theater (Kokuritsu Gekijô) in Tokyo and the National Bunraku Theater in Osaka. This is important especially for providing a structure and stipends for recruitment and initial training. Regular performances at the two national theaters for middle and high school students, which include demonstrations of the elements of performance, have made *bunraku* (and *kabuki*) more accessible. The troupe today has less than one hundred members and performs regularly in two-to-three week runs at these theaters for most months of the year, and otherwise tours Japan and usually, once a year, performs abroad. Amateur activities are still to be found in Tokyo, Kyoto, and Osaka, including "women's *gidayû*," but even with increasing interest there simply are very few experienced teachers around. *Bunraku* has maintained its popularity and is acknowledged by all as an important cultural heritage. Like opera or other classical music, however, it is difficult; but unlike classical Western music it is not taught in Japan's schools. Most young Japanese are far more familiar with classical piano and violin than with the shamisen.

We are fortunate that *bunraku* has survived as a living tradition. The level of skill of the men who devote a lifetime to their art is incredible. As many have noted, *bunraku's* disparate elements of voice, music, puppet head, hands, and feet—all performed by different individuals—create a marvelous ensemble that has the power to create moments of magic, moments when the artificial elements of human expression produce an impact that brings tears of awe to the audience. This impact can only be achieved by the full participation, the full performance of the audience's imagination. The exhibition gives us an opportunity to view up close the diverse elements, the bits that make up a whole. For us, as Roland Barthes might have said, these are a score for our minds to play on, to bring to life.

1. Traditionally known as *ningyô jôruri* (puppet jôruri), *bunraku*, originally the name of a *jôruri* troupe founded by Uemura Bunrakuken in the 19th century, is now the generic name for *jôruri* puppet theater. *Jôruri* is a general term for various kinds of musical narrative and is also used in *kabuki*. Other names for *bunraku* include *ningyô shibai* (puppet theater), *ayatsuri shibai* (manipulators' theater), and so on.

2. Barthes (1982), 60. Barthes (1977) also discusses *bunraku*.

3. Translated in Copeland (1992), 124-125. Original in Uno (1943) 61-64. Kumagai appears in the play *Ichinotani Futaba Gunki* (Chronicle of the Battles of Ichinotani, 1751), translated in Brandon (1975).

4. Translated in Keene (1956), 386. Original in Shuzui (1959), 356.

5. Translated in Gerstle (1990), 105.

6. Translated in Keene (1956), 389.

7. Gerstle (1990), 1-7 and 103-121, discusses the changing relations of playwrights and performers.

8. Adachi (1978), 54.

9. Ibid., 54-56.

10. Translated in Gerstle (1986), 189-196. Original in *Nihon Shomin Bunka Shiryô Shûsei* (1975), 130-134.

11. Translated in Keene (1961). Gerstle (1986) contains an analysis of this cyclical structure. Each act of a five-act play has several scenes. Later plays, such as *Kanadehon Chûshingura*, are sometimes in multi-act (scene) format, but these in fact are usually still essentially within *gidayû's* five-act (each act with several scenes) structure.

12. Jones (1993).

13. Jones (1985).

14. Keene (1971).

15. The second and third acts of the *kabuki* version are translated in Brandon (1975).

16. See Gerstle (1990) for information on this play and the period 1760-1790.

17. See Gerstle (1990) for more on the development of *bunraku* music.

18. See Gerstle (1995) for more information on the amateur *gidayû* phenomenon.

19. Ibid., 45-49.

20. Ibid, 49-53.

6.1

PLATE 50

6.21

PLATE 51

6.23 B

PLATE 52

5.2, 6.10

PLATE 53

7.68

Plate 54

VII. THE ACTOR'S ART: *Kabuki*

Torigoe Bunzô
Translation and adaptation by James R. Brandon

Kabuki performances are no longer limited to Japan, but have become familiar in many countries of Europe and the American continent. Beginning with a tour of China in 1955, large *kabuki* companies have performed abroad thirty-five times since the end of World War II. Thanks to their success, *kabuki* is now known as Japan's "traveling ambassador," and the term *kabuki* has taken on international currency.[1] On the other hand, the opportunity to carry out an exhibition of kabuki is rare. Indeed, this comprehensive exhibition of Japanese theater art in New York and Munich will be the first ever held in America or Europe. What follows is a brief elucidation of some of the major characteristics of *kabuki* and a discussion of the reasons for the appeal of this extraordinary theater.

Today in Tokyo, twelve monthly *kabuki* productions are staged at the Kabuki-za each year. In addition, the National Theater (Kokuritsu Gekijô) in Tokyo mounts eight *kabuki* productions yearly. Together with the Minami-za in Kyoto, the Misono-za in Nagoya, and the Shôchiku-za in Osaka, these big-city theaters offer some 600 days of *kabuki* annually. The standard run is twenty-five days, a practice that began early in the 20th century. *Kabuki* troupes also tour to small- and medium-sized cities for runs of one or a few days' duration, but, in general, because of its monumental scale, today's *kabuki* is a theater of Japan's largest cities.

The theaters mentioned above naturally vary in size, but, to take one example, the Kabuki-za is extremely large, seating 2,276 spectators in five ticket-price categories, ranging from about $150 (¥16,000) to $23 (¥2,500), with special productions costing more. This seems very expensive to the average Japanese person. Even so, the audience is not restricted to an elite that can afford steep ticket prices. Because almost everyone is pleased to be invited to attend *kabuki*, Japanese companies offer complimentary tickets as a perk to favored customers and clients. The ratio of invitees to paying spectators is a business secret, but I think it is likely that a majority of spectators today receive complimentary tickets.

These invited spectators do not come for the enjoyment of appreciating the drama; rather, their aim is to taste *kabuki's* novel atmosphere. Because *kabuki* dialogue is not in contemporary Japanese and because the subject matter of most scenes is different from modern life experiences, the invited one-time spectator has a poor understanding of the dramatic content of the play. Earphone guides have been adopted to ameliorate the situation. By listening to explanations of the play's plot and acting techniques through earphones, the spectator gains a better understanding of the performance. An English-language earphone guide is available for foreign audience members as well. A theater expert from Mexico once asked me, after attending a performance, "Since Japanese spectators have to request an earphone guide, wouldn't it be better to perform in modern Japanese translation?" I immediately voiced a contrary opinion. The meaning of *kabuki's* existence lies precisely in holding as closely as possible to the "forms of original performance," including language. Looked at from this point of view, *kabuki* is a traditional art form.

I should clarify what I mean by "forms of original performance." We commonly speak of *kabuki* as if it were a fixed, known object, but, in fact, the art has changed continuously during its nearly 400-year history. Let us look quickly at a brief history of *kabuki*. By the 17th century, the hundred-year period of civil war (*sengoku jidai*) had ended and common people in the cities, who had long dreamed of peace, were at last able to pursue their own lives. At the same time, a number of young men who had come to Kyoto to fight in the wars were now masterless samurai (*rônin*). With no work to do, these *rônin* carried on in a scandalous manner, earning the nickname "*kabuki* people" (*kabukimono*), the word "*kabuki*" meaning something abnormal or askew.[2] Their number was not large—had *kabukimono* been more numerous they would have become the new normality—but they constituted an explosive social and artistic force.

As an example of this, at the beginning of the 17th century a bath house opened for business opposite the front gate of the mansion of Lord Hori Tango in the Kanda district of Edo. Because wooden houses posed a constant fire hazard, baths were not permitted in private homes in the city at this time, so public bathhouses became places where common people could congregate and socialize. Among the customers of this new bathhouse were bold—we might even say courageous—young *kabukimono* who loved to draw people's attention by wearing conspicuous clothes and by walking with a peculiar strutting gait. Because the new bathhouse was located "before (*zen*) Tan(go)," it was nicknamed Tanzen, and the *kabukimono's* bath-house stride was called "*tanzen*" as well. Shoulders pulled up and arms swinging up and down, it was truly an eye-catching swagger. We can even say that *kabuki* drama began when this public bathhouse parade was theatricalized. Somewhat exaggerated for the stage, the *tanzen* walk became a part of early *kabuki* acting and has been transmitted down to the present day.

As another example, low-ranking servants in a samurai household were called *yakko*. When they accompanied their lord on a journey, their task was to carry his baggage and possessions. In *kabuki* today, we can still see the *yakko's* style of walk in the dance play *Tomo Yakko* (Accompanying Servant) (1828). We might think the walking style was exaggerated when taken into *kabuki* dance, but we have evidence to show this was not the case. The German Englebert Kaempfer (1651-1716), who came to Japan around 1690, observed *yakko* when he traveled between Nagasaki and Edo on two occa-sions. He describes the *yakko's* costume: "Indeed, you had to laugh. The hem of the kimono was tucked up at the back extremely high, so that his underwear, try as it would, could not completely fulfill its duty of concealment and the entire lower body was publicly exposed." Kaempfer was greatly amused by the manner of walking: "At each step, one foot is raised so high it nearly touches the buttocks and, at the same time, one arm is thrust straight forward. It looks like nothing so much as swimming in air." Of course, the *yakko* did not continuously execute this show-off walk, but only, as Kaempfer notes, "when they passed a busy intersection or they approached another procession."[3] The *yakko* style of walk seen on the *kabuki* stage today is exactly like this.

Some modern Japanese criticize *kabuki* for being exaggerated and conventionalized, but from these examples we can see that *kabuki* is rooted in reality. The theater form called *kabuki* started when the outrageous behavior of *kabukimono* was put on stage. A woman, Izumo no Okuni (active c.1600-1615), a shrine dancer from Izumo Province, is known as the founder of *kabuki*. During the years of civil war (1490-1573), it was difficult for women to come forth. But when Japan entered an era of peace at the beginning of the 17th century, Okuni, who shared the sensibility of the *kabukimono*, was able to express in performance the lively urban spirit of that time. When she dressed as a male *kabukimono* and danced in Kyoto on a temporary stage set up in the dry bed of the Kamo River or on the grounds of Kitano Shrine, town sophisticates called her fledgling drama "*kabuki*."

Although history books say Okuni founded *kabuki*, she did not create something out of nothing. Okuni's correct position, I believe, is that she was the first great performer to put Edo-period social customs on stage. Over the generations, artists have consistently preserved the idea that *kabuki* was a dramatization of urban social customs, following the examples of Okuni, *tanzen*, and *yakko*; they thus kept *kabuki* a "contemporary drama" well into the 19th century.

The Tokugawa shogunate (1603-1868) issued numerous prohibitions and restrictions to suppress *kabuki* out of fear that a flourishing popular theater would stimulate social change, which it deeply abhorred. It is significant that edicts were issued year after year, indicating they were not honored. It is fair to see in this the townsman's "spirit of resistance" against an oppressive government. However, that resistance was limited. Two stringent policies of the government changed *kabuki* drastically in the mid-17th century. In 1629, performances by women were banned, thus ending a third of a century of women's *kabuki* (*onna kabuki* or *yûjo kabuki*). During the following two decades the only performances were by troupes of adolescent and preadolescent boys (*wakashu kabuki*). In 1652, the government ordered a total ban on *kabuki* performance. Theater owners, backers, producers, musicians, choreographers, costumers, and actors had created a professional theater over the period of half a century. To what new profession could these artists turn? In 1653, they appealed to the government to let *kabuki* continue, even if it was under severe conditions. The government agreed to their petition with two conditions: (1) actors must be adult males, and (2) performances must be of serious drama (*monomane kyôgen zukushi*), rather than the customs of deviant *kabukimono*. The *kabuki* passed down to us today has its origin in those two requirements.

If, as Hamlet says, a play is a mirror of society, then a drama in which women do not appear will surely not survive. In *kabuki*, a solution was found in the creation of the *onnagata*, the male actor of female roles. One important characteristic of Japanese theater is that performers who do not speak dialogue share the stage with those who do. In *nô*, for example, musicians (*hayashikata*) accompany the singing, singers form a chorus (*jiutai*), and stage assistants (*kôken*) watch from behind the actors, on stage in full view of the audience. *Kabuki* follows this pattern as well. *Kabuki* musicians are called *jikata* (lit., "ground people") because they sit on the floor, while the actors who speak and move about are called *tachikata* (lit., "standing people"). When actresses were banned, someone had to play the female roles, so the *tachikata*, now all male, were divided into actors who played male roles, referred to as *tachiyaku*, "standing roles," and actors who played female roles, called *onnagata*, literally "female style." At the time of the birth of the *onnagata*, it was enough for actors to merely show the "figure of a woman." But culture is never static; it develops and grows over time. When the theatrical culture of *kabuki* evolved into a genre that expressed complex human relationships, audiences were no longer satisfied with an *onnagata* who showed only the outer appearance of a woman. Audiences demanded that a woman's feminine psychology be depicted. For this reason *onnagata* were forced to establish their acting as an art. Thus the *onnagata* became a unique feature of *kabuki*. Looking back at the historical record, we can see that *kabuki* flourished remarkably in periods when famous *onnagata* took the lead. It is a fact that *onnagata* propelled *kabuki* to great prosperity.

With the dawn of the Meiji era (1868-1912), the old regime's theater restrictions were repealed one by one. It is extremely interesting to note that when the ban on actresses was lifted and it became possible for women to act on the *kabuki* stage, actresses did not enter the *kabuki* world. Several reasons can be suggested, but the most compelling is that male actors, in their pursuit of the art of the *onnagata*, had constructed an acting form that was completely unsuited to women's quite different physical features. Let me give an example: the sleeves of a woman's kimono became longer until a style of kimono known as *furisode* (swinging sleeve) had sleeves that nearly reached to the ankles. Today, *furisode* is a dress-up garment worn mostly by young, unmarried girls, but the long sleeves were a device created by *onnagata* to conceal their masculine bodies. Similarly, *onnagata* widened the kimono's sash (*obi*) to accomplish the same purpose. Costumes and acting techniques designed to conceal the masculine anatomy and suggest feminine attractiveness were developed by *onnagata* to such a point that women could not imitate them. That is why even today women do not perform *kabuki* and female roles remain the province of *onnagata* actors.

We should note that there are one or two restrictions on the *onnagata*. One of the earliest male actors of female roles, Yoshizawa Ayame I (1673-1729), was so famous he was called the "god of *onnagata*." In his writings on acting, *Ayamegusa* (The Words of Ayame),[4] he insisted that the *onnagata* should show a woman's sensibility not only on the stage but in daily life as well. This is not only Ayame's opinion. If you read what other *onnagata* have written, they too describe the great effort required for a man to create the art of appearing like a woman. But they do not say the *onnagata* should become a woman completely. For example, because women are generally shorter than men, does this mean a tall actor cannot be an *onnagata*? The answer is no. Or because a man speaks in a voice that is different from a woman's, is he unsuited to play a woman's role? Again, the answer is no. My personal experience

attending *kabuki* in the postwar period leads me to believe that *onnagata* now utilize a special style of speech production. However, I have been told that before the early 20th century they did not. If we note that the *nô* actor plays both male and female roles using the same natural voice register (*jigoe*), we can imagine that *onnagata* actors previously used their natural voice register as well.

One rule of *onnagata* acting is that the *onnagata* must not be closer to the audience than the actor of male roles. Social etiquette of the Tokugawa period dictated that a woman should follow behind a man, and characters on the *kabuki* stage naturally expressed this feudalistic idea. It is interesting to look at the situation aesthetically. A female wig is larger than a male wig, and the wig of a magnificent courtesan (*keisei* or *oiran*) is especially enormous. An *onnagata* dressed in this fashion unquestionably appears oversize alongside a *tachiyaku*. Therefore, in order to make the *onnagata* appear somewhat smaller to the audience, he will take a position several steps upstage of the male character. In this we see an important aesthetic concept of the Edo period. Another example is the *mie*, a *kabuki* acting technique in which the actor poses motionless in the posture that most effectively expresses the feelings of the character. To make a *mie* especially conspicuous, the actor will mount a small platform, three steps high for a *tachiyaku*, but just two steps high for an *onnagata*. In *kabuki* aesthetics, the *onnagata* should not appear overly large. One famous *onnagata* active through the 1930s was quite tall. People still talk about how he consulted a doctor to find out if his legs could be cut off to make him shorter. The basic body stance of the *onnagata* on stage, standing or walking, is with knees pressed together and hips lowered, a posture that is almost imperceptible beneath the kimono. This particular body posture was created only because of the nature of the Japanese kimono. We can imagine Ophelia coming on stage in slacks; a *kabuki onnagata* dressed in trousers or short skirt would not work. This is one fundamental reason that original performance styles have to be preserved.

Another special characteristic of *kabuki* is its spectacular nature. As I mentioned earlier, *kabuki* acting absorbed the highly exaggerated styles of *tanzen* and *yakko* walking. Even after *kabuki* acting become more sophisticated, it continued to include acrobatic stunts, such as tightrope walking and somersaults. An extreme example is flying in the air (*chûnori*): acting his role, gesturing and speaking dialogue, the actor is lifted on ropes and swung across the stage or over the audience. To achieve the maximum of artistry and beauty in such stunts, the *kabuki* actor's own power is not enough. Striking stage devices and machinery were invented to enhance his physical expressiveness. I will mention just three.

First, a rampway, the *hanamichi* ("flower path"), was constructed running from the stage into the house, allowing actors to enter and exit in the midst of the spectators. With this invention, a unique *kabuki* stage was created, clearly differentiated from any previous Japanese stage. This occurred around the end of the 17th century. Second, a revolving stage (*mawari butai*) was built into the center of the main stage. The source of this invention

中村鴈治郎さん江

先斗町
末榮
市扇

was the desire to show two events simultaneously. This was around 1758. Third, also in the 1750s, elevator stage traps (*seri*) were devised to raise or lower separate portions of the stage floor independently. A section of the stage floor can be lowered to make a depression that holds a pool of water. With such a pond, the playwright is certain to include an active scene of fighting, with many combatants. Actors will fall into the water, splash about, and either crawl out or drown. Thanks to the *seri*, the water will be a practical stage device, not merely water painted onto scenery.

Here is another example. When the curtain opens, no one is on stage. Then, accompanied by music, a figure rises into view on a *seri*. Instead of finding the character standing in full view when the curtain opens, the audience is led to gaze intently as the actor appears, viewing him gradually from the top of his head down to his feet. We all know that the closeup is one of the conventions of modern cinema; the *kabuki* actor's appearance on the *seri* is analogous to a closeup. The elevator is not limited to actors, of course. Scenery can be raised and lowered on a large elevator (*ôseri*) as well. In one use, a character is lifted high in a building that is transformed into a lofty structure; at the same time, another elevator lifts a second character to stage level. The two characters exchange dialogue from above and below. The conventions of bodily expression and the use of stage machinery mentioned here were perfected by the second half of the 18th century and have been carried forward into *kabuki* performances today.

But what of the content of the plays? Let me turn now to the *kabuki* play script where communication is through words. As I have mentioned several times, in its formative period *kabuki* merely put contemporary social customs on the stage. As a consequence, written play scripts did not exist. The play text became important only from the start of the 18th century, a hundred years after *kabuki* began. During that hundred years when specialist playwrights did not exist, talented actors like Ichikawa Danjûrô I (1660-1704) doubled as authors. The professional playwright at last emerged at the end of the 17th century, but he had little authority. Another hundred years would pass before the playwright's position would equal or exceed the actor's. We finally find evidence of the playwright's increased status in a passage from *Sakusha Shikihô Kezairoku* (Rules for Playwriting: Dramatic Gems for Neophytes), an important 1801 treatise on the theory of *kabuki* playwriting by the Osaka playwright Namiki Shôzô II: "The theater is the castle walls, the financial backer (*kinshu*) or theater manager (*zamoto*) is the shôgun, the actor is the samurai, and the playwright is the military strategist." [5] From this comment we can appreciate that the actor, the samurai, remained at the heart of *kabuki* theater.

We can identify another reason that it was so difficult to foster playwrights of true ability. The puppet theater (see the essay "Margins Between the Real and Unreal: *Bunraku*") developed side-by-side with *kabuki* in Edo, Kyoto, and Osaka throughout the Edo period. This genre of theater appealed to adult audiences with its sophisticated manipulation techniques. Also, the narrative story supporting the puppets, expressed

through music, was highly appreciated as literature and became the most widespread and deeply rooted commoners' literature of the time. In the mid-18th century, puppet theater masterpieces were publicized and performed one after the other, such as "Kumagai Jinya" ("Kumagai's Battle Camp") from *Ichinotani Futaba Gunki* (Chronicle of the Battle of Ichinotani) (1751), by Namiki Sôsuke, et al. The *kabuki* world eagerly adapted the puppet texts and staged them as *kabuki* plays. To put it extremely, *kabuki* playwrights of that period were no more than puppet play adaptors; they were not original authors. Only from the last half of the 18th century, after talented puppet theater playwrights had disappeared and puppet masterpieces were no longer being written, did *kabuki* playwrights, such as Namiki Gohei I (1747-1808), finally began to attract notice. Major *kabuki* playwrights in the 19th century include Tsuruya Namboku IV (1755-1829), Segawa Jokô III (1806-1881), Kawatake Mokuami (1816-1893), and Fukuchi Ôchi (1841-1906), author of *Kagamijishi* (The Lion Dance) (1893).

Throughout the Edo period, puppet theater and *kabuki* playwrights were attached to theaters, that is, they were house playwrights (*zatsuki sakusha*). Playwrights did not exist independently of the theaters. In the late 19th century, this system of house playwrights finally broke down and *kabuki* companies began to stage plays written by authors who had no connection with *kabuki*. Because of the unusual nature of these new plays, the period of *kabuki* history after 1890 is known as the *shin kabuki* ("new kabuki") era. Today house playwrights do not exist. We have been waiting for powerful works by outside playwrights, but a playwright must deeply understand *kabuki* before he or she can bring its centuries-old performing conventions to life. As a result, there is no person today who can produce new *kabuki* scripts. We wait hopefully for a new generation of playwrights.

One further point needs to be considered beyond what has been said about the performance conventions and content of *kabuki* plays. Even when house playwrights of the Edo period used figures from the distant past as heroes in history plays (*jidaimono*), they psychologically portrayed them within the context of Edo period culture. It goes without saying that current urban incidents and scandals were put on the *kabuki* stage as well, in domestic plays (*sewamono*). We can say with confidence that audiences today are passionate about *kabuki* because they find embodied in its traditions of performance the thoughts, customs, and behavior of the Edo period.

This seems certain for two reasons. First is the evidence that *kabuki* is still a living theater. And second is the wealth of documentation that describes *kabuki* in the past. Many paintings and graphic illustrations show us what *kabuki* was like from its very beginnings. When serious *kabuki* developed, following the government edicts of 1653, books about actors were published in profusion. Among these were biographies, critiques of acting (*yakusha byôbanki*), and autobiographical actors' commentaries (*geidan*). Somewhat later, descriptions of the stage and stage machinery were often published. Within this multifaceted literature on *kabuki*, the weakest area was published play scripts. Some play synopses have come down to us, but not many full play scripts exist today, especially in comparison to the vast number of *kabuki* plays produced. The reason is simple. Each *kabuki* play script was handwritten by the house playwright. Playwrights had no motive to mass produce copies: a production required no more than three copies of the complete script. An actor was given an excerpt (*kakinuki*) that contained only his own dialogue, the equivalent of "sides" in Western theater. If you came across an actor's excerpt, you could not understand the full play from the content of the excerpt alone. The few complete scripts that reached book dealers were not published: rather, in hand-copied form, they became the merchandise of rental libraries. Because *kabuki* play scripts did not get into the publishing system, extremely few remain today. Obviously, the underlying problem of *kabuki* scripts' low literary value is involved as well. In contrast, although puppet plays were also written by house playwrights, from the beginning they were intended to be published; consequently, printed puppet scripts from the Edo period are preserved in large numbers.

Such was the attitude during the Edo period itself, but, entering the modern era, *kabuki* plays of the 18th and 19th centuries came to be considered classics. Puppet theater scripts had been mass produced and were easily obtained, so they drew little attention. But complete *kabuki* texts, or performance scripts (*daihon*), were aggressively searched out and published in modern type because they were hard to find. Although the absolute numbers of existing scripts is quite different, about a thousand plays each of puppet theater and *kabuki* can be read today in published editions.[6]

Each *kabuki* and puppet production was publicized by *banzuke*. *Banzuke* are the equivalent of today's posters or programs, introducing the cast, place, and time of the play, usually on a single printed sheet. *Banzuke* were first published in the late 17th century. I once made a study of puppet theater *banzuke*, visiting every collection in the world. In the process, I examined some 10,000 examples, if duplicates are included. From this experience, I think that as many as 200,000 *kabuki banzuke* may exist, based on the ratio of puppet theater to *kabuki banzuke* observed in the collections and on my intuition.

Banzuke were published for 180 years during the Edo period, from 1688 through the first year of the Meiji period, 1868. Each year, the basic rule was to publish *banzuke* for each production in the five-play season, starting in the 11th lunar month and continuing in the 1st, 3d, 5th, and 9th months. Three types of *banzuke* were published for a production: one to be posted at street corners (*tsuji banzuke*), one that listed actors and roles (*yakuwari banzuke*), and one that gave a plot synopsis (*ehon banzuke*). These kinds of *banzuke* were separately published in the cities of Edo, Kyoto, and Osaka, and in provincial cities such as Nagoya, making four regional "blocks." The large number of *banzuke* over such a long period of time suggests the flourishing of *kabuki*. If all the *kabuki* theaters are included—major licensed theaters (*ôshibai*), middle-ranking theaters (*chûshibai*) in Kyoto and Osaka, small theaters (*koshibai*), and shrine and temple theaters (*miyaji shibai*)—perhaps twenty

existed in each large city.[7] It may be presumptuous to conclude that *kabuki* was prosperous based on the possibility of twenty theater buildings in a city, but it is surely evidence that *kabuki* was deeply loved at every level of Edo society.

From the *kabuki* repertory, eighteen plays have been singled out and given the name *kabuki jûhachiban*, or "eighteen famous *kabuki* plays." *Jûhachiban* has come to mean "something you are good at," so that, for example, if you are called on to sing at a party you will say "this is one of my *jûhachiban*." It is used especially by restaurants and stores. After the phrase *"kabuki jûhachiban"* became well known, the general term *"jûhachiban"* entered colloquial speech. But why were the eighteen plays selected? This is a puzzle for which complex explanations have been offered. Here it is sufficient to note that the grouping was established by the actor Ichikawa Danjûrô VII (1791-1859) at the time he first performed in the dance-drama *Kanjinchô* (The Subscription List) in 1840. He chose the most popular plays premiered by Danjûrô I and Danjûrô II (1689-1758) and, when that was not enough to make eighteen, he added three plays premiered by Danjûrô IV (1712-1778). Among them, *Shibaraku* (Wait a Moment) (1697), *Sukeroku Yukari no Edo Zakura* (Sukeroku: Flower of Edo) (1714), and *Ya no Ne* (Arrowhead) (1725) are illustrated in the exhibit.

What were the circumstances of *kabuki* in 1840 when the eighteen famous plays were selected and publicized? As I have mentioned, after *kabuki* had been totally banned in 1652 it was reborn the following year in the form of adult-male (*yarô*) *kabuki*. Thereafter, *kabuki* operated under constant government controls. The most intrusive interference after 1652 occurred under the Reforms of the Tempo Era, 1841-1843. In Edo, theaters were driven almost to the point of closing. As part of the reforms, the city's three large licensed theaters—the Nakamura-za, the Ichimura-za, and the Morita-za—were forced to move from Sakai-chô and Kobiki-chô in the heart of the city to Saruwaka-chô in the suburbs. The theaters managed to survive, but harsh controls continued. Restrictions were placed on the plays that were staged as well as on how the theaters were run. In this hostile environment *kabuki* was being forced into a corner. It may be that Danjûrô VII revived *Kanjinchô* as a clever stratagem designed to reverse *kabuki's* declining fortunes: because the story had been performed by Danjûrô I in 1702, it was considered a "classic" and the government was unlikely to reject it. Of course, Danjûrô's personal ambitions were involved as well.

Now, what kind of actor was Danjûrô VII? Undeniably a star, he was also inordinately proud of his fame. Danjûrô lived on such a luxurious scale that in 1842 the government exiled him from Edo for "seventeen miles in four directions." When his sentence was lifted seven years later, he staged a play based on the legend of the Rock Cave, in which the goddess Amaterasu Omikami, ancestor of the imperial family, hides herself in a cave, thus plunging the land into total darkness. When a rock blocking the cave entrance is removed and she is able to return, light is restored to the nation. Through this play, Danjûrô boasted to everyone that his return brought light again to the city of Edo. He was indeed a man of vast self-confidence.

Some of the eighteen famous plays are rarely performed and even the popular ones are not staged today exactly as they were originally. For example, today *Kanjinchô* is a complex, one-hour dance-drama. But in Danjûrô I's premier performance in 1702, the basic episode of Benkei reading from the subscription list was one scene within the all-day play *Hoshiai Jûnidan* (The Weaver and the Cowherd).[8] Because records of that first production were scanty and because Danjûrô VII aspired to bring a *nô* quality into his performance, he asked the playwright Namiki Gohei III (1790-1855) to expand *Ataka*, the *nô* dramatization of the story. The script Gohei wrote is used for productions of *Kanjinchô* today.[9] In Danjûrô VII's time, attending and performing *nô* was a privilege reserved for samurai; to a lowly *kabuki* actor, *nô* was like a flower on a lofty peak. One of Danjûrô's great ambitions was to assimilate *nô* into his art.

One of the most popular of the eighteen famous plays is *Shibaraku*, whose exaggerated costumes and powerful, bravura acting style (*aragoto*) are illustrated in prints and objects in the exhibit. It was created under unusual circumstances. Danjûrô I, annoyed by the acting of a recalcitrant colleague just before he entered the *hanamichi*, ad libbed, "Wait a moment! Wait a moment!" (*shibaraku, shibaraku*). The play was a great success and, from the time of Danjûrô II, it became customary to perform it as the opening scene of the first production of the new season. This was the *kaomise* ("face showing") production, so called because it introduced to the audience the acting company assembled for the year.[10] The common title for the play, *Shibaraku*, was fixed when Danjûrô VII included the play in the collection of eighteen famous plays. Counting only the Edo period, *Shibaraku* was repeated each year for 170 years. The hero's eloquent and poetic self-introduction (*tsurane*) was newly written for each production. The text in current use is the revision written for Danjûrô IX by Kabuki-za manager and playwright Fukuchi Ôchi in 1895. The appeal of *Shibaraku* is difficult to explain in words, but this short play exemplifies *kabuki*'s rich conventions in its brilliant visual display and superb theatrical construction.

Sukeroku Yukari no Edo Zakura[11] came into being in a still different manner. It is said that Ichikawa Danjûrô II created the role of Sukeroku in 1713 in Edo in the play *Hana Yakata Aigo no Sakura* (Castle of Flowers, Cherry Blossoms of Compassion). However, a hero of love-suicide plays named Sukeroku was already popular on Kyoto and Osaka *kabuki* stages. When the figure of Sukeroku came to the Edo stage his nature gradually changed: in Danjûrô II's 1716 production of *Shikirei Yawaragi Soga* (The Example of Gentle Soga), Sukeroku had a double identity, being "in reality" (*jitsu wa*) the 12th-century samurai Soga Gorô, whose depiction was influenced by the gentle acting style (*wagoto*) of Kyoto-Osaka. In Danjûrô's third production, in 1749, Sukeroku was portrayed as a man who enjoys picking quarrels in the licensed quarter; he is still presented this way in current productions. Refinements that have accumulated over some fifty later productions have come down to us, the general shape of the play forming in the 1750s-1760s. Authorship is credited to Tsuuchi Jihei II (1683-1760), who was active

at the time of the first and second productions, but we also recognize that Jihei's written dialogue and characterization have been altered and numerous changes made in the manner of performance. We cannot say what sections have been changed, when, or by whom. When a new piece of business or interpretation introduced by one actor was accepted by his successors, it would then continue. In this way new *kata*, or patterns of performing, arose. In *Sukeroku*, if an old pattern is "*kata* A" and a new pattern is "*kata* B," a successor is able to choose A or B, whichever he likes. It is also all right if he creates a new "*kata* C." As a consequence, the more a play is performed the more variant *kata* are created. But the number is not unlimited. It seems that two or three variations of one pattern is a natural upper limit.

We can see variant *kata* in "Kumagai Jinya." Two styles of acting the play have been transmitted: the style of the Ichikawa Danjûrô line of actors and the style of the Nakamura Utaemon line. In the Danjûrô style, the hero, Kumagai Naozane, wears a plain woven kimono, while in the Utaemon style the costume is red-and-gold brocade. When Kumagai returns to the battle camp and the narrator sings "He ignores his wife Sagami . . . ," in the Danjûrô style the actor quietly strikes his thigh and poses, while in the Utaemon style the actor places one foot on the steps, turns back, and glares at Sagami. Further, an actor in the Danjûrô style strikes the "signboard *mie*" pose when he jabs the upside down signboard into the floor, while an actor in the Utaemon style poses holding the signboard in the opposite way. These and other differences can be noted.[12] In cases like these, *kata* are normally identified by the name of the actor who first created them, so that *kata* created by Danjûrô VII or Danjûrô IX (1839-1903) are "Danjûrô *kata*." However, *kata* created by Nakamura Utaemon III (1778-1838) are called "Shikan *kata*" because Utaemon's successor Nakamura Shikan IV (1830-1899) preserved and transmitted them.

When I wrote about *kabuki*'s history and the theater's charm for audiences, my description pertained to *kabuki* of Japan's great cities—Kyoto, Osaka, and Edo. However, this was only my preface to wanting to say that *kabuki* was also widely performed throughout Japan, even in remote farming and fishing villages. It was not limited to the large cities.

The report of an investigation of country *kabuki* stages was released in 1971. Although some were undoubtedly missed, this report confirmed the existence of approximately 1,000 rural *kabuki* stages throughout Japan.[13] Who used these stages, we may ask? People who loved *kabuki*, that is certain. People who, when they had the chance to visit Kyoto, Osaka, or Tokyo, saw *kabuki* performances without fail. When their obsession with *kabuki* grew, they invited actors to their village to teach acting to the locals. Then they performed *kabuki* themselves. They were people whose passion was so powerful that they constructed their own stages. Not a few records tell of villagers who became so obsessed with *kabuki* that they joined professional troupes and left home, causing great anxiety to their families.

7.103

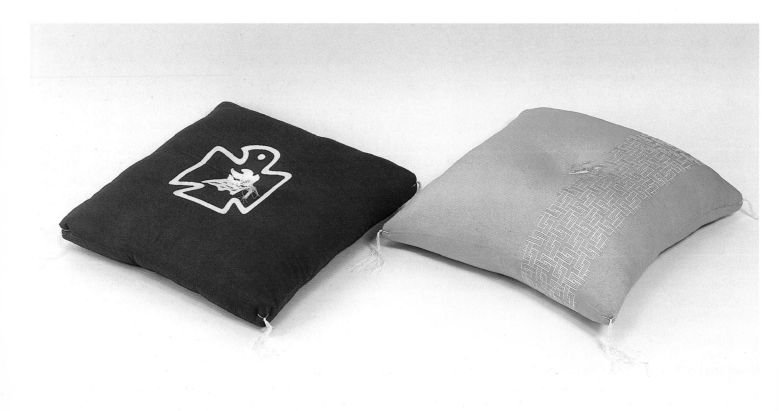

7.104, 7.105

PLATE 56

The men who even abandoned their homes were pillars of their families, but children were also involved in *kabuki*. Even today children perform *kabuki* on religious festival days in many places in the countryside. We can readily appreciate the charm of amateur *kabuki* in which all of the roles are played by local children. However, children's *kabuki* was not only performed by village amateurs, professional troupes of children (*kodomo shibai*) were popular in large cities as well. At the end of the 19th century, children's *kabuki* flourished in Tokyo. This was during the time of Nakamura Matagoro I (1885-1920), father of today's veteran actor Nakamura Matagoro II (b.1914).

The broad appeal of *kabuki* can be seen in educational performances staged in foreign languages. In the United States, students regularly perform *kabuki* in English translation at the University of Hawaii, sometimes under the direction of Nakamura Matagorô II, at Pomona College, and at other universities and institutions as well. We occasionally read newspaper reports of English-language *kabuki* being staged in Japan, acted by the offspring of foreigners living there.

We have seen that, during the Edo period, a large number of amateurs performed *kabuki* and some semiprofessionals turned professional. However, in present-day Japan such people are rare. In order to train more successors, a school for *kabuki* acting was established at the National Theater (Kokuritsu Gekijô) under Matagorô II's direction twenty-five years ago. It produces a number of graduates on a regular basis; yet, even so, the problem of educating enough young *kabuki* actors causes deep concern.

Japanese are fond of amateur accomplishments that involve physical training, which we call *okeikogoto*, "rehearsal arts." Traditional rehearsal arts embrace the tea ceremony, flower arrangement, archery, and fencing, among others, while modern rehearsal arts include ballet and piano. *Nô*, *kyôgen*, and Japanese dance (*nihon buyô*) are very popular rehearsal arts. *Kabuki*, on the other hand, is not included in this category. No system exists for the amateur to learn *kabuki* as an artistic hobby. Perhaps, in this, there lies hidden one more illustration of *kabuki's* unique nature.

Some *kabuki* theaters preserved in the countryside can be traced back to the 1770s. The oldest that retains its full stage machinery is the Kanamaru-za in Kotohira, Kagawa Prefecture, Shikoku. Constructed in 1836, it was modeled on a licensed *kabuki* theater in Osaka. It was in terrible disrepair, but, after being renovated in 1976, it is now used for traditional theater performances. We are extremely fortunate to have the Kanamaru-za, a fully equipped theater dating from the time when *kabuki* was a lively, contemporary entertainment. A *kabuki* program is staged at the Kanamaru-za for ten days or two weeks each year.[14] Actors unanimously say they enjoy the experience of being on this stage, because it is so different from today's Kabuki-za in Tokyo. One actor told me the following: "My elders' words of advice and their teaching become real to me when I stand on the Kanamaru stage." Actors appreciate the intimate size of the Kanamaru-za. *Kabuki* theaters in the mid-19th century were only about twenty-one

meters wide and held some 1,000 spectators.[15] *Kabuki* acting techniques were created and established in this relatively small space. But the modern Kabuki-za, operating in a capitalist economy, has to be as large as possible to maximize seating capacity (and therefore income), and acting has had to accommodate this change.

As I have suggested, upwards of twenty *kabuki* theaters operated in a single large city during the Edo period. Each theater was operated independently by different people. The actors, contracted to a theater for a year, strove to eclipse rival actors at other theaters. A spirit of competition blazed and the possibility that a great star might emerge enlivened the *kabuki* world. But at the beginning of this century, a capitalist monopoly was created when the Shôchiku Theatrical Corporation purchased all the *kabuki* theaters in Tokyo, Kyoto, and Osaka. *Kabuki* actors were hired as salaried employees of this business enterprise. As a result, the energetic spirit of Edo *kabuki* has been lost. But the fault is not Shôchiku's alone. Perhaps the powerful current of modernization in our time makes such change inevitable. One truth is certain—people in the *kabuki* world today lack the competitive spirit.

As we prepare to greet the 21st century, the sensibilities of the 17th and 18th centuries continue to live in Japan. Their form and content are present before our eyes in *kabuki*.

1. Araki (1992), 218.

2. The Japanese-Portuguese dictionary, *Vocabvlario da Lingoa de Iapam*, published by the Jesuit Mission in Japan in 1603, contains the entries "Cabuqimono Cabuqi, u" and "Cabuqi, u, uita." This is glossed as "doing deviant acts" in Doi, et al. (1980), 71.

3. Saito (1977), 53.

4. Dunn and Torigoe (1969), 53.

5. Nyûgatei (1972), 497.

6. It is immaterial whether there are ten copies of the original script (as there might be in the case of the puppet theater) or one copy (in the case of *kabuki*) in order to publish a script. In either instance, a modern edition can be produced.

7. Records of small theaters are scanty, but on the basis of maps, government edicts, and commentaries of the time, 20 *kabuki* theaters in each of the large cities is a reasonable estimate. For example, lists compiled in 1825 and 1840 give the names of 130 and 150 theaters throughout the country (Moriya [1988], 250-257) and a commentary of around 1800 notes that, in Edo, "theaters are permitted in the precincts of more than 20 shrines and temples throughout the city" (Moriya [1985], 376).

8. The "subscription list" (*kanjinchô*) of the title was a scroll (*chô*) containing the names of people who had contributed a donation (*kanjin*) to repair a temple or shrine,

9. An English translation is in Brandon (1975).

10. The theater season began in the 11th lunar month with the face-showing production. Four or five productions usually followed: New Year (1st lunar month), spring (3d lunar month), 5th month, summer (7th or 8th lunar month), and sometimes autumn (9th lunar month).

11. For a detailed history of the play and an analysis of Sukeroku-Gorô's "double identity" see Thornbury (1982) and Blumner, et al. (1995). A translation of the play is in Brandon (1975).

12. See Leiter (1991) for an account of the variations in this play's *kata*.

13. Tsunoda (1971), unpaginated.

14. A detailed, illustrated description of the theater is given in Leiter (1997), 56-92.

After being burned down several times, the Nakamura-za was rebuilt in 1834, with a frontage of 24 meters. When the theater was ordered to relocate in Saruwaka-chô, Asakusa, in 1842, its frontage was 20 meters, depth 38 meters, and ground area 778 square meters. See Suda (1957), 307.

7.83

7.2

74

PLATE 57

7.117

7.116

7.119

7.118

PLATE 58

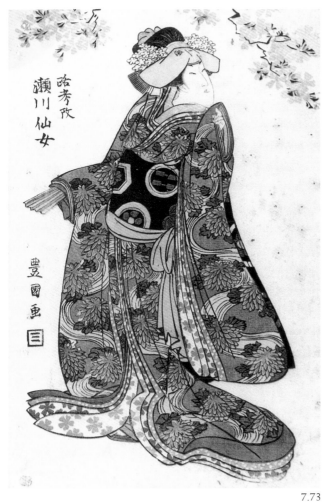

7.73

7.75

7.76

7.76

PLATE 59

7.63

7.82

PLATE 60

7.93

7.94

7.125

PLATE 61

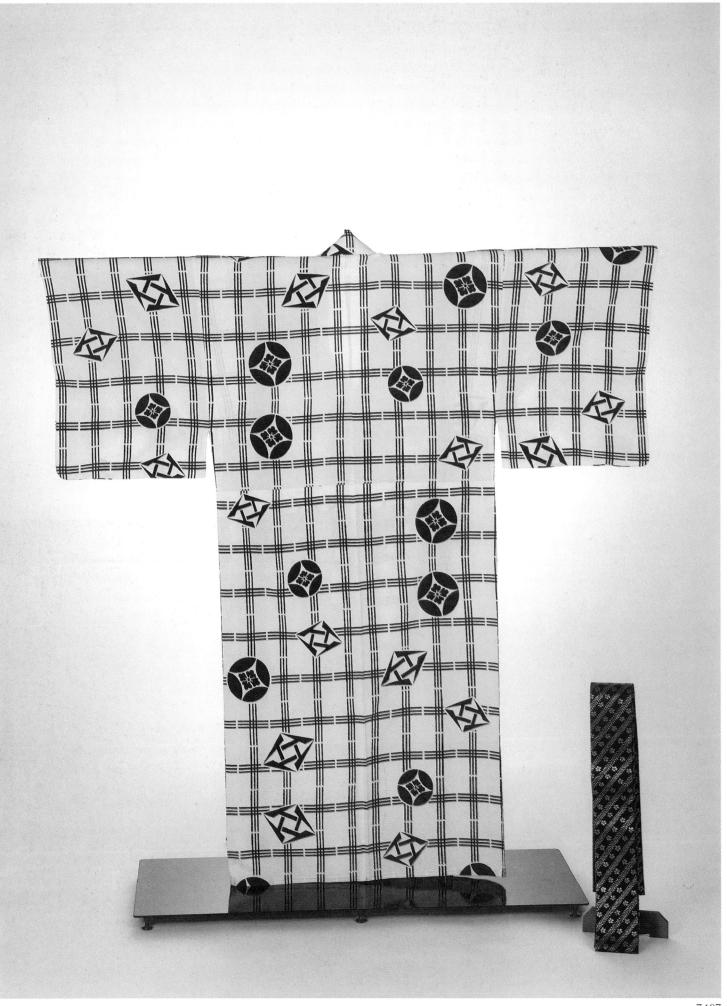

7.107

PLATE 62

7.111

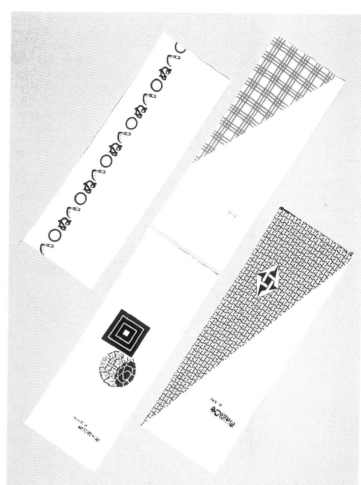

7.108, 7.109

7.55

7.110

PLATE 63

7.16

7.114 A

7.114 B

7.114 C

PLATE 64

7.16

7.114 D

7.114 E

7.115

PLATE 65

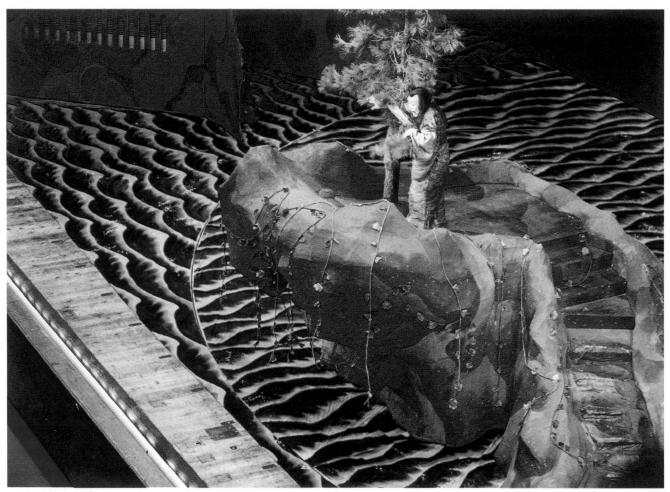

7.32

7.57

PLATE 66

PLATE 67

7.134

PLATE 68

7.137B

PLATE 69

世阿彌
ぜあみ／四幕とエピローグ
世阿彌生誕六百年記念
作・山崎正和／演出・千田是也・観世栄夫

俳優座
日曜劇場 NO.17
9・10・11月

世阿彌……千田是也
滝田裕介／山本　清
横森久井川比佐志／三戸部スエ
神山寛田中邦衛／秋好光果
内田透菅貫太郎／野中マリ
山崎直衛可知靖之／岩崎加根子
近藤洋介原田清人／尾瀬俊子
佐伯赫哉前島幹雄／樋口年子
ほか

俳優座劇場

9月8日初日　毎日曜夜6時30分
¥500　¥400／前売8月20日

8.54

VIII. JAPAN AND THE MODERN WORLD:
Shingeki

Kishi Tetsuo

The term *"shingeki"* may not be familiar to people who are not specialists of drama. Literally, the term means "new theater" or "new drama" and it is applied to modern theater in Japan, which began its life about a century ago. Fundamentally it is (or at any rate was) a paradoxical form because it began by dreaming an impossible dream. On one hand it tried to break itself away from the indigenous traditions, and on the other it tried to reproduce contemporary Western theater in the Japanese climate. Of course, the truth is not quite as simple as this, but any discussion of *shingeki* would be futile unless it considered the ambivalent relations it has had with traditional Japanese theater as well as Western theater (and Western culture in general).

When Japan began to "modernize" itself, the most popular form of theater in the country was *kabuki* (which was the old theater). Both thematically and aesthetically it was quite the opposite of contemporary Western theater, namely the theater of modern realism, which was taken as the model by Japanese innovators. For instance, *kabuki*, rather like nineteenth-century Western melodrama, depended very heavily on the dexterity of its actors, although many *kabuki* plays did have literary merit. Thus many people, especially intellectuals, felt that the form could not properly cope with the kind of "serious" themes with which contemporary Western drama deals. Technically speaking, theater of modern realism is closely connected with the proscenium arch stage with its invisible "fourth wall," and actors, at least in theory, are expected to behave as if the audience were not there. Then again, a production of *kabuki* is unthinkable without the *hanamichi*. In a performace of *kabuki*, actors often speak directly to the audience.

Besides this, in a number of *kabuki* plays, a small dais on which a narrator is seated is placed on the stage left side of the forestage, and, to the accompaniment of the shamisen—the musician is also on the dais—comments on the action and describes the inner feeling of the characters. All this was intolerable to some Japanese intellectuals who wanted to "reform" Japanese theater, and so they advocated for total abolishment of such "uncivilized" features as the *hanamichi* and the narrator.

Fortunately, such a simplistic theory was never put into practice, and it gradually became clear that there cannot be any experiment or innovation which has absolutely no connection with tradition. One good example of this is *shimpa* ("new school"), the first major attempt to "modernize" Japanese theatre. This mixed form of performance had become popular by the 1890s and dominated the Japanese popular theater during the first decade or so of this century; indeed, *shimpa* performances continue today. *Shimpa* productions made use of contemporary stories and modern settings, yet retained many conventions of "old school" *kabuki*, such as the frequent use of *onnagata*, or men playing women. As actresses became increasingly available, however, many of them began to perform leading parts, even sharing the stage with *onnagata*. Some of them, notably Mizutani Yaeko (1905-1979), had long and notable careers. Important writers, such as Izumi Kyôka (1873-1939), wrote dramas for these troupes to perform, and the combination of politics, melodrama, and slice-of-life realism created a nostalgia that still manages to attract audiences.

More serious attempts to create a truly modern Japanese theater resulted in *shingeki*, which was started by two leading companies, the Jiyû Gekijô (Free Theater) and Bungei Kyôkai (Literary Society). The Jiyû Gekijô was organized by Osanai Kaoru (1881-1928), director and playwright, who, perhaps, had more firsthand knowledge of contemporary European theater than anyone in Japan. But it is ironic that his closest collaborator was the *kabuki* actor Ichikawa Sadanji II (1880-1940). After all, the only professionally adequate performers were *kabuki* actors. Tsubouchi Shôyô (1859-1935), the leader of the Bungei Kyôkai, did not think so. He thought that *kabuki* actors lacked the kind of training necessary for the performance of plays with high literary quality depicting complex human psychology; he founded the group in 1906 to begin training amateurs. In a way, this would show how well Shôyô knew and understood *kabuki*, which was exactly the case.

The Jiyû Gekijô's first production was Ibsen's late play, *John Gabriel Borkman*. The Bungei Kyôkai's first production for the general public was Shakespeare's best-known work, *Hamlet* (in Shôyô's translation), but it was immediately followed by an Ibsen play, *A Doll's House*. It is both interesting and disturbing that the two Western dramatists who played decisive roles in the formation of *shingeki* were Shakespeare and Ibsen. We all know that they are among the greatest of European dramatists. We also know that they each wrote for almost completely different types of theaters and, technically speaking, share very little with each other. But they were the two writers who caught the attention of *shingeki* artists more than anyone else. Here we can detect the same lack of historical perspective that can be seen in many aspects of the so-called modernization of Japan.

The Bungei Kyôkai became defunct due to a rather trivial incident. Shimamura Hôgetsu (1871-1918), who was Shôyô's protégé and would have become a distinguished scholar like Shôyô, fell in love with the company's leading actress, Matsui Sumako (1886-1919), and deserted his family. The affair became a public scandal, and in 1913 the Society's activity came to an end. Hôgetsu and Sumako formed their own company, Geijutsu-za (Art Theater), which thrived for a few years offering *shingeki* productions with popular appeal. It too was disbanded after Hôgetsu's sudden death in 1918 and Matsui Sumako's suicide in the following year.

The Jiyû Gekijô gave its last production in 1913, but in 1924, the year after the great earthquake in Tokyo, Osanai Kaoru founded another company, the Tsukiji Shôgekijô (Tsukiji Little Theater), together with five other artists, including Hijikata Yoshi (1898-1959), a wealthy aristocrat who had spent some time in Europe studying contemporary theater. The Tsukiji Shôgekijô, which was by far the most influential *shingeki* company in the prewar period, showed from the very beginning an inclination toward the European avant-garde. Its first production was a German expressionist play, *Seeschlacht* (A Sea Battle) by Reinhard Goering. In the meantime, Osanai publicly announced that the company would produce no Japanese play for the time being, since there was no original work that interested them; until 1926, when Tsubouchi Shôyô's *En no Gyôja* was produced, the company did not modify its principle.

The company's adherence to the European avant-garde would no doubt seem naive to our eyes but it was typical of Japanese culture at that time. To mention a rather superficial example, Tsukiji actors tried to look as Caucasian as possible putting on false noses and blue eyeshadow. But, of course, they spoke Japanese. It is easy to take a patronizing attitude to them, but the matter is concerned with a deep-rooted dilemma in modern Japanese civilization in general.

After Osanai's death in 1928, the Tsukiji Shôgekijô's political orientation became clearer. In the 1920s and 1930s, Marxism fascinated intellectuals of many countries, and Japan was no exception. Eventually, the Tsukiji Shôgekijô was divided into smaller groups along political lines, but the differences among them were negligible. Militarists were becoming the central power on the Japanese political scene, and for some time *shingeki* was almost synonymous with the left-wing antigovernment movement.

However, this is not the whole story. In 1932, some former members of the Tsukiji Shôgekijô formed the Tsukijiza (Tsukiji Theater) together with playwrights Kishida Kunio (1890-1954) and Kubota Mantarô (1889-1963). We can safely say that Kishida played the most decisive part in the establishment of the nonpolitical *shingeki*. He had studied with Jacques Copeau and understood Western theater more profoundly than most members of the Tsukiji Shôgekijô. He certainly did not share their naive fascination with the avant-garde. It seems that he was a competent teacher, and several young writers who studied with him eventually became the leading playwrights of postwar *shingeki*. Their work in the 1930s regularly appeared in a magazine called *Gekisaku* (Playwriting), and it is a pity that the plays of such authors as Kawaguchi Ichirô (1900-1971), Tanaka Chikao (1905-1995), Koyama Yûshi (1906-1962), Morimoto Kaoru (1912-1946), Taguchi Takeo (1909-1948), and Tanaka Sumie (b.1908) are little known outside Japan. In 1937, the Tsukiji Shôgekijô evolved into the Bungaku-za (Literary Theater), this time with Kishida, Kubota, and another playwright-director, Iwata Toyô (1893-1969), as leaders. The Bungaku-za is still regarded as having had standards that were among the highest of all *shingeki* companies.

In the meantime, there was a significant move among small left-wing companies. In 1934, an influential playwright-director, Murayama Tomoyoshi (1901-1977), advocated for an amalgamation of the small troupes. Thus Shinkyô Gekidan (New Cooperative Troupe) was formed. One of the finest productions of the troupe was *Yoake Mae* (Before the Dawn), a dramatization of a novel by Shimazaki Tôson. The stage version was prepared by Murayama and it was directed by Kubo Sakae (1900-1963). Kubo was among the best of left-wing playwrights as well and his masterpiece, *Kazambai-chi* (Land of Volcanic Ash)(1937), was also produced by the troupe.

The end of the war in 1945 gave new freedom to politically oriented artists, so *shingeki*, until the second half of 1960s, was dominated by Mingei (People's Theater), Haiyû-za (Actor's Theater), and the less political Bungaku-za. There were other smaller companies as well, but they were not really able to compete with the three leading powers. This does not mean that the three companies, especially the Mingei and the Haiyû-za, in spite of their technical competence, were not free from the kind of ambivalent relations with Western theater which their predecessors were unable to overcome. If we may make a sweeping generalization, they stuck, artistically, to modern realism, and politically, to socialism. Neither of them was an indigenous product, and *shingeki* came under fierce attack, both artistic and political, from artists of the so-called underground (*angura*) theater from the late 1960s on.

But before we end our story we should mention two significant changes which took place after the war. One has to do with *shingeki*'s relations with Western theater. Before World War II, virtually no *shingeki* writer was known outside Japan. Probably the only significant exception was Kori Torahiko (1890-1924), whose plays were produced (in his own English translations) in Europe. But then—and it is sobering to consider—very little was known about the literature of modern Japan, no matter what the genre was. There was a serious imbalance between imports and exports. Only after the end of the war were Western readers given a chance to get to know novels by authors such as Tanizaki Jun'ichirô (1886-1965), Kawabata Yasunari (1899-1972), and Mishima Yukio (1925-1970). The last of these, Mishima, was an accomplished playwright as well, and some of his plays were also translated. The best known is probably a series of short plays, *Kindai Nôgaku Shû* (1956, published in Donald Keene's translations as *Five Modern Nô Plays*), which are *shingeki* adaptations of traditional *nô* plays. The title is deceptive because Mishima used only the basic premises and the stories of the original versions, and retained virtually no conventions of *nô*. Still, they caught the attention of relatively uninitiated Western readers, who expected something reminiscent of *nô*. They then realized that Japanese theater is not limited to more familiar forms like *nô* and *kabuki*. Another author who, like Mishima, first came to fame as a novelist was Abe Kôbô (1924-1993), whose plays, especially the Kafkaesque fable *Tomodachi* (Friends) (1967), have been produced widely outside Japan.

Mishima and Abe were followed by younger playwrights, many of whom were born in the 1930s. Today, works by such authors as Yamazaki Masakazu (b. 1934), Shimizu Kunio (b.1936), and Betsuyaku Minoru (b. 1937) are readily available in translation (see the bibliography). There is another significant phenomenon. To Japanese people before the 1950s, going abroad was almost like an adventure: something that happens once in a lifetime to a lucky few. Now it is the sort of thing any college student can experience. So even *shingeki* artists, who are still financially underprivileged, can sometimes afford to bring their productions to other countries, often to arts festivals of various kinds. The audience that expects the kind of "exotic" theater which comfortably fits their preconceived image of Japan tends to be disappointed because it feels exposed to a secondhand imitation, but unprejudiced audiences are likely to realize that theater which deals with serious themes exists in Japan as it does in their own countries.

The second significant change after the war has to do with *shingeki*'s relation with Japan's indigenous traditions. If the earliest *shingeki* depended (however reluctanctly) on *kabuki* actors— for instance, some of the first productions of Shakespeare in Japan were *kabuki* adaptations—the form developed trying to keep as much distance as possible from the traditions. It was simply unthinkable for *nô* or *kabuki* actors to perform on the same stage with *shingeki* actors. Artists of traditional forms regarded *shingeki* actors as people who were less than professional and politically "dangerous" because of their left-wing ideologies. *Shingeki* artists often felt that artists of traditional forms were not enlightened enough to appreciate *shingeki*.

This unfortunate separation slowly disappeared and it became more and more common for *kabuki* actors (and sometimes *nô* and *kyôgen* actors) to perform together with *shingeki* actors. Perhaps the epoch-making production was *Richard III* (1964), directed by Fukuda Tsuneari (1912-1994), in his own translation. Shakespeare has always been the most prominent site where different conventions meet. This makes perfect sense because Elizabethan drama shares many features with traditional Japanese drama. Both are supposed to be produced on an open stage. Both are "audience-conscious" in that they do not pretend to ignore the audience, as theater of modern realism does. To take a simple example, *kabuki* actors seem quite comfortable delivering Shakespeare's soliloquies, which they treat as direct addresses to the audience, whereas Stanislavsky-trained *shingeki* actors tend to cope with them rather unsuccessfully, pathetically trying to justify them according to their doctrine of modern realism.

Today, the "crossover" between various forms is simply taken for granted. Nobody would be shocked anymore if an eminent *nô* actor or a well-known *kabuki* actor appeared in an experimental production of a play by an obscure European playwright, but we should never forget that this is strictly a recent phenomenon and there was a time that such a thing as this was regarded as a near-crime.

Altogether, *shingeki* seems to have come to terms with its initial problems, that is, its relations with indigenous traditions and Western theater, and I think we can expect a maturer, if less pure, form in the future. But the prospect is not so rosy as it may look. Since the late 1960s, *shingeki* has been coming under fire from the artists of the younger generation. In a way, this was inevitable. In spite of many reservations, *shingeki* has been the kind of theater that takes drama seriously as a form of literature. Also, it has been essentially a theater of realism. Both of these premises were unforgivable to artists who were preoccupied with the actor's body rather than language, and who did not believe in the representational function of drama. I think *shingeki* has survived all this furore and has assimilated some elements of the so-called underground theater, but this is a topic for a separate essay.

Finally, as a kind of postscript, I would like to mention the reception of musicals in Japan. Japanese theater was always congenial to music, as anyone will realize who has attended a performance of *nô* or *kabuki*, but here I am concerned with productions of Broadway (and West End) musicals in Japanese translations.

It used to be simply impossible to produce Western musicals in Japan, as there were very few actors and actresses who were also competent singers and dancers. But the situation has changed drastically over the last couple of decades, and two organizations can take the credit. One is Tôhô, which has produced numerous plays and films, and controls theaters in such major cities as Tokyo and Osaka. The company has a very close connection with the all-female Takarazuka Revue Company. It may be rather difficult to imagine that Takarazuka has mounted all-female productions of such classics as *Show Boat*, *Guys and Dolls*, and *West Side Story*, but it has. More importantly, Takarazuka has produced a great number of actresses, and there is virtually no Tôhô musical in which highly-trained ex-members of Takarazuka do not play central roles.

The other organization is Shiki (Four Seasons), led by an exceptionally active director-producer, Asari Keita (b. 1933). Originally the company specialized in modern French plays, but now it is known for its productions of such mega-hits as *A Chorus Line*, *Cats*, and *Beauty and the Beast*.

But neither Shiki nor Tôhô, or other less active companies, has succeeded in creating an original musical by a Japanese writer and a Japanese composer. As far as musicals are concerned, there is still a serious imbalance between import and export.

8.32 A

8.11

8.12

8.14

8.36

PLATE 71

8.2 A

8.22 C

8.24

8.25

PLATE 72

8.27

8.28

8.29

8.33

PLATE 73

8.26

8.31

PLATE 74

8.32B

PLATE 75

8.42

8.44

8.51

8.57A

PLATE 76

8.43

8.47

8.48

8.49

8.50B

8.61

8.52

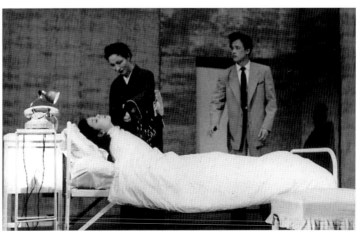

8.53

PLATE 77

9.39

PLATE 78

9.20A

9.24B

9.25B

IX. THE PAST IN THE FUTURE: Explosion of the Japanese Avant-Garde

Kusuhara-Saitô Tomoko
Translated by Arthur Birnbaum

DEAD-END IN THE PRESENT

In order to discuss the latest trends in Japanese theater–those that may be said to have a "future"–we first need to draw up a mental map of the state of the art "in the present," so as to grasp the interrelationships among various coexisting schools of performance.

Theater in Japan today, excluding traditional theatrical forms, spans three main currents. The first is *taishû engeki* (so-called "popular theater"), largely centered around major corporate-funded production companies, and characterized by plays appealing to popular sentiments, star "showcasing," "flamboyant staging," and "big productions" (with particular emphasis on maximizing the number of viewers per single sitting, not to mention lavish interior and exterior venue decor to evoke a "showtime" mood). The production system may be very up-to-date, but the themes and channels of expression remain wholly grounded in an emotional schema of human relations long accepted by the Japanese public; it never ventures to advance the popular imagination. In this sense, it is dead-end theater.

The second current in Japanese theater today is *shingeki* ("new theater"). Heavily influenced by the early- to mid-modern Western theater preferred by intellectuals, with marked tendencies toward literary textualism, an emphasis on ensemble over the individual star, non-commercial theater values, and with no relationship to the fostering of Western popular theater, *shingeki* provided a model of theatrical innovation. In fact, even after *shingeki* itself became an established tradition, it actively embraced new trends from the West. And by then its iconoclastic stance was directed against not only *taishû engeki*, but against society at large. Yet up until the 1960s, when elitism came under fire, *shingeki* cultivated a knowing posture of innovation as the proud bearer of cutting-edge ideas from abroad– a theater of the elite. If *shingeki* has hit a dead-end, it is because the outreach of mass education and broad diffusion of cosmopolitan influences has undermined the special stature of that elite, making it impossible to maintain a more-up-to-date-than-thou posture.

FLEXIBLE INITIATIVES

At this point, we can begin to appreciate our main interest, a third current in Japanese theater following a course distinct from the previous two. This avant-garde theater, which had its beginnings in the 1960s, has exerted surprisingly profound influences across the whole of today's highly diversified world of contemporary theater, and in many ways lives on as a model to the present day. Actually, not everything about it has been avant-garde. Even so, when we consider the future of Japanese theater, this is the sole direction that holds any promise, however indistinct. The troupes that fall under this heading—convenience dictates that we group them together as *shôgekijô* ("little theaters")—are otherwise diverse in their subject matter, organization and operations, scale, technical competence, and methodologies; they even resist classification as either professional or amateur. Each sprang from different backgrounds, with hardly any common lineage. In other words, most troupes—though not all—grew out of university theatrical circles. All do, however, share a common birthright in their refusal to be bound to existing theatrical forms and their search, under their own individual leadership, to find their own way toward some independent vision of theater. Most center on author-directors who, with a strong management base, pulled together two or three talented people into concerted opposition to existing theater. In this sense, they are avant-garde. Yet even so, recent trends indicate that group directives and ideals may no longer take such precedence over individual member activities, and that many such theater groups are now really more akin to loose networks flexibly interchanging participants project by project. As a result, the boundaries between various theater groups have blurred, which, together with a greater diversity in themes and means, makes them more and more impossible to grasp as a whole.

Increasingly, for better or worse, as groups take on the character of collectives of individual talents, the ascendance and very continuity of the group beyond the individuals is called into question. Yet conversely, the absence of conventional *sempai-kôhai* (senior-junior) hierarchies has also brought liberation from dated obsessions with the West, an end to elitism, and, moreover, a wave of self-styled *kawara kojiki* ("riverbank beggar")[1] free-thinking throughout the theatrical world. Granted all this started from contra-*shingeki* initiatives of the 1960s, newer generations since then have gradually wearied of indiscriminate anti-establishment assertions. While still radical in their own way, politically speaking, they have turned curiously conservative.

It is difficult then to situate *shôgekijô* in relation to the previous two currents in contemporary Japanese theater. It must at least be said that the university theater of the 1960s grew up on *shingeki*. And *shingeki* circles of the late 1950s to early 1960s saw the introduction of Brecht and Beckett, followed by Artaud with the 1965 translation of *The Theatre and Its Double*, and also the avant-garde tendencies of American Off-Off Broadway. So that even these standard bearers of newer theater, conceptually ignited by this world, may be said to be latter-day acolytes of *shingeki*. But because most remained outside the fold of *shingeki*, they were free from its curses and flexible enough to react to new anti-establishment thinking coming from the West. In other words, as Japanese who swept aside any pseudo-Western pretensions, they could directly appreciate the West of the 1960s, which was then storming protests against Western modernist civilization and seeking "lost roots" in the theater of the non-Western world. They thus found themselves in a prime position to incisively re-evaluate their own premodern Japanese roots, radicalizing them from the ground up.

Interestingly, this search for the roots of theater led them to reassess the physical body and existential nature of the Japanese, which also meant that they came face-to-face with the inner reality of the masses that was the original mainstay of Japanese theater. Thus, in this one sense at least, though quite paradoxically, most young, new, first-time performers now had a direct line to emotive themes and means of expression, not to mention the boisterous aesthetics, that have continued into present-day *taishû engeki*. It is all there—the melodramatic subjects (i.e., popular hero sagas), the heavy-handed musical excesses to underscore emotions, the bold lighting changes, the artificial performing style beyond anything resembling naturalism, the focus on the star. And so, seen from the perspective of the emotively charged *taishû engeki*, as opposed to the intellectualized *shingeki*, they came closer to popular theater.[2] Strictly speaking, however, this was only within the non-commercial contexts of "beggar's theater" in the most literal sense—cramped, dirty venues, outdoor or tent performances, ragged costumes, and poor props.

The same can be said about the "selling" of this theater. Similarly harking back to how the "riverbank beggars" sold their art, they draw upon past traditions in which actors back-handedly flaunted the unusual, disdainful regard the public held for them. As if subscribing to the *taishû engeki* motto, "The audience is god," entire casts are often seen kowtowing on the stage after a performance in an open show of thanks. Moreover, now that there is public funding for the arts, they are apt to have no use for the hesitant objections of the anti-establishment elitist *shingeki*; most of them actively and unflinchingly "sell out," going after any and all support they can get.[3] Thus, by way of promoting their productions, they share a vital common thread with commercial theater, although coming from the opposite extreme. Is this another token of the fluid adaptability of this new theater generation?

ORIGINS AND GROWTH

Granted that this current in Japanese contemporary theater had its beginnings in the avant-garde theater movement that swept the world in the 1960s, it still developed along its own unique course in the half-Westernized, half-unmodernized "primitive" climate of Japan. The forefront stimulus in this direction came from that strange circle of acquaintances—Europhile intellectuals, literary figures, artists seminal and unknown—surrounding *butô* pioneer Hijikata Tatsumi (1928-1986). From the time of his 1959 production of "Kinjiki" (Forbidden Colors), he and other dancers, such as Ôno Kazuo (1906-), became the focus of a diverse milieu of young artists and thinkers—including writer Mishima Yukio (1925-1970), author of the original novel *Kinjiki*—and their gatherings assumed the character of avant-garde salons. One of the central figures at these sessions, Shibusawa Tatsuhiko (1928-1987), French-speaking literary eccentric and translator of Sade, is credited with first introducing Hijikata to Artaud, then urging him to get back to the roots of Japanese body-based expression. So it was that from the end of the 1950s up until the start of the 1970s, Hijikata's *butô* performances became a concrete model for a generation of successors. It is altogether possible that dramatist Kara Jûrô (1941-) and poet-playwright Terayama Shûji (1935-1983) were inspired early on by these salon sessions. Also in attendance were photographer Hosoe Eikô (1933-), whose wealth of photographs of Hijikata and Ôno, and graphic designer-artist Yokoô Tadanori (1936-), whose posters for Kara's Jôkyô Gekijô (Situation Theater) and Terayama's Tenjô Sajiki (Les Enfants du Paradis)[4] have since proven invaluable documents of the charged atmosphere of those days.

The posters in particular are essential to any discussion of the later *shôgekijô* movement. Poor as they always appeared in their performances, the companies always spent sizable sums on posters, downscaling the same design onto handbills that they distributed by the thousands to their nexus of small theaters, an activity both conspiratorially theatric and culturally emblematic of the unaligned, flourishing Japanese avant-garde theater.

To return to those early days, however, it was Terayama Shûji who is reputed to have suggested the idea of a tent to Kara, whose Jôkyô Gekijô took to staging outdoor performances in disused corners of the urban night from the middle part of the 1960s. A red octagonal tent was needed "to evoke the comfort and raw nakedness of being in a womb," he was heard to confide, and so a red tent was pitched on the grounds of Shinto shrines, construction sites, off to the side of parks, or wherever they could get a permit to bear forth their alienated efforts into the city. It was Kara who first adopted the *kawara kojiki* moniker, his plays typically featuring the lone outcaste-wanderer at odds with society. Within an overall narrative framework (somehow Brechtian in its re-invention of Oriental theater—Kara's tent was said to have a natural "estranging effect"), leaps of time and space interpose the protagonist's reality and illusions. When, by the last scene, the protagonist hits rock bottom, the depths of despair are transformed into a magical dreamscape as the back of the tent pulls open and our hero walks away in a spotlit blaze—the sort of thing that drove young audiences wild. Others who later utilized a tent include the Jiyû Gekijô (Free Theater) with its black tent, a group headed by Satô Makoto (1943-) from this same first generation, whose plays are heavily influenced by Brecht. Today, the young Jôkyô Gekijô splinter group Shinjuku Ryôzanpaku (Shinjuku Den of Wild People) continues in this tradition with a purple tent.

Nonetheless, Kara's greatest impact was not in his use of the tent, but in his dramaturgy and the means of expression required of his actors. Both Noda Hideki's (1955-) Yume no Yûminsha (Dream Drones) and Kôgami Shôji's (1958-) Daisan Butai (The Third Stage)—leading lights through the 1970s on into the 1980s—evidence his influence on one level or another. Hallucinatory sequences brutally invading reality, narrative cutting abruptly into dialogue causing the players to transform the quality of their stage presence mid-delivery . . . anything was sanctioned to maintain dramatic suspense while sculpting a zanily free time-space. And since Noda and Kôgami both come from the post-1970s generation that grew up on moon landings and computers, it is perfectly understandable that they set their pieces in a not-so-distant, science-fiction—though not yet cyberpunk—future. This is a vision facilitated by Kara's school of disjointed dramaturgy and acting. Furthermore, because this supradimensionality allows for vigorous movement all over the length and breadth of the stage, actors in these younger theater groups need to undergo harder physical training than for any *shingeki* production. The resultant spectacle is a uniquely Japanese development.

Closer still to the roots of a unique Japanese bodily expression are the productions of Suzuki Tadashi (1939-). In this sense he is a successor to Hijikata. Starting in the 1960s, he joined together with playwright Betsuyaku Minoru (1937-)—sometimes called Japan's Beckett—to form a small theater group that performed upstairs over a coffee shop. Soon the two parted company, with Suzuki intent upon developing that aspect of bodily expression Beckett termed "the loss of the dramatic"; hence, while indirectly influenced by Artaud, he sought to disprove him via a rigorous reassessment of the physical character of the Japanese performer. His late 1960s production of *Shôjo Kamen* (Girl Mask), a specially commissioned body-based piece by Kara Jûrô, belongs to this period. Quickly tiring of this direction, however, Suzuki went on to stage his *Gekiteki na Mono wo Megutte* (On Things Dramatic), a collage of short, radically theatrical fragments from various plays and fiction texts, a shift which set him on a definitive career course. His technique, which works from a lower center of gravity, stands on common ground with that of Hijikata. To Suzuki's further credit, he also discovered Shiraishi Kayoko (1931-), Japan's "quintessential underground actress," whose haunting shamanistic presence brought the troupe to wide public attention. Meanwhile, in the same generation, Ôta Shôgo (1939-) and his Tenkei Gekijô (Transform Theater) developed methods—sharp motions constricted within the bounds of the body, lines "spoken" in silence—that seem to be variations upon Suzuki's. Tenkei Gekijo's tiny venues were always filled to capacity with die-hard young fans. This quest for the theatrical essence of Japanese physicality exerted an incalculable influence over the *shôgekijô* movement of the 1970s and 1980s (and, even later, abroad); the traces can still be detected.

On a slightly different note, from the 1970s, in sync with trends in the international avant-garde, Japan also had its woman-led and women-only theater groups. These did not signal a feminist current per se, though they did contribute to a relative improvement of the status of women in theatrical circles and achieved a measure of recognition. Seen in broader perspective, however, this was probably only because the art world is already considered an outsider's sphere by most of Japanese society. Even so, the fact that women of talent were able to establish a place for themselves was surely due to other unusual precedents of the *shôgekijô* movement.

Re-evaluating Sensibilities

With the 1990s and the popularization of the computer, artificial technologies began to filter into people's lives. New perspectives arose out of issues that had not even figured in the 1980s. Concurrent with this was the emergence of a new generation of theater groups more attuned to "performance art." Let us survey these developments briefly, and end upon the suggestion that the future may see the possibility of humans sharing the stage with robotic coperformers.

The principal forerunner to performance art in Japan—or what were then called "happenings"—was Terayama Shûji, who long before launching his own experimental theater group in 1967, was known as a poet of genius; he also wrote internationally acclaimed radio plays and even original *shingeki* pieces. With the founding of Tenjô Sajiki, however, he created an entire world of his own both in scale and lyric quality, a world that might be described as a poet's adventure into street theater. Yet the sad truth is that his heirs—the group Engeki Jikkenshitsu Banyûinryoku (Universal Gravitation Theater Laboratory)—have hit a dead end without, in fact, going beyond him. This is because he made no attempt to strive for disciplined characterization, relying instead on physical types—the beauty, the fat person, the midget, etc. In this regard, the performances of Papa Tamahumara are much more thoroughly polished, combining swift, physically demanding movements and beautiful vocals with all blending together to imagistic visual effect. A marked contrast is struck by the performances of Dumb Type, a group whose collaborative efforts span art, music, architecture, and other genres to construct tableaux where live performers interact in discontinuity with computer-controlled mechanisms and projections. Diverse as they are, there is yet some commonality between the two groups in their search for an existential human response to an increasingly artificial environment. It is here that we may look for the future of Japanese performance.

Today, we may even find attempts to readdress the long-discredited aesthetics of *shingeki* by such relatively new groups as Sakate Yoji's (1962-) Rinkôgun (Phosphorescent Group), or Kaneshita Tatsuo's (1964-) The Gazilla, which strive for a bone-piercing "authenticity" in their textual delivery. On the other hand, Hirata Oriza's (1962-) Seinendan (Youth Club) uses ordinary everyday expressions, spoken in casual conversational tones, to explore new dramatic possibilities influenced by film director Ozu Yasujirô (1903-1963). These are among the most promising new lights on the scene.

Lastly, we should mention the rather exceptional efforts of Yûki-za, which has continually put on new works by avant-garde authors and directors since the 1970s. Utilizing traditional Japanese "marionette" theater staging[5] with the puppeteer fully visible on stage, the interaction between automata and live performers in their productions seems to presage yet newer currents and possibilities in Japanese theater. Let us hope this is only one of many more new directions to come.

1. In the 16-17th centuries, before and during the early days of the Edo era, the shores of rivers in big cities and the inhabitants thereof were under the control of Buddhist temples or Shinto shrines. Among those riverside people were groups who were privileged to "sell" their art of performance at riverbanks. Their innovative arts attracted citizens and became forerunners of diverse kinds of Japanese popular theater, including *kabuki*. Eventually actors or performers were called riverbank vagrants or beggars. They were disrespected on the one hand, but, as outcastes, were free from social restrictions on the other; at the same time, as privileged people, they had something of a religious aura about them and wielded a strangely shamanistic power over their audience. This double concept of *kawara kojiki* as a disrespected yet privileged group is what avant-garde theater practitioners took into their theatrical activities.

2. This also relates to the tendency for radical youth of the time to be serious fans of *yakuza* gangster movies.

3. Japan is said to be an advanced country, but when it comes to public funding for the arts, it is a developing country: there were no public funds for avant-garde theatrical productions before the end of the 1980s. Besides, most funding goes only to groups who have achieved international reputation or to newcomers who have recently won critical acclaim. Most avant-garde groups get no support, a bias especially true of older generations whose spirits and attitudes betray an anti-authoritarian, supposedly dangerous marginality.

4. The literal English translation of *tenjô sajiki* is "ceiling gallery." But Terayama named his group after Marcel Carne's film, *Children of Paradise*, called *Tenjô Sajiki no Hitobito* (People in the Ceiling Gallery) in Japan. It seems that Terayama introduced his group as "Les Enfants du Paradis" when he was abroad. The group is therefore known in Europe as *Tenjô Sajiki* or Les Enfants du Paradis.

5. Yûki-za, a traditional marionette theater company, founded in 1634, still preserves techniques of one of the oldest types of Japanese puppetry. Yûki-za uses strings in contrast to the method of *bunraku*, whose puppets are manipulated directly by the operators' hands.

犬姫

風煉ダンス
第6回公演
『犬姫』

作　林周一
演出　笠原真志
音楽　不破大輔

1993年10月25日[月]～30日[土]
7:00pm開演
（整理券発行5:00pm）
法政大学学生会館大ホール
料金　￥2200（全席自由）

問合せ　風煉ダンス事務所　03-5351-2428
　　　　黒いスポットライト　03-3264-9470

FÜREN DANCE
風煉ダンス

9.21B

PLATE 79

IX. The Nakedness of Life: *Butô*

Gerhard Hackner
Translated by Dewar Adair

Nearly 400 years ago a new theater form—*kabuki*—appeared in Japan for the very first time. Its beginnings are attributed to a dancer, the legendary Okuni. Almost forty years ago the time was yet again right for the emergence of a new art form, a dance theater which was at that time unique in Japan. It went by the name of *butô* and was to conquer the world. The founders of *butô*, Hijikata Tatsumi (1928-1986) and Ôno Kazuo (1906-), who initially were completely ignored by the Japanese public, started exploring new avenues toward the end of the 1950s.

The path taken by Hijikata, who died all too prematurely in 1986, proved full of privation. State patronage of the arts used to be virtually unknown in Japan, except for those who had made it to stardom. And so it is that even to this day—with the single exception of the privately run Haiyû-za—there is no theater with its own ensemble.[1] The Japanese state indirectly forces its up-and-coming talents to finance their art by performing in night clubs. Since the economic boom of the 1980s, many prefectures and municipal bodies have built their own cultural emporia—many of them by renowned architects—which the artists refer to, not without reproach, as mere "hardware." Yet no one is intent on equipping them with "software." For an artist to be able to perform, they must be solely reliant on private sponsors or be damned to lead the life of a vagabond. Hijikata, for example, was left during some stages of his "career" with no alternative but to sleep for weeks on end in public parks. Ôno Kazuo was obliged to earn his living as a gym instructor at a grammar school in Yokohama until he was sixty and then as a school janitor at the same school until 1980.

Despite all these difficulties, Hijikata was soon to gain widespread fame on the artists' scene for his revolutionary work. Avant-garde theater figures such as Terayama Shûji (1935-1983) and Kara Jûrô (1941-), star designers such as Yokoô Tadanori, or the world-famous author Mishima Yukio (1925-1970), worked together with Hijikata, as indeed did Ôno Kazuo (on "Kinjiki" [Forbidden Colors], 1959).

Ôno Kazuo, who is now ninety-one years old and the grand old man of *butô*, is not quite certain about the exact time of *butô's* birth. However, he feels that important steps along the way were the performances of "Rôjin to Umi" (The Old Man and the Sea) (1959), an adaptation of Hemingway's novel, and "Nôtre Dame des Fleurs" (1960), based on the novel by Jean Genet. Both performances were worked on jointly with Hijikata.

Whereas Ôno Kazuo sees the central motif of his dance in the attempt to "experience an existence between death and life,"[2] not in a logical-rational sense, but "somehow as a feeling,"

Hijikata is primarily concerned with the expression the dark side of our existence as human beings. He calls his dance *ankoku butô* ("dark *butô*"). He strives to raise from the lower depths of consciousness those memories and gestures that have been lost in the monotony of our humdrum existence.

Hijikata used the term *butô* for the first time in 1959. He formed it from *bu* for dance and *fumu* or *tô*[3] for "to step," "to place one's feet," which itself is derived from *buyô*, the term for traditional dance forms. The roots of *buyô* go back to ancient, ritual, preclassical dance forms, to the *kagura* of Shinto shrines, to shamanistic dances, right back to the dawn of Japanese culture. The prehistoric and the ritualistic are sources which almost all *butô* choreographers draw on intensively.

Through avant-garde performances in his small *Asbestokan* (Theater Asbestos) in the Meguro district of Tokyo, Hijikata commented on contemporary events. New things were also taking place on other stages. Avant-garde theater groups sprang up literally all over the place. It was the beginning of a new age, one in which the body was experienced intensely. *Nikutai* (body) was the buzzword. It was all about the body and what can be experienced through its senses. The feelings of the time exploded in the streets in the form of violent riots with the police. On stage, Hijikata portrayed the violence. In "Nikutai no Hanran" (Rebellion of the Body) (1968), he killed a cock during the performance. He came on stage wearing a bridal kimono and proceeded to take off his garb and continue his performance, dressed only in a towering, golden penis.

Hijikata—who gave *butô* the impulses permitting modern Japanese expressive dance to experience its renaissance in the 1960s, thus lending it its predominant form—explains the need for his dance to adopt this form as follows:

> Japanese bodies are so different from those of Europeans. Japanese have their own form. I cannot move my body using it just as a piece of material. The body is life itself. The origin of my dance lies in rice paddies. Farmers are forced to work so hard that finally there is no energy left in their bodies. They pretend to move. It is the origin of my dance. I shrink my body as I dance, making it as small as possible to avoid the winter coldness. I could not find such a dance anywhere in the world.[4]

This is why *butô* dancers move low and close to the ground, their legs bent in like crabs or lying on their backs with their legs pulled toward them and turned outwards. Kafka in Japan. *Butô* is, in intrinsically Japanese fashion, firmly rooted in the earth. Crouching, cowering characters are to be found in ancient Japanese myths. Not only do the dancers weigh down heavily on the ground, with their center of gravity low, their feet flat, or standing on the sides of their feet, but they also seem to come out of the very earth itself. They roll around and squirm on the ground, ash-grey, ruffled, and their costumes torn to shreds. They are bald, to all intents and purposes naked, devoid of all the attributes of civilization, dull in color like the earth of a dim and distant past, like so-called primitive tribes who use clay and earth in their ritual body painting to achieve spiritual self-denial.

Nudity is frequently used as a means of expression, not to depict eroticism that has been mercilessly deprived of its meaning, but to demonstrate bodily mastery almost to the point of insufferable pain. Central to this art form is the attention that is drawn to the corporeal essence, the animalistic in people. One has the impression that the spirit is trying indefatigably to free itself from the body's shell. Beauty is not the goal, but authenticity. *Butô* consciously undermines the cliché, "keep smiling." Hopes for peace and harmony are brutally dashed. Each troupe creates pictures of pain and suffering which flood the audience with violence and shocks them. Hieronymous Bosch is omnipresent. And yet, as Anna Kisselgoff [5] has stated, *butô* is a compound of the grotesque and the beautiful, the nightmarish and the poetic, the erotic and the austere, the streetwise and the spiritual. *Butô* is a highly theatrical dance form.

One of the most important themes found in *butô* is the creation and destruction of the universe. Although the troupes are disparate, they seem to have one thing in common: the feeling of being drawn inescapably toward portraying life in its inception, seen as a painful process. *Butô* deals as much with destruction as it does with rebirth. It confuses the senses and shakes the foundations of traditional ideas of what constitutes theater. It is undoubtedly a theater of protest.

The dancers demonstrate extraordinary bodily mastery in the way they change the form of their bodies in excruciating slow-motion. They distort their bodies and faces such that they take on the appearance of costumes and masks. It was even claimed of Hijikata's most famous student, Ashikawa Yôko (1947-), long the leading light in the Hakutôbô troupe, that she had her teeth extracted to achieve the ultimate in grotesqueness— a claim that has since been proved incorrect.

A critic of *butô* once said it looked either like the world at its genesis or the world directly after World War III. The dancers are white-painted creatures who have either just learned to move or are in some post-atomic age, hopelessly maimed.[6] "Guernica" live on stage. The apocalypse casts its shadows.

One of the few dancers still capable of portraying this self-denial and of mesmerizing the audience is Namerikawa Gorô (1950-). His back looks as if it is not just one piece, but rather composed of three limbs. He dances, creating space, as if bent back and forth by the whispered insinuations of a light breeze, then again mystically and ritually, as if born of Mother Earth, frozen in an embryonic position, doubling up on the ground, to finally dance himself free of it. A face devoid of motion, a

mask or mirror, humanity pained by torture and terror, a replica of the dehumanization of our modern society. Twitching, jerky movements as if shaken by electric shocks. Then, yet again, the dancer appears to be remote-controlled, inwardly indifferent. On the outside, movement, on the inside, numbness. The Dead appear as the Living; the Living as the Dead. Humanity suffering in madness. Madness is the norm. The human form appears as if metamorphosed to a point where mutation seems more normal than the normal itself.

It is not by accident that Gorô's favorite theater venues are caves:

> I believe our origins lie at the heart of our Earth. In the darkness underground the air moves and sound reverberates despite the apparent underground void. It is here that our bodies awake for the first time. And so I wanted to descend into the depths to commune with the darkness.[7]

This is how Namerikawa Goro saw his performance in "Aborigine," in the subterranean quarries of Ôya in Tochigi Prefecture.

A founding member of the Sankai Juku troupe, he has been working independently for more than ten years. He conceives himself as an Earth Child, a child of the earth. He understands the earth as both our Mother and the ultimate beginning. That is why, for a while, he called his troupe Earth Child Co.

Butô can be seen performed by solo dancers and by dance theater groups with sometimes lavish choreography. Both forms share the same beginnings—the solo dances of the first advocate of modern Japanese expressive dance, Ishii Baku (1886-1962), who was active back in the 1920s. The further development toward dance theater was to take place in several stages and under various influences.

Like other early advocates of the new dance forms, such as Takada Masao and Hara Seiko, Ishii had previously danced in opera productions at the Tokyo Imperial Theater (Teikoku Gekijô). He felt the way in which bodily expression is reduced to fixed forms in Western classical ballet to be inadaquate. This opened his eyes to modern dance, particularly to the German expressive dance of someone such as Mary Wigman, which is characterized by the strong expression of emotions and loud music.

When *butô* blossomed in the 1960s, Japanese dancers could look back on three generations of German-style dance expressionism. Yamada Kôsaku (1886-1965), the famous composer, who also composed the favorite Japanese children's song "Akatonbo" (Red Dragonfly), returned from Berlin in the 1920s and soon after published the book *Kindai Buyô Hôka* (Beacon of Modern Dance)[8] He studied the new form together with Ishii Baku. In 1934, he met Harold Kreutzberg in Tokyo. Ôno Kazuo took lessons, even before World War II, from a student of Mary Wigman's, Eguchi Takaya. In 1929 he saw the famous flamenco dancer, Antonia Mercé, nicknamed La Argentina, perform at the Tokyo Imperial Theater. These influences led

PLATE 80

him to develop his own special style. In 1977, almost fifty years later, he dedicated his most famous dance, "Ra Aruhenchina Shô" (Admiring La Argentina), to Mercé.

Kasai Akira (1943-) and Hijikata were both instrumental in further developing solo dance. However, Hijikata was soon to do the choreography for group performances, as well. Maro Akaji (1943-), a student of Hijikata, was the one who took the decisive step toward dance theater in a grand style. In 1972, he founded Dairakudakan (Big Camel Battle Ship), the first large-scale *butô* troupe, which was, in turn, to spawn a series of other troupes. When Maro Akaji was asked why *butô* is so fixated on the portrayal of the abnormal, he said:

> *Butô* shows movements from every aspect of life, so it must not exclude abnormality. Disfigurement, abnormality, etc., give the dancers the opportunity to broaden their experience. To portray physical disability and madness is the aesthetic of *butô*. The perspectives of an animal, insect, fetus, dwarf, are also important. We want to show life from different viewpoints. How things look from upside down, through a hole in a curtain, with certain lighting effects, are equally valid. In presenting such images we aim to change the audience's perspective, shock them perhaps, strike a chord. We try to create images never to be erased from their minds.[9]

Born of the feeling of alienation and rebellion, developed further from modern dance, enriched by the avant-garde theater that was unfolding at the same time, *ankoku butô* was preoccupied with raising to the surface of our consciousness those things that had hitherto been buried in shame. This brought up questions concerning the darker sides of our all too glittering, affluent society. As Maro pointed out, they were concerned with the abnormal, and also with minorities and underprivileged groups.

It is not completely by accident that some troupes, such as the Paris-based Sankai Juku, have taken up residence abroad. Following their fame abroad, today's well-known troupes have at last found well-deserved recognition at home, too—a trend that is typical for the Japanese art scene outside of the traditional areas.

Amagatsu Ushio (1949-), the leading figure in Sankai Juku, describes the meaning behind his *butôs*: "*Butô* belongs to life and death. It is a realization of the distance between a human being and the unknown. It also represents man's struggle to overcome the distance between himself and the material world."[10]

"Ankoku," if it ever played a part in the various styles at all, has now been dropped from the generic name. In the case of some troupes, it has long since disappeared from their productions. All that is left is the simple term *butô*, which covers the entire breadth of this genre. Spectacular actions such as those of Sankai Juku are no longer to be seen. Their hallmark was performances that culminated in the dancers, strapped by their feet, dangling from tall buildings: the world turned topsy-turvy. The idea behind such altered perspectives à la Georg Baselitz was to draw attention to the absurdities of this world.

In the 1970s, one new *butô* troupe after another was founded, and in the 1980s, newspapers in the U.S.A. and Europe were packed with theatrical reviews full of praise for the increasingly frequent, spectacular performances. Consequently, *butô* extended its influence abroad on the art scene in general and theater in particular. In Brunswick, Germany, Furukawa Anzu, for example, even holds a professorship at the university. Foreign dancers in Europe as well as in Japan joined the various *butô* groups or took up solo *butô* dance, but with varying success. Yet, in the middle of the 1990s, relatively little is heard of *butô*. Will it still be around in the next forty years? The answer depends largely on whether a new generation of talented dancers with the artistic intensity of someone like Hijikata takes up center stage or not.

1. One should not be confused by the fact that there exist "National Theaters" (Kokuritsu Gekijô) in Japan. These buildings are in fact more like empty shells; i. e., they lack permanent ensembles. In Japan, theater halls are rented for a fee to any group who can afford it either through the help of sponsors or by selling enough tickets. In contrast, a theater in any city in Europe would not be complete without its own team of actors.

2. Kennedy (1995), 18-21.

3. In Japanese, most Chinese characters have multiple readings. Thus the same character meaning "to place one's feet" or "make a step" can be read *fumu* or *tô*.

4. Takahashi (1986), 5.

5. Kisselgoff (1984), 9-10.

6. Richie (1984), 15-17.

7. "Interview" (1986), 9.

8. Yamada (1992).

9. Myerscough (1983), 10.

10. Kisselgoff.

9.9

9.13 A,B

9.16 B

9.14 B

PLATE 81

9.25A

9.26B

9.27A

9.34

PLATE 82

9.31/1

PLATE 83

9.36/1

9.36/9A

9.36/10

9.36/12

PLATE 84

I. Japanese Theater in the World

Europe Discovers Japan

1.1 Photograph of section of scroll showing Europeans viewing early kabuki
Early 17th c.
Color on silk [original]
36.7 x 1550 cm [original]
Important Art Object [original]
The Tokugawa Art Museum, Nagoya

A portion of a scroll painting depicting an early performance of the kind of dance play that eventually became *kabuki*. Two Europeans stand at the rear watching the spectacle. Note that one of the actresses wears a rosary, reflecting the fashion for things European at the time.

Growing Relationship between Japanese and Western Theater: Late 19th and Early 20th Century

1.2 A-B Two photographs of Sada Yacco
Photographer: Atelier Zander & Labisch, Berlin
A) Photograph of Sada Yacco pasted on cardboard
Signature on cardboard, "Sada Yacco"
1901
20.2 x 11 cm; cardboard size 23.9 x 12 cm
B) Photograph of Sada Yacco, her husband Kawakami, her son Otojirô, and Loïe Fuller
1901 or 1902
22.8 x 22.6 cm
Theaterwissenschaftliche Sammlung, Universität zu Köln, Cologne, Germany

These photographs were taken in Berlin during the tour through the United States and Europe by the entrepreneur, actor, and producer Kawakami Otojirô. His wife, Sada Yacco, a former geisha, did not originally intend to perform but merely assumed she would accompany her husband. Eventually, when she acted in simplified versions of traditional Japanese plays, she became an international star virtually overnight. One of her ardent admirers, the famed American dancer Loïe Fuller, is pictured in the second photograph.

1.3 Playbill for a Berlin performance of the Kawakami Troupe
Title: "Guest Performance: Sada Yacco, O. Kawakami, with the Ensemble of the Imperial Court Theatre in Tokio consisting of real Japanese"
1901
Paper
31.5 x 22.6 cm
Theaterwissenschaftliche Sammlung, Universität zu Köln, Cologne, Germany

The program features two perennial favorites performed by Kawakami's troupe on tour. "The Geisha and the Knight" and "Kesa" might be considered, at best, vague adaptions of classical Japanese plays. Nevertheless, American and European audiences loved these dramas (which Japanese found embarrassing) and believed them to be authentic. There was no "Imperial Court Theatre" in Tokyo at this time, but Kawakami, ever the masterful publicist, did not hesitate to find a way to add luster to his group's international reputation.

1.2 A

1.2 B

1.1

1.4 A-C TORII KUNISADA AND TORII KIYOTADA VII
Woodblock prints showing the actor Ichikawa Danjûrô IX in his Eighteen Famous Roles
ca. 1896
Printed paper
43.3 x 27.6 cm
Museum für Ostasiatische Kunst, Berlin, Germany

The Shochiku Girl's Operetta Troupe was founded in Osaka in 1921 as an all-girl review to rival the already-popular Takarazuka Revue, featured in Section VIII of the exhibition. One of their early successes was a musical adaption of the ever-popular drama "The Blue Bird" by the Belgian playwright Maurice Maeterlinck. To honor the playwright, officials of the troupe presented him with this elegant collection of *kabuki* actor prints of Ichikawa Danjûrô IX, the leading performer of the Meiji period. The Shochiku troupe was finally disbanded in 1996.

1.5 HEADDRESS FOR COSTUME WORN BY GENIA GUSZALWISCA IN "THE GEISHA" AT BERLIN'S DEUTSCHES VOLKSTHEATER
1929
Tin, painted in gold, textile rose at each end
31 x 37 x 3 cm
Theaterwissenschaftliche Sammlung, Universität zu Köln, Cologne, Germany

"The Geisha," written by the British theater composer Sidney Jones, was one of many musicals that sought an exoticism in the "mysterious Japan" first chronicled by writers like Lafcadio Hearn as well as by painters such as Manet, Degas and Van Gogh, who helped create the romance of Japonisme. The operetta, first staged in London in 1896, soon became popular in the United States and all over Europe, its fame lasting through the 1930s. This Berlin production of 1929 was, according to contemporary accounts, one of the finest and most elaborate ever presented.

1.3

1.8

1.9 B

1.9 E

1.6 PHOTOGRAPH OF GENIA GUSZALWISCA IN "THE GEISHA"
Photographer: Atelier Lotte Jacobi, Berlin
1929
Paper
11.9 x 8.9 cm
Theaterwissenschaftliche Sammlung,
Universität zu Köln, Cologne, Germany

A photograph of Genia Guszalwisca in the title role of this celebrated production directed by Hans Winge.

1.7 PHOTOGRAPH OF MAX PALLENBERG AS KOKO IN "THE MIKADO"
Photographer: Atelier Willinger, Berlin
1927
Paper
16 x 21 cm
Theaterwissenschaftliche Sammlung,
Universität zu Köln, Cologne, Germany

Since its first production in London in 1885, Gilbert and Sullivan's "The Mikado" has remained the most popular of the light stage entertainments based (however loosely) on Japanese themes. Gilbert and Sullivan has always been performed in England and the United States. This photograph serves as a reminder of the popularity of "The Mikado," even in translation. The star Max Pallenberg played Koko in this 1927 production at Berlin's Grosses Schauspielhaus.

1.8 DRAMES D'AMOUR BY OKAMOTO KIDO
1929
Paper
19.1 x 12.7 x 2 cm
J. Thomas Rimer

This first edition, published by Librairie Stock in Paris in 1929, contains French-language versions of three plays by Okamoto Kidô, an important Meiji dramatist who wrote modern *kabuki* plays in a new, psychological style. Although a few modern plays in English translation were published in Japan during the 1920s, this is one of the very first collections to be published directly in Europe. One of the dramas, "A Tale of Shuzenji," is often regarded as the author's masterpiece.

1.9 ILLUSTRATIONS BY EDMUND DULAC IN FOUR PLAYS FOR DANCERS BY WILLIAM BUTLER YEATS
1921
Paper
20.3 x 14 x 2 cm
Hillman Library, The University of Pittsburgh

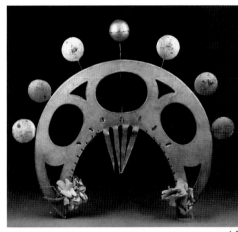

1.6

1.5

1.7

In 1916, William Butler Yeats, inspired by his reading of a series of translations of *nô* plays made by Ernest Fenollosa and revised by the American poet Ezra Pound, decided to write a series of dramas making use of certain elements he found compatible with his perception of the medieval Japanese style. Reproductions of the striking costume sketches by the gifted artist and illustrator Edmund Dulac for the first of these plays, "At the Hawk's Well," are included in *Four Plays for Dancers*, published in New York by The Macmillan Company in 1921.

Western Interpretations of Japanese Theater

1.10 A-C THREE COSTUME SKETCHES FOR PUCCINI'S "MADAMA BUTTERFLY"
A) No. 29: women's chorus, Act I
B) No. 33: women's chorus, Act II
C) No. 53: costume details
Early 20th c.
Gouache on paper
25.4 x 39.4 cm
Metropolitan Opera Archives, New York

Puccini's "Madama Butterfly," which had its disastrous première in 1904, soon became a worldwide success in a revised version, and has remained a staple of the operatic repertory ever since. The firm of Ricordi, which published Puccini's music, received many requests from opera companies for help in costuming and other production details of what was then highly unusual Japanese material. These three sketches are among those made to assist designers to create an "authentic" staging of the opera, set in the southern port of Nagasaki at the end of the 19th century.

1.11 A-B PHOTOGRAPHS OF TWO STAGE SETTINGS FOR "IRIS"
Photographers: A) Byron, New York and
B) White Studio
1915
Paper
22.9 x 33 cm
Metropolitan Opera Archives, New York

Pietro Mascagni first became famous for his early 1890 opera "Cavalleria Rusticana," his only work to remain in constant performance today. His "Japanese" opera "Iris," premièred in 1898. After its first production at the Metropolitan Opera, it was considered a great success and receives an occasional mounting even today. The music is certainly more successful than the melodramatic libretto by Luigi Illica (one of Puccini's librettists for "Madama Butterfly"), which curiously contains characters named for Japanese cities, including the villain, Kyoto (baritone), and the protagonist, Osaka (tenor).

1.10 A

1.10 B

1.10 C

1.11

1.12 Box cover for CD recording of "Iris"
1989
Paper
15.2 x 14 x 3.8 cm
J. Thomas Rimer

A modern recording of the Mascagni opera, conducted by Giuseppe Patané and starring such vocal luminaries as Ilona Tokody, Placido Domingo and Juan Pons, helped restore the attention of music lovers to Mascagni's lyrical score.

1.13 A-B, 1.14 Three photographs of the Weill-Brecht opera "Der Jasager"
Berlin première, 1930; New York première, 1933
Paper
1.13A): 19.1 x 22.9 cm; B) 12.7 x 16.5 cm;
1.14: 16.5 x 24.1 cm
Courtesy of the Weill-Lenya Research Center, Kurt Weill Foundation for Music, New York

In 1930, Bertolt Brecht, having read a German translation made from Arthur Waley's English renderings of medieval Japanese *nô* published in 1921, decided to write his own drama in this abbreviated style, which Kurt Weill set to music. The title, which might be roughly translated as "The One Who Says Yes," was written to be performed by high school students as what Brecht called a "learning piece." The instrumentation and vocal parts are simple, but the work is musically and dramatically compelling, as might be expected from the composers of "The Threepenny Opera" and "Mahagony."

1.15 Cover painting by Yama Moto on LP recording of "Der Jasager"
Music by Kurt Weill; text by Bertolt Brecht
Original recording, 1955; this reissue 1966
Paper
30.5 x 30.5 cm
J. Thomas Rimer

The first recording of "Der Jasager" was made in Dusseldorf in 1955 under the supervision of Lotte Lenya, the widow of Kurt Weill. The recording has been reissued several times, including a CD version in 1989.

1.12

1.15

1.13A

1.13B

1.14

JAPANESE THEATER IN THE WEST

1.16 A-C THREE SKETCHES BY ROLF
CHRISTIANSEN FOR A PRODUCTION OF
MISHIMA YUKIO'S "THREE MODERN NO
PLAYS"
1958
32.5 x 50 cm
Theaterwissenschaftliche Sammlung,
Universität zu Köln, Cologne, Germany

The celebrated postwar novelist Mishima
Yukio is also highly respected in Japan as a
playwright, and many of his works have
been produced abroad, thanks to translations by Donald Keene, which have often
served as the basis for further adaptions in
German, French, and other European languages. These stage designs, created for a
1958 production in Kiel directed by
Wolfgang Blum, show designs for "The
Damask Drum" and two others of Mishima's
evocative one-act adaptions of these medieval Japanese dramas. A photograph of a
Japanese production of modern *nô* by
Mishima can be found in Section VIII.

1.17 KARIGINU ROBE FOR HAMLET IN
"NO HAMLET"
1982
Silk
10 x 170 x 25 cm
Munakata Kuniyoshi, Shizuoka National
University, Shizuoka Prefecture

In 1982, Munakata Kuniyoshi, a professor of
English at Shizuoka National University and
the founder, director, and leader of the *Nô*
Shakespeare Group of Japan, created a
production of *"Nô Hamlet."* The production
was later seen at the National *Nô* Theater in
Tokyo, as well as in Europe and the United
States. The costume, in *kariginu* (so-called
"hunting robe") style–actually a courtier's
usual costume–is worn by the protagonist.

1.18 POSTER FOR MUNAKATA'S "NO
HAMLET" AT TOKYO'S NATIONAL NO
THEATRE
1985
Paper
60 x 40 cm
Munakata Kuniyoshi

1.19 STAGE SET MODEL BY ASAKURA
SETSU FOR "ANGELS IN AMERICA"
1994
Wood, paper
60 x 60 x 40 cm
Toyama City

Asakura Setsu, one of the top set designers
in contemporary Japan, has worked in

1.16 C

theaters around the world. This model shows
the set prepared for the Japanese-language
première in 1994 of Tony Kushner's prize-
winning drama "Angels in America."

1.20 SET DESIGN BY HANS SCHAVERNOCH
FOR "SATOMI AND THE EIGHT DOGS"
1992
Paper
Hans Schavernoch

Hans Schavernoch, one of the most significant of contemporary European stage designers, is perhaps best known for his opera
settings, in particular a Bayreuth production
of Wagner's Ring cycle and, in the United
States, a startling visual realization of
Wagner's "The Flying Dutchman" for the
Metropolitan Opera in New York. The actor
Ichikawa Ennosuke, famous for his productions of "super-*kabuki*," was struck by the
imaginativeness of the the Bayreuth settings
and invited Mr. Schavernoch to design a
Tokyo production of a new-style *kabuki*
drama based on the famous early 19th-
century romantic novel by Takizawa Bakin,
Satomi and the Eight Dogs.

1.21 POSTER FOR BERGMAN PRODUCTION
OF "MADAME DE SADE"
1989
Paper
99.1 x 69.9 cm
Gift of Royal Dramatic Theatre of Stockholm

Another work by the novelist and playwright
Mishima Yukio which found favor abroad is
his play "Madame de Sade," which was given
a brilliant production in 1989, directed by
the famed film director Ingmar Bergman for
the Royal Dramatic Theatre of Stockholm.
This mounting, revived several times, was
also seen in the United States, to considerable acclaim.

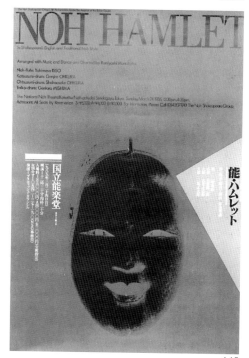

1.18

1.21

1.22 POSTER FOR THE U.S. TOURING PRODUCTION OF "SOTOBA KOMACHI"
1991
Paper
35.6 x 52.1 cm
J. Thomas Rimer

A brilliant production of Mishima Yukio's modern *nô* play "Sotoba Komachi," first staged in Tokyo by Ninagawa Yukio, the celebrated avant-garde director, toured the United States in 1991. The play is a trenchant psychological retelling of the original medieval drama in which Komachi, a famous beauty in her youth, now lives out her wretched life as an aged beggar crone. Other Ninagawa productions are pictured in Section VIII of the exhibition.

1.23 ROSE
Puppet used by Lee Breuer in his Mabou Mines production "An Epidog"
Designed and built by Julie Archer
1995
Fabric, wood, paper, pulp
8.9 x 2.5 x 6.4 cm
Mabou Mines

Lee Breuer, one of the most innovative figures in contemporary avant-garde theatre, was a founding member of the Mabou Mines Company in 1970 and has been associated with a variety of avant-garde productions at LaMama in New York. Long fascinated by Japanese theater, and in particular the puppets of *bunraku*, he asked Julie Archer to create the puppet Rose, which has appeared in a variety of productions.

1.24 PHOTOGRAPH FROM "WOMAN IN THE DUNES"
1996
Paper
Sara O'Connor, Milwaukee Repertory Theatre

Highly successful bilingual productions of Japanese plays have become more common in recent years. In this 1996 dramatization of Abe Kôbô's novel *Woman in the Dunes*, staged by the Omsk State Drama Theatre in Russia, the director, Vladimir Petrov, chose a Russian actor, Michael Klounev, for the protagonist and a Japanese actress, Araki Kazuko, for the mysterious "woman," with each speaking in their respective languages. The stage designer, Matsushita Ryô, was also from Japan.

1.23

1.29

1.24

THE CONTEMPORARY WESTERN FASCINATION WITH JAPAN

1.25/1.26 POSTERS FOR TWO PRODUCTIONS OF STEPHEN SONDHEIM'S "PACIFIC OVERTURES"
1976 and 1984 (© Faver)
Paper
35.6 x 55.9 cm
Japan Society, Inc.

In 1976, the composer Stephen Sondheim and the writer John Weidman created a striking musical and dramatic version of the coming to Japan of Commodore Matthew Perry in 1853, an event usually considered to have been instrumental in opening Japan up to foreign influences after some two hundred years of seclusion. In the view of these two gifted men, the cultural trauma caused by this event has never really stopped. "Pacific Overtures" has also been popular in England, where it has been given several important productions.

1.27 PHOTOGRAPH FROM THE ORIGINAL PRODUCTION OF STEVEN SONDHEIM'S "PACIFIC OVERTURES"
Photographer: Carol Rosegg
1976
20.3 x 25.4 cm
Carol Rosegg

A striking scene from "Pacific Overtures" showing Commodore Perry at the bow of his ship. His pose is redolent of the *mie* (climax poses) in the traditional *kabuki* theater.

1.28 RECORD COVER FOR ORIGINAL CAST RECORDING OF "PACIFIC OVERTURES"
1976
30.5 x 30.5 cm
J. Thomas Rimer

1.29 COSTUME SKETCH BY ANNENA STUBBS FOR THE FERRYMAN IN THE PRODUCTION OF "CURLEW RIVER" BY THE OPERA THEATRE OF SAINT LOUIS
1986
Color on paper
57.2 x 38.1 cm
Colin Graham

The British composer Benjamin Britten, when visiting Japan in 1956, became intrigued by what he found to be the strangeness and unique beauty of the *nô* theater. He later asked his collaborator William Plomer to adapt the text of the *nô* play Britten had particularly admired –"The River Sumida"– into the text for a one-act opera. Britten's version, set in medieval England, uses Christian plainsong to replace the original *nô* chanting in order to create a work that, while deeply indebted to the beauty of medieval Japanese theater, is altogether authentic and one of the most moving works by this master stage composer.

1.30 A-D FOUR PUPPETS USED IN MIKI MINORU'S OPERA "JORURI"
1985
Wood, wire, cloth, with wooden stands
A) 73.7 x 50.8 cm; B) 43.2 x 27.9 cm;
C) 81.3 x 45.7 cm; D) 53.3 x 30.5 cm
Courtesy of Opera Theatre of Saint Louis

For its 10th anniversary season, the Opera Theatre of Saint Louis commissioned Miki Minoru, a leading contemporary Japanese composer, to compose a new opera especially for the company. Miki, who had already written several successful operatic scores, teamed up with the noted opera director Colin Graham, who wrote the libretto, to create a moving and evocative evening. The story, which concerns a doomed pair of lovers, draws on conventions of both *kabuki* and *bunraku*. The company later toured the production to Japan, with great success.

1.31 SOUVENIR PROGRAM FOR THE 10TH ANNIVERSARY SEASON OF THE OPERA THEATRE OF SAINT LOUIS
Featuring designs for the première of the Miki Minoru opera "*Jôruri*;" cover by Walter Cooper
1985
Paper
28.6 x 21.6 x 3.2 cm
J. Thomas Rimer

1.31

1.32 A-B TWO PHOTOGRAPHS OF MAYUZUMI TOSHIRO'S OPERA "KINKAKUJI"
Photographer: Jerome Sirlin
1995
Music from Japan, Inc.

Mayuzumi Toshirô, one of the postwar Japanese composers best known internationally, wrote "*Kinkakuji*" based on the celebrated 1956 novel of Mishima Yukio, entitled in English *The Temple of the Golden Pavilion*. Set to a text in German by Claus H. Henneberg, the opera was premièred in Berlin in 1976. The elaborate production given at the New York City Opera, in 1995, was its first staging in English. Widely known internationally as a film composer, Mayuzumi wrote a number of symphonic works, as well

as ballet scores for George Balanchine's "*Bugaku*" and Maurice Béjart.

1.33 A-B A) DRAWING BY ASAKURA SETSU FOR THE STAGE SETTING OF "THE WOMAN WITHOUT A SHADOW"
B) Photographs of the production
A) 1993; color on paper; 103 x 73 cm
B) Photographer: ©Anne Kirchbach
A) Asakura Setsu; B) Bavarian State Opera, Munich, Germany

In 1993, Asakura Setsu was asked to design the settings for a spectacular production in Munich of the 19199 Richard Strauss opera "The Woman without a Shadow" (*Die Frau ohne Schatten*). Set in a mythical country, a Japanese mise-en-scène was used. Costumes were by Mohri Tomio, and the production was directed by Ichikawa Ennosuke, the famed "super-*kabuki*" performer, mentioned elsewhere in this section in connection with his production of "Satomi and the Eight Dogs." The Strauss production was later taken to Nagoya to inaugurate the new opera house there, and remains in the repertory of the Bavarian State Opera.

1.34 COSTUME BY MOHRI TOSHIO FOR "THE WOMAN WITHOUT A SHADOW"
1993
Cloth
Bavarian State Opera, Munich, Germany

1.33A

II. ANCIENT ROOTS: *Kagura* and *Minzoku Geinô* (Folk Theater)

KAGURA

A) *KAGURA* MASKS

2.1 OKAME ("BEAUTIFUL WOMAN")
Mask used for young women or goddesses in *Kagura* dances
Late Meiji-Taishô period (late 19th-early 20th c.)
Wood, *gofun*
18 x 14 cm
Günter Zobel

2.2 HYOTTOKO (FUNNY MAN, CLOWN)
Mask used for buffoonery by a farmer
Taishô or Shôwa period (20th c.)
Wood, *gofun*
20 x 14 cm
Günter Zobel

In several kinds of what is known as *Satô-Kagura*–that is, *Kagura* performed in the countryside–Okame and Hyottoko form an amusing couple. As a drunken farmer, whose mouth is bent to the side from blowing into a charcoal fire to fan it every morning, Hyottoko attempts to approach Okame with erotic movements during his dance. The latter, also known as Otafuku, who has a face representing an attractive, rural woman, tries to escape by hiding his bottle and even beating him.

2.3 AMATERASU (THE SUN GODDESS)
Mask used for the mythical scenes of *Iwato-iri* and *Iwato-biraki*
Shôwa period (1926-88)
Wood, *gofun*
20.6 x 13 cm
Tsubouchi Memorial Theatre Museum, Waseda University

2.4 SUSANO-O (SHINTO GOD; BROTHER OF THE SUN GODDESS AMATERASU)
Mask
Shôwa period (1926-88)
Wood, *gofun*
21 x 14.5 cm; beard length: 15 cm
Tsubouchi Memorial Theatre Museum, Waseda University

2.5 KAMI (WAKA-OTOKO)
Mask used for gods such as Izanagi and Tachikara-ô
1891 (inscription: Meiji 24th year)
Wood, *gofun*
21 x 11.5 cm
Günter Zobel

2.1

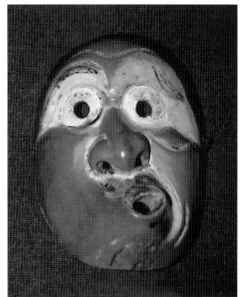

2.2

2.4

2.5

2.6

2.6 KAMI (JO)
Mask used for old gods
End of Meiji period (early 20th c.)
Wood, *gofun*
18 x 13 cm
Günter Zobel

Because of vulgar jokes directed towards her by her wild brother Susano-o, Amaterasu-Omikami, the sun goddess, is offended. According to Shinto mythology, she goes into hiding in a rock cave, thereby causing total darkness in the world. (This dance is usually called *Iwato-iri*.) Myriads of gods gather in front of her hiding place to find a way to lure her out. Finally it is decided to let the lovely young goddess Ama-no-uzume perform an amusing and erotic dance that will entice the sun goddess. To most of the assembled old gods, the dance of the half naked Uzume is so funny that they burst out laughing. Curious, Amaterasu peeps out of her cave, is instantly enthralled by the strong young god Tachikara-o, and the world is again in possession of sunlight.(The dance is *Iwato-biraki*.) This scene, usually referred to as the mythological origin of Japanese theater, stresses once more that its oldest and most basic roots lie in dancing.

2.7 KISHIN/ONI (DEMONIC GOD/DEMON)
Mask
Edo period (1603-1868)
Wood
23.5 x 18.5 cm
Matsushita Art Museum, Kagoshima;
inv. no. E2-16

2.8 TA-NO KAMI (RICEFIELD GOD)
Mask
End of 16th-beginning of 17th c.
Wood
21 x 15.5 cm
Matsushita Art Museum, Kagoshima;
inv. no. E6-1

2.9 TENGU (MOUNTAIN GOBLIN)
Mask used for the role of the god Saruda-hiko
Edo period (1603-1868)
Wood, *gofun*, human hair
31 x 20 cm
Matsushita Art Museum, Kagoshima; inv. no. E1-15

In early times, no masks were used in ritual *Kagura*. Since the beginning of the early modern age (about 1568-1867), masks related to figures of Japanese mythology and the folklore tradition were introduced for performances. Out of the abundant variety of old masks that were inherited, some were

chosen as patterns and models for the *Kagura* masks which have been produced since in unlimited variety.

The mask collection of the late Kensuke Matsushita is rich in all sorts of Japanese masks. The old examples of *oni* and *kami* masks in the exhibition not only represent the roots of *Nô* masks, but also reveal traditional conceptions of demons and gods in Japan.

B) *KAGURA* HANDPROPS AND MUSICAL INSTRUMENTS

2.10 A-B TORIMONO I
Kagura handprops: a) *shaku* (scepter);
B) *sensu* (fan)
Umezu-Kagura performed in Umeji-mura, Honkawane-machi, Shizuoka Prefecture
Wood, paper
A) 41 x 6.5 cm; B) 28 cm long
Ikeda Masao

2.11 A-D TORIMONO II
Kagura handprops: A,B) *yumi, ya* (bow and arrow of Hachiman); C) *hana-zutsu* (paper bag); D) *oni-no-nusa* (demon's scepter)

2.11 D

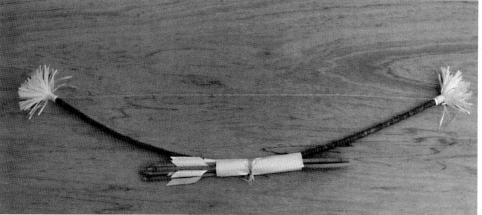

2.11 A, B

2.8

2.54

New; made by hand for the *Kagura* performance at the winter festival of Umeji, the so-called *Umezu-Kagura*, performed in Umeji-mura, Honkawane-machi, Shizuoka Prefecture
Wood, paper, foil, string
A,B) Large bow: 120 cm, arrow 52 cm long; small bow: 54 cm, arrow 30 cm long; C): 43 cm long; D): 80 cm long
Ikeda Masao

2.12 A-F SIX GOHEI (SYMBOLIC OFFERINGS)
Shintoistic *Kagura* handprops
New
Bamboo, paper
60 x 60 cm (single height: 55.8 and 65.4 cm)
Tsubouchi Memorial Theatre Museum, Waseda University

2.13 A-B A) SUZU (HANDSTICK BELLS) AND B) HINOMARU ÔGI (FAN)
Shintoistic *Kagura* handprops
1973, Shiogama Shrine, Miyagi
A): wood, lacquer, metal; B): paper, wood
A): 33 x 12 cm
Günter Zobel

Many handprops for the performances of *Sato-Kagura* are simply made objects, prepared just before the festival. In addition to a *shaku* and a *gohei*, which are carried by dancers as Shintoistic ritual requisites, there is the suzu used to call on the gods through sound. To characterize the gods to whom a dance may be dedicated, simply modeled miniatures of their iconographic attributes are manufactured in wood and paper. The bow and arrows of Hachiman, god of warriors and war, exemplify this. Among the handprops of *Umezu-Kagura*, the paper bag fixed on a bamboo grip, called *hana-zutsu*, is very special: a rain of gold glitter is sprinkled on the believers as a blessing which is said to be derived from Buddhist custom. This proves that in some regions the term *suijaku-honzui* (all Shinto *kami* are incarnations of the Buddha and Bodhisattvas) is as applicable to *Kagura* as it is to other forms of folk belief (*minkan shinkô*). The triangular framework for the demon in the *Oni-mai* (demon's dance) is called *oni-no-nusa* (demon's scepter) and is found only in the *Umezu-Kagura*, which was performed at various places in Germany and Europe in the summer of 1996.

2.14 TAIKO (STICK DRUM)
Musical instrument of Shiiba-Kagura
Shôwa period (1926-88)
Wood, leather, rope
55 x 43 cm
Tsubouchi Memorial Theatre Museum, Waseda University

2.15 YOKUBUE (FLUTE)
Musical instrument for *Kagura*
Shôwa period (1926-88)
Wood, lacquer and strings
44.5 x 2 cm
Günter Zobel

2.16 DOBYOSHI OR TEBIRAGANE (HAND CYMBALS)
Musical instrument for *Yamabushi-Kagura*
1996, Ôhazama-cho, Iwate
Metal
16.8 cm (diameter of each part)
Tsubouchi Memorial Theatre Museum, Waseda University

2.12

2.12

2.12

2.12

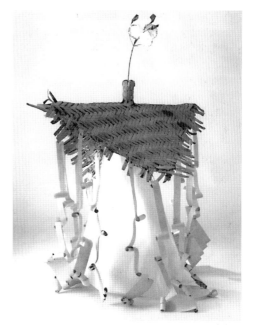

2.21C

2.21A

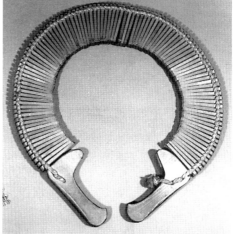

2.24A

c) HATS AND COSTUMES

2.17/2.18 TORI-KABUTO (HEADGEAR)
Hats for *Yamabushi-Kagura* in Take-mura, Ôhazama-cho, Iwate-ken, with a male and female chicken on top
Shôwa period (1926-88)
Cloth and paper
Each: 73.6 cm (high) x 35 cm (wide)
Hayachinedake Kagura Hozonkai

One of the most famous *Kagura* performances in Japan is held every year on August 1 in front of the Hayachine Shrine at the foot of Mount Hayachine—a *rei-zan*, a mountain where the souls of the dead are believed to dwell-as part of the ritual festival of the so-called *Yamabushi*, an esoteric sect of mountain ascetics. The *Yamabushi-Kagura* at that location has a history of about 500 years. In addition to the flute (*yokobue*), which remains behind the curtain throughout the dances as the voice of the invisible gods, a big drum is located just at the front of the *Kagura* stage. It is vigorously beaten on both sides with long sticks to provide the dancers with the rhythmical pattern for their ecstatic steps and jumps. The drummer facing the stage, who sometimes recites a ritual text, is flanked by two players of the *dobyôshi* (hand cymbals) which yield a loud metallic sound reminiscent of the bell at the entrance of a Shinto shrine, where one tries to evoke the gods by similar sounds to listen to one's prayers.

A special headgear of the *Yamabushi-Kagura* is the so-called *torikabuto* which, with its flaps on both sides of the dancer's head, recalls a similarly shaped helmet of the *Bugaku* tradition. However, here it is topped by the colorful figure of a chicken. For the dance called *Tori-no-mai*, the dancers represent the mythological first pair of gods, Izanami and Izanagi. A female and a male chicken symbolize the beginning of this world's reproductive nature, thus forming the Yin-Yang complex. Moreover, in Japanese folk belief it is said that the cry of the chicken has the power to drive evil and bad spirits away. In many cultures, however, birds represent the souls of the dead who became gods, according to beliefs manifested in their successors' shamanistic rites.

2.19/2.20 KAGURA-ISHO (KAGURA COSTUMES)
Kariginu (hunting cloak) and *happi* (jacket) for the Sambasô ritual dance of *Kagura* performed at the Ageô Andô-Shashû-*Kagura*, Ageô City, Saitama Prefecture
Shôwa period (1926-88)
Linen, silk embroidery
Kariginu: 170 cm wide x 134 cm long; *happi*: 220 cm wide x 105 cm long
Andô Gisaku

This *kariginu* for the Okina and *happi* for the Senzai-Sambasô worn in the ritual opening dance of a *Kagura* program belong to the costumes of the Andô-Shashû-*Kagura* in Ageô, Saitama Prefecture. Its tradition belongs to the so-called Edo-*Kagura*, famous for interweaving comical characters with slapstick-like acting among the more formal mythological figures of gods and heros.

DENGAKU

2.21A-C DENGAKUMAI-ISHO (COSTUME FOR RICEFIELD DANCE)
Costume from Môtsû-ji, Hiraizumi, Iwate Prefecture
Shôwa period (1926-88)
Wool, linen; straw hat
Upper garment: 157 x 92 cm; trousers:

2.19/20 C

87 x 37 cm on wooden frame
Tsubouchi Memorial Theatre Museum, Waseda University

2.22 DENGAKUMAI-TAIKO (DRUM FOR
RICEFIELD DANCE)
Drum and drumsticks from Môtsû-ji,
Hiraizumi, Iwate Prefecture
Beginning of Shôwa period (1920s-30s)
Wood, paper, strings
Drum: 56 cm diameter, 8 cm deep;
drumsticks: 50 cm long
Tsubouchi Memorial Theatre Museum,
Waseda University

The costume and drum are used for the
"Ennen-no mai," a ritual dance performed as a
prayer for long life at the Môtsû-ji of
Hiraizumi, a town in the northeastern part
of Japan. The earliest record of the "Ennen,"
still very much celebrated today at that temple, is from the early 16th century. The drum
is a rare example of one made of paper.

2.23 BINZASARA I (MUSICAL INSTRUMENT
FOR RICEFIELD DANCES)
Instrument to provide rhythmical sounds at
Dengaku dances at Môtsû-ji
Shôwa period (1926-88)
Wood, rope
50 cm diameter, 130 cm long, 9.5 cm wide
Tsubouchi Memorial Theatre Museum,
Waseda University

2.24A-B BINZASARA II (MUSICAL
INSTRUMENT FOR FESTIVAL DANCES)
Instrument to provide rhythmical sounds at
the Yuki-matsuri (snow festival) of the Izu
Shrine in Niino, Nagano Prefecture
Shôwa period (1926-88)
Wood, strings
50 cm diameter, 150 cm long, 13 cm wide
Tsubouchi Memorial Theatre Museum,
Waseda University

The binzasara, a major instrument for
Dengaku-related ritual dances, is made of
pieces of wood bound together. Dancers
take hold of two handles and make a rattling
sound while dancing.

2.25 HIRAGASA (UMBRELLA HAT)
Headgear of a Dengaku dancer at the Ôji
Shrine in Tokyo
Shôwa period (1926-88)
Paper
55 x 60 x 94 cm
Tsubouchi Memorial Theatre Museum,
Waseda University

2.26 HANAGASA (FLOWER HAT)
Headgear of a Dengaku dancer at the Ôji
Shrine in Tokyo
Shôwa period (1926-88)
Paper
60 x 45.5 cm
Tsubouchi Memorial Theatre Museum,
Waseda University

2.25   2.26

2.25 B

2.27 B

A flower hat for the role of the Komagaeshi (one who plays a drum) in the *Dengaku* at the Ôji Shrine, Tokyo. The hat was made anew each year and people competed to get it afterwards since it was regarded as a bringer of luck. This piece has survived because the dance was omitted in the 1942 festival, due to the war. The dance has not been performed since then.

2.27A-B DAISEN-JI EMAKI
Two copied paintings from a handscroll (*emaki*) originally at Daisen-ji, showing scenes of a) Dengaku and b) Taue
Colors on paper
A) 62.5 x 42 cm; B) 79.4 x 43 cm
Tsubouchi Memorial Theatre Museum, Waseda University

The original *emaki* of Oe 5th year (1398) was destroyed by fire in 1928 at the Daisen-ji in Tottori Prefecture. Copies of the two scenes were made shortly before that accident for the purpose of displaying them in the newly opened Tsubouchi Memorial Theatre Museum at Waseda University.

2.28 NISHI-KANASA-DENGAKU-ZU (HANGING SCROLL OF THE KANASAYAMA DENGAKU)
Hanging scroll depicting scenes of the Lion Dance, *Dengaku* dance, and a stilt acrobat
Meiji 23rd year (1890)
Colors on silk, mounted as hanging scroll
170 x 78 cm
Tsubouchi Memorial Theatre Museum, Waseda University

2.29A-B TAKA-ASHI (STILT)
Prop from Nishiure-*Dengaku*, Shizuoka Prefecture
Shôwa period (1926-88)
Wood
160.2 x 29.5 cm
Tsubouchi Memorial Theatre Museum, Waseda University

Examples of *Dengaku* which still include hopping on *taka-ashi* (a kind of pogo stick) are nowadays rare. In the medieval era, they were often included among the entertaining arts at temples. At present they can be observed at the Wakamiya Grand Festival in Nara and at the Sumiyoshi *Dengaku* in Hyôgo Prefecture.

RITUALS IMPORTED FROM CHINA

2.30 TSUINA
Mask for exorcistic ritual performance
End of 16th-beginning of 17th c.
Wood
27.5 x 21 cm
Matsushita Art Museum

2.31A-B TSUINA
Masks for exorcistic ritual performance
18th c.
Wood, *gofun*
A) 35 x 23 cm; B) 31.5 x 23 cm
Matsushita Art Museum, Kagoshima;
A) inv. no. E2-22; B) inv. no. F1-11

Tsuina masks are not *Sarugaku* masks. The Tsuina ritual originated in China and was imported in the 9th century. Members of the *Sarugaku* tradition were very often involved at the Tsuina ritual, usually held on the last day of the year to exorcize demons, especially those connected with epidemics. They used this kind of demon mask for that ritual. In addition to Tsuina masks, *In-Yô* masks appeared for a dance connected with Taoistic Yin-Yang (Jpn.: *In-Yô*) symbolism.

2.32 YO-NO-MEN (YANG MASK)
Mask for *Sarugaku* ritual performance of Jushi origin
18th c.
Wood, *gofun*
21.5 x 15 cm
Matsushita Art Museum, Kagoshima;
inv. no. G2-1

2.33 IN-NO-MEN (YIN MASK)
Mask for *Sarugaku* ritual performance of Jushi origin
18th c.
Wood, *gofun*
17 x 14 cm
Matsushita Art Museum, Kagoshima;
inv. no. G2-2

2.34 YO-NO-MEN (YANG MASK)
Mask for *Sarugaki* ritual performance of Jushi origin
18th c.
Wood, *gofun*
21 x 14 cm
Matsushita Art Museum, Kagoshima;
inv. no. E2-34

SARUGAKU

2.35 OKINA (BLESSING-BRINGING ANCESTOR)
Mask for *Sarugaku* ritual performance
17th c.
Wood, *gofun*
17.7 x 14.9 cm
Hakusan Shrine, Kuzemura, Gifu Prefecture

2.36 ONNA (CHUNEN; MIDDLE-AGED WOMAN)
Mask for *Sarugaku* ritual performance
17th c.
Wood, *gofun*
20 x 14.2 cm
Hakusan Shrine, Kuzemura, Gifu Prefecture

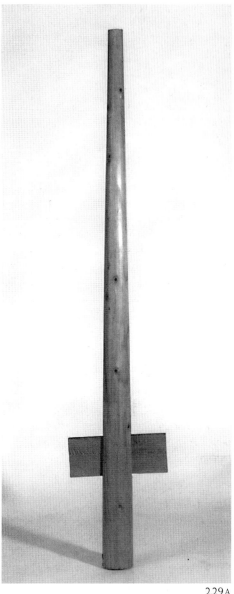

2.29A

2.29B

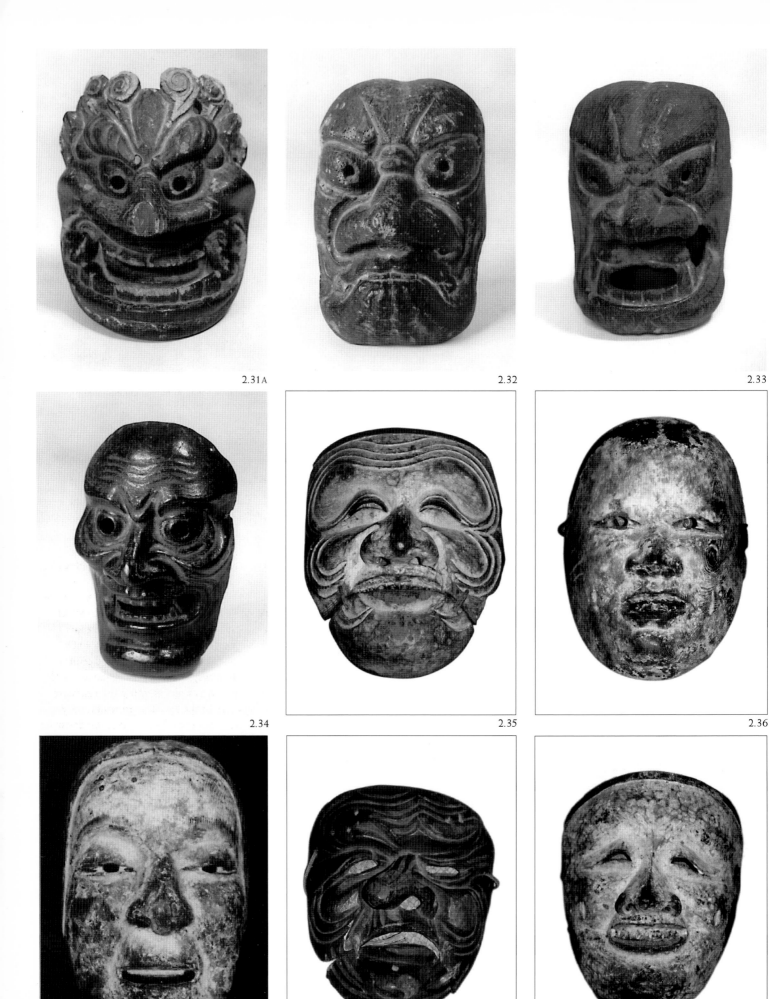

2.31A

2.32

2.33

2.34

2.35

2.36

2.37

2.38

2.39

2.40

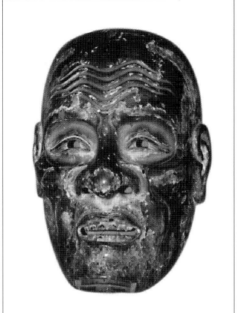

2.41

2.42

2.44

2.43

2.40 OTOKO (HYOTTOKO; MAN)
Mask for *Sarugaku* ritual performance
17th c.
Wood, *gofun*
21.8 x 14.7 cm
Hakusan Shrine, Kuzemura, Gifu Prefecture

2.41 JO (OLD MAN)
Mask for *Sarugaku* ritual performance
17th c.
Wood, *gofun*
20.9 x 15.8 cm
Hakusan Shrine, Kuzemura, Gifu Prefecture

2.42 KISHIN (HACHIMAKI; DEMONIC GOD)
Mask for *Sarugaku* ritual performance
17th c.
Wood, *gofun*
19.2 x 16.4 cm
Hakusan Shrine, Kuzemura, Gifu Prefecture

2.43 KI-MEN (JAKAN; DEMON MASK)
Mask for Sarugaku ritual performance
17th c.
Wood, *gofun*
25.6 x 21 cm
Hakusan Shrine, Kuzemura, Gifu Prefecture

2.44 TSUINA
Mask for exorcising-ritual performance
17th c.
Wood, *gofun*
28 x 23 cm
Hakusan Shrine, Kuzemura, Gifu Prefecture

The masks inherited by the Hakusan Shrine
in the mountain region of Gifu Prefecture
were created during a period just before *Nô*
masks began to be made in Kyoto and its
surrounding area. Masks for representing
demons, gods, and spirits were carved with
the intention of representing the dramatic
characters of the epic text in which they
appeared. Some of them reflect the desire to
copy the human face. It is appropriate to call
them "old *Nô* masks."

FURYU

2.45A-L DENGAKU-SARUGAKU-FURYU
Photo panel of four places with famous
Dengaku festivals having different perform-
ing characters and features: Sumiyoshi-Jinja,
Hyôgo; Nishiure, Shizuoka; Fujimori,
Shizuoka; *Yuki-matsuri*, Nagano
Günter Zobel

2.46 DAIHANNYA (GRAND DEMON)
Mask for exorcistic purposes (*akuma-barai*)
from Yamaguchi Prefecture
Meiji period (1868-1912)
Wood, *gofun*
36 x 29 cm
Thomas Immoos, Tokyo

2.37 WAKA-ONNA (YOUNG WOMAN)
Mask for *Sarugaku* ritual performance
17th c.
Wood, *gofun*
21.6 x 13.7 cm
Hakusan Shrine, Kuzemura, Gifu Prefecture

2.38 SAMBASO (KUROSHIKI-JO)
Mask for *Sarugaku* ritual performance
17th c.
Wood, *gofun*
17.4 x 14.6 cm
Hakusan Shrine, Kuzemura, Gifu Prefecture

2.39 ENMEIKAJA
Mask for *Sarugaku* ritual performance
17th c.
Wood, *gofun*
17.8 x 14.1 cm
Hakusan Shrine, Kuzemura, Gifu Prefecture

2.47 KANNAGARA-SHIKA-ODORI-GASHIRA (KANNAGARA DEER DANCE MASK)

Mask and cloth for representing a deer head and body from Tôno in Iwate Prefecture
Shôwa period (1926-88)
Colors on wood, linen
Mask: 61.5 cm wide x 63 cm high
Thomas Immoos, Tokyo

2.48 SASARA-SHISHIMAI-GASHIRA (SASARA LION DANCE MASK)

Mask and cloth for representing a lion's head and a face covering, for a dancer from Yokozawa village, Ôta-machi, Akita Prefecture
Meiji-Taishô periods (1868-1926)
Colored lacquer on wood, linen cloth
42 cm wide x 37 cm deep x 28 cm high
Tsubouchi Memorial Theatre Museum, Waseda University

This deer mask is an authentic one from the village of Tôno which became famous through Kunio Yanagita's Legends of Tôno (Tôno-*monogatari*).The dance of the deer (*shika-odori*) is an exorcistic festival rite mimicking the banning and hunting of deer which, like wild boars, were not welcome in ricefields.

2.49 KUROSHISHI-GASHIRA (BLACK LION MASK)

Mask and cloth for representing a lion's head and body from Nagai City, Okitama, Yamagata Prefecture
1996-97
Carved by Masato Shibuya; lacquered and colored by Tadahiro Eguchi
Head: wood, black and red lacquer, gold leaf, and horsetail hair; body: cotton and linen
Head: 35 cm high x 51.5 cm wide (ear to ear) x 43 cm long; body: 9.55 x 3.5 m
Masato Shibuya and Tadahiro Eguchi, Nagai

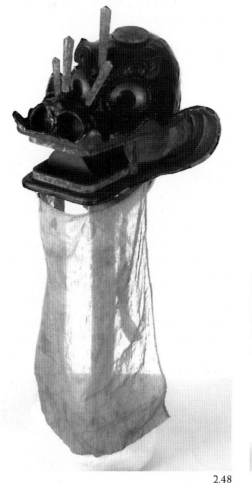

2.48

2.52

2.51

In the mountain regions of the western part of Yamagata Prefecture there are more than 140 villages for which the main event of their annual festivals is the lion dance. Ritual purification of all houses is accomplished by a "lion" running through the streets. Up to twelve dancers are under the linen "*maku*" (curtain) that forms the long body of the lion. The group changes constantly as the dancers carry the heavy (7-10 kg) lion head.

The rare black "lion" of Nagai City, where 42 varying traditions are still alive, is especially wild and aggressive. The outer appearance of this mystical creature resembles a serpent more than a lion. In fact, its creeping movements and the sudden attacks it makes while dancing are called "*ja-no-mai*," serpent's dance. Its deceptiveness is closely watched

by a guard who represents the strongest man of the village. He wears the costume (*keshi-mawashi*) of a *rikishi*, a powerful Sumo wrestler who in former times was discovered by the gods in the final bout of a Sumo competition held before the festival. This lion head, carved exclusively for the exhibition, replicates the oldest form preserved at the Somiya Shrine in Nagai, where the tradition dates back to the 14th century.

2.50 SURIZASARA

Instrument consisting of two bamboo sticks to create rhythmical sounds during the lion dance
Lower piece: 40 cm long, 3.5 cm diameter; upper piece: 29.5 cm long, 3 cm diameter
Tsubouchi Memorial Theatre Museum, Waseda University

This instrument of Japanese folk art is made of bamboo and makes a rustling sound when its split head is rubbed with a notched stick. This one is used at the Shiramatsu Festival in Chiba Prefecture.

2.51 KOKIRIKO

Rhythmic dancing batons from: A) *Kokiriko* Dance in Gokayama, Toyama Prefecture; B) *Ayako-mai* in Kashiwazaki, Niigata Prefecture; C) *Bon-odori* in Hirano, Shizuoka Prefecture

Three sets of two bamboo sticks each: A) plain bamboo (22.5 cm long); B) with color stripes (40 cm long); C) with white paper tassels at both ends of the sticks (65 cm long)
Tsubouchi Memorial Theatre Museum, Waseda University

While dancing, a player makes dry sounds by striking the sticks together, or he shakes and twirls them to augment the effect of his dance. Although the *Kokiriko* was a popular instrument during the Muromachi era (15th-16th centuries), it is now used only at a few festivals.

2.52 KANNOGAKU-NO ÔUCHIWA (LARGE FAN OF KANNOGAKU)
Handprop of Kannôgaku festival in Buzen City, Fukuoka Prefecture
Shôwa period (1926-88)
Paper, bamboo
81.8 cm diameter, 135.2 cm long
Tsubouchi Memorial Theatre Museum, Waseda University

In a large group of young drummers who perform the dance rite of begging for rain with loud sounds, there are two men waving these large fans up and down as if getting rid of insects. Indeed, this was the other purpose of former ricefield rites to which this popular present-day festival belongs.

2.53A-C ÔNIKENBAI-NO MEN AND ISHO
A) White and red masks; b) one costume set of Iwasaki-Ônikenbai, Iwate Prefecture
A) Masks
ca. 30th year of Shôwa (1955)
Wood, *gofun*, colors
White mask: 21 x 17 cm; red mask: 21.5 x 17.2 cm
Owner: Masumi Oikawa
B) Costume set (5 pieces)
Wool
Migoro 83 x 120 cm; *hakama* 70 x 56 cm; *oguchi* 56 x 71 cm; *muneate* 60 x 178 cm; *nugitare* 65.5 x 60 cm
Owner: Yuichi Wada
All parts of this loan made possible with the assistance of the Oni Museum, Kitakami City, Iwate Prefecture

At more than 120 places in the prefecture of Iwate in northern Japan, a form of dance that calls on and praises Buddha (*nembutsu-odori*) is performed in six different guises. One of these consists of four or five terrifying demons masks called *"oni-kenbai."* The word *kenbai* derives from an exorcistic term used by *Yamabushi* priests when banning evil spirits and purifying the places where they have been. The four colors of the masks–blue, red, white and black–represent the four seasons and directions. In some cases, a fifth mask in yellow is added as a symbol of the center, at the point where the four directions intersect, in accordance with ancient Taoistic iconography. The masks are also regarded as incarnations of the Five Great Myôô (*Godai Myôô*), the great, fearsome Kings of Wisdom of Esoteric Buddhism.

They consist of Fudô and the four deities who surround him.

KAZARI-MONO (SPECIAL ORNAMENTS)

2.54A-C CHI-NO-WA (RING OF REED)
Festival properties for exorcistic rites, from the Akunami Shrine in Fujieda, Shizuoka Prefecture
A) *Chi-no-wa*: new; reed, bamboo; 210 cm diameter, 15 cm thick layer of reed
B) *Chi-no-wa-kazuri*: attributes in the form of two dolls (*hitogata*) made of string and cloth in red and white; 70 x 80 cm
C) *Chi-no-wa-waku*: 3 bamboo rings that form the frame of the *chi-no-wa*; 3-4 m long, 7 cm wide
Ikeda Masao

On the last day of June, a purification rite called *"nagoshi"* is held at local Shinto shrines. Part of this rite entails passing through a ring of reeds; after doing so, all evils and diseases are believed to have been eliminated. Here in the middle of the ring, two figures in human shape (*hitogata*) hang. When a person passing through the ring comes into physical contact with these red and white fetishes, he or she is believed to have been freed of any evil influences from the past six months.

2.55 ERINU; KAGURA-BUTAI-KAZARI (KAGURA STAGE ORNAMENTS)
18 paper cut-outs (*erimono*) from the canopy over the Katsura-*Kagura* stage in Morozuka-mura, Miyazaki Prefecture
Shôwa period (1926-88)
White paper
17 pieces: 43 x 32 cm
Tsubouchi Memorial Theatre Museum, Waseda University

At some *Kagura* in the countryside there is a custom of suspending a kind of canopy, called *biyatsukai*; i.e., a square wooden frame to which paper ornaments are fixed on strings, over the stage or floor where the dances will be performed (*mai-komi*). Sometimes these ornaments are only small paper leaflets in five colors, representing the five kinds of crops in the fields, as is the case with the Umezu-*Kagura* (nos. 2.10, 2.11). At the end of the program, members of the public are allowed to grab them and take them home for good luck.

At the Katsura-*Kagura*, paper cut-outs called *erime* are hung from a small canopy called *"clouds for the dragon's image"* (*ryûzu-no kumo*). There are nineteen types of pictorial motifs including a swinging dragon, the sun and moon above a decorated Shinto shrine

2.53A

2.53B

2.53C

gate (*torii*), a foal in bamboo grass, deer under patterns of maple leaves, and a dragon under the rising sun. All these figures, artistically cut out by the villagers, are a form of offering to the gods who protect their shrine. Thus, the paper cutouts function not merely as ornaments, but also greet and celebrate the gods, who supposedly visit that night to enjoy the *Kagura* performance and bring blessings to the village.

III. COURT, SHRINE, AND TEMPLE:
Gigaku, Bugaku, and *Gyôdô*

CHIDO AND SHISHI

CHIDO (CLEARING THE WAY)

The purification of the route taken by a procession is an important part of performances and is related to many events in Japan. At the beginning of a festival (*matsuri*) or a theatrical performance, such a procession (*michiyuki*) is considered to be an integral part of the whole occasion. This purification of the way entered Japanese folk theater with *gigaku*. Masks with prominent phallic noses, as can be seen from the Chidô of *gigaku* to the Tengû of *kagura*, are characteristic of all these events.

The wild lion dances of Shishi, imported from the Asian continent, also became an integral part of Japanese theatrical arts. Even with a piece like Kagami-jishi ("Mirror of Lions"), they entered *kabuki*. Shishi lion dances are popular throughout Asia. The few examples selected here are important for a better understanding of the history of the diffusion of these dances.

2/3.1 GIGAKU MASK OF CHIDO
Replica of an 8th-c. original from the Shôsôin Imperial Repository, Nara
Wood, pigments, *gofun*
31.5 cm high
Tsubouchi Memorial Theatre Museum, Waseda University

2/3.2 DANCER OF CHIDO: MASK AND DRESS
Reconstructed by Yoshiaka Sachio according to original 8th-c. masks and costumes from the Shôsôin Imperial Repository
Fabrics dyed with vegetable dyes
Life-size
Tôdai-ji, Nara

2/3.3 GYODO MASK OF HANATAKA ("HIGH NOSE") OR ÔBU ("KING'S DANCE")
One of a set of three masks
Kamakura period, 13th c.
Wood, *gofun*
21.8 x 15.4 x 17.5 cm
Tamukeyama Hachiman Shrine, Nara

As the dancer with the Tengû mask in processions of later times, Chidô, as well as Hanataka, rid the processional route of bad influences. This mask is one of the most important masks of this type preserved in Japan.

SHISHI (LION DANCE)

2/3.4 SHISHI FROM SHISHI DANCE; WITH TWO DANCERS HIDDEN UNDER A FUR-LIKE REPRESENTATION OF THE BODY
Photograph
Terracotta figurine (original); excavated in Turfan, Central Asia
T'ang period (618-907)
Courtesy of Tanabe Saburosuke

2/3.5 CHINESE LION DANCE; WITH TWO DANCERS HIDDEN UNDER A FUR-LIKE REPRESENTATION OF THE BODY
Photographer: Inoue Hiromichi
Contemporary
Courtesy of Kokuritsu Minzokugaku Hakubutsukan

2/3.6 SHISHI DANCERS OF A GIGAKU IN FRONT OF THE DAIBUTSU-DEN, TODAI-JI, NARA
Photographer: Inoue Hiromichi
Courtesy of Tôdai-ji

Several attempts have been made over the years to revive the extinguished *gigaku*. Based on scientific analyses, costumes have been rewoven with the same materials and dyed with the vegetable dyes used in the 7th and 8th centuries. Contemporary *busshi* (sculptors of Buddhist images) have recreated the old masks. A re-enactment of *gigaku* was held on the occasion of the restoration of the roof of the Daibutsu-den at Tôdai-ji. The script for these new performances doesn't follow exactly the description given by the only written source, the *Kyôkunshô* of 1233 by Koma Chikazane (1177-1242). He was a member of the Dancers of the Right, related to Korean heritage.

2/3.7 GIGAKU MASK OF SHISHI-KO,
Nara Period, 8th c.
Wood with traces of pigment
28.8 high x 19.3 cm
British Museum, London

This is one of the few examples of an authentic *gigaku* mask in a Western collection. Until 1954, it was in the collection of Tomitarô Hara and was originally in the possession of the Tôdai-ji, Nara.

2/3.1

2/3.9

2/3.4

2/3.8

2/3.8 MASK OF SHISHI (SHISHI-GASHIRA)
USED IN GYODO
Kamakura period, 13th c.
Wood with red lacquer
38 x 47 x 51 cm
Tamukeyama Hachiman Shrine, Nara

02/3.9 SHISHI DANCE; DETAIL FROM THE
ILLUSTRATED HANDSCROLLS OF NENJU
GYOJI (EVENTS OF THE YEAR)
Photograph
Courtesy of Tanabe Saburosuke

The long history of Shishi, the lion dance,
is shown in this small section from a handscroll. It portrays a few examples ranging
from Central Asia to modern China; 7th-8th
century gigaku; and handscrolls describing
the role of Shishi in the sequence of annual
events.

COURT, SHRINE, AND TEMPLE: GIGAKU, BUGAKU, GYODO

INTRODUCTION

3.1 SHINZEI-KOGAKU-ZU
Artist: Fujiwara Michinori (–1159)
Modern copy of 1755 handscroll showing
theatrical performances of the mid-Heian
Period
26.3 x 1420 cm

Tsubouchi Memorial Theatre Museum,
Waseda University University

The scroll is named after Michinori's name
as a monk, Shinzei. This most important
12th-century testimony of representations
of early continental theater imports is preserved in a copy of 1755, today at the Art
University, Tokyo. The copy contains an
additional section with other representations
of bugaku dancers.

3.2 SCREEN (BYOBU) WITH REPRESENTA-
TION OF TWELVE BUGAKU DANCES
Modern copy of an unknown screen
Probably 18th c.
Paper, pigments
93.5 x 319 cm
Tanabe Saburosuke

Shown, from right to left, is part of the
orchestra, with the great drum and gong.
Two Ama dancers with ornamental paper
masks are paired with the old couple of Ni-
no-mai. This was required by the rule pairing dances with dancers in a performance.
Next to Ni-no-mai, dancers of Shinnô-raku
appear in armor, nowadays used for
Taiheiraku. On the top of the fourth and
fifth panels, the children's dances – Kochô
(Butterfly) and Karyôbin (Heavenly Bird) –
are represented. At the bottom of panel four,
the Saisôrô dancer is visible in his white
costume. Ônintei, (panel four), Taishukutoku
(panel five), as well as Komaboko, a dance
with long sticks, comprise part of the Koma-
gaku, dances supposedly imported from
Korea. The atmosphere of courtly dances is
well represented here.

3.3 BUGAKU: KOKONCHOMONSHU
Author: Tachibana Narisue
Block-printed books (7 vols.)
1770 (copy); original: 1230-31, finished in
1254
22.5 x 16.1 cm
Bayerische Staatsbibliothek, Munich; inv.
no. 12-L Jap. 1352

The Kokonchômonshu is a large collection of
events of court life, assembled by Tachibana
Narisue, a 13th-century courtier. The book
was published in a most useful, annotated
translation by Hans Eckardt in 1956.

3.4 SHUKO JISHU
Block-printed books (17 vols.)
1800
Bayerische Staatsbibliothek, Munich

The purpose of this important collection of
printed books was to publish information
about antique objects from famous collections. Paintings, inkstones, and arms and

3.5 A

3.5 B

armor are depicted. Most important are the
numerous woodcuts illustrating the gigaku
and bugaku masks of many old temples and
shrines, including Hôryû-ji, Tôdai-ji,
Tamukeyama Shrine, and Itsukushima
Shrine, Hiroshima. Masks which have been
destroyed since 1800 are preserved as
images in this collection of books.

3.5 A-H EIGHT STENCIL PRINTS WITH
REPRESENTATIONS OF BUGAKU DANCES
Artist: Emma Bormann (1887-1974)
A) Ringa in front of the Great Drum
(dadaiko); B) Sanju; C) Bairo-hajin-raku;
D) court dance of the Right style;
E) Komaboko; F-G) court dance of the Left
style; H) Dancer of Ryô-ô
ca. 1967
Paper, colors, stencil-print techniques
A) 53.5 x 38.2 cm; B) 43 x 34 cm; C) 40.5 x
30.5 cm; D) 42.5 x 36.7 cm; E) 32 x 49.4 cm;
F) 28 x 56.6 cm; G) 35.7 x 69.7 cm;
H) 43 x 30.8 cm
Uta Schreck, Tokyo

3.5 C

3.5 E

3.5 F

3.8

3.5 D

3.5 G

3.9 A,B

In the 1960s, the Austrian artist Emma Bormann, well-known for her grand landscape paintings and prints of the late 1920s from Europe, America, China and Japan, was invited to performances of dancers and musicians of the Imperial Court, represented here. These artists are, and were, descendants of the old families practicing *bugaku* and *gagaku* (concerts without dancing) since the Heian period.

THE SIGNIFICANCE OF HEAVENLY MUSIC

3.6 MUSICIANS FROM SHINZEI-KOGAKU-ZU
Photograph (see no. 3.1)

The orchestra members depicted in the Shinzei-kogaku-zu wear Chinese costumes and their instruments are of continental Asian provenance.
3.7 BUGAKU COSTUME FOR MUSICIAN
20th c.
Silk
Life-size
Kunaicho (Imperial Household Agency)

White trousers (*sashinuki*) are worn under the white *shita-kasane*, which is embroidered with Imperial crests and has red seams. A long

train embellishes the back. The costume is held together by a Chinese-style lacquered belt with jade-like stone applications (*ishitai*). The shoes (*shikai*) made of textile strings are used only in *bugaku*. A pointed headdress with an extension down the back is called *tori kabuto*. The *tori kabuto* of Hayachine Kagura, in section II of the exhibit, imitate this type of courtly headgear.

3.8 BUGAKU: DADAIKO, THE BIG DRUM
ca. 1970
Wood, colors
Miniature of actual *dadaiko*
44 cm high
Japan Society, Inc.

3.9 A-B A) BUGAKU: SHO, PERCUSSION INSTRUMENT
Contemporary
Wood, bamboo, lacquer, metal
B) BUGAKU FLUTE
Contemporary
Wood
Tsubouchi Memorial Theatre Museum, Waseda University

String, wind, and percussion instruments are used in *gagaku* (concerts without dancers) and *bugaku* dance performances. String

instruments are used only in *gagaku*. The *shô*, made of bamboo, needs to be warmed before being used and produces an especially harmonious sound. The music is divided into that of the Left and that of the Right. Music of the Left consists of: Tô-gaku (all music imported from T'ang-period China); so-called Rinyû-gaku (Indian music); and Shinsei-gaku (music created in Japan). Music of the Right consists of Koma-gaku (Korean music); music from the Korean state of Bokkai (P'o-hai; 712-926); and the *gigaku*. In Asia, the left side is considered more important than the right. Therefore, "modern" music, brought back by a member of the last official embassy to the T'ang court in 838, was assigned to the Left in the 9th century. As a consequence, foreign music performed at the Imperial court underwent a complete change and was adapted to these new rules.

IN THE CONTEXT OF HEAVENLY BEINGS

3.10 GYODO MASK OF BODHISATTVA (BOSATSU-MEN)
Kamakura Period, 13th c.
Wood, traces of pigment
23 cm high
British Museum, London

3.11 GYODO MASK OF BODHISATTVA
(BOSATSU-MEN)
Kamakura Period, 13th c.
Wood, traces of pigment, metal
British Museum, London

3.12 GYODO MASK OF BUDDHA
(NYORAI-MEN)
Edo Period (1615-1868)
Wood, gold paint
39.7 x 19.3 x 24.2 cm
Jôshin-ji, Tokyo

3.13 GYODO MASK OF BODHISATTVA
(BOSATSU-MEN)
Edo period (1615-1868)
48.4 x 18.1 x 24.3 cm
Jôshin-ji, Tokyo

3.14 GYODO MASK OF BISHAMON-TEN
From an original set of 28 masks of
Nijûhachi-bushu
Kamakura Period, 14th c.
Wood, pigments
25.8 x 18.6 cm
Tokyo National Museum; inv. no. CO449

As described by Tanabe Saburosuke in his
essay, masked dancers represented various
sacred beings of the Buddhist pantheon.
This mask is a unique masterpiece. This type
of Buddhist mask and those of *bugaku* were
carved by sculptors of Buddhist images, not
by specialized mask carvers, as was the case
with *nô* masks.

3.15 BUGAKU: BATO DANCED BY A BOY
DANCER, YACHI HACHIMAN SHRINE,
KAHOKU CITY, YAMAGATA PREFECTURE
Poster
85 x 65 cm
Japan Society, Inc.

Two of the eleven dances preserved for centuries in the Hayashi family are children's
dances (*dôbu*). The Hayashi family *bugaku* was
designated an Intangible Cultural Asset of
Folk Art. This performance took place on the
occasion of the Yashi Donga Matsuri, 1994.

3.16 BUGAKU DISPLAY FIGURINE (NINGYO)
OF KOCHO, THE BUTTERFLY DANCE—THE
DANCE PAIRED WITH KARYOBIN, DANCE
OF THE HEAVENLY BIRDS
Contemporary
Paper, wood, silk
23 cm high
The Ayervais Collection

One delightful feature of *bugaku* is the
graceful dances of children. The most
important of these, the pair dances of the
Heavenly Birds (Karyôbin) and the Butterfly
(Kôcho), are described in the *Genji-monogatari*.

3.10

3.11

3.13

3.12

THE TRAJECTORY OF ASIAN PERFORMANCES

3.17 CASE FOR SHAKA RELICS FROM
KUCHA, CENTRAL ASIA
Two Photographs: Complete view; detail
with dancers wearing animal masks
6th c.
Wood, pigments
32.3 cm high
Tokyo National Museum

Very few remains of Chinese theater traditions before the Yüan period (1278-1368)
have been preserved. A wooden casket
decorated with a circle of masked dancers,
found in Central Asia, is one of these rare,
surviving examples. It is especially interesting because of the dancers disguised as
animals.

3.15

3.19A,B

3.28A,B

3.29A,B

3.31A,B

3.23

3.18 MASK FOR EXORCISM FROM
KUEICHOU PROVINCE, CHINA
Replica of a Chinese original
Wood, pigment
Gotô Hajime

This demon mask belongs among those few
preserved Chinese wooden masks that bear a
striking similarity to Japanese demon masks
(*kishin*).

3.19/3.20 BUGAKU COSTUME FOR BAIRO-
HAJIN-RAKU
Two sets of *ikan-hô* (vests) and *hô* (blouses)
19th c.
Silk
Life-size
Tokyo National Museum

The *bugaku* dance Bairo, or Bairo-hajin-raku,
which does not require masks, is performed
in a red costume with a vest called *ikan-hô*,
which is adorned with wave-like ornaments.
The dress was used during the Heian Period

by the Imperial Guards. In the Shinzei-
kogaku-zu, the dancers of Bairo still wear
armor similar to that worn nowadays in the
Taiheiraku dance. The Bairo dance is
performed with a long spear and rectangular
shield embellished with a flame-like ornament on the top. Such a shield can be found
in Tunhuang wall paintings (cave 217). The
dance also belongs to the so-called *bu-no-mai*
(Ch.: *wu-wu*; "martial dances"). In China, wu-
wu has been a classical music term since the
end of the 6th century. In contrast to these
dances which have a military character,
those having a peaceful character are called
bun-no-mai (Ch.: *wen-wu*; "literature dances").

Bairo also forms part of the so-called Rinyû
Hachi Gaku, ("Eight Musical Pieces from
Rinyû"), eight dances grouped together after
1500. Rinyû is the term used for Southeast
Asia, or sometimes India. According to
historical sources and traditions, the music
was introduced in the 8th century by the
first Indian reaching Japanese soil, the priest

Bodhisena. Other sources attribute this
introduction to Buttetsu, a legendary monk
coming from Campa (Jpn.: Rinyû; Ch.: Lin-
yi), a Southeast Asian state in the area of
today's Vietnam. Hints of a remote Indian
origin are preserved in a kind of prelude
played only in dances supposedly having an
"Indian" provenance.

3.21 FOUR BUGAKU DANCERS OF
TAIHEIRAKU
18th c.
Painting, paper, mineral pigments
16 x 43 cm
Gunhild Avitabile

Taiheiraku ("Music of Great Peace"), now
with the accoutrements of the martial dance
Shinnô-hajin-raku, was originally a lion
dance, but was performed since the Heian
Period in armor and with weapons. The
"Music of Great Peace" belongs also to the
group of martial dances mentioned before.
The armor and weapon represented in this

3.18

3.26

3.27

3.29

painting were transferred in 1690 to Taiheiraku from the time of the Shinnô-hajinraku dance represented in the Shinzei-kogaku-zu. They did not survive this period. This latter dance was imported in the Nara Period from China, where it was known as P'o-chen-yüeh-chü and described a martial event of 620. It was performed in grand style at the T'ang Imperial Court on official occasions and was known throughout Asia.

3.22 A-B BUGAKU DANCERS: A) RA RYO-O AND B) NASORI

Pair of hanging scrolls
Artist: Tsuruzawa Moriyuki (?-1816)
Signed: Hôgen Tansen Fujiwara Moriyuki *hitsu* ("painted"); and seal: Tsuruzawa. Signed on near margins by the calligrapher: Tsune san e ("to Mr. Tsune")
Late 18th–early 19th c.
Ink and colors on silk
A) 96.8 x 41 cm (without mounts); B) 97.8 x 40.6 cm
Translations of poems by Naoko Yaegashi
Collection of The Newark Museum, Gift of Edith Kurstin, 1982

A) Poem from Ra Ryô-ô:
As a flower trembles
to a shining light
the dancer's sleeves shimmer;
lost in his own movement,
we feel our spirit refreshed.

B) Poem from Nasori:
From the isolated countryside,
now we remain in Miyako [Kyoto]
the beauty of this *bugaku* form
is a wonder to my eyes.

3.23 FIGURE OF A BUGAKU DANCER OF RYO-O,

19th c.
Hirado porcelain
32 cm high
Barbra Okada

3.24 BUGAKU RA RYO-O, YACHI HACHIMAN SHRINE, KAHOKU CITY, YAMAGATA PREFECTURE

Poster
85 x 65 cm
Gunhild Avitabile

This poster was created on the occasion of the Yachi Donga Matsuri in 1992 (see no. 3.15).

3.25 BUGAKU: MASK OF RYO-O

18th c.
Wood, lacquer, gold leaf
Courtesy of the British Museum, London

3.26 BUGAKU MASK OF RYO-O

18th c.
Wood, lacquer, gold leaf
38.3 cm high
Gunhild Avitabile

3.27 BUGAKU MASK OF RYO-O

Contemporary
Wood, lacquer, gold leaf
Tsubouchi Memorial Theatre Museum, Waseda University; inv. no, 3763

3.28 Bugaku costume for Ryô-ô; Set of Ryôtô (vest) and Hô (Blouse)

19th c.
Silk
Life-size
Tokyo National Museum

(Ra) Ryô-ô, the most famous dance of the Left, together with Nasori, its Right-style partner piece, has been the most popular *bugaku* dance over the centuries. It belongs to the great ceremonial works for the *bugaku*. Masks are preserved in many temples. The dancer wears a golden mask with a dragon on top. In addition to the rich, red brocade dress, bound at the wrists and ankles, the dancer holds a long stick and performs an "in" (*mudrâ*), named hand gestures that reveal a probable origin in India. The oldest defi-

3.29

nitely identified *bugaku* mask, a dry lacquer one from the Ryûsen-ji in Nara, is now in the Fujita Art Museum, Osaka, and can be dated to the 8th century. The dance is closely connected with rain and is often performed in temples and Shintô shrines when there is excessive rain or drought. Its history is one of the most complex of all dances imported from the continent. The golden mask with a dragon on top of the head reveals a dance provenance of multiple sources. The dragon is an old Asian symbol for water, transformed in China from the original Indian snake (*nâgâ*) into a mythical dragon. Such an origin explains the relationship of the dance to the above-described functions.

The golden face, with deeply carved, stylized wrinkles, which look as if they had been created in metal, is also reminiscent of metal masks used to protect the faces of warriors in battle. It inspired one of the

3.25

3.30

3.32

3.33

historical interpretations of this dance, which is that it is the Japanese version of the famous dance "The King of Lan-ling Exits to Battle." This interpretation from the 6th century describes the triumph of the young king of Chou, who hid his beautiful face behind a ferocious-looking mask in battle. This description of the dance reveals a characteristic element of *bugaku*'s early history, when many attempts were made to connect preserved traditions with elements of Chinese culture, which was considered superior.

3.29 BUGAKU MASK AND COSTUME OF NASORI
Contemporary
Mask: wood, lacquer, pigments; costume: silk
Life-size
Tsubouchi Memorial Theatre Museum, Waseda University

3.30 BUGAKU MASK OF NASORI
19th c.
Wood, lacquer, pigment
28.1 x 18 cm
Tokyo National Museum; inv. no. C1128-2TNM

3.31 BUGAKU COSTUME OF NASORI; SET OF RYOTO (VEST) AND HO (BLOUSE)
19th c.
Silk
Life-size
Tokyo National Museum

Nasori, pair dance of Ryô-ô, a dance of the Right style, is supposed to be of Korean origin. One or two dancers in blue-green costumes, similar in cut to the ones of Ryô-o, and wearing blue or green masks, perform this work. The name of the dance appears in a 780 temple inventory, but no representa-

tion of Nasori can be found in the Shinzei-kogaku-zu. Although Nasori is one of the most popular dances, very little is known about its origin. One interpretation explains the dance as two dragons playing in the sun. Nevertheless, its pairing with Ryô-ô leads us to conclude that it must have been an important dance, strongly connected with shamanistic elements. In its original form, it was probably brought over from the Korean peninsula during the early historical period. The construction of the masks, with moveable eyeballs and a loose chin, adds to the drama of the representation.

3.32 REPLICA OF A MASK CALLED SONBI ("SCHOLAR") FROM HAHOE VILLAGE IN SOUTHEAST KOREA
Wood
Pre-16th c.
Tsubouchi Memorial Theatre Museum, Waseda University

In the 1960s, a group of masks was discovered in the village of Hahoe. Their existence could be documented as far back as the 16th century; according to the Korean scholar Chewon Kim, these masks may well go back to the Koryo period (935-1392). All show characteristics which relate them to *bugaku* masks. Technical criteria such as the loose or inserted chin are reminiscent of a mask like the Nasori, and the slit half-moon-shaped eyes are similar to *bugaku* masks from the Koma-gaku (Korean music) group, considered to be among the earliest imports from the continent because of their style and iconography. One of the female masks is marked on the cheeks with a stylized flower similar to that found on each cheek of Shintoriso as well as on contemporary Korean folk masks.

3.33 BUGAKU MASK OF SHINTORISO, KASUGA SHRINE
Photograph
1185 (original mask)
Wood, pigments
21.5 x 16.5 cm
Gunhild Avitabile

3.34 KOREAN MASK OF "SMALL SORCERESS"
1930s
Papier-mâché
25 x 24 cm
Tsubouchi Memorial Theatre Museum, Waseda University

3.35 BUGAKU DANCER OF AMA-MAI AT SHITENNO-JI, OSAKA
Photograph
Courtesy of Shitennô-ji Kongakubu (Cultural Treaure Administration), Osaka

3.36 BUGAKU PAPER MASK (ZO-MEN) OF AMA-MAI
17th–19th c.
Paper, ink
30.4 x 22.1 cm
Tokyo National Museum; inv. no. C 1149

Masks nos. 3.33, 3.34, 3.35 have in common an ornament on the cheeks; no. 3.36 shows a stylized form of this ornament. The *bugaku* mask Shintoriso, identified as a male mask because of the moustache, is also adorned with this type of female cosmetic attribute. In Korea, this feature is found not only on female masks of folk theater, but also on the shamanistic pillars called Tchangsöng ("spirit pillars") at the entrance to many Korean villages. The history of these ornaments goes back to Central Asia. The dance Shintoriso was considered comical and might contain cross-sexual references.

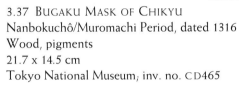

3.36A

3.36B

3.39

3.37 BUGAKU MASK OF CHIKYU
Nanbokuchô/Muromachi Period, dated 1316
Wood, pigments
21.7 x 14.5 cm
Tokyo National Museum; inv. no. CD465

Chikyû is one of the dances of good luck believed to be of Korean origin. Its pair dance also manifests good luck. The laughing face reveals the characteristics of the mask's provenance. Formerly, it was at the Amano Shrine, Koya-san.

3.38 BUGAKU MASK OF KITOKU
Formerly at Amano Shrine, Koya-san
Nanbokuchô Period (1333-92)
Wood, pigments, lacquer
21.8 x 15.2 cm
Tokyo National Museum; inv. no. CD1147

3.39 BUGAKU: KITOKU
Painting; segment from a handscroll
18th c.
Paper, mineral pigment
33.4 x 38.5 cm
Gunhild Avitabile

Kitoku is mentioned as early as 937 and belongs to dances having shamanistic meaning, which are probably of Korean origin. The dancer is dressed in a green dress, in the style of Dances of the Right. His important prop is a spear, which he uses as an instrument to pacify the spirits of the earth, in a way similar to that of Sanju, his Right-style pair dance. While the red mask of Sanju reveals a dignified but friendly expression, the Kitoku face of white or blue is severe, with firmly closed lips or with golden teeth biting into the lower lip. Kitoku's eyes, which are supposed to be golden, underline his demonic character, just as such eyes would in *nô*. As in many other pieces of

bugaku, interpretations of classical Chinese origin obscure the original meaning.

3.40 BUGAKU MASK OF AYAGIRI
From Sumiyoshi Taisha Shrine
Photograph
1161 (original)
19.9 x 15.3 cm (original)
Courtesy of Gunhild Avitabile

3.41 BUGAKU DANCER OF AYAGIRI AT SHITENNO-JI, OSAKA
Photograph
Courtesy of Shitennô-ji Kangakubu
(Cultural Treasure Administration), Osaka

Only two female dances using masks are known in *bugaku*: the comical dance Ni-no-mai, in which a woman with a grotesque swollen face appears, and the dance Ayagiri ("Cutting Silk Damask") of the Koma-gaku. The dance Ayagiri was mentioned for the first time in the 10th century. Originally performed by women, it became a dance for male dancers wearing female masks from the Heian Period on. The few preserved masks (in the Hôryû-ji, Nara, and also, originally, in Tsurugaoka-hachiman Shrine, Kamakura) show features which have led to the acceptance of an early Korean provenance for the dance.

Seen in the photograph, no. 3.40, the most beautiful masks for this dance are preserved in the Sumiyoshi Shrine close to the Shintennô-ji in Osaka. These masks are strongly influenced by the ideals of sculptural representations of Bodhisattva.

As can be seen from this short survey, the various masks included in the repertoire of *bugaku* well reflect different geographical origins.

3.40

3.41

3.43   3.46

3.47 A   3.47 B

3.49   3.50

Theatricality and Comical Sense in Continental Imports

A strong sense of comical entertainment runs like a thread through the history of Japanese theater. Early documentary proofs can be found in scenes of *gigaku*, which clearly reveal the Asian continent as the provenance of the theatrical presentation.

3.42 Gigaku Procession with Gojo at Todai-ji
Photographer: Inoue Hiromichi

3.43 Gigaku Mask and Costume of Gojo ("Woman from [the Chinese State of] Wu")
Replica of mask from the Shôsôin Imperial Repository
Original signed: "Made by Master Kishi"
8th c. (original mask)
Mask: wood, pigments; costume: silk
Life-size
Tôdai-ji, Nara

3.44 Gigaku Mask of Konron
Nara Period, 8th c.
Wood, traces of pigment and fiber
35.6 high x 27.9 wide x 24.1 cm
Philadelphia Museum of Art: Given by John H. Converse and Samuel Vauclain

3.45 Gigaku Mask of Konron in Netsuke form
Maker: Kanya Tsujimoto, after an original in the Tôdai-ji
Signed: "Kanya Koku"
Contemporary
Wood (*tsugi*), lacquer
4.3 x 3.2 cm
Barbra Okada

Netsuke masks form a special category in this miniature art. Many of the representations are exact copies of real masks.

3.46 Gigaku Mask and Costume of Konron
Photograph of replicas created by Yoshioka Sachio after originals in the Shôsôin Imperial Repository; in the possession of Tôdai-ji, Nara
Life-size
Courtesy of Tôdai-ji, Nara

3.47 Gigaku Mask and Costume of Kongo and Rikishi
Photograph of replicas created by Yoshioka Sachio after originals in the Shôsôin Imperial Repository; in possession of Tôdai-ji, Nara
Life-size
Courtesy of Tôdai-ji, Nara

The story of the woman, or women, from the Chinese state of Wu (222-77 AD) has given rise to much speculation. The masks of these women with classical 7th-century hair styles are the only female *gigaku* masks. The *Kyôkunshô* (1233) is our only written source of information about the woman (women), apart from the preserved masks, costumes, props, and temple inventories. According to this text, two or more women appear in front of the great stone lantern of a Buddhist temple. While flirting with their leaf fans, the ugly, dark Kuron (or Konron) appear, who are described as being *gedô*. According to Chinese sources, *gedô* were those who stood outside the Buddhist law; they were supposedly from Southeast Asia where the Shiva cult with its emphasis on the phallus is common. The Konron approach the women with sexually explicit gestures. At this moment, Kongô and Rikishi, the two guardians of Buddhist law, appear to expel them. While modern retellings have transformed this story into morally presentable versions, the *Kyôkunshô* describes Kongô and Rikishi as appearing, then ripping the penis off each Konron. Then these two guardians of the Buddhist law perform a dance called "Swinging around the Phallus."

Scenes of sexual character have been popular in Japanese folk theater until the present day, although the interpretation of this particular one is difficult to verify. The slapstick-like scene described in the *Kyôkunsho* could also be considered a parody of a non-Buddhist religion such as Shivaism. Other scenes, such as the Baramon (Brahman) who comes on the stage to wash baby diapers, support such a theory.

3.48 GIGAKU SCENE OF SUIKO-O AND SUIKO-JU ("THE DRUNKEN HU BARBARIAN KING AND HIS FOLLOWERS") ON A STAGE IN FRONT OF THE DAIBUTSU-DEN, TODAI-JI, NARA
Photographer: Inoue Hiromichi
Courtesy of Inoue Hiromichi

3.49 GIGAKU MASK AND COSTUME OF SUIKO-O
Replicas created by Yoshioka Sachio after originals in the Shôsôin Imperial Repository; in the possession of Tôdai-ji, Nara
8th c. (original)
Mask: wood, pigment, lacquer; costume: various materials rewoven and dyed with original vegetable dyes
Life-size
Tôdai-ji, Nara

3.50 GIGAKU MASK AND COSTUME OF SUIKO-JU
Replicas created by Yoshioka Sachio after originals in the Shôsôin Imperial Repository; in the possession of Tôdai-ji, Nara
8th c. (original)
Mask: wood, pigment, lacquer; costume: various materials rewoven and dyed with original vegetable dyes
Life-size
Tôdai-ji, Nara

3.51 BUGAKU: MASK OF KOTOKURAKU
Woodblock print illustration in the *Shukô Jishû*; based on an original mask from Tôdai-ji, Nara
12th c. (original mask)
Courtesy of Gunhild Avitabile

The bearded man in no. 3.49, with a prominent nose, is identified as Hu Barbarian King. He is portrayed in colorful dress and characteristic headgear with his followers (no. 3.50) drinking on the stage. Their long noses make it difficult to drink from flat bowls. Some have bent their noses to the side, some of them exhibit frustration because they are not able to do so. In *bugaku*, the dance was taken over as Kotokuraku ("Virtue of the Hu Barbarians," or "Virtue of the Nose-Turning Hu Barbarians"). The *Shûko Jishû* describes how the mask's long phallic nose was separately carved and fixed to the face with a string, making it easy for the wearer to move the nose to the side while drinking.

This presentation is one of the most stunning scenes of *gigaku*. It is a parody of a Central Asian (probably Samarkand) wine-drinking ritual by followers of the cult of Mithras-Mihira at the spring festival Nowroz. The king represents the god. The custom was known in 6th-century China and representations can be found in Chinese tombs of the period (examples at Boston Museum of Fine Arts and Musée Guimet, Paris). With their prominent noses and beards, the features of the *gigaku* masks show a clear Central Asian provenance. The beautifully decorated cap of the Suiko-ô can be found in 6th-century Chinese representations. In China, the term Hu Barbarian (pronounced "ko" in Japanese) was clearly associated with inhabitants of Central Asia. As in the other scenes of *gigaku* described in these entries, this is also a parody of a non-Buddhist religion, brought to the stage as a kind of religious propaganda.

3.43 B

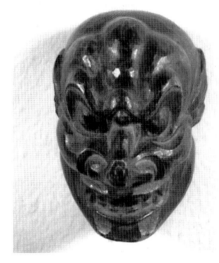

3.45

3.49 B

3.51 A

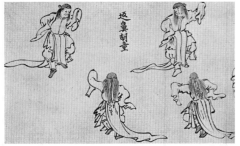

3.51 B

3.52

揉桑老

3.53 B

3.52 GIGAKU MASK OF TAIKOFU
Photograph
Mid-8th c.
Wood
30 cm high
Formerly in the collections of Tomitarô
Hara (1939) and Tôdai-ji; present owner
unknown; published in Shukô Jishû (1801)
Courtesy of Gunhild Avitabile

Datable *gigaku* masks of the Taikofu ("Great
Orphan Father") or Kojifu ("Father of the
Stepchildren") types are the oldest representations of elderly men, so popular in Japanese theater history. The rare tradition
describes an old man supported by his two
stepchildren as he is brought to the temple
to be near Buddha.

3.53 BUGAKU MASK OF SAISORO
Nanbokuchô/Muromachi Periods (1333-
1568)
Wood, pigment, lacquer
21.6 x 15 cm
Tokyo National Museum; inv. no. C0295

The Saisôrô ("Old Man Plucking Mulberry
Leaves") mask shows the dignified face of an
elderly bearded man and in many aspects is
reminiscent of the Okina mask of *nô*. If one
compares the two masks, Okina seems like a
rural grandchild of Saisôrô. The oldest dated
Saisôrô mask (1249) recalls an event at the
Itsukushima Shrine in Hiroshima. The dance
is first mentioned in a 867 temple inventory.

The dancer wears a white dress, purple
according to other sources, with a brocade
cap, and special trousers (*hakama*) and shoes.
He carries a stick on which a dove rests and
a branch of bamboo. In the 1133 *Ryûmeishô*,
the dance is described in writing as an
auspicious one, with the dancer coming on
to the stage as someone who is very elderly
and who is accompanied by an armed
helper. The *Kyôkunshô*, written in 1233,
speaks of an old man in purple dress who is
hardly able to move because of his advanced
age. Mulberry leaves are associated with the
cultivation of the silkworm.

Although the dance is affiliated with the
Dances of the Left, considered to be of
Chinese or other non-Korean origin, the
black headband, the recognizable iconographic formation of the wrinkles, the
construction of the mask, and the white
costumes seem to point to Korean sources.
A stick with an attached bird image also
belongs to the accoutrements of Siberian
shamans.

A song of the Saisôrô dancer describes the
different ages of a man—from his 30th to
100th year. Interestingly, the last three
stages, from the 80th to the 100th year, are
considered "taboo." The iconography of
various gigaku masks of Taikofu show similar wrinkles and types of hoods. Although
reference to Chinese origin is made in
different sources, no Chinese connection
has been proven for Saisôrô, the court and
temple dance. The meaning of Saisôrô
might indicate that it is a predecessor of
Okina, which assumed such an important
role in *nô*.

Representations of old men are a popular
subject in Japanese theatrical history. The
two examples presented above show the
relationship with the dance of Okina, which
was popular later on.

3.54 HOLY GHOST RITUAL AT HORYU-JI
Illustrations showing different kinds of
theatrical representations at special events,
as described in medieval literature
Provided by Tanabe Saburosuke

IV. Snow in a Silver Bowl: *Nô* Theater

The Stage

4.1 Miniature of Nô Stage
Model of the *nô* stage in Edo Castle, built in 1860 and destroyed by fire in 1863. Made by Yonekichi Banba, based on the original stage plan at one-twentieth of the original size.
Wood, metals, and colors
109 x 109 cm
Tsubouchi Memorial Theatre Museum, Waseda University

4.2 A-B Diagrams of Nô Stage
Photograph showing two sections: A) front view, B) aerial view, with explanations of essential stage parts
Japan Society

4.3 Rakuchu-rakugai-zu Byobu (Screen picturing scenes in and around Kyoto)
Photograph with detail of an early Kanze *nô* performance
60 x 40 cm
Gotô Hajime

4.4 Floor plan of stage and seating arrangement of patrons for subscription Nô performance in 1464
Photograph of drawing
60 x 40 cm
Gotô Hajime

4.5 Woodblock Print of the large-scale subcription Nô performance of Hosho-dayu in 1848 (Koka-gonen Hosho-dayu Kanjin No Kogyobasho Ryakuzu)
Photograph of the print
36.8 x 51.2 cm
Tsubouchi Memorial Theatre Museum, Waseda University

Hôshô-dayû, the leader of the Hôshô School of *Nô*, received a special permit from the government of the shôgun for a public *nô* performance only once in his life. These public subcription performances, called *Kanjin-nô*, were held to raise money for the construction or repair of shrines and temples. This original purpose later became only a pretext for *nô* actors to earn money.

4.6 Indoor and Outdoor Nô stages in Japan today
Photographs showing the The National *Nô* Theater and its stage; the stages of the five *nô* schools in Tokyo and Kyoto; the outdoor stages of the Itsukushima Shrine in Miyajima, Hiroshima; of Nishi-Hongan-ji, Kyoto; the one in Hiraizumi; as well as one of the remaining outdoor stages on Sado Island.
Japan Society

Musicians, Instruments, and Chorus

4.7 Musicians and Chorus on stage
Photograph of the beginning of a performance
45 x 30 cm
Günter Zobel

4.8 A-D Nô musical instruments
A) *Nô-kan* (flute; 39 x 2.5 cm); B) *ko-tsuzumi* (shoulder drum; 25 x 15 cm); C) *ô-tsuzumi* (hip drum; 30 x 22.8 cm); and D) *taiko* (floor drum; 35.6 x 15.5 cm);
drum mounts (35 x 30 cm; 6 x 25 cm); drum stick (33 x 2.4 cm)
Bamboo, wood, leather, string
Tsubouchi Memorial Theatre Museum, Waseda University

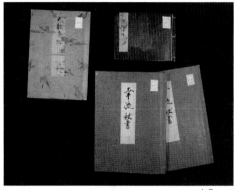

4.9 A-C

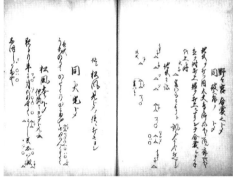

4.9 A-C

4.9 A-C Three Books with Nô Music scores
A) Manual for Hip Drum from the Ôkura School
Copy: ca. 1860 [date of original not known]
23 x 16 cm
Tsubouchi Memorial Theatre Museum, Waseda University

The Ôkura School is one of five present-day schools that teach the hip drum playing of *nô*. So-called *tezuke* are the books that show the arrangements of *nô* instruments.

B) Scores for the Nô Flute (*nô-kan-no fu*)
Copy: ca. 1680 [date of original not known]
12.4 x 16.6 cm

Tsubouchi Memorial Theatre Museum, Waseda University

Written scores for the *nô* flute are derived from oral ones called *shôka* ("the singing"). In this book, the oral tradition for the flute of the Issô School, one of three present-day schools, were laid down in writing.

c) Secret Writings of the Kô School (*Kô-ryû bishô*)
Copy: ca. 1860 [date of original not known]
26 x 19 cm
Tsubouchi Memorial Theatre Museum, Waseda University

The Kô School is one of four present-day schools training shoulder drummers. This book was a secret one, describing how to play the shoulder drum in the many plays of *nô*, as well as providing information about the variations connected with the different schools of *nô*.

STAGE PROPS (TSUKURIMONO)

4.10/4.11/4.12 TSUKURIMONO I
Full-size stage props: 4.10) *fune* (boat frame; 302.1 cm long x 94.3 cm wide); 4.11) *shiokumi-kuruma* (cart for sea water; 97.5 cm long x 38.2 cm wide x 32.5 cm high), exhibited with *mizu-oke* (buckets for sea water [no. 4.73A-B] from the play "*Matsukaze*"; 21.1 cm high x 21 cm wide and 21.1 cm high x 18.7 cm wide); 4.12) *kakko-dai* (drum stand; 170.3 cm long x 121.7 cm wide), exhibited with *kakko* (miniature drum [no. 4.70] used in the plays "*Tenkô*" and "*Fuji-daiko*"; 18.3 x 14.5 cm); ground frame: 61 x 50 cm
Bamboo, white and red cloth
Tsubouchi Memorial Theatre Museum, Waseda University (A, B, D)
Hikone-jô Hakubutsukan (Hikone Castle Museum) (C, E)

4.13A-E TSUKURIMONO II
Stage props in small-model form: A) *moto-no matsu-no tatechiki* (fundamental form of stand for a pine tree; 18.3 cm high x 7.8 cm wide x 7.8 cm long); B) *moto-no kuruma* (fundamental form of an ox cart; 21 x 9.4 x 23.8 cm); C) *hikitate-omiya* (protective roof over a shrine or palace; 24.3 x 9.8 x 18.3 cm); D) *susuki-tsuki-no izutsu* (rim of a well with reed grass attached in one corner; 17.6 x 10 x 10 cm); E) *kumo-zuka* (cave of the spider demon; 20 x 9.5 x 9.5 cm)
Wood, paper
Tsubouchi Memorial Theatre Museum, Waseda University

4.14 TSUKURIMONO ON STAGE
Photographs showing different kinds of props on stage during performance

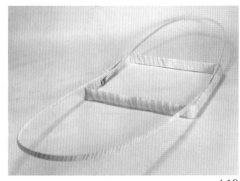
4.10

4.11

4.13A-E

4.14G

4.14A

4.14B

4.14C

4.14D

4.14E

4.14F

4.15 A-C TSUKURIMONO HANDBOOKS (HOSHO-RYU TSUKURIMONO-NO-SETSU)
Three books describing how to make stage properties
A) *Album of Nô Stage Properties in the Hôshô School* (*Hôshô-ryû Nô-tsukurimono-chô*)
Copy: ca. 1800 [date of original not known]
12 x 18 cm
Tsubouchi Memorial Theatre Museum, Waseda University

B) *Records of Stage Properties in the Hôshô School* (*Hôshô-ryû Tsukurimono-no-ki*)
Copy: 1857 [date of original not known]
15 x 21 cm
Tsubouchi Memorial Theatre Museum, Waseda University

C) *Stage Properties in the Hôshô School* (*Hôshô-ryû Tsukurimono*)
Copy: ca. 1860 [date of original not known]
25.4 x 18.5 cm
Tsubouchi Memorial Theatre Museum, Waseda University

Tsukurimono are used during a *nô* performance in accordance with the requirements of the play's content. For example, if a sea or river must be crossed, a simple boat model will be on stage. It is characteristic that a *tsukurimono* is not a realistic model of an object, but rather that it conveys only the essential contours of the object. This is done by creating a bamboo model covered with cloth. These books of the Hôshô School, one of five schools of *nô*, explain the nature of many different forms of *tsukurimono* through drawings.

4.15

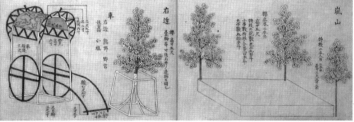

4.15

NO MASKS

4.16 BASIC TYPES OF NO MASKS
Photographs of the 24 basic types. The masks were carved by Irie Binoru and are owned by the Tsubouchi Memorial Theatre Museum, Waseda University.

At present there are about 250 or 260 different kinds of *nô* masks; although the basic masks, which are the ones most often used, are are few in number. *Nô* masks are commonly divided into the following groups: *okina* (divine old men); *kishin* (divine demons); *jô* (old men); *dan-jo* (women and men); and *rei* (ghosts).

A. *Okina* Group
The masks of the *okina* group (divine old men) can be regarded as *kami* masks, that is ones representing Shinto gods which give blessings to humans. Of all the masks, the most sacred is the *okina* (no. 4.22). It is the mask of an old man with a healthy, broadly smiling face. The *sambasô* mask (see Section

V: *kyôgen*) looks like an imitation of the *okina* but, compared with it, the *sambasô* has a more comical expression. *Sambasô* can also be regarded as a role which explains the *okina* in a simple way. Today the styles of the *sambasô* and *okina* masks are the same, but the *okina* is white, while the *sambasô* is painted black. Both have eyebrows, a moustache made of hair, and look somewhat vulgar. The characteristic form in which their eye parts are hollowed out does not exist in any other *nô* mask. Another special feature is their lower jaw, carved as a separate piece and attached by strings at both sides. This is not typical for *nô* and *kyôgen* masks, and it is not clear what meaning the carved chin has. But it is said that the separated chin is the symbol of a role which brings blessings. *Okina* masks are the oldest *nô* masks.

B. *Kishin* Group
Masks of the *kishin* group (divine demons), like those of the *okina*, are old ones. Whereas *okina* masks show laughter, *kishin* masks convey strength and fear. For the *kishin* group, there are names such as: *tobide* (lit., "protruding"); *beshimi* (lit., "clamped, firmly shut mouth"); *akujô* (fierce old man; nos. 4.17, 4.27); *tenjin* (young deity); *shikami* (lit., "scowling face"); *yakan* (fox with human face); *ikazuchi* (lit., "thunderbolt"; no. 4.31); *shishiguchi* (lit., "lion's jaw"); *tsurimanako* (lit., "slant-eyed"); and *kurohige* (lit., "black beard"; no. 4.26).

C. *Jô* Group
Jô masks portray old men, sometimes with dignity and sometimes with none. Many kinds of *jô* masks were created for the roles of the various elderly men who appear in *nô*. When a god or spirit took human form, and this was expressed through the appearance of an old man, a *jô* mask was used. The beard was made of natural hair, or painted with ink. The way it was painted revealed the relative degree of dignity of the role. Types of *jô* masks include: *kojô* (small mask of an old man, also called *koushi-jô* after the carver Koushi); *sankôjô* (named after the artist-priest Sankô-bô); *waraijô* (lit., "laughing old man"); *maijô* (lit., "dancing old man"); *shiwajô* (old man with wrinkles); and *ishiôjô* (a type created by the carver Ishiô).

D. *Dan-Jo* Group
Whereas the role of the *jo* (man) is to express sadness and loneliness, the role of the *dan* (woman) is to express beauty. There are numerous types of *dan* masks to show young women, middle-aged women, or old women. There is, of course, a distinction shown between characters who have dignity or have been burdened by personal experience, and those who have not yet had any such experiences. As the dramatic content of the plays progressed through the generations, the masks changed, too. Female masks include: *ko-omote* (lit., "little face"); *waka-onna* (lit., "young woman"), *zô-onna* (a type created by Zôami); *fukai* (lit., "deep well");

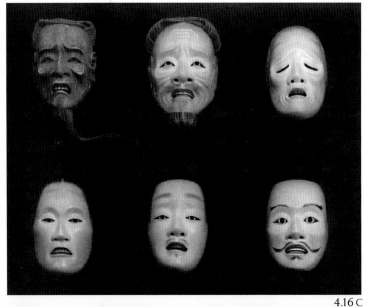

4.16 C

4.16 B

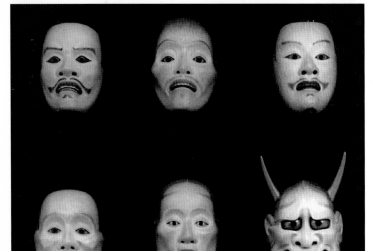

4.16 E

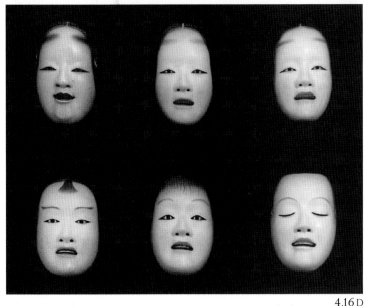

4.16 D

shakumi (lit., "seeing the curvature"); *uba* (old woman); and *rôjo* (old lady).

Male masks express the roles of aristocrats and warriors, young boys, and pages. Both the male and the female masks are generally used when a god or spirit appears in human form. Male masks include: *chûjô* (a man holding the second highest rank in the Imperial Guard); *imawaka* (lit., "being young now"); *kasshiki* (kitchen boy); *yoroboshi* (blind, weak temple boy; no. 4.24); *dôji* (boy); *shôjô* (the elf and spirit of wine; no. 4.25); *kagekiyô* (the mighty warrior Kagekiyo who became a blind beggar; no. 4.20); *shunkan* (the bitterly suffering, exiled priest Shunkan; no. 4.19); and *yorimasa* (the defeated warrior of that name).

E. *Rei* Group
Ghost (*rei*) masks which express the *yûrei* (apparition) role can be considered a very special category among Japanese masks. There are various kinds: masks such as *ayakashi*, *mikazuki*, and *awa-otoko* portray the

departed spirits of warriors; masks such as Fudô and Shaka portray Buddha; special masks such as the so-called *deigan* masks (no. 4.23), whose eyeballs are painted in gold; and many others which express horror or apprehension.

Typical *nô* masks that are generally well known include: *hannya* (a female demon, a devil of jealousy); *ja* (the demonic female snake; no. 4.30); *namanari* (lit., demons with "horns still growing"; see no. 4.29 for a special form); and *yamauba* or *yamanba* (lit., "the old mountain woman"; no. 4.21). Masks such as *yase-otoko* (lit., "skinny man"); *ryô-no-onna* (lit., "the ghost woman"); *yase-onna* (lit., "emaciated woman"); and *hashihime* (named after the beautiful Hashihime, who became a demon through jealousy; no. 4.18) are used to show gloomy fear. Usually, demonic deity and ghostly spirit masks have a ring of metal in their eyes. On the other hand, *jô* masks and those representing usual men and women, have no metal attached to their eyes. Their eyes are simply painted black.

NO MASKS WITH SPECIAL THEATRICAL FEATURES I

4.17 WASHIBANA-AKUJO (GRIM FACED OLD MAN WITH AN "EAGLE'S NOSE")
15.6 x 20.6 cm; with beard: 43.4 cm
Tsubouchi Memorial Theatre Museum, Waseda University

4.18 HASHIHIME ("THE LADY ON THE BRIDGE," JEALOUS DEMONIC WOMAN)
By Irie Binori
14.6 x 20.6 cm)
Tsubouchi Memorial Theatre Museum, Waseda University

4.19 SHUNKAN (THE EXILED, DESPERATE BUDDHIST PRIEST SHUNKAN)
By Irie Binori
14.6 x 20.6 cm
Tsubouchi Memorial Theatre Museum, Waseda University

4.20 KAGEKIYO (THE LONELY AND BLIND FORMER HERO KAGEKIYO)
By Irie Binori
14.6 x 21.0 cm
Tsubouchi Memorial Theatre Museum,
Waseda University

4.21 YAMANBA (DIVINITY OR WITCH OF THE MOUNTAIN)
By Irie Binori
13.8 x 20.4 cm
Tsubouchi Memorial Theatre Museum,
Waseda University

4.22 OKINA (OLD MAN AS A REPRESENTATIVE OF GODS, ANCESTORS)
By Nomura Manzô
15.6 x 18.6 cm
Tsubouchi Memorial Theatre Museum,
Waseda University

4.23 DEIGAN ("DIM GOLD-FLECKED EYE"; FOR SPIRITS, GODDESSES)
By Irie Binori
13.6 x 20.6 cm
Tsubouchi Memorial Theatre Museum,
Waseda University

4.24 YOROBOSHI (THE BLIND BOY-MONK)
13.5 x 19.8 cm
Tsubouchi Memorial Theatre Museum,
Waseda University

4.25 SHOJO (THE DANCING SPIRIT OF RICE WINE)
By Irie Binori
13.5 x 20.4 cm
Tsubouchi Memorial Theatre Museum,
Waseda University

4.26 KUROHIGE ("BLACK BEARD"; FOR DRAGONS AND GODS)
By Irie Binori
14 x 20 cm
Tsubouchi Memorial Theatre Museum,
Waseda University

NO MASKS WITH SPECIAL THEATRICAL FEATURES II

4.27 MYOGA-AKUJO
Possibly by Shunwaka Tadatsugu at end of 15th c.
Wood
21.2 x 15.3 cm
Tokyo National Museum

The eyes of this strong, old man are slanted like the ginger plant (*myôga*), hence the name. This mask was used in a *nô* play such as *"Dômyôji."*

4.28 IKKAKU SENNIN
Wood
21.8 x 15.3 cm
Tokyo National Museum
Used only in the *nô* play *"Ikkaku Sennin."* The single deer horn (*ikkaku*) in the middle of his forehead became the characteristic feature of the mask because it was said that this magic man living in the mountains (*sennin*) was born from a deer.

4.29 FUKUROZUNO NAMANARI
Replica by Nakamura Naohiko
20th c.
Wood
20.4 x 12.9 cm
Tokyo National Museum

This mask has the expression of a female avenging spirit. Compared with the famous mask of a female devil of jealousy called Hannya depicted on the photo panel, no. 4.16, these horns are short and truncated. (*Fukuro* means bag.) As a *namanari*, the urge for revenge is relatively minor.

4.30 JA (SERPENT)
Possibly carved by Yamato, descendant of the Iseki Dynasty of carvers
Edo Period (1615-1868)
Wood
21.3 x 16.2 cm
Tokyo National Museum

This mask has to express the face of a dragon or serpent. It fully conveys a thirst for revenge and, therefore, is used as the Hannya mask for the *nô "Dôjôji,"* or other plays with similar themes.

4.31 IKAZUCHI (THUNDER GOD)
Possibly carved by Shunwaka Tadatsugu at end of 15th c.
Wood
20.4 x 17.2 cm
Tokyo National Museum

The face expresses thunder (*kaminari*). On the head, in the eyebrows, and around the mouth are carved signs which signify lightning. The mask is used, for example, in *"Raiden."*

4.32 HOW TO MAKE A NO MASK
The process is shown at various stages. The mask shown here, as an example, is "Magojiro," depicting a young female.
I. Sculpting and painting (from right to left):
A) Material: a dry zelkova block, without knots
B) "*Kidori*": the outline is roughly cut, usually imitating the measurements of "*Komen,*" famous masks transmitted and treasured from the 15th and 16th centuries.
C) "*Konashi*": rough-carving. A block is cut with a chisel into the shape of a mask.
D) Carving: the positions of the eyes, mouth, and hair are marked on the "*Konashi,*" and then the mask is sculpted smooth with small chisels. The inside of the mask is also carved at this stage, and the artist's signature and name of the mask are usually branded on it. Chisel traces on the reverse side are important for judging the mask's authorship, especially on an old mask with no artist's signature.
E) Coating: *gofun* is applied. After the paint has dried, the surface is polished. The process of coating and polishing is usually

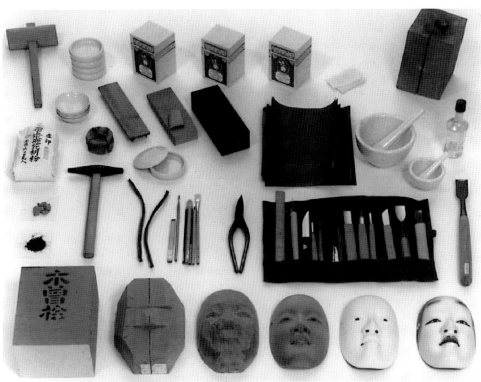

4.32

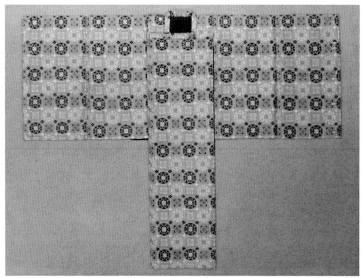

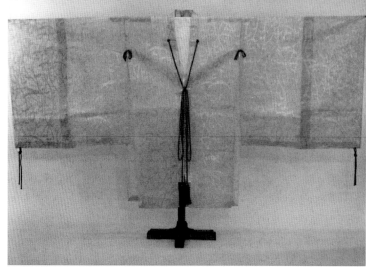

4.33 A, B

4.42

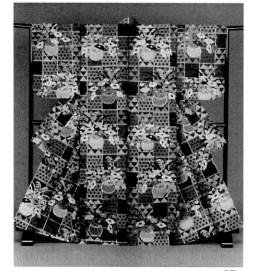

4.36 A

4.37 A

4.38 A

repeated more than ten times. Sometimes a special technique is used to give an antique effect.

F) Coloring: The eyes, mouth, and hair are painted with black and red. "*Kegaki*," the hairline around the face, is most carefully drawn. Each type of female mask has its own "*Kegaki*" style. Artists of *nô* masks ingeniously invented techniques to catch the delicate differences in various female looks and personalities in terms of the styles of the hair.
II. *Gofun* and other paints, with tools for coating.
III. Instruments for carving.
Tsubouchi Memorial Theatre Museum, Waseda University

No Costumes

Most of the old *nô* costumes that remain today are from the Momoyama Period (latter half of the 16th century); there are few costumes older than these. Most of the older costumes still used today are extravagant ones of high quality. This is because *nô* became the formal entertainment of the warriors and therefore was always present, supported by the upper-class culture, during

this period. Momoyama and Genroku (1688-1703) cultures seem to have had both a direct and indirect influence.

Among these costumes are items which express varying degrees of dignity. There are also designs for expressing the content of a play. For example, there are kimono which have a snakeskin pattern like that worn in "*Dôjôji*," a famous play in which a young girl becomes a snake through her jealousy. But it must be remembered that, because *nô* basically expresses *yûgen-bi*, there are various ways in which *nô* costumes differ significantly from those of *kabuki*. The different types of *nô* costumes can be divided roughly into two categories: 1) *ôsode*, an outer garment with broad, double-width sleeves and open cuffs; 2) *kosode*, kimono with single-width sleeves and small cuff openings. The most representative examples are:
1) *Ôsode*
Kariginu is a round-necked hunting cloak with double-width sleeves. The *happi* is a cloak for men in which the front and back panels are connected by a strap at the hem. *Chôken* is worn by dancing female figures and, like *maiginu*, has a gauze weave in unglossed silk with a design woven in gold and colors,

or overall in gold. The *mizugoromo* (lit., "water robe") is worn by men and women as a plain-colored traveling cloak. Worn over something else, it is designed especially for the *nô* stage. *Suô*, a suit of matching jacket and long trailing divided skirts, is woven in fiber, and *kamishimo* (lit., "upper-under"), an ensemble worn by samurai from the end of the 15th century, are garments of the members of the chorus and orchestra, as well of the stage assistants.
2) *Kosode*
Karaori (lit., "Chinese weave") is a brocade kimono with single-width sleeves, which forms a gorgeous dress for women. *Atsuita* (lit., "thick board") is a robe with similar sleeves and small cuff openings; it is thick like a plank and is worn by men. *Atsuita-karaori* is a brocade kimono primarily for warrior-courtiers. *Surihaku* is an under-kimono of plain white satin weave, on which gold foil is imprinted. Costumes which have colored embroidery are called *nuihaku* and are worn as outer robes. For the lower half of the costumes, there are items such as: the *ôguchi*, plain-colored divided skirts with large pleats in front and stiffened, gathered panels in the back; *hangire*, broad divided skirts with

4.40

4.46   4.47

4.48

dynamic gold or silver designs; *sashinuki*, a courtier's pleated pantaloons, gathered at the ankles and worn over *ôguchi*; and *nagabakama*, long trailing divided skirts.

4.33 A-B OKINA KARIGINU (LIT., "HUNTING CLOAK" OF OKINA)
Costume: *shokkô-monyô, asagi-iro* (*shokkô* [tortoise] design on pale blue; reserved for *Okina* garments)
Silk replica
224 x 167 cm
Yamaguchi Nô Costume Research Center

4.34 A-B CHOKEN (LIT., "LONG SILK" SLEEVES) FOR FEMALE ROLES
Costume: *susuki-ni chô-monyô, murasaki* (butterflies in *susuki*-grass pattern; purple)
Silk replica
214 x 117 cm
Yamaguchi Nô Costume Research Center

4.35 CHOKEN FOR FEMALE ROLES
Costume: *hanakago-ni seigai hana-eda chirashi-monyô, hana-iro* (design of flower baskets and scattered blue waves with flower sprigs; light blue)
Silk replica
214 x 117 cm
Yamaguchi Nô Costume Research Center

4.36 A-B ATSUITA-KARAORI (LIT., "THICK BOARD OF CHINESE WEB") FOR WARRIOR-COURTIERS
Costume: *yuri-nôzenkazura-monyô, shiro-murasaki* (pattern of lilies and great trumpet flowers on design of alternating white and violet blocks)
Silk replica
147 x 143 cm
Yamaguchi Nô Costume Research Center

4.37 A-B ATSUITA-KARAORI FOR WARRIOR-COURTIERS
Costume: *moniri-ishitatami-ni yushoku hanakago-monyô, kuro-aka* (pattern of flower baskets on checkered design; browns)
Silk replica
153 x 142 cm
Tsubouchi Memorial Theatre Museum, Waseda University

4.38 A-B KARAORI (LIT., "CHINESE WEB") FOR FEMALE ROLES
Costume: *kiku-karakusa-iri higaki-ni botaneda-monyô, kuro-aka* (design of peony sprigs on a lattice pattern filled with chrysanthemum arabesque; brown)
Silk replica
153 x 162 cm
Tsubouchi Memorial Theatre Museum, Waseda University

4.39 KARAORI FOR FEMALE ROLES
Costume: *dangawari fuji-dana-monyô*
(changing color blocks with pattern of
wisteria hanging from a lattice)
Silk replica by Yamaguchi Nô Costume
Research Center
153 x 162 cm
Tsubouchi Memorial Theatre Museum,
Waseda University

4.40 KARAORI FOR FEMALE ROLES
Costume: *kasumi-ni omodaga aoi-monyô* (swamp
sections in haze under patterns of stick roses)
Silk replica by Yamaguchi Nô Costume
Research Center
153 x 162 cm
Tsubouchi Memorial Theatre Museum,
Waseda University

4.41 KARAORI FOR FEMALE ROLES
Costume: *shiroji-aoi-monyô* (on white ground
patterns of stick rose sprigs)
Edo Period (1615-1868)
Silk
153 x 162 cm
Tsubouchi Memorial Theatre Museum,
Waseda University

4.42 CHOKEN FOR FEMALE ROLES
Costume: *kinshiori-yukimochi karakusa-monyô*
(arabesque pattern of sprigs burdened with
snow in gold-thread web)
Edo Period (1615-1868)
Silk
130 x 170 cm
Tsubouchi Memorial Theatre Museum,
Waseda University

4.43 A-B EXPLANATIONS OF COSTUMES
A) Female *nô* figure with a *karaori* outfit and
B) male figure in an *atsuita-karaori* warrior's
garment

WIGS, HEADGEAR, FANS, WIG-BANDS, AND HANDPROPS

4.44 KATSURA-OBI (WIGBANDS)
Five wigbands for elderly women
Silk reproductions
235.6 x 3.9 cm each
Yamaguchi Nô Costume Research Center

4.45 KATSURA-OBI (WIGBANDS)
Five wigbands for younger women
Silk reproductions by Yamaguchi Akira
235.6 x 3.9 cm
Tsubouchi Memorial Theatre Museum,
Waseda University

**4.46/4.47 KURO-KASHIRA, AKA-KASHIRA
(LONG WIGS)**
Black and red examples of long hair wigs
Taishô-Shôwa Period (1912-88)

4.49

4.50

4.51

Horse hair
150 cm long each
Hikone-jô Hakubutsukan (Hikone Castle
Museum)

4.48 TO-KANMURI (CHINESE HAT)
Taishô-Shôwa Period (1912-88)
Wood, lacquer

16.9 cm high
Hikone-jô Hakubutsukan (Hikone Castle
Museum)

4.49/4.50 TENGAN (HEAVENLY CROWN)
Two examples of golden heavenly crowns
1) Edo Period (1615-1868); 19.9 cm high
2) Taishô-Shôwa Period (1912-88); 23.4 cm
high
Metal, paper, colors
Hikone-jô Hakubutsukan (Hikone Castle
Museum)

4.51 RYUGAN (DRAGON CROWN)
Crown with the colored shape of a dragon
Taishô-Shôwa Period (1912-88)
Metal, paper, colors
36.8 cm high
Hikone-jô Hakubutsukan (Hikone Castle
Museum)

4.52/4.53 KAZAORI-EBOSHI
Two examples of a black folding cap for
officials
1. Edo Period (1615-1868); 17.8 cm high x
30 cm long
2. 1930; 18.7 x 30.5 cm
Silk
Hikone-jô Hakubutsukan (Hikone Castle
Museum)

4.54 HO-O-TENGAN
Crown with a miniature bird of paradise
1939
Metal, colors
28.4 cm high
Hikone-jô Hakubutsukan (Hikone Castle
Museum)

4.55 RYU-DATEMONO
Colored shape of a dragon to insert into a
headgear crown
Taishô-Shôwa Period (1912-88)
Paper, colors
71 cm high x 81.5 cm wide
Hikone-jô Hakubutsukan (Hikone Castle
Museum)

4.56/4.57 OKINA-EBOSHI
Two dance caps for *Okina*
1930
Silk
4.56) 21.1 x 30 cm; 4.57) 23.4 x 31.3 cm
Hikone-jô Hakubutsukan (Hikone Castle
Museum)

4.58/4.59 SAMURAI-EBOSHI
Two caps for warriors
Taishô-Shôwa Period (1912-88)
Silk
4.58) 21.5 cm long; 4.59) 24.4 cm long
Hikone-jô Hakubutsukan (Hikone Castle
Museum)

4.52

4.54

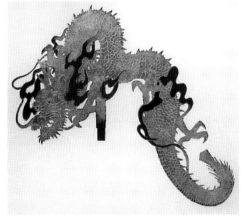

4.55

4.56

4.60 SUI-KANMURI
Pierced lacquer hat for a Chinese character
1930
Leather, lacquer
16.4 cm high
Hikone-jô Hakubutsukan (Hikone Castle Museum)

4.61 KITSUNE-KANMURI
Crown with the shape of a fox on top
Taishô-Shôwa Period (1912-88)
Metal, paper, colors
41.5 cm high
Hikone-jô Hakubutsukan (Hikone Castle Museum)

4.62 RYU-KO-DATEMONO
Paper shapes of dragon and tiger for wearing in a crown
Taishô-Shôwa Period (1912-88)
Paper, colors
71 cm high x 75.5 cm wide
Hikone-jô Hakubutsukan (Hikone Castle Museum)

4.63 A-B TSURU-KANMURI AND KAME-KANMURI
Two crowns with miniatures of a crane and a turtle on top
1926
Metal, colors
A) crane: 17.9 cm high; B) turtle: 16.3 cm high
Hikone-jô Hakubutsukan (Hikone Castle Museum)

4.64 A-D TACHI (SWORDS)
Four examples of swords as handprops
Edo Period (1615-1868)
Metal, wood, lacquer
A) 91 cm long; B) 79.4 cm long; C) 124.6 cm; D) 124.7 cm long
Hikone-jô Hakubutsukan (Hikone Castle Museum)

4.65A-D JUZU (BUDDHIST ROSARY)
Four Buddhist rosaries as handprops
Taishô-Shôwa Period (1912-88)
Stones, silk strings
A) 44 cm long; B) 46 cm long; C) 49 cm long; D) 46 cm long
Hikone-jô Hakubutsukan (Hikone Castle Museum)

4.66 A-B TO-UCHIWA (CHINESE ROUND FAN)
Two round fans for Chinese characters
Edo Period (1615-1868)
Wood, silk
A) 48 cm high; B) 47.6 cm high
Hikone-jô Hakubutsukan (Hikone Castle Museum)

4.57

4.58

4.59

4.60

4.67 HANE-UCHIWA (FEATHER FAN)
Round fan, constructed using a circle of feathers
1927
Wood, feathers
89.5 cm high with grip, 79.5 cm wide
Hikone-jô Hakubutsukan (Hikone Castle Museum)

4.68 HA-UCHIWA
Fan made with leaves
Taishô-Shôwa Period (1912-88)
Wood, silk
51.5 cm long
Hikone-jô Hakubutsukan (Hikone Castle Museum)

4.69/4.70 KAKKO (DRUM)
Two examples of drums as hand props
4.69) 1924; 18.5 cm high x 14 cm wide
4.70) Taishô-Shôwa Period (1912-88);
18.3 cm x 14.5 cm
Wood, leather, leaf gold
Hikone-jô Hakubutsukan (Hikone Castle Museum)

4.71 A-B UCHI-ZUE
Two sticks for striking magic (catalpa bow)
Edo period (1615-1868)
Wood, silk
A) 63.1 cm long; B) 67.8 cm long
Hikone-jô Hakubutsukan (Hikone Castle Museum)

4.62 B

4.72

4.72 A-D EMA
Four votive tablets
1926
Wood, colors
17.4 cm x 27.3 cm each
Hikone-jô Hakubutsukan (Hikone Castle Museum)

4.73 A-B MIZUOKE
Two examples of sea water pails as stage and hand props
Taishô-Shôwa Period (1912-88)
Wood, colors
A) 21.1 cm high x 21 cm wide; b) 21.1 cm high x 18.7 cm wide
Hikone-jô Hakubutsukan (Hikone Castle Museum)

4.74 A-B HIGAKI-MIZUOKE
Water pail with lattice pattern as stage and hand prop
1933
Wood, color
14.4 cm high x 15.1 cm wide

4.65A

4.65B

4.65C

4.65D

4.64A

4.64B

4.64C

4.64D

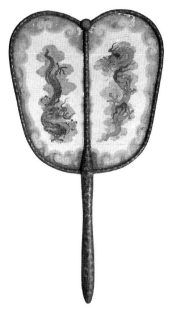

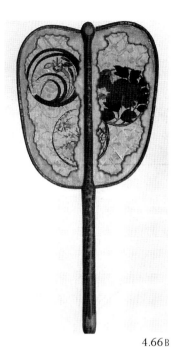

4.66 A   4.66 A   4.66 B   4.66 B

4.67

4.68

Hikone-jô Hakubutsukan (Hikone Castle Museum)

4.75 SUZUKAKE
Special outfit for *Yamabushi* priest: shoulder bands
Taishô-Shôwa Period (1912-88)
Wool, silk
113.9 cm [total length]
Hikone-jô Hakubutsukan (Hikone Castle Museum)

4.76 TOKIN
Cap of *Yamabushi* priest
Edo Period (1615-1868)
wood, lacquer
8.8 cm diameter
Hikone-jô Hakubutsukan (Hikone Castle Museum)

4.77 HORAGAI
Trumpet shell, signal horn of *Yamabushi* priest
Taishô-Shôwa Period (1912-88)
Shell
33.3 cm total length
Hikone-jô Hakubutsukan (Hikone Castle Museum)

4.78/4.79/4.80 CHUKEI
Three examples of dance fans with different painted patterns
4.78) crows; 4.79) Chinese sages; 4.80) pine and bamboo
Wood, paper
35 cm x 45 cm
Tsubouchi Memorial Theatre Museum, Waseda University

TEXTBOOKS, DANCE TEACHINGS, AND WRITINGS ON NO

4.81 A-B KOETSU-UTAIBON AND UTAIBON (TEXTBOOKS OF NO PLAYS)
A) *Nô* textbooks created by Kôetsu
ca. 1610
24 cm high x 18 cm wide
Tsubouchi Memorial Theatre Museum, Waseda University
B) Present-day *Nô* textbooks. Titles of plays: *"Warei"* (22.8 x 16.4 cm); *"Senju"* (21.2 x 14.9 cm); *"Sôshi-arai* Komachi" (23.2 x 16.2 cm); *"Nonomiya"* (23.6 x 16 cm; *"Shunkan"* (12.8 x 9.1 cm)
Collection of Gotô Hajime

The *utaibon* is the libretto of a *nô* play. Beside the words, pneumatic marks called *fushi* are written, which are melodic commands to guide the voice. These books are used for *nô* performance as well as for study. In the 17th century, Hon'ami Kôetsu made his own designs for *nô* textbooks and created beautiful *utaibon*. These Kôetsu-*utaibon* fully reveal his characteristic writing form as well as the fashionable writing style of his time. The present-day textbooks are from different schools of *nô*. A small pocket-book format is also included.

4.82 A-B SHIMAIZUKE (DANCE INSTRUCTIONS)
This copy ca. 1800 [date of original book not known]
25 x 17.2 cm
Tsubouchi Memorial Theatre Museum, Waseda University

When a man has mastered the art of *nô* and he is able to dance alone, that dance is called *shimai*. On this occasion, the dancer

4.69

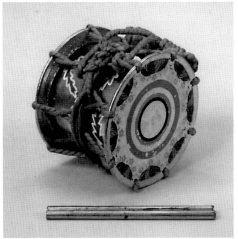

4.70

4.73

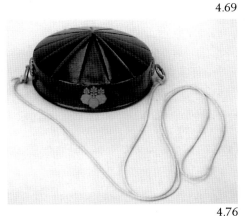

4.76

4.77

4.74 A,B

4.78

4.79

4.80

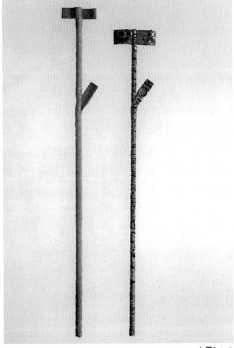

4.71 A,B

does not wear a regular *nô* mask and costume. Clad instead in a crested ceremonial cloak and divided skirts, he performs to the chanting of the *nô* chorus. He does not stage a whole *nô* play, just a brief part of it. The patterns of movements for a *shimai* are given in the book called *Shimaizuke*.

4.83 A-C THREE EDITIONS OF SCRIPTURES
BY ZEAMI
A) *Fûshikadenshô* (Book of the Transmission of the Flower)
Original writing by Zeami Motokiyo, 1400-18; this copy ca. 1800
27.8 x 12.2 cm
Tsubouchi Memorial Theatre Museum, Waseda University

B) *Fûshikaden* (The Transmission of the Flower)
Original writing by Zeami Motokiyo, 1400-18; this copy ca. 1860
27.8 x 19 cm
Tsubouchi Memorial Theatre Museum, Waseda University

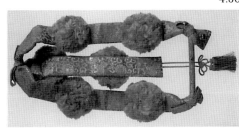

4.75

C) KAKYO (The Mirror of the Flower)
Original writing by Zeami Motokiyo, 1424; this copy ca. 1768
27 x 18.8 cm
Tsubouchi Memorial Theatre Museum, Waseda University

Zeami Motokiyo (163-1443) brought *nô* to its full flowering. He wrote down what *nô* is and ought to be, primarily in terms of the style of acting. The *Fûshikaden* contains not only his own ideas, but probably also those of his father Kan'ami Kiyotsugu (1333-1384). In *Kakyô*, he summarizes his own experi-

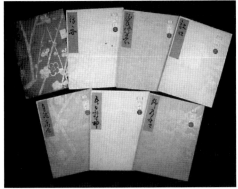

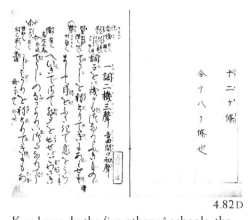

4.81 A,B

4.81 B

4.82 D

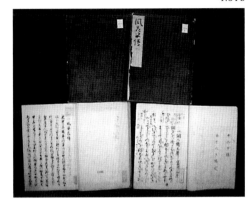

4.82 A,B

4.83 A-C

ences in *nô* and reveals that his thoughts had widened to include fundamental aesthetic questions which included concerns about the relationship between performer and auditorium–how to reach into it not only with words, music and dance, but also with the strength of the master actor's mind (*kokoro*). Another question he ponders is how to create ultimate beauty (*yûgen*), the ideal of the art of *nô*.

KUROKAWA-NO (NO IN THE RURAL TRADITION)

4.84 HASHIHIME
Mask of Kurokawa nô (Kamiza)
16th c.
Wood
21 x 14.5 cm
Kurokawa Nô Denshû-kan

4.85 TSUCHIGUMO
Mask of Kurokawa nô (Shimoza) for the nochijite in nô "Tsuchigumo"
15th c.
Wood
20.7 x 18 cm
Kurokawa Nô Denshû-kan

It is certainly a myth that the origin of Kurokawa *nô* goes back to the Muromachi Period when the son of Emperor Gokomatsu, at the end of the 14th century, came to the region of Kurokawa near the city of Tsuruoka in Yamagata Prefecture, and his retainers taught the art of *nô* to the local people. Presently, performances are held on several set annual occasions, which suggests

how thoroughly *nô* has been integrated into the daily lives of Kurokawa farmers. The performers belong to two troupes, an upper (*Kami-za*) and lower (*Shimo-za*) one, which alternate performances in the local Kasuga shrine in front of their guardian gods, in a kind of competition. During the first night of February each year, at newly chosen farmers' houses, they do their best in performing both ritual worship and their old art. But Kurokawa *nô* is not simply a folk theater form derived from *nô*. Instead, it is a unique kind of *nô*, which has been passed down from generation to generation among local farmers who are not professional *nô* performers. Having followed an existence completely isolated from the highly refined style of the five schools of *nô* based largely in the cities, Kurokawa *nô* still maintains techniques as well as plays which have been lost or dropped by the five schools. Thus, it plays an extremly important role in reflecting the history of *nô*.

The masks of Kurokawa, in terms of both quality and quantity, are significant. Many of the approximately 215 masks are made by very well-known mask carvers, and some can be dated back to times before the completion of the types of typical *nô* masks well known today. As a whole, the Kurokawa collection is by no means inferior to the standard of many of the collections of feudal lords or those maintained by the five dynasties of *nô*.

The mask Tsuchigumo of the *Shimo-za* is a good example of an old mask unique to

Kurokawa. In the five other *nô* schools, the *maejite* (the main actor in the first half of the play) is without a mask (hitamen), while the *nochijite* (the main actor in changed appearance in the second half) in this play usually wears a Shikami demon mask. In Kurokawa *nô*, for both the *maejite* and *nochijite*, there are special, very old masks used only for "Tsuchigumo." Here, its ancient form and expression reminds us of a kind of demonic god mask (*kimen*) of *Sarugaku* (see section II in exhibit), from which the *nô* tradition developed. In addition, there are various demon and other masks whose names are no longer precisely remembered. In the case of the mask Hashihime of the *Kami-za*, presently used only by the *nochijite* of the play "Kanawa," it could be a *Ryû-nyo* (lit., "dragon's wife"), an even more demonic type female than *Deigan* (nos. 4.18, 4.23). This mask is named after the legendary woman who became the wife of the Dragon King, living in his palace on the floor of the sea, as related in the old *nô* play "Ama."

SHAKESPEARE IN NO STYLE

4.86/4.87 KING LEAR, MACBETH: TWO MASKS FOR SHAKESPEARE PERFORMANCES IN NO STYLE
Carved by Otsuka Ryôji
Wood, *gofun*, colors
4.86) King Lear: 12.5 x 12.5 cm (including beard, 41 cm)
4.87) Macbeth: 18 x 12 cm
Otsuka Ryôji, Shimada, Shizuoka Prefecture

Both masks were made for performances of Shakespearean dramas in *nô* style that were adapted by Munakata Kuniyoshi. Performances took place in the National Nô Theater in Tokyo as well as abroad. Otsuka's masks were favorably received at the Japanese Culture Center, Sydney, Australia, and at four other major venues in 1994. Born in 1945 in Shimada, Shizuoka Prefecture, where he still lives, Otsuka is devoted to carving *nô* and *kyôgen* masks. The Iemoto Dynasty of the Izumi Kyôgen School frequently performs using his *kyôgen* masks with their very modern expressions.

V. Satire, Parody, and Joyous Laughter: *Kyôgen*

Introduction

5.1 Tsukinami Fuzokuzu Byobu (Sambaso)
Photograph of painting
Late 16th c.
61 x 40 cm [original painting]
Tokyo National Museum

Sambasô dance performed during a rice planting festival.

5.2 Rakuchu Rakugaizu Byobu (play: "Asahina")
Photograph of painted screen (*byôbu*)
ca. 1610
162 x 58 cm [original screen]
Tokyo National Museum

"Asahina" (Asahina, the Warrior) performed on a temporary stage on the Shijô river bank in Kyoto.

5.3 a-b Kyogen Kozu Harikae Byobu
Painted screen (*byôbu*)
1620s-30s
Paper, wood
129 x 178 cm
Tsubouchi Memorial Theatre Museum, Waseda University

Scenes from several Ôkura school *kyôgen* plays are depicted, including plays that can be clearly identified as *"Su Hajikami"* (Vinegar and Ginger), *"Kitsunezuka"* (The Fox Mound), "Asahina" (Asahina, the Warrior), *"Senjimono"* (The Tea Seller), *"Tsuto Yamabushi"* (The

5.1

5.5 A

5.3 B

Lunchbox Thief), "Shûron" (A Religious Dispute), "Gan Nusubito" (The Goose Thief), and "Jizô Mai" (The Dance of the God Jizô). Note that the actors' clothing and properties are similar to those used in daily life in the early 1600s. They are not specialized theater costumes and properties.

5.4 A-B ISE MONSUI
Ise Monsui kyôgen zu byôbu (pair)
Painted screens (byôbu)
Late 19th c.
Paper, wood
332 x 153 cm
Tsubouchi Memorial Theatre Museum, Waseda University

Scenes from various plays are depicted, including "Kusabira" (Mushrooms), "Sanbonbashira" (Three Poles), "Tsuribari" (The Magic Fish Hook), and "Taue" (Rice Planting Ceremony). Note that by the 19th century, costumes and properties designed for exclusive use on the stage have been developed for kyôgen plays. The positioning of the actors is more formalized than in no. 5.3.

5.5A KYOGENKI (KANBUN EDITION)
Book
ca. 1660
26 x 19 cm [original]
Gakushûin University, Japanese Language and Literature Center

Illustrated play texts in five volumes. This illustration shows the play "Nukegara" (Shedding the Demon Shell).

5.5B YAMAWAKI IZUMI MOTONARI
Kumogatabon
Book
ca. 1820s
24 x 17 cm
Nagoya Kyôgen Kyôdôsha

Annotated play texts used by the Izumi School of kyôgen.

COSTUMES

5.6 KATAGINU (VEST) WITH RICE PLANT AND CLAPPER MOTIF
19th c.
Paint-resist dyed and painted hemp
83.5 x 71 cm
Shigeyama Sengorô
This is an autumn scene in the country. Motifs like this are suitable for Tarô Kaja, the archetypical servant.

5.7 KATAGINU (VEST) WITH ARRAY OF INSECTS AS MOTIF
19th c.
Paint-resist dyed and painted hemp
78.5 x 68 cm
Shigeyama Sengorô

A mantis, a butterfly, a wasp, a snail and a spider are resisted in white with paste, then painted in sumi ink and colors. Note that the mantis has two too many legs. The insects are largely destructive and abhorrent ones, and this costume would be worn by a bad character such as a shyster or slave trader.

5.8 KATAGINU (VEST) WITH MOON AND AUTUMN GRASSES MOTIF
19th c.
Paint-resist dyed and painted hemp
77.5 x 73 cm
Shigeyama Sengorô

This autumn design of pampas grass, bell flowers and the rising full moon shows a lyrical strain in kyôgen costume design.

5.9 KATAGINU (VEST) WITH CRAB MOTIF
Edo Period (1615-1868)
Paint-resist dyed, stencilled and painted hemp
70 x 61 cm
Nagoya Kyôgen Kyôdôsha

A Chinese-brocade pattern is stencilled with sumi ink on a yellow ground, and on it seven crabs are resisted with slightly colored paste. The crabs are contoured with sumi.

5.10 KATAGINU (VEST FOR CHILD ACTOR) WITH A MOTIF OF A MONKEY REACHING FOR THE MOON'S REFLECTION
19th c.
Paint-resist dyed and painted hemp
56 x 51 cm
Shigeyama Sengorô

The monkey is drawn in the style of Mu Ch'i of the Southern Sung Dynasty. This design is both allegorical and humorous. The little monkey of course cannot scoop the moon up from the water, and it is foolish to think that he can, but the sincerity of his effort to do so (the moon symbolizes enlightenment) is laudable. The allegory perfectly suits the child actor who is striving to excel at kyôgen, but is too young to do so.

5.11 KATAGINU (VEST) WITH ARRAY OF TOYS AS MOTIF
Edo Period (1615-1868)
Yuzen-dyed and painted hemp
65.5 x 68 cm
Nagoya Kyôgen Kyôdôsha

Yuzen dying makes possible brilliant colors and subtle gradations of color. The toys depicted on this costume include tops, a demon mask, dolls, pinwheels, and a carp pull toy.

5.12 KATAGINU (VEST) WITH SPEARHEAD POCKETS MOTIF
19th c.
Paint-resist dyed and painted hemp
79 x 62 cm
Shigeyama Sengorô

Each spear cover is represented by a komon— a fine, stencilled pattern.

5.13 KATAGINU (VEST) WITH HORSE IN BRUSH PAINTING STYLE BY TANIGUCHI KOKYO
Costume
Late 19th or early 20th c.
Paint-resist dyed and painted hemp
82 x 63.5 cm
Shigeyama Sengorô

5.4 A

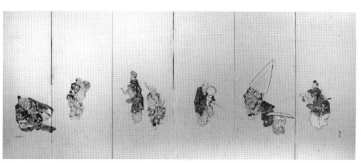

5.4 B

5.6

5.14

5.7

5.9

5.16

The design was painted by Kyoto artist Taniguchi Kokyo (1863-1915). The Shigeyama family uses this *kataginu* when playing the monkey trainer in *"Utsubôzaru"* because of an old association between monkeys and horses, which included keeping a monkey in the vicinity of a stable as a talisman to protect horses.

5.14 KATAGINU (VEST) WITH DISTANT MOUNTAIN AND RAPE BLOSSOM DESIGN
19th c.
Paint-resist dyed and colored hemp
78.5 x 60 cm
Shigeyama Sengorô

The design depicts a spring evening and the white Shigeyama family crest suggests the moon rising over the mountains.

5.15 NUIHAKU (KIMONO) WITH WRITING AND FLOWER DESIGN
Costume for women's roles
19th c.
Silk
150 x 65 cm
Tsubouchi Memorial Theatre Museum, Waseda University

5.16 KATAGINU (VEST) WITH SPACE SHIP MOTIF
1978
Linen (hemp)
approx. 70 x 60 cm
Shigeyama Sengorô

Used in the new *kyôgen* play "The Fox and the Alien."

5.12

5.13

5.15

5.17 ONO TOSHIAKI, TAKEUCHI KOICHI, HAKOZAKI MUTSUMASA, HATANAKA KOSHO, HATTA TETSU
Kosode and *suo kamishimo* (robes) with design of poems and paintings on square and rectangular cards and slips
1993
Silk
approx. 150 x 70 cm
Shigeyama Akira

Commissioned by Shigeyama Akira for his debut as the *daimyô* in the play "Hanago."

SPECIAL ROLES

5.18 A-E DAIMYO (FEUDAL LORD)
Costume and accoutrement ensemble: *suo kamishimo* (overrobe & trousers, spider web pattern); *dan noshime* (striped kimono); *daimyô* hat; sword; fan
Various dates
Cloth, wood, paper, steel, bamboo
approx. 213.4 x 91.4 cm
Nagoya Kyôgen Kyôdôsha

5.19 A-I and 5.20 A-B TARO KAJA (SERVANT, FROM PLAY "BO-SHIBARI" (TIED TO A POLE)
Clothed life-sized figure with: 5.19) *kataginu* (vest); *shima noshime* (kimono); *hakama* (trousers); *dôgi* (underkimono); *tabi* (socks); *koshi obi* (sash); pole; 2 ropes; 5.20) *oke* (barrel), lid
Various dates
Cloth, wood, lacquered wood, etc.
approx. 182.9 x 152.4 x 121.9 cm

Tsubouchi Memorial Theatre Museum, Waseda University (5.19 A-I) and Zenchiku Jûrô (5.20 A-B)

Tarô Kaja is the archetypical clever *kyôgen* servant. At this point in "Tied to a Pole," he is attempting to drink *sake* even though he has been tied to a stave by his master.

5.21 A-C WOMAN
Costume ensemble: A) *nuihaku* (kimono: blue with butterflies & flowers); B) *binnan* (headdress [drapes over kimono]); C) *obi* (woman's sash: red [not displayed at full length])
Various dates
Cloth (silk and flax)
approx. 152.4 x 121.9 cm
Nagoya Kyôgen Kyôdôsha

5.22 A-G THUNDER GOD
Costume, mask, and accoutrement ensemble:
A) *atsuita* (kimono: lightning pattern);
B) thunder god mask; C) *akagashira* (red wig);
D) *hakama* (trousers); E) cap; F) hip drum with sticks; G) *happi* (jacket)
Cloth, wood, paper, bamboo
Various dates
approx. 182.9 x 121.9 cm
Nagoya Kyôgen Kyôdôsha

For use in the play "*Kaminari*" (The Thunder God).

5.19/20

5.23 A-C SAMBASO
Costume and accoutrement ensemble:
kokushikijo (black, old man's mask); *atsuita* (kimono: diamond-crane pattern); *hitatare* (overrobe & trousers: tortoise-crane pattern); *kensaki eboshi* (cap); *suzu* (bells on a stick); fan
Various dates
Cloth, wood, paper, bamboo, metal
approx. 213.4 x 152.4 cm
Zenchiku Jûrô

For use in the ceremonial dance Sambasô.

5.23

MASKS

5.24 SAMBASO MASK
Tsubouchi Memorial Theatre Museum,
Waseda University

5.25 FUKU NO KAMI (GOD OF HAPPINESS)
Mask
20th c. replica of classical mask
Wood, gesso, and pigment
14.1 x 23 x 7.21 cm
Shigeyama Sengorô

5.26 OJI (OLD MAN)
Mask
20th c. replica of classical mask
Wood, gesso, and pigment
14.7 x 18.3 x 7.9 cm
Shigeyama Sengorô

Used in *"Makura Monogorui"* (Grandfather in Love).

5.27 OTO (WOMAN)
Mask
Edo Period (1615-1868)
Wood, gesso, and pigment
20.7 x 16 cm
Nagoya Kyôgen Kyôdôsha

Used in *"Tsuri Bari"* (The Magic Fish Hook) and in many other plays with women.

5.28 BUAKU (DEMON)
Mask
Edo Period (1615-1868)
Wood, gesso, and pigment
21 x 16.5 cm
Tsubouchi Memorial Theatre Museum,
Waseda University

Used in *"Oba ga Sake"* (Auntie's Sake) and in many other plays.

5.29 BUAKU (DEMON)
Mask
20th c. replica of classical mask
Wood, gesso, and pigment
16.8 x 20.5 x 9.9 cm
Shigeyama Sengorô

Nicknamed the leering (*tsukebe*) buaku by the Shigeyama family, it is used in roles such as *"Setsubun"* in which a demon falls in love with a human lady.

5.30 USOBUKI (MINOR SPIRIT)
Mask
Edo Period (1615-1868)
Wood, gesso, and pigment
13.5 x 18 cm
Tsubouchi Memorial Theatre Museum,
Waseda University

Used in *"Kazumo"* (Wrestling with a Mosquito), the fruit spirits in *"Konomi Arasoi"* (The War Between the Fruits and the Nuts) and in *ai-kyôgen* interludes in *nô* plays.

5.31 KENTOKU (SPIRIT OR ANIMAL)
Mask
Wood, gesso, and pigment
18.5 x 14.7 cm
Tsubouchi Memorial Theatre Museum,
Waseda University

Used for horses, cows, dogs, and nut spirits in *"Konomi Arasoi"* (The War Between the Fruits and the Nuts).

5.32 SARU (MONKEY)
Mask; signed by the mask carver Yamato
Edo Period (1615-1868)
Wood, gesso, and pigment
18.5 x 14.5 cm
Nagoya Kyôgen Kyôdôsha

Used in *"Utsubo Zaru"* (The Monkey Quiver).

5.33 MASK BY TAKATSU KOICHI
Kitsune (fox)
Mask
Contemporary
Wood, gesso, and pigment
20 x 15.9 x 13 cm
Takatsu Kôichi

Used for the fox in the second act of *"Tsurigitsune"* (Fox Trapping).

5.34 HAKUZOSU (FOX IN GUISE OF MAN)
Mask
Edo Period (1615-1868)
Wood, gesso, and pigment
14.2 x 21.3 x 8.3 cm
Shigeyama Sengorô

Used for the fox disguised as the trapper's uncle in the first act of *"Tsurigitsune"* (Fox Trapping).

5.35 SAGARIHIGE (OLD MAN)
Mask
Edo Period (1615-1868)
Wood, gesso, and pigment
20 x 14.5 cm
Nagoya Kyôgen Kyôdôsha

Used for Shinto sub-deities in *ai-kyôgen* interludes in *nô* plays.

5.36 AMA (OLD WOMAN)
Mask
Edo Period (1615-1868)
Wood, gesso, and pigment
21.7 x 16 cm
Nagoya Kyôgen Kyôdôsha

5.24

5.25

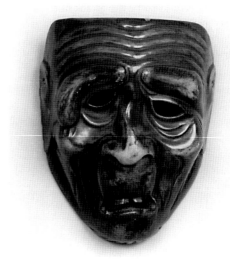

5.26

Used in *"Naki Ama"* (The Crying Nun) and other plays about nuns and old women.

5.37 NOBORIHIGE (OLD MAN)
Mask
Edo Period (1615-1868)
Wood, gesso, and pigment
21 x 14 cm
Tsubouchi Memorial Theatre Museum, Waseda University

Used for Shinto sub-deities in *ai-kyôgen* interludes in *nô* plays.

5.38 *"UTSUBO ZARU"* (THE MONKEY QUIVER)
Photograph
Shigeyama Sengorô

The monkey trainer (Shigeyama Akira) uses a stick to set the tempo for the monkey's (Shigeyama Shigeru) dance, while the feudal lord (Shigeyama Shimei) imitates the monkey's movements.

5.39 *"KAMINARI"* (THE THUNDER GOD)
Photograph
Shigeyama Sengorô

The quack acupuncture doctor (Shigeyama Akira) helps the thunder god (Shigeyama Shimei) stand up after finishing his ministrations. This is an Ôkura School, Shigeyama family *kyôgen* play.

5.40 *"KONOMI ARASOI"* (THE WAR BETWEEN THE FRUITS AND THE NUTS)
Photograph
Shigeyama Sengorô

The tangerine (Shigeyama Sengorô XIII) uses his stave to parry the attack of the persimmon (Kimura Masao), a rank-and-file member of the nut army, who is wielding pruning clippers. This is an Ôkura School, Shigeyama family *kyôgen* play.

5.28

5.29

5.30

5.31

5.34

5.37

KYOGEN IN THE MODERN WORLD

5.41 "THE HIKOICHI STORY"
Photograph
Post-World War II
12.7 x 17.8 cm
Shigeyama Sengorô

Original *kyôgen* based on a Kumamoto folk story, directed by Takechi Tetsuji.

5.42 "THE OLD FARMER ASSAULTS SOCRATES"
Photograph
1978
27.9 x 38.1 cm
Shigeyama-Takarazuka joint production
Shigeyama Sengorô

5.43 A-D NOHO PRODUCTIONS OF BECKETT'S "ACT WITHOUT WORDS I" AND "THEATRE I"
Four photographs
1980s
20.3 x 25.4 cm
Jonah Salz

NOHO, founded by Jonah Salz and Shigeyama Akira in 1981, is an international theater group dedicated to utilizing *nô* and *kyôgen* techniques, structures, and spirit to interpret western texts.

A) "Theatre I" directed by Jonah Salz, with Shigeyama Akira as the blind man and Maruishi Yasushi as the lame man. Tokyo, 1982.
B) "Act Without Words I" directed by Jonah Salz, featuring Shigeyama Akira, Kyoto, 1981. "He gets up [on the cubes] and is about to reach a carafe [of water] when it is pulled up a little way and comes to rest beyond his reach."
C) "Act Without Words I" directed by Jonah Salz and Shigeyama Akira, featuring Shigeyama Sennojô. This is the same scene as above, with different *kata*. Kyoto, 1985.
D) "Act Without Words I" directed by Jonah Salz and Shigeyama Akira, featuring Shigeyama Sennojô and Maruishi Yasushi as the stage assistant. "A pair of tailor's scissors descends from the flies and comes to rest before a tree, a yard from the ground."

5.44 NOHO PRODUCTION OF "THE MOON VIEWING BLIND MAN" (IN ENGLISH)
Photograph
Photographer: Muranaka Osamu
1985
20.3 x 25.4 cm
Jonah Salz

5.45 A-C

5.45 A-C

Directed by Shigeyama Akira and presented at Kyoto's Mumonkan, this play features Dan Furst as the blind man and Laurence Kominz as the city man.

5.45 A-C THEATRE OF YUGEN KYOGEN FUSION PLAYS
Three photographs
Photographers: A, B) Robert Isaacs;
C) David Allan
A)1985; B)1987; C)1996
27.9 x 35.6 cm
Courtesy of Theatre of Yugen, San Francisco

Theatre of Yûgen, led by Yuriko Doi, is a San Francisco-based theater group dedicated to experimental fusion plays.

A) Yuriko Doi in the lead role in the English-language *kyôgen* play, "The Melon Thief," 1987.
B) Brenda Wong Aoki as Pozzo in Beckett's "Waiting for Godot" in *kyôgen* style, 1985; directed by Yuriko Doi.
C) Mikio Hirata as Scrooge and Kinji Hayashi as the ghost of Christmas future in "*Noh* Christmas Carol," 1996; directed by Yuriko Doi.

5.46 A-B TWO PRODUCTIONS BY THE KENNY AND OGAWA KYOGEN PLAYERS
Two photographs
A)1983; B)1988
Poster size
Kenny and Ogawa Kyôgen Players

The Kenny and Ogawa Kyôgen Players began in 1975 to perform *kyôgen* plays and other experimental works in English. Since then, they have performed at numerous venues in Japan and elsewhere.

A) Don Kenny and Shichirô Ogawa as the lame man and the blind man in Yeats's "The Cat and the Moon" (*kyôgen* play), directed by Don Kenny, Tokyo, 1983.
B) Don Kenny in the title role in his original *kyôgen* play, "A Slight Flaw or The Deputy Death Deity," Tokyo, 1988. Directed by Don Kenny; mask by Rebecca Teele.

5.41

5.47 A-D

5.42

5.44

5.43

5.47A-D WORLD PREMIERE OF MISHIMA YUKIO'S MODERN KYOGEN PLAY "BUSU" (DEADLY POISON)
At the University of California/Davis, Wyatt Pavilion Theater; directed by Barbara Sellers-Young
Photographs
May 1995
20.3 x 25.4 cm
Barbara Sellers

A) Raspotinov (Jason Rothbart), an émigré Russian antique shop proprietor gives instructions to his two servants, Keith (Tim Redmond) and Chiz (Dave Kapoor). Megan Evans and Jennifer Quinn are display cases.
B) Chiz fans air away from the supposed poison while Keith investigates it.
C) The poison is, in fact, caviar, which the master is concealing from his employees. Chiz and Keith eat it all up.
D) Keith has just finished smashing a valuable antique vase in preparation for the elaborate excuse he will give the master for eating up the "poison."

5.48 POSTCARD FROM SAMUEL BECKETT TO JONAH SALZ
1980s
12.7 x 16.5 cm
Jonah Salz

Message concerns influence of Yeats on Beckett's writing of "Theatre I."

5.49 POSTER FOR A SHOW OF KYOGEN PLAYS KENNY AND OGAWA KYOGEN PLAYERS

A publicity poster for a Kenny and Ogawa Kyôgen Players performance in French at L'institut Franco-Japonais de Tokyo.

VI. MARGINS BETWEEN THE REAL AND UNREAL: *Bunraku*

PUPPET THEATER AS PART OF THE FOLK TRADITION

6.1 EBISU-MAWASHI PUPPET
Wood, cloth
70 x 35 cm
Tsubouchi Memorial Theatre Museum,
Waseda University

Ebisu-mawashi was a form of folk puppet theater originating in Hyogo Prefecture. Ebisu is a god of the sea and was therefore revered by fishermen who prayed for successful catches. Itinerant puppeteers performed auspicious dances around the country from at least the 16th century onwards. This was important as a precursor of *bunraku* puppet theater

6.2 A-D SADO NOROMA PUPPETS
Wood, cloth
30 x 15 cm
Tsubouchi Memorial Theatre Museum,
Waseda University

These are examples of a folk puppet from Sado Island, where traditions have survived from the 17th century. Noroma are comic puppets held by one puppeteer and were used in interludes between acts. They survive as part of performances in festivals in villages around Japan. This is part of the tradition from Niigata Prefecture.

6.3 SADO BUN'YA PUPPET (SAMBASO)
Maker: Nishihashi Takeshi
Contemporary (made for this exhibition)
Wood, cloth
50 x 20 cm
Nishihashi Takeshi

Bun'ya was a type of puppetry and chanting dating from the 17th century in Osaka and Kyoto that gave way to bunraku. It has survived on remote Sado Island off the west coast of Japan in Niigata Prefecture. Each puppet was worked by one man. The Sambasô puppet is used at the beginning of performances in an auspicious dance.

6.4 SADO BUN'YA PUPPET: YASHA (SHE-DEVIL)
Maker: Matsunosuke
Contemporary
Wood, cloth
30 x 15 cm
Tsubouchi Memorial Theatre Museum,
Waseda University

6.2 A-D

6.4-6.7

6.3

6.5 SADO BUN'YA PUPPET (DAUGHTER)
Maker: Matsunosuke
Contemporary (made for this exhibition)
Wood, cloth
30 x 15 cm
Tsubouchi Memorial Theatre Museum,
Waseda University

6.6 SADO BUN'YA PUPPET (OLD MAN)
Maker: Kono
Contemporary; made in Sado for this exhibition
Wood, cloth
30 x 15 cm
Tsubouchi Memorial Theatre Museum,
Waseda University

6.7 SADO BUN'YA PUPPET (YOUNG SAMURAI)
Contemporary; made in Sado for this exhibition
Wood, cloth
30 x 15 cm
Tsubouchi Memorial Theatre Museum,
Waseda University

6.8 SADO NOROMA PUPPET (DEMON)
Wood, cloth
30 x 15 cm
Tsubouchi Memorial Theatre Museum,
Waseda University

6.9 PAINTING OF SCENE OF MID-17TH C. PUPPET THEATER
Color on paper
81 x 35 cm
Tsubouchi Memorial Theatre Museum,
Waseda University

The scene is most likely in Kyoto, but this has not been confirmed. The backdrop shows a castle, and various warrior puppets are visible.

6.10 RAKUCHU-RAKUGAIZU (PHOTOGRAPH OF PAINTING OF KYOTO AREA IN EARLY 17TH C.)
Tokyo National Museum

This painting shows a scene along Shijo-kawara where there are two puppet theaters. On the left, the play shown is "Munewari" and on the right, "Yamanaka Tokiwa." Puppeteers work the puppets from behind the screen.

6.8

6.9

CHIKAMATSU MONZAEMON AND TAKEMOTO GIDAYU

6.11 PHOTOGRAPH OF PORTRAIT OF CHIKAMATSU MONZAEMON (1653-1725)
73 x 30 cm (original portrait)
Osaka Municipal Museum

Chikamatsu is the most famous playwright of *bunraku* and *kabuki*. His real name was Sugimori Nobumori and he was born a samurai in Fukui Prefecture. When he was about fifteen or sixteen, his father lost his position as an employed samurai and became a *rônin*. Chikamatsu moved with his family to Kyoto where he served in an aristocratic house for a time. He gave up his samurai status and entered the world of theater, working backstage and then writing plays for *bunraku* (*jôruri*) and *kabuki*. Initially he wrote for Uji Kaganojô, and then for Takemoto Gidayû. He also wrote *kabuki* for Sakata Tôjûrô during the 1690s, until about 1703. Over his long career he wrote about ninety *bunraku* and thirty *kabuki* plays. He is best known for his twenty-four *sewamono* (contemporary-life plays), which depict tragedies of individuals from Kyoto and Osaka; for example, "Love Suicides at Sonezaki," first performed in 1703. After his death, he was called the "god of writers." He is famous for his sympathetic depiction of the passions and crimes of ordinary men and women.

6.12 PHOTOGRAPH OF PORTRAIT OF TAKEMOTO GIDAYU (1651-1714)
88 x 28 cm (original portrait)
Osaka Municiplal Museum

Gidayû is considered the founder of the *bunraku* (*jôruri*) tradition. His name Gidayû came to be the term for *bunraku*-style music. His birthname was Gorobei and he was born in Tennoji in Osaka. He was a disciple of various chanters such as Inoue Harimanojô and Uji Kaganojô before opening his own theater (Takemoto-za) in Osaka in 1684 in the Dotonbori area, which is still Osaka's major entertainment district. Success came with his first performance, which was of Chikamatsu's play "The Soga Successors." The combination of Chikamatsu and Gidayû ushered in the golden age of *bunraku*. In 1698, Gidayû received the royal title Chikugonojô. He left several important and influential short treatises on the art of chanting. Chikamatsu wrote all of his *bunraku* plays for Gidayû until the chanter's death.

6.11

6.12

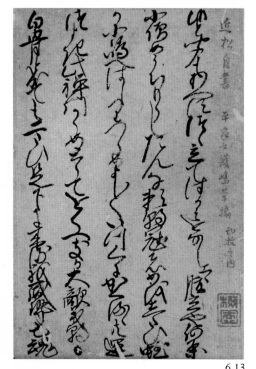

6.13

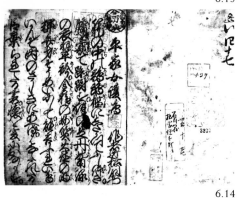

6.14

6.15

6.16

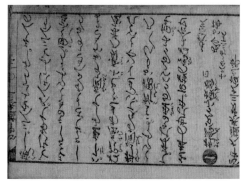

6.18

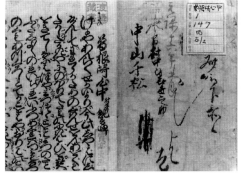

6.19

6.20 B

6.13 Manuscript in the hand of Chikamatsu for the 1719 play "Heike nyogo shima"
Hanging scroll
Ink on paper
48 x 38 cm
Tsubouchi Memorial Theatre Museum, Waseda University

Since Chikamatsu's plays were almost always published in authorized editions at the time of first performance, we have very few examples of his manuscripts. The words of this manuscript are different from the published version.

6.14 Authorized printed book (maruhon) of text for the play "Heike nyogo shima"
1719
Print on paper
23.5 x 17 cm
Tsubouchi Memorial Theatre Museum, Waseda University

Each page has seven lines. The book is open to a section of Chikamatsu's manuscript.

6.15 Chikamatsu's desk (replica)
1890
Wood
25 x 91.5 cm
Tsubouchi Memorial Theatre Museum, Waseda University

Chikamatsu's actual desk is in the hands of a private individual in Gifu Prefecture. Tsubouchi Shôyô had this desk, modeled on the original, made in 1890.

6.16 Photograph of re-creation of one-man puppets (Ohatsu and Tokubei)
1970
National Bunraku Theater

We have no one-man puppets from Chikamatsu's era. This re-creation was made in 1970 by the Bunraku Kyôkai (Bunraku Association), based on various traditional illustrations of "Love Suicides at Sonezaki."

6.17 Photograph of re-creation of one-man puppet in pilgrimage scene from "Love Suicides at Sonezaki"
Waseda University Library

This scene portrays Ohatsu's pilgrimage to the thirty-three Kannon temples in Osaka. "Love Suicides at Sonezaki" was revived in the modern era in 1955, although with a revised text. In 1990, a version faithful to Chikamatsu's original text was performed.

6.18 PHOTOGRAPH OF BOOK GREAT MIRROR OF LOVE SUICIDES (SHINJU OKAGAMI)
1704 (original)
National Bunraku Theater

The book is open at the section describing the actual incident upon which Chikamatsu based his play "Love Suicides at Sonezaki." On the seventh day of the fourth month of 1703, Tokubei, a 25-year-old clerk in an oil merchant's shop, and Ohatsu, a 21-year-old prostitute from the Tenma House of Shinchi, committed love suicide in the Tenjin woods at Sonezaki. Exactly one month later, Chikamatsu's play was performed at the Takemoto-za in Dotonbori, Osaka. The *Great Mirror* describes more than twenty such love suicides, attesting to what was in vogue at the time.

6.19 LOVE SUICIDES AT SONEZAKI
Book: authorized complete edition (*maruhon*)
1703
Waseda University Library

Each page has seven lines. The book was published at the time of the play's first performance. The texts contain the chanter's code of musical notation, which is a guide to how the lines are to be delivered and where musical cadences should fall, marking paragraphs. These texts were aimed at amateur chanters, who had requested that the notation be included so that the books could be used as practice texts. This play was Chikamatsu's first *jôruri* (*bunraku*) play dealing with contemporary life (*sewamono*). In all, he was to write twenty-four *sewamono*.

6.20 A-B PHOTOGRAPHS FROM A CONTEMPORARY BUNRAKU PERFORMANCE OF "LOVE SUICIDES AT SONEZAKI"
National Bunraku Theater

After its initial run in 1703, Chikamatsu's original play was not performed in *bunraku* until 1955, when it was revived. Since then, both in Japan and abroad, it has become one of the most popular pieces in the repertory, having been performed in *bunraku* more than one thousand times. However, it is performed with three-man puppets, which were developed in the 1730s after Chikamatsu's death, and the text has been rewritten to fit current *bunraku* conventions.

6.22

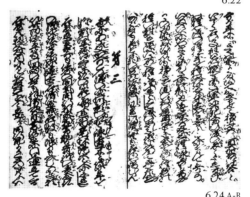

6.24 A-B

"CHRONICLE OF THE BATTLES OF ICHINOTANI"

6.21 BUNRAKU PUPPET IN ROLE OF KUMAGAI, FROM "CHRONICLE OF THE BATTLES OF ICHINOTANI" (1751), ACT THREE
Maker: Ôe Minosuke (1907-1997)
Wood, cloth
135 x 65 cm
Tsubouchi Memorial Theatre Museum, Waseda University

The costume is said to be modeled on the *shikan* style of *kabuki*, named after the family of actors with the name Nakamura Shikan or Nakamura Utaemon. The puppet head is called *bunshichi*, and both the eyes and eyebrows move. Kumagai must sacrifice his own son in place of the high-ranking Atsumori. Act three is the depiction of this tragedy and its impact upon Kumagai and his wife Sagami.

6.22 BUNRAKU PUPPET IN ROLE OF SAGAMI FROM "CHRONICLE OF BATTLES OF ICHINOTANI" (1751), ACT THREE
Maker: Ôe Minosuke (1907-1997)
Wood, cloth
125 x 50 cm
Tsubouchi Memorial Theatre Museum, Waseda University

This type of puppet head is called *fuke-oyama* (middle-aged woman). The costume has strands of gold thread. It was prepared by the puppeteer Kiritake Monjûrô II (1900-1970).

6.23 A-C PHOTOGRAPH OF CURRENT BUNRAKU PERFORMANCE OF ACT THREE, KUMAGAI'S CAMP, FROM THE PLAY "CHRONICLE OF BATTLES OF ICHINOTANI"
Lent by the puppet maker: Aoki Shinji

6.24 A-B PRINTED BOOK (MARUHON) OF "CHRONICLE OF BATTLES OF ICHINOTANI"
1751
24 x 17 cm
Tsubouchi Memorial Theatre Museum, Waseda University

This book has seven lines to a page and was published at the time of the first performance. Namiki Sôsuke (1695-1751), the senior playwright of the Toyotake-za, died after completing act three of this play. Under the name Namiki Senryû, he was the senior playwright for a period in the 1740s at the rival Takemoto-za. There he wrote, with others, the three most famous plays of the *kabuki* and *bunraku* repertories, including the story of the forty-seven *rônin*, "Chûshingura."

6.25 A-B PHOTOGRAPHS OF PLAYBILLS (BANZUKE) OF THE FIRST PERFORMANCE (1751) OF "CHRONICLE OF BATTLES OF ICHINOTANI"
Osaka College of Music

These playbills were used as advertising, in the manner of posters or notices today. They usually were printed in two sheets, one with the list of chanters and *shamisen* players, the other with the puppeteers.

6.26 PHOTOGRAPH OF ILLUSTRATED EDITION (EZUKUSHI) OF THE FIRST PERFORMANCE (1751) OF "CHRONICLE OF BATTLES OF ICHINOTANI"
National Diet Library

Full-text *maruhon* editions were read as novels or used as practice texts, and were often kept in print until the late 19th century. Playbills and illustrated editions tended to be printed at the time of performance as part of an advertising campaign. Each of the five

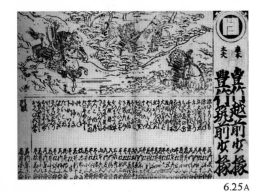

6.25A

6.25A

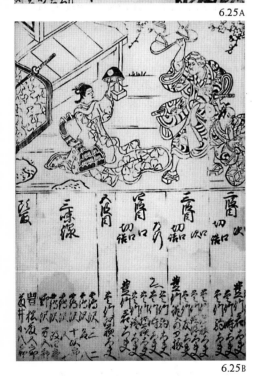

6.25B

6.26A

6.26B

6.26C

6.26D

6.26E

6.26F

acts was illustrated in two to three pages. These editions are valuable sources about the plays because, unlike *kabuki*, there are not many illustrations of the *bunraku* versions of plays.

Bunraku Music (Gidayu)

6.27 Kendai (stand) used in performance by Toyotake Yamashiro no Shojo (1878-1967)
Wood
48 x 50 x 35 cm
Tsubouchi Memorial Theatre Museum, Waseda University

Yamashiro no Shôjô, a collector of *bunraku* objects, at one time had more than twenty *kendai*, but these were destroyed in World War II. He obtained this after the war; it was the favorite of Toyotake Roshô (1874-1930), the famous women-*gidayû* performer.

6.28 Shirihiki (stool for chanter in performance)
Wood
15 x 25 x 25 cm
Takemoto Miwadayû

A chanter never uses a microphone in performance. He sits on a stool, such as this one, to get maximum power for his voice from a seated position.

6.29 Haraobi (sash wrapped tightly around chanter's waist)
Cloth
15 x 200 cm
Takemoto Miwadayû

The focus of a chanter's voice is said to be in his stomach. The sash is wrapped tightly so that the chanter can put force into his diaphragm.

6.30 Kataginu costume of chanter
Cloth
75 x 115 cm
Takemoto Miwadayû

This formal "coat" of a chanter or *shamisen* player is worn over the shoulders of a kimono. The chanter and *shamisen* player are in full view of the audience, to the right of the stage. It is customary for the chanter to prepare a matching pair of *kataginu* and *hakama* for the *shamisen* player, who then returns them at the end of the month's performances.

6.31 Hakama costume of chanter
Cloth
63 x 80 cm
Takemoto Miwadayû

These are the formal trousers of a chanter or *shamisen* player, worn over the kimono. It is customary for the chanter to prepare a matching pair of *kataginu* and *hakama* for the *shamisen* player, who then returns them at the end of the month's performances.

6.32 YUKAHON (TEXT USED IN PERFORMANCE BY CHANTER)
Paper
27 x 40 cm (open)
Takemoto Miwadayû

Traditionally, a chanter wrote out the text of the particular scenes of each performance. Each page has five lines and has a musical notation code for voice (*kuroshu* or *fu*). A chanter may also use a text by his teacher or other more experienced performer.

6.33 OTOSHI (A SMALL BEAN OR SAND BAG)
Takemoto Miwadayû

A chanter places this next to his stomach for pressure when chanting.

6.34 SHAMISEN (MUSICAL INSTRUMENT)
Maker: Shiba Ken
Wood, leather, ivory
23 x 102 cm
Tsubouchi Memorial Theatre Museum, Waseda University

The neck is made from a red wood (*kôki*) found only in India. The body is made from Chinese quince (*karin*). A *bunraku* (*gidayû*) *shamisen* has the thickest neck of any type of *shamisen*, and is referred to as *futozao*. This was used by Tsuruzawa Seiroku IV (1889-1960) and has the name "Takitsuse." He played with Yamashiro no Shôjô for a long time, and on 14 March 1947, he used this instrument when performing before Emperor Shôwa.

6.35 A-B KEIKOBAN (SHAMISEN PRACTICE TEXT) WITH RED NOTATION MARKS
Paper
25 x 20 cm
Tsubouchi Memorial Theatre Museum, Waseda University

The red notation is called *shu*. *Samisen* notation was never published and has far more detail than the code used by chanters. This book is in the hand of Toyozawa Shinzaemon II (1867-1943) and is the Kumagai Camp scene from the play "Chronicle of the Battle of Ichinotani."

6.28, 6.29, 6.33

6.32

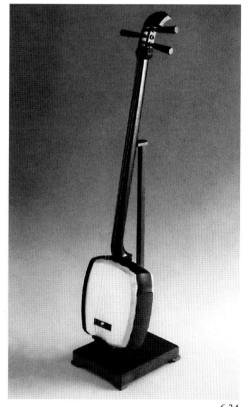

6.34

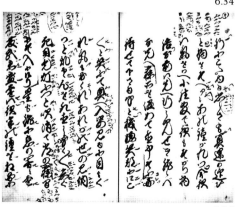

6.35

PUPPETS AND PUPPETEERS

6.36 OSOME
Head is by Tengu Kyû (Hisa); body was put together by Kiritake Monjûrô II
Wood, cloth
57 x 107 cm (head and body)
Andrew Gerstle

In 1942, this puppet was given to the author Kawabata Yasunari (1899-1972). Osome is a popular role in several sewamono plays dealing with contemporary life, such as "Shinpan utazaemon" (1780), the earliest version of which dates from 1711.

6.37 BUNRAKU PUPPET; BODY FRAME AND FEET OF MALE PUPPET
Wood, bamboo, cloth
85 x 30 cm
Tsubouchi Memorial Theatre Museum, Waseda University

The frame has "shoulders" (*kataita*) and a "waist" (*koshiwa*), but the inside is empty space with a cloth covering. Legs are attached with strings to the frame. The kimono is fitted over the frame.

6.38A-E PHOTOGRAPHS OF ILLUSTRATIONS FROM THE BOOK SHIBAI GAKUYA ZUE SHUI (ILLUSTRATIONS OF BACKSTAGE IN KABUKI AND BUNRAKU)
1802
National Bunraku Theater

These show the preparation of a *bunraku* puppet for performance. What is evident is that *bunraku* puppets in late 18th-century Osaka were almost exactly the same as they are today.

6.39 PHOTOGRAPHS OF THE PROCESS OF CARVING A PUPPET HEAD
National Bunraku Theater

6.40 EXAMPLE OF A PUPPET HEAD AT DIFFERENT STAGES OF CARVING
Wood
50 x 60 cm
Tsubouchi Memorial Theatre Museum, Waseda University

1. Block of wood (*koso-e*) is dried and prepared for carving by being cut into a square.
2. Side for puppet face is chosen and the outline of face is drawn.
3. Initial carving follows outline of face.
4. When puppet is almost finished, it is cut in two just in front of the ears, and the mechanisms for moving the eyes, mouth, etc., are fitted.
5. The finished head is then glued together.

6.36

6.37

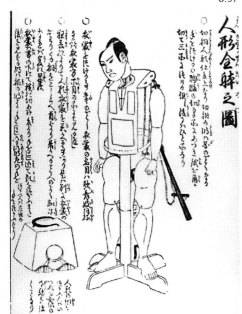

6.38E

Japanese traditional paper (*washi*) is pasted all over the face and then several light coats of *gofun* (chalk whitewash) are applied. Finally, the eyes and other features are painted on.

6.41 BUNRAKU PUPPET HEAD "KUCHI-AKI (MOVEABLE MOUTH) BUNSHICHI"
Maker: Ôe Minosuke
Wood
38 cm high
Andrew Gerstle

Bunshichi is a main role, often of a tragic samurai character. The "moveable-mouth" variation is often used for grand villains, such as Fujiwara Shihei in the 1746 play "Sugawara and the Secrets of Calligraphy."

6.42 BUNRAKU PUPPET HEAD "GENTA"
Maker: Tengu Kyû (Hisa)
Wood
35 cm high
Andrew Gerstle

This type of head is used for the roles of handsome young men. Eyes and eyebrows move. The wig would be fitted for a particular role.

6.43 BUNRAKU PUPPET HEAD "TSUME"
Wood
26 cm high x 8 cm
Tsubouchi Memorial Theatre Museum, Waseda University

This head is for minor roles. It has no moving parts or wig, and is handled by a single puppeteer.

6.44 COSTUME (UCHIKAKE OUTER KIMONO) FOR AKOYA ROLE IN THE PLAY "DANNOURA KABUTO GUNKI"
1947
Cloth
130 x 105 cm
Tsubouchi Memorial Theatre Museum, Waseda University

This was used by the puppeteer Kiritake Monjûrô (1900-1970).

6.45 COSTUME (KIZUKE, INNER KIMONO) FOR AKOYA ROLE IN THE PLAY "DANNOURA KABUTO GUNKI"
1947
Cloth
96 x 115 cm
Tsubouchi Memorial Theatre Museum, Waseda University
This was used by the puppeteer Kiritake Monjûrô (1900-1970).

6.39A

6.39B

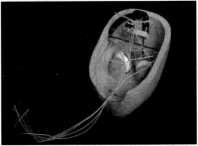

6.39C

6.39D

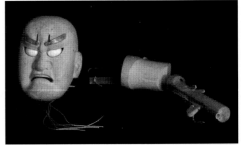

6.39E

6.39F

6.44/46

6.47

6.51

6.48

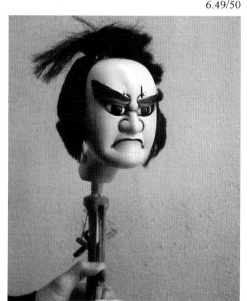

6.49/50

6.41

6.46 COSTUME (OBI, SASH) FOR AKOYA ROLE IN THE PLAY "DANNOURA KABUTO GUNKI"
1947
Cloth
20 x 69 cm and 33 x 65 cm
Tsubouchi Memorial Theatre Museum, Waseda University

This was used by the puppeteer Kiritake Monjûrô (1900-1970).

6.47 COSTUME (KATAGINU AND HAKAMA) OF PUPPETEER FOR AKOYA ROLE IN THE PLAY "DANNOURA KABUTO GUNKI"
Cloth
Kataginu: 75 x 115 cm; hakama: 63 x 80 cm
Tsubouchi Memorial Theatre Museum, Waseda University

Puppeteers are, in principle, hooded and veiled and in black kimono; but the main puppeteer in the climax or dance scenes will be without a hood or veil, and sometimes will wear a decorative kimono. This costume was used by the puppeteer Kiritake Monjûrô (1900-1970) in 1947.

6.48 STAGE GETA (CLOGS) WORN BY SENIOR PUPPETEERS (OMO-ZUKAI)
Wood
24 x 16 x 18 cm
Tsubouchi Memorial Theatre Museum, Waseda University

The floor surface (funazoko) upon which the puppets seem to walk is about 36 cm from the stage floor. The senior of the three puppeteers holds up the puppet so that it is at the correct height. Each stage geta must suit the particular height of the puppeteer.

The geta bottom is wrapped in straw to permit smooth and quiet movement.

6.49 PUPPETEER'S HOOD (ZUKIN) IN "YOSHIDA" STYLE
Cloth
67 x 30 cm
Tsubouchi Memorial Theatre Museum, Waseda University

There are two puppeteer surnames, Yoshida and Kiritake, each of which has a different style of hood.

6.50 PUPPETEER'S HOOD (ZUKIN) IN "KIRITAKE" STYLE
Cloth
52 x 30 cm
Tsubouchi Memorial Theatre Museum, Waseda University

6.51 BUNRAKU PUPPETEER'S BLACK COSTUME (KUROGO)
Cloth
60 x 165 cm
Tsubouchi Memorial Theatre Museum, Waseda University

In *Bunraku*, "black" by convention means to be invisible. In general, all the accoutrements of a puppeteer are his personal possessions.

VII. The Actor's Art: *Kabuki*

History

7.1A Kabuki Scroll (Kabuki Zukan)
Horizontal picture scroll; photographic
reproduction
First half, 17th c.
Paper
37 x 1600 cm
The Tokugawa Reimei Foundation

The founder of *kabuki*, actress-dancer Izumo
no Okuni (active ca. 1596-1610), is shown in
an early dramatic sketch in which a young
samurai dandy, played by Okuni, dallies
with a prostitute. This rare picture scroll
depicts the flamboyant life of commoners in
Kyoto before the banning of Christianity in
1612. Note the Christian rosary, as
fashionable decoration, around Okuni's
neck.

7.1B-C Okuni Kabuki Screen (Okuni
Kabuki-zu Byobu)
Pair of six-fold screens; photographic
reproduction

Paper
147.8 x 330.2 cm
Idemitsu Museum of Art

The oldest screen painting (*byôbu*) to depict
kabuki performance shows the actress Izumo
no Okuni, her face covered in disguise,
performing her popular "visiting a prostitute"
(*chaya asobi*) sketch. The stage set up in the
precincts of Kitano Shrine in Kyoto, is
typical of early *kabuki* around 1610.

7.2 The Actor Ichikawa Danjuro IV
(1712-1778) in "Wait a Moment"
("Shibaraku")
Votive plaque
1764
Wood
122 x 151.5 cm
Yamaguchi Kannon Temple

A major religious offering to temples and
shrines in ancient times was a living horse,

in later times replaced by a picture (*e*) of a
horse (*ma*) painted on a wooden votive
plaque (*ema*). Images of *kabuki* actors were
also often painted on votive plaques.

7.3 Mitsukoshi Costume Department
"Wait a Moment" ("Shibaraku")
Costume; worn by Ichimura Uzaemon XV
(1874-1945)
Linen
256 x 136, 72 x 270 cm
Tsubouchi Memorial Theatre Museum,
Waseda University

7.4 Takahashi Hiroaki
Twelve Zodiac Votive Plaque Screen
(Junishi Ema-zu Byobu)
Two-fold screen
1930
Wood and paper
185 x 212 cm
Tsubouchi Memorial Theatre Museum,
Waseda University

7.1 B-C

7.5

7.1 A

7.6

7.7

7.8

This wooden votive plaque painted by Ippitsusai Bunchô in 1773 and preserved at Kumano Shrine, Tokyo, was reproduced on this folding screen in 1930 by Takahashi Hiroaki.

7.5 UTAGAWA KUNISADA I
"WAIT A MOMENT" ("SHIBARAKU")
Color woodblock print
1833
Paper
Ôban
Actors Ichikawa Ebizô V (top) and Ichikawa Danjûrô VIII (bottom)
Tsubouchi Memorial Theatre Museum, Waseda University; acc. no. 100-2447

7.6 UTAGAWA TOYOKUNI III
"WAIT A MOMENT" ("SHIBARAKU")
Color woodblock print
1864
Paper
Ôban
Actor Kawarasaki Gonjûrô I (later Ichikawa Danjûrô IX)
Tsubouchi Memorial Theatre Museum, Waseda University; acc. no. 100-2463

7.7 TOYOHARA KUNICHIKA
"WAIT A MOMENT" ("SHIBARAKU")
Two-panel color woodblock print
1864
Paper
Ôban

Actors Kawarasaki Gonjûrô I, Bandô Hikosaburô V (insert)
Tsubouchi Memorial Theatre Museum, Waseda University; acc. nos. 100-2437, 2438

7.8 UTAGAWA TOYOKUNI III
"WAIT A MOMENT" ("SHIBARAKU")
Three-panel color woodblock print
Paper
Ôban
From right: actors Ichikawa Kodanji IV, Iwai Kumesaburô III, Kawarasaki Gonjûrô I
Tsubouchi Memorial Theatre Museum, Waseda University; acc. nos. 100-2448, 2449, 2450

| 7.10 | 7.14 | 7.9 | 7.11 | 7.12 | 7.13 |

7.9 IPPITSUSAI BUNCHO
"MIRROR POND IMAGE OF THE SOGA"
("KAGAMI GA IKE OMOKAGE SOGA")
Color woodblock print
1770
Paper
Hosoban
Actors Ichikawa Komazô II (top), Ichikawa
Yaozô II (bottom)
Tsubouchi Memorial Theatre Museum,
Waseda University; acc. no. 030-0149

7.10 IPPITSUSAI BUNCHO
THE ACTOR SEGAWA KIKUNOJO II (1742-
1773) IN "CHRONICLE OF GREAT PEACE:
A SERVANT GIRL'S TRAILING SLEEVE"
("TAIHEIKI SHIZUME NO FURISODE")
Color woodblock print
1767
Paper
Hosoban; nishiki-e
Tsubouchi Memorial Theatre Museum,
Waseda University; acc. no. 030-0012

7.11 IPPITSUSAI BUNCHO
"THE SOGAS' STRATAGEM: THE SNOWS OF
FUJI" ("FUJI NO YUKI KAIKEI SOGA")
Color woodblock print
1770

Paper
Hosoban
Actors Onoe Tamizô I (top), Ichimura
Uzaemon IX (bottom)
Tsubouchi Memorial Theatre Museum,
Waseda University; acc. no. 030-0091

7.12 IPPITSUSAI BUNCHO
"THE ARCHERY CONTEST AT OTOKOYAMA"
("OTOKOYAMA YUNZEI KURABE")
Color woodblock print
1768
Paper
Hosoban
Actors Ichimura Uzaemon IX (top),
Nakamura Matsue I (bottom)
Tsubouchi Memorial Theatre Museum,
Waseda University; acc. no. 030-0090

7.13 IPPITSUSAI BUNCHO
THE ACTOR ÔTANI HIROJI III (1746-1802)
Color woodblock print
Unknown date
Paper
Hosoban
Tsubouchi Memorial Theatre Museum,
Waseda University; acc. no. 030-0008

7.14 IPPITSUSAI BUNCHO
THE ACTOR ÔTANI HIROJI III (1746-1802)
IN "EDO FASHION ROPE-PULLING INCLINE"
("EDO KATAGI HIKEYA TSUNA-SAKA")
Color woodblock print
1772
Paper
Hosoban
Tsubouchi Memorial Theatre Museum,
Waseda University; acc. no. 030-0004

7.15 PICTURE HALL, NARITA-SAN TEMPLE
Photograph of the building
Constructed 1861
Wood
18.9 x 9.9 m
Narita-san Shinshô-ji
Building donated by Ichikawa Danjûrô VII

7.16 MIYAKO MANDAYU THEATER
SCREEN (MIYAKO MANDAYU-ZA BYOBU)
Six-fold screen
Early Edo Period
Paper and wood
90.2 x 281 cm
Tsubouchi Memorial Theatre Museum,
Waseda University

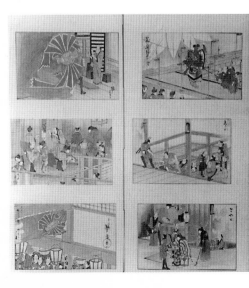

7.18

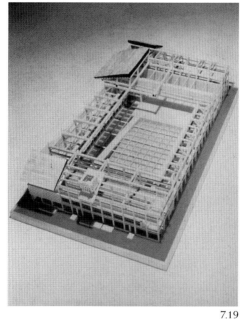

7.15

7.19

One of Kyoto's large *kabuki* theaters, the Miyako Mandayû-za, around 1690. The stage is still largely a copy of the *nô* stage, although somewhat larger, and it does not yet have a *hanamichi*. This screen is a valuable document illustrating urban customs and the lively atmosphere of an early theater district.

7.17 ICHIMURA THEATER SCREEN (ICHIMURA-ZA GEKIJO-ZU BYOBU)
Four-fold screen
1733
Paper and wood
93.4 x 262 cm
Tsubouchi Memorial Theatre Museum,
Waseda University

A scene from one of the many plays about the Soga brothers staged at the New Year season in Edo. In this print of the Ichimura Theater, 1733, the actor playing the hero, Soga Gorô, posed on the *hanamichi*, is probably Ichikawa Danjûrô II (1688-1758). The stage's gabled roof and pillars, remnants of *nô* architecture, can be seen.

7.18 A-B NANSUISHA YOSHIYUKI
SCENES FROM THE OSAKA THEATER SCREEN (OSAKA SHIBAI FUZOKU HARIMAZE BYOBU)
One of a pair of six-fold screens
Early Meiji Period
Paper and wood
375 x 147.4 cm
Tsubouchi Memorial Theatre Museum,
Waseda University

Detailed illustrations of Osaka *kabuki* at the end of the Edo period show the practical workings of the theater from offstage and backstage. Eighteen paintings are arranged, three to a panel, on this six-fold screen. The actor Kataoka Nizaemon X (1851-1895) served as Nansuisha's model.

KABUKI THEATERS AND DOCUMENTS

7.19 ÔSAWA NOBUMOTO
THE ICHIMURA THEATER IN THE EARLY 19TH C.
Model
1982
Wood

W. 101.2, D. 65, H. 30 cm
Tsubouchi Memorial Theatre Museum,
Waseda University

A model of the Ichimura-za, one of Edo's three major licensed *kabuki* theaters, showing typical architectural features of the stage and auditorium in the period 1800-30. The building was about 23 meters wide and 36 meters deep.

7.20 UTAGAWA TOYOHARU
KABUKI THEATER INTERIOR (UKIE KABUKI SHIBAI NO ZU): EDO'S ICHIMURA THEATER
Color woodblock print
ca. 1781-88
Paper
Ôban
Tsubouchi Memorial Theatre Museum,
Waseda University; acc. no. 118-0093

Woodblock prints show us lively scenes inside *kabuki* theaters (*gekijô naibu*). Besides showing the actors on the *hanamichi* and on the main stage, the audience fills every

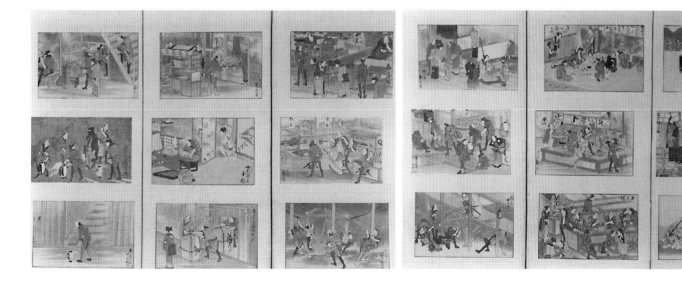

7.18

7.20

7.21

matted square on the floor (*masu*) and two tiers of boxes (*sajiki*). The *nô* stage roof and pillars remain, but they are now dwarfed by the scale of the large surrounding structure.

7.21 REKISENTEI EIRI
KABUKI THEATER INTERIOR: EDO'S SAKAI WARD THEATER DISTRICT (EDO SAKAI-CHO, SHIBAI NO ZU)
Color woodblock print
ca. 1789-1803
Paper
Ôban
Tsubouchi Memorial Theatre Museum, Waseda University; acc. no. 118-0012

The actor playing the superhuman hero of "Wait a Moment" ("Shibaraku"), posed on the *hanamichi* in the midst of audience, is probably Ichikawa Danjûrô V. Two Chinese characters reading "full house" (*ôiri*) are displayed over the stage (left).

7.22 ATTRIBUTED TO UTAGAWA TOYOKUNI I
KABUKI THEATER INTERIOR: A PICTURE OF GREAT PROSPERITY IN THE THEATER (SHIBAI ÔHANJO NO ZU)
Three-panel color woodblock print
Paper
Ôban

Tsubouchi Memorial Theatre Museum, Waseda University; acc. nos. 118-0001, 0002, 0003

This close-up view of a play-in-progress, spread over three sheets, provides wonderful detail of the *kabuki* theater interior. Audience members move about, gossip, eat, and drink as they wish. The play is so popular, spectators are jammed on stage (audience left) in two tiers, while musicans can be seen watching the action (audience right). The *nô* roof and pillars are now gone, opening the stage for full use by the actors.

7.23 UTAGAWA TOYOKUNI I
KABUKI THEATER INTERIOR: A PICTURE OF GREAT PROSPERITY IN A THEATER (ÔSHIBAI HAN'EI NO ZU)
Three-panel color woodblock print
1859
Paper
Ôban
Tsubouchi Memorial Theatre Museum, Waseda University; acc. nos. 118-0026, 0027, 0028

The bravura scene, "Pulling the Carriage Apart" ("Kurumabiki"), adapted from the puppet play, "Sugawara and the Secrets of Calligraphy" ("Sugawara Denju Tenarai Kagami").

7.24 ATTRIBUTED TO UTAGAWA TOYOKUNI I
KABUKI THEATER INTERIOR: A PICTURE OF GREAT PROSPERITY IN THE THEATER (SHIBAI ÔHANJO NO ZU)
Three-panel color woodblock print
Paper
Ôban
Tsubouchi Memorial Theatre Museum, Waseda University; acc. nos. 118-0100, 0101, 0102

Stereotyped views of the theater might be repeated in the side panels, but the center panel always illustrated a specific scene from the current play.

7.25 KABUKI THEATER AUDIENCE
Photograph; detail of no. 7.22
Tsubouchi Memorial Theatre Museum, Waseda University

7.26 UTAGAWA HIROSHIGE
THEATER STREET SCENE: FAMOUS PLACES IN THE EASTERN CAPITAL, THE "TWO WARD" THEATER DISTRICT (TOTO MEISHO NICHOCHO SHIBAI NO ZU)
Color woodblock print
ca. 1830-42
Paper
Ôban

7.26

7.27

7.22

7.23

7.24

7.28

7.29

7.30

Tsubouchi Memorial Theatre Museum,
Waseda University; acc. no. 118-0112

Some woodblock prints show the bustling
activities on the street in front of a theater
(gekijô-gai). Hawkers sell tickets, customers
enter by the small front doors, and passersby
and workers make up the dense crowd.
Theater teahouses (shibai jaya) flank the
theater building, which is easily identifiable
by the drum tower (yagura) and advertising
sign boards (kanban) over the entrance. This
scene is of the theater district in Edo's "two
ward town" (nichôcho) comprised of adjoining
Sakai-chô and Fukiya-chô near Nihonbashi.

7.27 UTAGAWA HIROSHIGE
THEATER STREET SCENE: FAMOUS PLACES
IN EDO, THREE THEATERS OF SARUWAKA
WARD (EDO MEISHO SARUWAKA-GAI SANZA)
Color woodblock print
1858
Paper
Ôban
Tsubouchi Memorial Theatre Museum,
Waseda University; acc. no. 118-0113

Women looking from a balcony at decorations, actors' banners, and signs advertising *kabuki* productions in theaters across the street. The three main theaters in Edo were moved to Saruwaka Ward in Asakusa in 1842-43.

7.28 UTAGAWA HIROSHIGE
THEATER STREET SCENE: A PICTURE OF GREAT PROSPERITY IN THE EASTERN CAPITAL (TOTO HAN'EI NO ZU)
Three-panel color woodblock print
1854
Paper
Ôban
Tsubouchi Memorial Theatre Museum, Waseda University; acc. nos. 118-0125, 0126, 0127

The double comma design (*tomoe*) on the curtain of the drum tower (*yagura*) is that of theater licensee Kawarasaki Gonnosuke, and identifies the Kawarasaki Theater.

7.29 UTAGAWA HIROSHIGE
THEATER STREET SCENE: A PICTURE OF GREAT PROSPERITY IN THE EASTERN CAPITAL (TOTO HAN'EI NO ZU)
Three-panel color woodblock print
1854
Paper
Ôban
Tsubouchi Memorial Theatre Museum, Waseda University; acc. nos. 118-0122, 0123, 0124

The orange leaf (*tachibana*) crest that emblazons the curtain of the drum tower (*yagura*) is that of theater licensee Ichimura Uzaemon, and identifies the Ichimura Theater.

7.30 KEISAI EISEN
THEATER STREET SCENE: A PARTIAL VIEW OF THEATERS IN SARUWAKA WARD (SARUWAKA-CHO SHIBAI NO RYAKUZU)
Color woodblock print
1842-43
Paper
35 x 48 cm
Tsubouchi Memorial Theatre Museum, Waseda University; acc. no. 118-0115

When the three large *kabuki* theaters in Edo moved to Saruwaka Ward, Asakusa, in 1842-1843, they were built side-by-side. This print shows the Nakamura Theater (left) and the Ichimura Theater (right), while the Morita Theater is unseen behind the cloud at the right. The two smaller theaters at the bottom of the picture are puppet theaters.

7.31 YANAGISAWA MACHIO
"SHUNKAN"
Model
1995
Wood and paper
W. 89, D. 65.5, H. 45 cm
Tsubouchi Memorial Theatre Museum, Waseda University

A model of the stage set for "Shunkan." The ship that will take Shunkan's exiled companions back to Kyoto arrives at desolate Demon Island. Opposite, is a high cliff. When Shunkan climbs the cliff to watch the ship depart, the stage set turns on the revolving stage (*mawari butai*), bringing the cliff center-stage so that Shunkan can play his farewell scene directly to the audience.

7.32 YOSHIDA CHIAKI
ACTOR NAKAMURA KANZABURO XVII (1909-1988) AS SHUNKAN
Photograph
Late Shôwa Period
Yoshida Chiaki

7.33A-B YOSHIDA CHIAKI
A) REVOLVING STAGE (MAWARI BUTAI)
Photograph
Shôwa period
Actor Onoe Shôroku II as Kezori Kyûemon, in "The Girl from Hakata" ("Hakata Kojorô Namimakura")
Yoshida Chiaki

B) MODEL OF REVOLVING STAGE BY YOSHIDA CHIAKI
Photograph
Shôwa period
Yoshida Chiaki

7.34 YOSHIDA CHIAKI
"YOSHINO RIVER" SCENE FROM THE PLAY "MOUNT IMO AND MOUNT SE" ("YOSHINOGAWA," "IMOSEYAMA ONNA TEIKIN")
Photograph
Shôwa period
Yoshida Chiaki

The *hanamichi* provides a performing space running through the left part of the auditorium to the main stage. This space may be linked to the main setting or actors may use it as a separate acting area. In the "Yoshino River" scene in the play "Mount Imo and Mount Se," a main (*hon*) *hanamichi* on the left side of the auditorium and a temporary (*kari*) *hanamichi* on the right side represent the opposite banks of the Yoshino River separated by the imagined flowing stream.

7.31

7.33B

7.33A

7.34

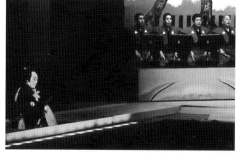

7.35

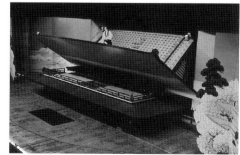

7.36

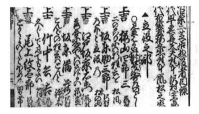

7.37
7.38

7.39
7.40

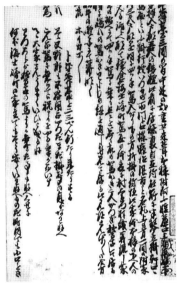
7.41

7.35 YOSHIDA CHIAKI
ELEVATOR TRAP (*SUPPON*) IN THE
HANAMICHI
Photograph
Shôwa Period
Yoshida Chiaki

A small elevator trap (*suppon*), approximately
1 meter x 1.5 meters, is built into the
hanamichi close to where it joins the main
stage. It is used for highly effective appear-
ances and disappearances of a spirit, demon,
or other supernatural figures. In this picture,
Onoe Shôroku II (1913-1989), as the spirit
of the fox Tadanobu in "Yoshitsune and the
Thousand Cherry Trees" ("Yoshitsune
Senbon Zakura"), stands on the elevator.

7.36 YOSHIDA CHIAKI
ELEVATOR TRAP (*SERI*) ON MAIN STAGE
Photograph
Shôwa Period
Yoshida Chiaki

A large elevator (*seri*) built in the center of
the main stage can slowly raise an entire set
before the audience's eyes (*seriage*), often
with characters posed in a pictorial composition. Or an elaborate set filled with characters can be gradually lowered out of sight
(*serisage*). It is said that the elevator was
invented by playwright Namiki Shôzô I in
1753, as well as the revolving stage (*mawari
butai*), to create spectacular stage effects. The
picture shows the "Gokuraku Temple" scene
in the play "Benten the Thief" ("Benten Kozô").

7.37 ACTORS' SALARY LIST (YAKUSHA
KYUBUNZUKE) OF THE ARAKI YOJIBEI AND
KATAOKA NIZAEMON THEATERS
Woodblock print, single sheet
1697
Paper
16 x 50 cm

Tsubouchi Memorial Theatre Museum,
Waseda University; acc. no. RO-18-00071-001

This invaluable salary list (*yakusha
kyubunzuke*) contains the amounts paid company actors in the year 1697; the size of an
actor's salary indicating his rank. The salaries
of actor-managers (*zamoto*) are not listed,
perhaps because the information was considered a privileged business secret. The
famous *onnagata* actor Yoshizawa Ayame I
(1673-1729) received an annual salary of 300
gold *ryô*, the equivalent today of $300,000.

7.38 ACTORS' CRITIQUE (YAKUSHA
HYOBANKI, YAKUSHA HATSU KOSHIN)
Book
1764
Woodblock printed
10.4 x 16 cm
Tsubouchi Memorial Theatre Museum,
Waseda University; acc. no. RO-11-01202

Books of actors' critiques (*yakusha hyôbanki*)
were published annually in Edo, Osaka, and
Kyoto beginning in 1660, and somewhat
later in Nagoya. They evaluated the personality, looks, and artistic ability of major
kabuki performers. After theatrical criticism
began to appear in daily newspapers from
around 1880, annual critiques lost favor and
they ceased being published.

7.39 SHIKITEI SANBA
ILLUSTRATED ATLAS OF THE THEATER
NATION (SHIBAI KINMO ZUI)
Book
Woodblock printed
1803
22.5 x 16 cm
Tsubouchi Memorial Theatre Museum,
Waseda University; acc. no. RO-01-00124

7.42

7.43

7.44

7.45

7.46

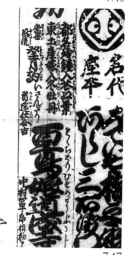

7.47

A humorous "atlas" in which aspects of *kabuki* are described in terms of a "nation"– the theater season as cosmology, rain and snow stage effects as climate, the stage as geography, the actors as independent principalities, and so on – eight sections in all. Written by satirist Shikitei Sanba (1776-1822) and illustrated by woodblock artists Utagawa Toyokuni I (1769-1825) and Katsukawa Shun'ei (1762-1819). Very popular when it first appeared, it was often republished.

7.40 ILLUSTRATED PLAY SCENARIO: "PROSTITUTE OF ASAMA MOUNTAIN" (EIRI KYOGENBON, "KEISEI ASAMA GA TAKE")
Book
Woodblock printed
1699
21.5 x 16.2 cm
Tsubouchi Memorial Theatre Museum, Waseda University; acc. no. RO-15-01881

In the period 1690-1720, before complete *kabuki* play scripts were written, readers purchased an illustrated play scenario (*eiri kyôgenbon*) to read, as in today's theater program, the plot synopsis of a current production. Some 300 of these booklets have been preserved, averaging twenty pages in length, with pictures of major scenes filling six pages.

7.41 KABUKI PLAY SCRIPT, "SONG OF A BUTTERFLY DREAM" ("YUME MUSUBI CHO NI TORIOI")
Book
Woodblock printed
1856
24.2 x 17.2 cm
Tsubouchi Memorial Theatre Museum, Waseda University; acc. no. I-12-01082

Early *kabuki* dramatic plots grew out of the interaction of actors improvising a scene in performance. In time, playwrights provided actors with just the opening speeches of each act, and from this practice fully scripted plays gradually evolved. The oldest existing complete *kabuki* play script (*daihon*) is "The Love Suicides at Devil's Gate" ("Shinjû Kimon no Kado"), dated 1710.

7.42 FAVORITE DIALOGUE FOR AMATEURS: "THE SONG OF ISE, A SWORD OF LOVE" (ÔMUSEKI, "ISE ONDO KOI NO NETABA")
Book
Woodblock printed
1863
23.6 x 15.5 cm
Tsubouchi Memorial Theatre Museum, Waseda University; acc. no. RO-06-00005-037

Mimicking *kabuki* actors' voices became a popular fad among townsmen, particularly in Edo, from around 1770. Amateurs learned famous speeches from booklets five-to-ten pages long, called appropriately "parrot pebbles" (*ômu seki*), that were published and widely sold. From around 1850, portraits of the actors were included.

7.43 TAKEDA IZUMO AND OTHERS FAVORITE DIALOGUE FOR AMATEURS: "THE FORTY-SEVEN LOYAL SAMURAI" (ÔMUSEKI, "KANADEHON CHUSHINGURA")
Book
Woodblock printed
1748
26.6 x 19 cm
Tsubouchi Memorial Theatre Museum, Waseda University; acc. no. RO-06-00004-015

7.44 NAKAMURA THEATER STREET POSTER (TSUJI BANZUKE)
Single sheet poster
First month, 23rd Day, 1833
Woodblock printed
27.4 x 38.2 cm
Tsubouchi Memorial Theatre Museum, Waseda University; acc. no. RO-22-0041-188

A variety of publications (*banzuke*) provided theatergoers with information about what was playing in the *kabuki* theaters around town. "Street posters" (*tsuji banzuke*), posted at busy intersections, gave the theater name, play title, and a list of major actors. It could be illustrated, as in this example.

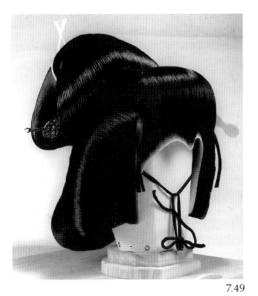

7.49

7.50

7.51

7.52

7.53

7.45 ICHIMURA THEATER CAST BOOK (YAKUWARI BANZUKE)
Booklet
Eighth month, 2nd day, 1849
Woodblock printed
23.5 x 15.5 cm
Tsubouchi Memorial Theatre Museum, Waseda University; acc. no. RO-24-00001-571

Another type of advertisement for a production was the "cast book" (yakuwari banzuke), that listed in detail who the actors were and what roles they were playing. Actors' crests (mon) were prominently displayed, making this an attractive book to purchase before or after seeing the production.

7.46 NAKAMURA THEATER ILLUSTRATED PLAY BOOKLET (EHON BANZUKE)
Booklet
Third month, 18th day, 1804
Woodblock printed
17.5 x 12.4 cm
Tsubouchi Memorial Theatre Museum, Waseda University; acc. no. RO-18-00050-001

An "illustrated play booklet" (ehon banzuke) consists of full-page illustrations of crucial scenes in a play. Each of the banzuke's eight to ten pages illustrates one of the program's acts, with each actor and his role identified. Stage scenery, properties, costuming, wigs, and makeup are all clearly shown.

7.47 FLYER FOR "ONE HUNDRED PLOVERS AND THE MAIDEN OF DOJO TEMPLE" ("MOMOCHIDORI MUSUME DOJO-JI" TSUJI BANZUKE)
Single-sheet flyer
1744
Woodblock printed
27.2 x 38.6 cm
Torigoe Bunzô

Actor Nakamura Tomijûrô I (1719-1786) is credited with premiering the well-known kabuki dance play "Maiden of Dôjô Temple" ("Musume Dôjô-ji") at the Nakamura Theater in Edo in 1753. This poster (tsuji banzuke) advertises a production of the play in Kyoto one year earlier, in 1752, starring Tomijûrô, under the title "One Hundred Plovers and the Maid of Dôjô Temple."

FAMOUS PLAYS

7.48 "MIRROR LION DANCE" ("KAGAMI JISHI")
COSTUME WORN BY SPIRIT OF LION IN PART TWO
Shôwa period
Silk
Shôchiku Costume Co., Ltd.

Actor Ichikawa Danjûrô IX (1839-1903) played the major role, Lady Yayoi, in the première of "Mirror Lion Dance" ("Kagami Jishi") in 1893, with his two daughters performing by his side as the two butterflies. This large, stiff costume, worn in the second part of the play, conveys the masculine nature of the lion spirit who has taken possession of Lady Yayoi.

7.49 OKADA YONEZO
"MIRROR LION DANCE" ("KAGAMI JISHI")
Wig worn by Lady Yayoi in part one
Shôwa period
Hair
W. 31.8, D. 36, H. 39.3 cm
Tsubouchi Memorial Theatre Museum, Waseda University

7.50 OKADA YONEZO
"MIRROR LION DANCE" ("KAGAMI JISHI")
Wig worn by spirit of lion in part two
Shôwa period
Hair
W. 50, D. 50, H. 162 cm
Tsubouchi Memorial Theatre Museum, Waseda University

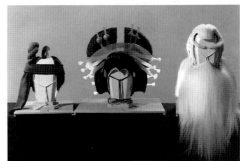

7.60-62

7.56

7.58

7.51 OKADA YONEZO
"MIRROR LION DANCE" ("KAGAMI JISHI")
Wig worn by butterfly
Shôwa period
Hair
W. 30, D. 32, H. 39 cm
Tsubouchi Memorial Theatre Museum,
Waseda University

7.52 "MIRROR LION DANCE" ("KAGAMI
JISHI")
Hand properties: pair of hand-held lion
masks; favorite properties of actor Onoe
Kikugorô VI
Early Shôwa period
Wood
W. 24.5, D. 23.5, H. 14 cm
Tsubouchi Memorial Theatre Museum,
Waseda University

In Edo Castle, Lady Yayoi manipulates two
small lion masks while she dances in celebration of the New Year season. As part one
ends, the lion spirit residing in the masks
takes possession of Lady Yayoi's body.

7.53/7.54 HAND PROPERTIES: PAIR OF FANS
Favorite properties of actor Onoe
Kikugorô VI
Early Shôwa period
Wood and paper
32 x 55 cm
Tsubouchi Memorial Theatre Museum,
Waseda University

7.55 FUJINAMI PROPS CO., LTD.
"MIRROR LION DANCE" ("KAGAMI JISHI")
Stage property: butterfly on bamboo pole
1990s
Wood and silk
27 x 227 cm
Tsubouchi Memorial Theatre Museum,
Waseda University

7.56 "MIRROR LION DANCE" ("KAGAMI
JISHI")
Onoe Baikô VII as the court lady Yayoi
Photograph
Yoshida Chiaki

7.57 "MIRROR LION DANCE" ("KAGAMI
JISHI")
Onoe Baikô VII (1915-1995) as the spirit of
the lion in part two
Photograph
Yoshida Chiaki

7.58 AGEMAKI IN "SUKEROKU: FLOWER
OF EDO"
Costume; worn by actor Nakamura
Utaemon VI
Shôwa period
Silk
Shôchiku Costume Co., Ltd.

The several costumes worn by Agemaki,
the high-ranking courtesan (oiran) who is
Sukeroku's lover in "Sukeroku: Flower of Edo"
("Sukeroku Yukari no Edo Sakura") are
among the most lavish and spectacular on
the kabuki stage.

7.59 IKYU IN "SUKEROKU"
Costume
Shôwa period
Silk
Shôchiku Costume Co., Ltd.

Ikyû's elegant costume, consisting of padded
kimono and outer robe, clearly conveys the
high status and the wealth of this samurai
villain in "Sukeroku."

7.60 OKADA YONEZO
SUKEROKU IN "SUKEROKU"
Wig
Shôwa period
Hair
W. 28.4, D. 32.4, H. 33 cm
Tsubouchi Memorial Theatre Museum,
Waseda University

7.61 OKADA YONEZO
AGEMAKI IN "SUKEROKU"
Wig
Shôwa period
Hair
W. 31, D. 36, H. 40 cm
Tsubouchi Memorial Theatre Museum,
Waseda University

7.62 OKADA YONEZO
IKYU IN "SUKEROKU"
Wig
Shôwa period
Hair
W. 30.4, D. 31.4, H. 41 cm
Tsubouchi Memorial Theatre Museum,
Waseda University

7.63 UTAGAWA TOYOKUNI III
"SUKEROKU"
Three-panel color woodblock print
1850
Paper
Ôban
Actors Ichikawa Kodanji IV, Ichikawa
Danjûrô VIII, Bandô Shuka I and others
Tsubouchi Memorial Theatre Museum,
Waseda University; acc. nos. 100-2551,
2552, 2553

Sukeroku (center panel, seated), the hero of
"Sukeroku: Flower of Edo," provokes quarrels
in the Yoshiwara licensed quarter in order to
discover the identity of the man who has his
family's precious heirloom sword. In costuming and makeup, the role of Sukeroku blends
the bravura Edo style of acting (aragoto) with
Kamigata's soft style (wagoto), making him
extremely attractive to women. Sukeroku is
the one kabuki role that everyone, not only
actors, would like to play.

7.64

7.65

7.66

7.70

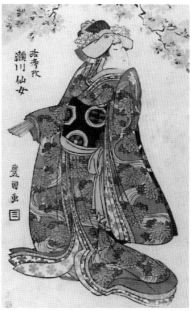

7.73

7.74

7.64 UTAGAWA TOYOKUNI III
"SUKEROKU"
Three-panel color woodblock print
1850
Paper
Ôban
From right, actors Ichikawa Kodanji IV,
Ichikawa Danjûrô VIII, Bandô Shuka I
Tsubouchi Memorial Theatre Museum,
Waseda University; acc. nos. 100-2648,
2649, 2650

7.65 UTAGAWA TOYOKUNI III
"SUKEROKU"
Three-panel color woodblock print
1850
Paper
Ôban
From right: actors Ichikawa Kodanji IV,
Ichikawa Danjûrô VIII, Bandô Shuka I
Tsubouchi Memorial Theatre Museum,
Waseda University; acc. nos. 100-2651,
2652, 2653

7.66 UTAGAWA TOYOKUNI III
"SUKEROKU"
Three-panel color woodblock print
1850
Paper
Ôban
From right: actors Ichikawa Kodanji IV,
Bandô Shuka I, Ichikawa Danjûrô VIII
Tsubouchi Memorial Theatre Museum,
Waseda University; acc. nos. 100-2654,
2655, 2656

7.67 UTAGAWA TOYOKUNI III
"SUKEROKU"
Three-panel color woodblock print
1850
Paper
Ôban
From right, actors Ichikawa Kodanji IV,
Bandô Shuka I, Ichikawa Danjûrô VIII

Tsubouchi Memorial Theatre Museum,
Waseda University; acc. nos. 100-2665,
2666, 2667

7.68 YOSHIDA CHIAKI
ACTOR ICHIKAWA DANJURO XII (B. 1946)
AS SUKEROKU
Photograph
Yoshida Chiaki

7.69 TAKATSU KOICHI, KANAI SCENERY
COMPANY
STAGESET FOR "SUKEROKU"
Model
Wood
W. 123, D. 36, H. 50 cm
Tsubouchi Memorial Theatre Museum,
Waseda University

The setting used for all current productions
of "Sukeroku" shows the curtained entrance
and grilled windows of the house of prosti-
tution, Three Harbors, and the water vat in
which Sukeroku eventually hides himself.

7.70 YAMATOYA GINKO
BATTLEDORE DEPICTING ACTORS IN
"SUKEROKU"
Toy
1886
Cloth and wood
61 x 24 cm
Tsubouchi Memorial Theatre Museum,
Waseda University

According to folk belief, a child who played
the game of battledore and shuttlecock at
New Year would be protected from sickness.
It was fashionable to decorate battledores
(oshie hagoita) with the images of popular
celebrities such as kabuki actors. Likenesses
of Ichikawa Danjûrô IX (1839-1903) as
Sukeroku and Nakamura Shikan IV (1830-
1899) as Ikyû adorn this battledore.

7.71 "MAIDEN OF DOJO TEMPLE"
("MUSUME DOJO-JI")
Costume
Shôwa period
Silk
Shôchiku Costume Co., Ltd.

Many versions of the *nô* play "Dôjô Temple,"
concerning a woman's jealousy and transformation, have been staged in *kabuki*, the most
popular being "Maiden of Dôjô Temple"
("Kyôganoko Musume Dôjô-ji"). The actor
playing the role of the beautiful dancer
Hanako changes costume six times before
the audience, gradually transforming him/
herself, with the help of a chorus of protest-
ing monks, into a monstrously beautiful
serpent.

7.72 UTAGAWA KUNIYASU
ACTOR NAKAMURA UTAEMON III
(1778-1838) IN "MAIDEN OF DOJO
TEMPLE" ("MUSUME DOJO-JI")
Color woodblock print
1812
Paper
Ôban
Tsubouchi Memorial Theatre Museum,
Waseda University; acc. no. 101-5977

7.73 UTAGAWA TOYOKUNI I
ACTOR SEGAWA SENJO (1751-1810) IN
"MAIDEN OF DOJO TEMPLE" ("MUSUME
DOJO-JI")
Color woodblock print
1807
Paper
Ôban
Tsubouchi Memorial Theatre Museum,
Waseda University; acc. no. 101-5975

7.78

7.74 Utagawa Toyokuni I
Actor Ichikawa Monnosuke III
(1794-1824) in "Maiden of Dojo
Temple" ("Musume Dojo-ji")
Color woodblock print
1821
Paper
Ôban
From right: actors Arashi Kanjûrô I,
Ichikawa Monnosuke III, Seki Sanjûrô III
Tsubouchi Memorial Theatre Museum,
Waseda University; acc. no. 101-5983

7.75 Utagawa Kunisada I
Actor Segawa Kikunojo V in "Maiden
of Dojo Temple" ("Musume Dojo-ji")
Color woodblock print
1829
Paper
Ôban
Tsubouchi Memorial Theatre Museum,
Waseda University; acc. no. 101-5988

7.76 Utagawa Kunisada I
Actor Ichimura Uzaemon XII (1812-
1851) in "Maiden of Dojo Temple"
("Musume Dojo-ji")
Two-panel color woodblock print
1839
Paper
Ôban
From right, actors Ichikawa Kuzô II, Arashi
Kichisaburô III, Ichimura Uzaemon XII
Tsubouchi Memorial Theatre Museum,
Waseda University; acc. nos. 101-5992, 5993

7.77 Yoshida Chiaki
Actor Nakamura Utaemon VI (b.1917)
as Hanako in "Maiden of Dojo Temple"
("Musume Dojo-ji")
Photograph
Yoshida Chiaki

7.78 Utagawa Toyokuni III
"Kumagai's Battle Camp" ("Kumagai
Jinya")
Three-panel color woodblock print
1850
Paper
Ôban
Actors Ichikawa Ebizô VI, Onoe Kikujirô II,
Bandô Hikosaburô IV and others
Tsubouchi Memorial Theatre Museum,
Waseda University; acc. nos. 100-4911,
4912, 4913

Following Lord Yoshitsune's hinted com-
mand written on the sign board, General
Kumagai Naozane has beheaded his own
son. In the "Kumagai's Battle Camp" scene
from the play "Chronicle of the Battle of
Ichinotani" ("Ichinotani Futaba Gunki") (1751),
Kumagai (center) must display his son's head
to Yoshitsune (upper left) for verification
(kubijikken). This tragic event takes place
before the horrified gaze of the child's
mother, Sagami (lower right), and court lady
Fuji no Kata (upper right). The play is
adapted from the jôruri puppet theater.

7.79 Toyohara Kunichika
"Kumagai's Battle Camp" ("Kumagai
Jinya")
Three-panel color woodblock print
1867
Paper
Ôban
From right, actors Sawamura Tosshô II,
Nakamura Shikan IV, Ôtani Tomoemon IV
Tsubouchi Memorial Theatre Museum,
Waseda University; acc. nos. 100-4898,
4899, 4900

Kumagai (center) narrates the supposed
death of Prince Atsumori (actually
Kumagai's son) to Yoshitsune (right), while
Sagami (left) listens.

7.80 Utagawa Toyokuni III
"Kumagai's Battle Camp" ("Kumagai
Jinya")
Three-panel color woodblock print
1854
Paper
Ôban
Actors Arashi Kichisaburô III, Nakamura
Fukusuke I, Nakamura Tomijûrô II and
others
Tsubouchi Memorial Theatre Museum,
Waseda University; acc. nos. 100-4887,
4888, 4889

7.81 Utagawa Toyokuni III
"Kumagai's Battle Camp" ("Kumagai
Jinya")
Three-panel color woodblock print
1851
Paper
Ôban
From right, actors Arashi Kichisaburô III,
Ichimura Takenojô V, Bandô Shuka I
Tsubouchi Memorial Theatre Museum,
Waseda University; acc. nos. 100-4879,
4880, 4881

Kumagai (center) narrates the supposed
death of Prince Atsumori to Yoshitsune
(right), while Sagami (left) listens.

7.82 Utagawa Kunisada I
"Kumagai's Battle Camp" ("Kumagai
Jinya")
Three-panel color woodblock print
1841
Paper
Ôban
From right, actors Ichikawa Danjûrô VIII,
Sawamura Tosshô I, Iwai Kumesaburô III
Tsubouchi Memorial Theatre Museum,
Waseda University; acc. nos. 100-4856,
4857, 4858

7.79

7.80

7.81

7.83 Yoshida Chiaki
Actor Onoe Shoroku II (1913-1989)
as Kumagai Naozane, in "Kumagai's
Battle Camp" ("Kumagai Jinya")
Photograph
Yoshida Chiaki

7.84 "Kumagai's Battle Camp"
("Kumagai Jinya")
Costume
Shôwa period
Silk
Shôchiku Costume Co., Ltd.

MUSIC

7.85 LARGE DRUM (ÔDAIKO)
Wood and leather
W. 53, D. 62, H. 53 cm
Tsubouchi Memorial Theatre Museum,
Waseda University

7.85

Kabuki is fundamentally a musical theater
and music plays almost continuously during
performance. *Kabuki* has two basic types of
musical ensemble: percussionists, *shamisen*
players, and singers seated offstage right
(*geza*) who play background music, and
onstage musicians (*degatari or debayashi*) who
accompany dance plays. The large drum
(*ôdaiko*) is one of the major *geza* instruments.
Varied drum patterns indicate by convention wind, snow, rain, and waves, and
dramatic situations such as danger, mystery,
alarm, or battle.

7.86 TEMPLE BELL (HONTSURI)
Bronze
W. 29, D. 29, H. 49 cm
Tsubouchi Memorial Theatre Museum,
Waseda University

The temple bell (*hontsuri*) is a *geza* instrument
that tolls the time, or can indicate a Buddhist
temple locale.

7.87/7.88 BUDDHIST WOODEN DRUM
(MOKUGYO) WITH DRUMSTICK
Wood
W. 28, D. 29, H. 28 cm
Tsubouchi Memorial Theatre Museum,
Waseda University

A small fish- or gourd-shaped hollowed
wood drum (*mokugyo*) played during Buddhist
prayers that is part of the *geza* ensemble.

7.89 SHAMISEN, TOKIWAZU STYLE
Shôwa period
Wood, leather, and ivory
W. 22, D. 10.5, L. 98 cm
Tsubouchi Memorial Theatre Museum,
Waseda University

7.86

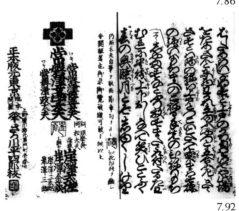

7.92

The *shamisen*, whose three strings are played
with a plectrum, can be classified by the size
of the neck and, hence, the quality of musical sound: the *nagauta shamisen* neck is narrow
and the sound light; the *gidayû shamisen* neck
is thick and the sound heavy; while the
tokiwazu shamisen neck is medium size and the
music sensuous.

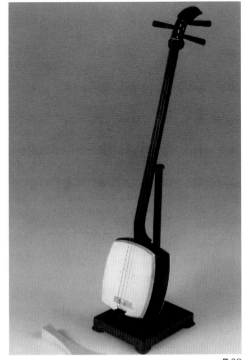

7.89

7.90

7.91

7.90 KI
Musical instrument
Meiji period
Wood
W. 5.1, H. 4.8, L. 28 cm
Tsubouchi Memorial Theatre Museum,
Waseda University

The piercing sound of a pair of *ki* (or *byôshigi*)
struck together by a stagehand (*kyôgen kata*)
can be heard throughout performance,

signaling the opening and closing of the curtain, changing scenery, the raising or lowering of the elevator, the turning of the revolving stage, and other technical actions.

7.91 TOKIWAZU SINGER'S MUSIC STAND (KENDAI)
Stage Property
Heisei Period
Wood
W. 47.2, D. 31.2, H.48 cm
Tsubouchi Memorial Theatre Museum, Waseda University

From the shape of the singer's music stand (*kendai*) you can identify the style of music that is being played and sung onstage. The *tokiwazu* style music stand has uniquely shaped "octopus legs" (*tako ashi*).

7.92 TOKIWAZU LIBRETTO (TOKIWAZU KEIKOBONSHU)
Book
Late Edo Period
Woodblock printed
14.2 x 21 cm
Tsubouchi Memorial Theatre Museum, Waseda University; acc. no. TO-18-00005

A libretto contains the lyrics sung by on-stage singers in *nagauta, tokiwazu, kiyomoto, katôbushi, gidayû,* or other musical style, during the performance of a dance play.

7.93 KATSUKAWA SHUNTEI
SCENE WITH TOKIWAZU MUSICIANS (TOKIWAZU DEGATARI-ZU)
Colored woodblock print
1807
Paper
Ôban
From right, actors Bandô Mitsugorô III, Iwai Hanshirô V
Tsubouchi Memorial Theatre Museum, Waseda University; acc. no. 101-7424

7.94 UTAGAWA KUNISADA I
SCENE WITH TOKIWAZU MUSICIANS (TOKIWAZU DEGATARI-ZU)
Two-panel colored woodblock print
1818
Paper
Ôban
From right, actors Bandô Mitsugorô III, Iwai Hanshirô V, Nakamura Shikan I
Tsubouchi Memorial Theatre Museum, Waseda University; acc. nos. 101-7429, 7430

7.95 UTAGAWA KUNISADA I
SCENE WITH TOKIWAZU MUSICIANS (TOKIWAZU DEGATARI-ZU)
Two-panel colored woodblock print
1838
Paper
Ôban

7.95

7.96

7.97

From right, actors Ichikawa Kuzô II, Iwai Shijaku
Tsubouchi Memorial Theatre Museum, Waseda University; acc. nos. 101-7438, 7439

7.96 Utagawa Kuniyoshi
Scene with Tokiwazu Musicians
(Tokiwazu Degatari-zu)
Two-panel colored woodblock print
1839
Paper
Ôban
From right, actors Onoe Eizaburô III,
Sawamura Tosshô I
Tsubouchi Memorial Theatre Museum,
Waseda University; acc. nos. 101-7440, 7441

7.97 Utagawa Toyokuni III I
Scene with Kiyomoto Musicians (Kiyomoto
Degatari-zu)
Two-panel colored woodblock print
1860
Paper
Ôban
From right, actors Onoe Kikugorô IV,
Nakamura Fukusuke I
Tsubouchi Memorial Theatre Museum,
Waseda University; acc. nos. 101-0277, 0278

This travel dance (*michiyuki*), using *kiyomoto*
music, is a version of Act IV, "The Forty-
Seven Loyal Samurai" ("Kanadehon
Chûshingura"). It depicts the young lovers
Kampei and Okaru in flight.

7.98 Yoshida Chiaki
Offstage Musical Ensemble (Geza Ongaku,
Kuromisu)
Photograph
Yoshida Chiaki

The important offstage musicians who play
in a small room stage right (hence the name
geza) watch a performance from behind a
black blind (*kuromisu*). From this position
next to the stage action, they are able to
time their instrumental music and singing to
match the dialogue and movement of the
actors.

The Dressing Room

7.99 Detail of a Theater (detail of
no. 7.23)
Photograph
Tsubouchi Memorial Theatre Museum,
Waseda University

The large *kabuki* theaters in Tokyo, Osaka,
and Kyoto offer two programs each day,
twenty-five consecutive days each month,
sometimes twelve months a year. So, the
contemporary *kabuki* actor will spend nearly
twelve hours a day at the theater, more time
than he has at home. Consequently, the
dressing room is the most important place,
after the stage, in the actor's life. The actor
surrounds himself with objects that are

7.100

7.101

7.106

useful to his profession and call attention to
his artistic lineage.

7.100 Yoshida Chiaki
Onnagata Makeup, Actor Onoe
Baiko VII (1915-1995) as the courtesan
Yugiri in "Love Letter From the
Licensed Quarter" ("Kuruwa Bunsho")
Photographic panel
Yoshida Chiaki

7.101 Dressing Room Curtain
(Gakuya Noren) of Actor Ichikawa
Danjuro XII (b. 1946)
Backstage property
Shôwa Period
Silk
128 x 104 cm
Ichikawa Danjûrô XII

The actor's dressing room is separated from
the common passageway by an elegantly
hand-dyed curtain (*noren*), made in loose
panels. Here the Danjûrô's name is prominently displayed on the left and his family
crest (*mon*) in the center, while the name of
the donor, the Tokiwazu Association of
Nagoya, is written in smaller characters on
the right.

7.102 Dressing Room Curtain
(Gakuya Noren) of Actor Nakamura
Ganjiro III (b. 1931)
Backstage property
Shôwa Period
Silk
128 x 104 cm
Nakamura Ganjirô III

7.103 Makeup Mirror and Cabinet
(Kyodai) of Actor Bando
Hikosaburo VI (1886-1938)
Backstage property
Meiji Period
Wood and glass
W. 138, D. 45, H. 88 cm
Tsubouchi Memorial Theatre Museum,
Waseda University

Probably the present-day *kabuki* actor's most
important professional possession is his
makeup mirror and cabinet (*kyôdai*). Many
hours are spent each day seated on a thick
cushion (*zabuton*) before the mirror applying
makeup for three, four, or even more roles
that he will play. The beautifully lacquered
surface is embellished with crests of the
actor's family.

7.104 DRESSING ROOM CUSHION
(ZABUTON) OF ACTOR ICHIKAWA
DANJURO XII (B. 1946)
Backstage property
Silk
62 x 62 x 15 cm
Ichikawa Danjûrô XII

7.105 DRESSING ROOM CUSHION
(ZABUTON) OF ACTOR NAKAMURA
GANJIRO III (B. 1931)
Backstage property
Silk
62 x 62 x 15 cm
Nakamura Ganjirô III

7.106 DRESSING ROOM ROBE (GAKUYA
YUKATA) OF ACTOR ICHIKAWA DANJURO XII
(B. 1946)
Costume
Cotton
Ichikawa Danjûrô XII

The actor wears a cotton kimono (yukata)
decorated with family crests when making up
or resting in his dressing room between roles.

7.107 DRESSING ROOM ROBE (GAKUYA
YUKATA) OF ACTOR NAKAMURA GANJIRO III
(B. 1931)
Costume
Cotton
Nakamura Ganjirô III

7.108 HAND TOWEL (TENUGUI)
Property
Shôwa Period
Cotton
30 x 90 cm
Ichikawa Danjûrô XII

A hand towel (tenugui) decorated with the
actor's crests has many uses, including presentation to a fan as a token of appreciation
for support.

7.109 HAND TOWEL (TENUGUI)
Property
Shôwa Period
Cotton
30 x 90 cm
Nakamura Ganjirô III

7.110 TEACUP (YUNOMI-JAWAN)
Property
Shôwa Period
Ceramic
8 x 8 x 10 cm
Ichikawa Danjûrô XII

The actor's large personal teacup, with lid
(yunomi-jawan), is decorated with family crests.

7.112

7.113A

7.113B

7.111 TEACUP (YUNOMI-JAWAN)
Property
Shôwa Period
Ceramic
8 x 8 x 10 cm
Nakamura Ganjirô III

7.112 MAKEUP KIT
Property
Shôwa Period
Wood, hair, powder
Tsubouchi Memorial Theatre Museum,
Waseda University

Each actor does his own makeup, working
from a personal makeup kit that contains
brushes of various sizes, water-based white
base (oshiroi), wax to cover eye brows, rouge,
powder, eyeliner, and other items. The
nuanced layering of onnagata makeup may
take an actor more than an hour to apply.

7.113A-C ACTOR'S EXCERPTED SCRIPT
(KAKINUKI) USED BY ICHIKAWA CHUSHA VII
(1860-1936)
Books
Meiji Period
Paper
24.6 x 17.5 cm
Torigoe Bunzô

Playwrights cared to write out no more
than two or three complete copies of a play
script—an actor was given an excerpt
(kakinuki), or "sides," that contained only the
lines spoken by his character.

7.114A-E ÔTA GAKO
Bravura Makeup Patterns (Kumadori)
Masks
Resin and paper
25 x 18 x 12 cm
Tsubouchi Memorial Theatre Museum,
Waseda University

Makeup of powerful male characters consisting of exaggerated and conventionalized
red, blue, and black patterns is called
kumadori, "follow the contour." These masks
have been made to illustrate five variations
of the appropriately 100 types of kumadori
makeup that delineate different role types
and characters.

7.115 YOSHIDA CHIAKI
ACTOR ICHIKAWA DANJURO XII (B. 1946)
Applying Makeup for his Role as Sukeroku
Photograph
Yoshida Chiaki

7.116 UTAGAWA TOYOKUNI III
ACTOR BANDO HIKOSABURO V (1832-1877)
Making Up in the Dressing Room
Colored woodblock print
1861
Paper
Ôban
Tsubouchi Memorial Theatre Museum,
Waseda University; acc. no. 120-0217

7.117 UTAGAWA TOYOKUNI III
ACTOR SAWAMURA TANOSUKE III (1854-
1878) Making Up in the Dressing Room
Colored woodblock print
1861
Paper
Ôban
Tsubouchi Memorial Theatre Museum,
Waseda University; acc. no. 120-0216

7.118 UTAGAWA TOYOKUNI III
ACTOR NAKAMURA SHIKAN IV (1830-1899)
Making Up in the Dressing Room
Colored woodblock print
1861
Paper
Ôban
Tsubouchi Memorial Theatre Museum,
Waseda University; acc. no. 120-0214

The actor does all or most of his own
makeup, but has assistance in putting on
costumes and wigs.

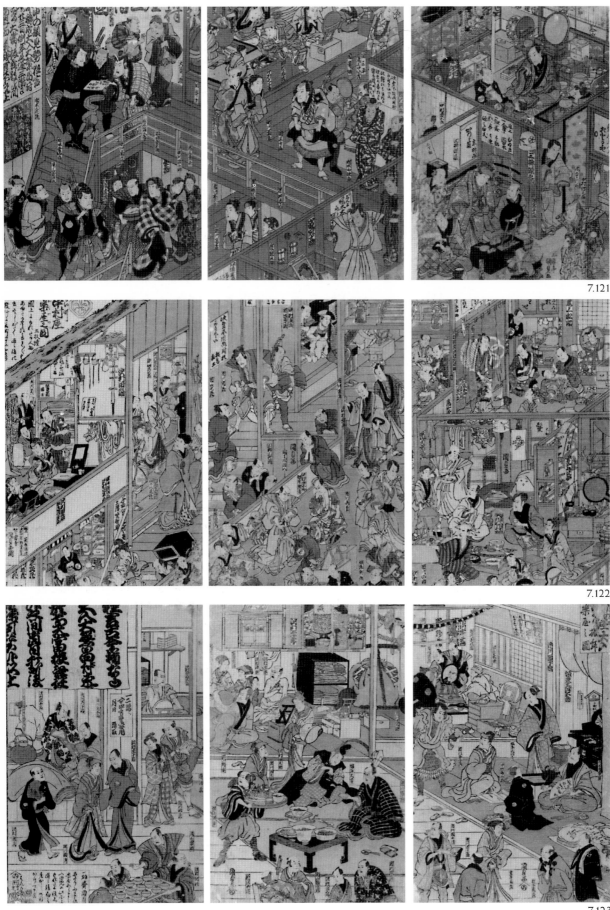

7.121

7.122

7.123

7.124

7.119 UTAGAWA TOYOKUNI III
ACTOR KAWARASAKI GONJURO I (LATER
ICHIKAWA DANJURO IX) (1839-1903)
MAKING UP IN THE DRESSING ROOM
Colored woodblock print
1861
Paper
Ôban
Tsubouchi Memorial Theatre Museum,
Waseda University; acc. no. 120-0222

7.120 UTAGAWA TOYOKUNI III
ACTOR SAWAMURA TOSSHO II (1838-1886)
MAKING UP IN THE DRESSING ROOM
Colored woodblock print
1861
Paper
Ôban
Tsubouchi Memorial Theatre Museum,
Waseda University; acc. no. 120-0223

7.121 UTAGAWA KUNISADA I
THE NAKAMURA THEATER IN SAKAI
WARD, DRESSING ROOM SCENE (SAKAI-
CHO NAKAMURA-ZA, GAKUYA NO ZU)
Three-panel colored woodblock print
Paper
Ôban
Tsubouchi Memorial Theatre Museum,
Waseda University; acc. nos. 120-0243,
0244, 0245

Artists created numerous woodblock prints
showing to an eager public the practical side
of the actor's life backstage: putting on
makeup before his mirror, being dressed or
wigged by assistants, rehearsing a scene with
fellow actors, discussing costume choices
with other actors, or smoking, eating, or
drinking tea between scenes.

7.122 UTAGAWA KUNISADA I
THE NAKAMURA THEATER, THIRD FLOOR
DRESSING ROOM SCENE (NAKAMURA-ZA,
SANGAI NO ZU)
Three-panel colored woodblock print
ca. 1824
Paper
Ôban
Tsubouchi Memorial Theatre Museum,
Waseda University; acc. nos. 120-0233,
0234, 0235

7.123 UTAGAWA KUNISADA I
THE ICHIMURA THEATER, BANQUETING IN
THE DRESSING ROOM TO CELEBRATE A HIT
PLAY (ICHIMURA-ZA ÔIRI ATARI-BURUMAI
GAKUYA NO ZU)
Three-panel colored woodblock print
ca. 1811
Paper
Ôban
Tsubouchi Memorial Theatre Museum,
Waseda University; acc. nos. 120-0227,
0228, 0229

7.124 UTAGAWA KUNISADA I
THE MORITA THEATER IN KOBIKI WARD,
DRESSING ROOM SCENE AT THE FACE-
SHOWING PRODUCTION (KOBIKI-CHO
MORITA-ZA, KAOMISE GAKUYA NO ZU)
Three-panel colored woodblock print
ca. 1812
Paper
Ôban
Tsubouchi Memorial Theatre Museum,
Waseda University; acc. nos. 120-0211,
0212, 0213

Backstage was particularly busy for the
actors when the first production of the
season, the "face-showing" (kaomise)
production, opened in the eleventh month
of the year.

7.125 UTAGAWA KUNISADA II
THE ICHIMURA THEATER, SECOND
BLOCK, SARUWAKA WARD, BANQUETING
IN THE DRESSING ROOM TO CELEBRATE A
HIT PLAY (SARUWAKA-CHO NICHOME
ICHIMURA-ZA NITE ÔIRI ATARI-BURUMAI
GAKUYA NO ZU)
Three-panel colored woodblock print
1865
Paper
Ôban
Tsubouchi Memorial Theatre Museum,
Waseda University; acc. nos. 120-0236,
0237, 0238

Delicacies in round wooden trays and sake
are being served backstage as the actors
remove makeup and change into their
dressing room robes (yukata).

7.126 ZOHIKO URUSHI ART
MAKEUP MIRROR STAND (KYODAI) AND
TOWEL RACK OF ACTOR NAKAMURA
TOKIZO III (1895-1959)
Backstage property
Shôwa Period
Wood and glass
Stand: W. 63.5, D. 40, H. 124.5 cm; Rack:
W. 28.8, D. 34, H. 40.9 cm
Tsubouchi Memorial Theatre Museum,
Waseda University

The delicately made mirror stand and small
towel rack decorated with flowers and
butterflies are beautiful examples of the art
of zôhiko lacquerware.

7.129

7.130

7.132

7.133

Rural Kabuki and Other Forms

7.127 Ogata Isamu
Village Kabuki, Kashimo Town, Gifu Prefecture
Photograph
Tsubouchi Memorial Theatre Museum, Waseda University

Kabuki performed by villagers is called *ji shibai*, "ground play," that is, theater rooted in the soil. Performances in winter, when villagers had free time, were usual. Today, an annual festival of village *kabuki* rotates among country theaters. Villagers in Kashimo Town, Gifu Prefecture, perform on a *kabuki* stage equipped with a *hanamichi*.

7.128 Village Kabuki: Kuromori Kabuki
Photograph
Tsubouchi Memorial Theatre Museum, Waseda University

The audience, seated outdoors on mats spread on the ground, watch local actors performing *kabuki* at Kuromori Village.

7.129 Model of a Rural Kabuki Theater in Ômomo Village
Photographic panel
Shôwa Period
Tsubouchi Memorial Theatre Museum, Waseda University

This model of a rural *kabuki* stage, without *hanamichi* or offstage areas, was made by Ôsawa Nobumoto.

7.130 Actor Nakamura Kichiemon I in Children's Kabuki (Kodomo Shibai):
Photograph
Tsubouchi Memorial Theatre Museum, Waseda University

Kabuki performed by troupes of child actors flourished in the 1770s and was revived briefly in the early decades of this century. Nakamura Kichiemon I (1886-1954) and Nakamura Matagorô I (1855-1920), who later became stars, began their careers in children's *kabuki*. Here Kichiemon, in his teens, poses as General Kumagai Naozane in "Kumagai's Battle Camp" ("Kumagai Jinya"). No professional children's troupes exist today, although amateur children's *kabuki* is popular in some villages.

Contemporary Kabuki

7.131 University of Hawai'i
English-Language Kabuki in America: "Sukeroku"
Photograph
University of Hawai'i, Department of Theater and Dance

7.132 Present-day Kabuki Theaters: Kabuki-za, National Theater, Minami-za, Kanamaru-za
Group of photographs
Shôchiku Co., Ltd., National Theater of Japan, Kotohira City Education Council

The Kabuki-za, located next to the elegant Ginza district in Tokyo, occupies an important place in 20th-century *kabuki* history. Opened in 1889, the theater was burned during the Kanto Earthquake in 1923 and again in the bombing of World War II, but was rebuilt in 1951. The movement to build a national theater, begun in 1873, at last bore fruit in 1966 when the National Theater of Japan was constructed in the center of Tokyo. Its large theater hosts *kabuki* most months of the year, and its small theater is a venue for *bunraku* puppet theater and other traditional performing arts. From around 1620, a *kabuki* theater has existed on the south side of Fourth Street at the Kamo River in Kyoto. The present theater at this location, the Minami-za (literally, "south theater"), was built in 1929 and rebuilt in 1992. The oldest extant *kabuki* theater in Japan is the Kanamaru-za, in Kotohira town, Shikoku island. It was built in 1835, modeled after a large Osaka theater, and reconstructed in 1970 in its Edo-period form.

7.133 Designer: Mori Tomio
Takeru in the Super-Kabuki Play "Yamato Takeru"
Costumes
1986
Cloth
Shôchiku Costume Co., Ltd.

Actor Ichikawa Ennosuke III (b. 1939) formed his own *kabuki* company to revive spectacular staging devices (*keren*) such as the flying in the air (*chûnori*) of traditional *kabuki*. In "Yamato Takeru," the first "Super-Kabuki" play, written by Umehara Takeshi and staged in 1986, Ennosuke moved beyond standard *kabuki* to create a contemporary "kabuki-esque" genre.

7.134 Actor Ichikawa Ennosuke III as Takeru in the Super-Kabuki Play "Yamato Takeru"
Photograph
1986
Shôchiku Co., Ltd.

7.135

TAKARAZUKA

7.135/7.136 DESIGNER: TODA IKUEI
TAKARAZUKA WOMEN'S OPERA, GRAND
REVUE, "GOLDEN DAYS" (TAKARAZUKA
SHOJO KAGEKIDAN, GURANDO REBYU,
"GORUDEN DEIZU")
Costumes
1997
Silk and wool
Takarazuka Revue Company

This all-female musical revue and opera
company established in 1913 now has four
troupes performing constantly. These
costumes for male and female roles were
worn in the Grand Revue "Golden Days," at
the Takarazuka Theater (Takarazuka
Daigekijô), Takarazuka City, Hyôgo Prefecture, March-May, 1997.

7.137 DESIGN: TSUJIMURA JUSABURO
TAKARAZUKA WOMEN'S OPERA
(TAKARAZUKA SHOJO KAGEKIDAN)
Costume
1994
Silk
Takarazuka Revue Company

An actress's costume for a male role, worn
on tour, London Colosseum, 1994.

7.138 TAKARAZUKA WOMEN'S OPERA
Photograph
Takarazuka Revue Company

7.136

7.137A

7.138B

VIII. Japan in the Modern World: *Shingeki*

Japanese Fascination with Western Theater: First Experiments

8.1 Kawanabe Kyosai
Actors as the One Hundred Demons
Curtain for the Shintomi Theater
1880
Ink and color on cotton
401 x 1704 cm
Tsubouchi Memorial Theatre Museum,
Waseda University

Supposedly painted in four hours by one of the Meiji period's greatest artists, this striking theater curtain mixes traditional Japanese folklore imagery of a night procession of demons with portraits of the leading actors of the time, identified both by their faces and by their crests.

8.2 A-B Photographs from
A) "Onna Keizu" (The Female Line) and
B) "White Threads of the Waterfall"
Early 20th c.
Tsubouchi Memorial Theatre Museum,
Waseda University

Early 20th-century photographs of *shimpa* ("New School") drama, an experimental form which dealt with contemporary Japanese life but retained many conventions from *kabuki*. The play, "White Threads of the Waterfall," was written by the leading romantic novelist and dramatist of the period, Izumi Kyōka.

8.3 Photograph from "John Gabriel Borkman"
1909 (November)
Tsubouchi Memorial Theatre Museum,
Waseda University

Shingeki (literally, "new theater") represented the first serious attempt to create a modern theater in Japan. One of the leaders of this movement, Osanai Kaoru, began the productions of his Free Theater in 1909 with a staging of "John Gabriel Borkman" by the Norwegian playwright Henrik Ibsen (1828-1906), in a translation by the distinguished novelist Mori Ōgai.

8.4 Photograph from "The Lower Depths"
1913 (October)
Tsubouchi Memorial Theatre Museum,
Waseda University

Osanai Kaoru had a particular success with his production of "The Lower Depths" by Russian playwright Maxim Gorky (1868-1936), first produced in 1910, then revived (as seen in this photograph) in 1913.

8.5 Photograph from "Hamlet"
1911 (May)
© Bungei Kyōkai; in the collection of the Tsubouchi Memorial Theatre Museum,
Waseda University

Tsubouchi Shōyō (1859-1935), Japan's first great translator of Shakespeare, began his company, which he called the Literary Society, in 1905. The photograph records a highly successful production of "Hamlet" in 1911. Ophelia (center) was played by Matsui Sumako, the company's leading actress.

8.6 Photograph from "A Doll's House"
1911 (November)
© Bungei Kyōkai; in the collection of the Tsubouchi Memorial Theatre Museum,
Waseda University

Tsubouchi Shōyō shared Osanai Kaoru's passion for Henrik Ibsen. Here, Matsui Sumako plays Nora in the 1911 production of "A Doll's House" by the Literary Society.

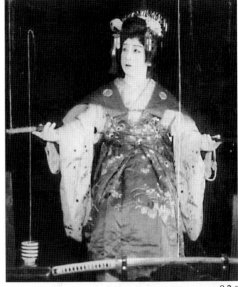

8.2 B

8.6

8.1

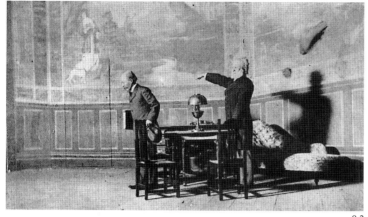

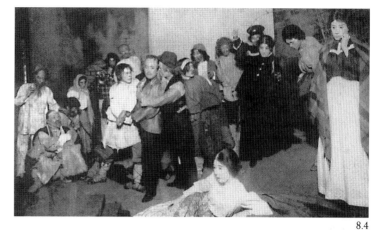

8.3

8.4

8.5

8.7

8.9

8.10

INTERWAR ACCOMPLISHMENTS

8.7 PHOTOGRAPH FROM "THE LOWER DEPTHS"
Photographer: Sakamoto Manhichi
1928 (May)
© Sakamoto Akiyoshi; in the collection of the Tsubouchi Memorial Theatre Museum, Waseda University

The final and most important phase of Osanai's attempts to create a modern Japanese theater were carried out in a new theater called the Tsukiji Little Theater. It was built especially for his company in 1924, after the Tokyo earthquake of 1923. In 1928, Osanai again directed his company in a revival of "The Lower Depths," one of his great early successes.

8.8 POSTER FOR "THE LOWER DEPTHS"
1928
Paper, cloth
59 x 43.5 cm.
Tsubouchi Memorial Theatre Museum, Waseda University

This poster advertises the 1928 production of Gorky's "The Lower Depths" by Osanai's company.

8.9 PHOTOGRAPH FROM "THE BLUE BIRD"
Photographer: Sakamoto Manhichi
1925 (December)
© Sakamoto Akiyoshi; in the collection of the Tsubouchi Memorial Theatre Museum, Waseda University

The 1925 staging by the Tsukiji Little Theater of that perennially popular theatrical fantasy by the Belgian playwright Maurice

8.8

Maeterlinck (1862-1949), "The Blue Bird," is now perhaps best remembered as the basis for a Shirley Temple film.

8.10 PHOTOGRAPH FROM "ROAR CHINA!"
Photographer: Sakamoto Manhichi
1931 (June)
© Sakamoto Akiyoshi; in the collection of the Tsubouchi Memorial Theatre Museum, Waseda University

"Roar China!," an anti-colonialist play by the Soviet playwright Sergei Tretyakov (1829-1939), was first produced in Moscow in 1926. It was soon mounted around the world-in New York, London, and, in 1931, in Tokyo by the Tsukiji Little Theater.

8.11 POSTER FOR "THE HERMIT"
1926
Paper, cloth
79 x 58 cm
Tsubouchi Memorial Theatre Museum, Waseda University

Osanai's first production of a modern Japanese play at the Tsukiji Little Theater, in 1926, was "The Hermit" (En no Gyôja) by Tsubouchi Shôyô, who had given up his own theatrical activities more than a decade before. The drama, dealing with the life of an ancient, charismatic Buddhist priest, was soon regarded as a masterpiece of modern Japanese drama.

8.12 POSTER FOR IBSEN'S "GHOSTS"
1928
Paper, cloth
60.3 x 44.5 cm
Tsubouchi Memorial Theatre Museum, Waseda University

One of Ibsen's strongest works, "Ghosts" received a powerful production by Osanai's company in 1925. The poster dates from the revival of this staging in 1928.

8.13 PHOTOGRAPH FROM "OPENING THE EYES OF THE BUDDHA"
Photographer: Sakamoto Manhichi
1940 (February)
© Sakamoto Akiyoshi; in the collection of the Tsubouchi Memorial Theatre Museum, Waseda University

With Osanai's death in 1928, the Tsukiji Little Theater eventually split into rival troupes. After several years, an important group to emerge was the New Cooperative Troupe. In 1940, the company produced "Opening the Eyes of the Buddha," an historical drama by Nagata Hideo, which impressed audiences with its spectacular stagecraft.

8.14 POSTER FOR "OPENING THE EYES OF THE BUDDHA"
1940
Paper, cloth
81.7 x 59 cm
Tsubouchi Memorial Theatre Museum, Waseda University

8.15 PHOTOGRAPH OF A "FROM MORN TO MIDNIGHT" STAGE DESIGN
Photographer: Sakamoto Manhichi
1924 (December)
© Sakamoto Akiyoshi; in the collection of the Tsubouchi Memorial Theatre Museum, Waseda University

A stage design by Murayama Tomoyoshi, the progressive playwright, director, and designer, for the 1924 production of German playwright Georg Kaiser's (1878-1945) "From Morn to Midnight" by the Tsukiji Little Theater Company. The title of the play and the Latin motif were painted directly on the stageset.

8.16 PHOTOGRAPH FROM "USHIYAMA HOTEL"
1954
© Bungaku-za; in the collection of the Tsubouchi Memorial Theatre Museum, Waseda University
In 1932, the Tsukiji Little Theater gave the first production of "Ushiyama Hotel" by Kishida Kunio, a leading playwright who lived in France for several years after World War I and studied with the famed Parisian director Jacques Copeau (1879-1949). Set in Vietnam, the play deals with the nihilistic lives of expatriated Japanese living there. The photograph was taken at a 1954 revival by the Literary Theatre troupe.

8.17 COPY OF PHOTOGRAPH FROM "EAST IS EAST"
1932
Owner: Shochiku Co., Ltd., Tokyo; in the collection of the Tsubouchi Memorial Theatre Museum, Waseda University

A photograph of a delightful comedy "East is East," written by a friend and colleague of Kishida Kunio, Iwata Toyoo. The play, which appropriates some techniques of traditional kyôgen, deals with the marriage of a Chinese man to a Japanese woman. This photograph shows an October 1952 performance.

8.18 PHOTOGRAPH FROM "ÔDERA SCHOOL"
Photographer: Sakamoto Manhichi
1928 (November)
© Sakamoto Akiyoshi; in the collection of the Tsubouchi Memorial Theatre Museum, Waseda University

A scene from the play "Ôdera School" by Kubota Mantarô, a writer known for his attempt to capture the older traditions of Japan, now quickly disappearing in the 1920s and after. The play was first staged by the Tsukiji Little Theater in 1928 and concerns the demise of a small, old-fashioned private school.

8.19 STAGE MODEL BY ITO KISAKU FOR "BEFORE THE DAWN"
This reproduction by the Haiyû-za Stage Art Department
1938
Wood, paper
60 x 30 x 30 cm
Tokyo Metropolitan Museum of Modern Japanese Literature

Itô Kisaku, the brother of the talented dancer Itô Michio, whose work is mentioned in Section I, was one of the leading set designers in Japan during his long career. Here is a model for a 1938 production of a play by Murayama Tomoyoshi based on the epic novel by Shimazaki Tôson of Japan's early modernization, Before the Dawn. It was performed at the Tsukiji Shô Theater.

8.20 STAGE DRAWING BY ITO KISAKU FOR "BEFORE THE DAWN"
1937
Paper
26 x 73 cm
Itô Hiroko

JAPAN'S LONG FASCINATION WITH SHAKESPEARE

8.21 FLYER FOR A PRODUCTION OF "THE MERCHANT OF VENICE"
1885
Paper
133 x 66.2 cm
Tsubouchi Memorial Theatre Museum, Waseda University

A flyer representing the program for the Ebisu Theater in Osaka for May 1885, which includes a kabuki adaption of Shakespeare's "The Merchant of Venice," here entitled "Cherry Blossom Time and Money Makes the World Go Around." Sketches of various scenes from the production are included as well.

8.22A-C THREE SCENES FROM "JULIUS CAESAR"
Three postcards
1913
Paper
10.2 x 15.2 cm
Theaterwissenschaftliche Sammlung, Universität zu Köln, Cologne, Germany

8.13

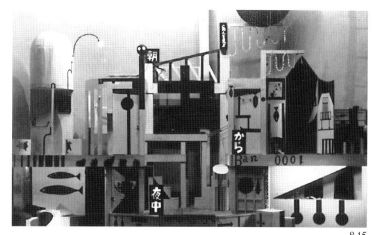

8.15

8.16

8.17

8.18

8.20

8.22B

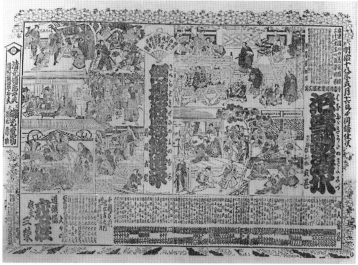

8.21

As a result of their "scancalous romance," the two leading performers in Tsubouchi Shôyô's Literary Society, Shimamura Hôgetsu and Matsui Sumako, left the company and began their own troupe. Shôyô, profoundly disheartened, managed to mount a final production in 1913 at the Imperial Theatre of Shakespeare's "Julius Caesar." The title role was undertaken by Katô Seiichi, and Caesar's wife was played by Ôura Masako. The company was then dissolved.

8.23 MANUSCRIPT IN JAPANESE OF "HAMLET"
With notes by translator (Tsubouchi Shôyô)
1933
Paper
24 x 502 cm
Tsubouchi Memorial Theatre Museum, Waseda University

The script was prepared by Tsubouchi Shôyô for a public reading of "Hamlet" in 1933. His notes accompany Act III, Scene I, which includes the famous soliloquy "To be, or not to be."

8.24 PHOTOGRAPH OF SENDA KOREYA AS HAMLET
Photographer: Sakamoto Manhichi
1938 (May)
© Sakamoto Akiyoshi; in the collection of the Tsubouchi Memorial Theatre Museum, Waseda University

Senda Koreya began his long and distinguished career as an actor and was to become a celebrated director in the postwar period. The photograph shows his assumption of the role of Hamlet in a 1938 production by the Tsukiji Little Theater.

8.25 PHOTOGRAPH OF THE FUKUDA TSUNEARI PRODUCTION OF "HAMLET"
1956 (January)
Owner: Bungaku-za; in the collection of the Tsubouchi Memorial Theatre Museum, Waseda University

Fukuda Tsuneari, the critic, director, writer, and translator, mounted many important productions of Shakespeare in the postwar period. In this photograph, the protagonist (left) is played by Akutagawa Hiroshi, son of the famous novelist Akutagawa Ryûnosuke, author of Rashômon, later made into a classic film by Kurosawa Akira. Gertrude is Sugimura Haruko, a major star in this period.

8.26 STAGESET MODEL BY KONO KUNIO for the production of "Hamlet" by Fukuda Tsuneari
1956

Wood, plaster
56.5 x 54.6 x 42.8 cm
Tsubouchi Memorial Theatre Museum, Waseda University

8.27 PHOTOGRAPH FROM "AKECHI MITSUHIDE"
1969 (March, at Teikoku Theater)
© Toho Co., Ltd.; in the collection of the Tsubouchi Memorial Theatre Museum, Waseda University

In 1969, Fukuda Tsuneari's staged his "Akechi Mitsuhide," an experimental adaption of Shakespeare's "Macbeth," set in Japan, and with the medieval warlord Akechi Mitsuhide as protagonist. The role was performed by the noted *kabuki* actor Matsumoto Kôshirô VIII (right). His son, Matsumoto Kôshirô, has become a major star in both Western drama and classic *kabuki*. Akechi Mitsuhide's wife was performed by Otowa Nobuko.

8.28 PHOTOGRAPH OF FUKUDA'S PRODUCTION OF "RICHARD III"
1964 (March, at Nissei Theater)
© Nissei Theater, Tokyo; in the collection of the Tsubouchi Memorial Theatre Museum, Waseda University

In Fukuda's experimental production of this Shakespearean play, he put the accomplished *kabuki* actor Nakamura Kanzaburô XIII in the title role and used regular *shingeki* actors for the rest of the cast.

8.29 PHOTOGRAPH OF ASARI KEITA'S PRODUCTION OF "OTHELLO"
1969 (April, at Nissei Theater)
© Gekidan Shiki; in the collection of the Tsubouchi Memorial Theatre Museum, Waseda University

Another well-known *kabuki* actor appeared in this production of Shakepeare's "Othello." Onoe Shôroku II plays Othello; Kusaka Takeshi (right), a *shingeki* actor, plays Iago.

8.30 DRAWING OF THE STAGE MODEL BY TAKEDA KAZURO FOR "ROMEO AND JULIET"
1971
Paper
77.7 x 90 cm
Tsubouchi Memorial Theatre Museum, Waseda University

In 1971, three well-known Japanese stage designers participated in a competition held in Prague by designing a set for Shakespeare's "Romeo and Juliet." Takeda's version emphasized the play's concerns with sexuality.

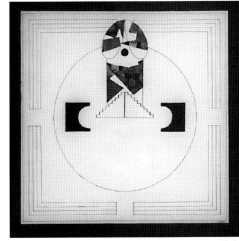
8.30

8.37

8.38

8.31 DRAWING OF THE STAGE MODEL BY
ASAKURA SETSU FOR "ROMEO AND JULIET"
1971
Paper
78 x 90 cm
Tsubouchi Memorial Theatre Museum,
Waseda University

Asakura Setsu, the second artist who contributed to the "Romeo and Juliet" project,
chose to project an atmosphere of simplicity.

8.32 A-B DRAWINGS OF A STAGE MODEL BY
KANAMORI KAORU FOR "ROMEO AND JULIET"
1971
Paper
78 x 90 cm
Tsubouchi Memorial Theatre Museum,
Waseda University

Kanamori Kaoru, the third of the designers
in the "Romeo and Juliet" project, revealed a
highly mobile conceptualization in his
design.

8.33 PHOTOGRAPH OF SENDA KOREYA'S
PRODUCTION OF "HAMLET"
1965 (February)
© Haiyû-za; in the collection of the
Tsubouchi Memorial Theatre Museum,
Waseda University

In this famous production directed by Senda
Koreya for the Actor's Theater, the protagonist was played by Nakadai Tatsuya, well-
known in the West for his roles in films
directed by Kurosawa Akira.

8.34 PHOTOGRAPH OF NINAGAWA
YUKIO'S PRODUCTION OF "MACBETH"
1980 (February)
© Toho Co., Ltd.; in the collection of the
Tsubouchi Memorial Theatre Museum,
Waseda University

A celebrated production of Shakespeare's
"Macbeth" set in medieval Japan. The tour-
ing production was later highly acclaimed in
Great Britain and the United States.

8.35 PHOTOGRAPH OF NODA HIDEKI'S
PRODUCTION OF "RICHARD III"
1990 (October)
© Yume no Yûminsha; in the collection of
the Tsubouchi Memorial Theatre Museum,
Waseda University

A fanciful adaption of Shakespeare's play by
the young writer, director, and actor Noda
Hideki, in which the central character
Richard is a master of flower arrangement,
whose ambition is to control a leading
school of this traditional art. Noda himself,

8.34

8.35

8.39

8.40

8.41

8.45 C/1

8.45 C/2

who took part in the production, is second from the left. This was the thirty-ninth production of the Yume no Yûminsha troupe.

8.36 POSTER FOR NODA HIDEKI'S PRODUCTION OF "RICHARD III"
1990
Paper
102.9 x 72.6 cm
Tsubouchi Memorial Theatre Museum, Waseda University

The poster for "Richard III" also features Noda himself, who maintains an enormous personal following even today.

8.37 POSTER FOR THE FIRST PRODUCTION OF "KANADEHON HAMLET"
1992
Paper
73 x 52.1 cm
Tsutsumi Harue

The poster for the original Tokyo production of "Kanadehon Hamlet," a delightful and touching play which recreates in a fanciful way the first attempt to produce Shakespeare's "Hamlet" in Japan in the late 19th century. The actors, used to performing in *kabuki*, often intersperse speeches and gestures from "Kanadehon Chushingura," the greatest of the traditional plays, shown in section VII of the exhibition.

8.38 SCRIPT FOR "HAMLET" IN KABUKI STYLE
Stage property
1992
Paper
24.1 x 17.8 x 1.3 cm
Tsutsumi Harue

An amusing prop for the play "Kanadehon Hamlet," a mockup of the script of "Hamlet" in *kabuki*-style lettering. The prop was also used in the 1997 production of the play at LaMaMa E.T.C. in New York, where it garnered excellent reviews.

POSTWAR DEVELOPMENTS

8.39 PHOTOGRAPH FROM "THE LIFE OF A WOMAN"
Photographer: Yôkichi Kojima
1954 (January)

© Bungaku-za; in the collection of the Tsubouchi Memorial Theatre Museum, Waseda University

Sugimura Haruko was an accomplished actress who played a variety of important roles in her long career. Here she enacts the heroine of the 1945 play by Morimoto Kaoru, "The Life of a Woman," which chronicles the complex life of a Japanese woman who suffers various vicissitudes from social ills, economic unrest, and war. The photograph was taken at the 1954 revival of the play.

8.40 PHOTOGRAPH FROM "LET NO AMERICAN RAIN WET MY SLEEVES"
1974 (April)
© Bungaku-za; in the collection of the Tsubouchi Memorial Theatre Museum, Waseda University

Here, Sugimura performs a role in a play set in the 19th century by the eminent woman writer Ariyoshi Sawako.

8.41 PHOTOGRAPH FROM "A STREETCAR NAMED DESIRE"
1969 (July)
© Bungaku-za; in the collection of the Tsubouchi Memorial Theatre Museum, Waseda University

One of Sugimura Haruko's most acclaimed roles was that of Blanche in "A Streetcar Named Desire" by American playwright Tennessee Williams (1911-83).

8.42 PHOTOGRAPH FROM "THE SUBSCRIPTION LIST"
1994 (April)
Matsumoto Kôshirô Office

A number of *kabuki* actors now play roles in modern dramas. Perhaps most important among them is Matsumoto Kôshirô IX, son of Matsumoto Kôshirô VIII (see his photo in "Akechi Mitsuhide"), who performs in many styles. Here, in the role of Benkei, he performs in a traditional *kabuki* play "The Subscription List" (*Kanjinchô*).

8.43 PHOTOGRAPH FROM "KING LEAR"
1975 (July, at Nissei Theater)
© Toho Co., Ltd.; in the collection of the Tsubouchi Memorial Theatre Museum, Waseda University

8.50 A

8.45

8.56

8.55

8.58

Matsumoto Kôshirô IX is the protagonist in this production of Shakespeare's "King Lear." Zaizu Ichirô plays a joker.

8.44 PHOTOGRAPH FROM "MAN OF LA MANCHA"
1969 (April, at Teikoku Theater)
© Toho Co., Ltd.
Matsumoto Kôshirô Office

Matsumoto Kôshirô IX achieved one of his great successes in the internationally popular musical about Don Quixote, "Man of La Mancha." He performed the role both in Japan and (in English) on Broadway.

8.45 PHOTOGRAPH FROM "EVENING CRANE"
1950 (October)
© Yamamoto Yasuenokai; in the collection of the Tsubouchi Memorial Theatre Museum, Waseda University

"Evening Crane," by the important postwar dramatist Kinoshita Junji, is based on a Japanese folktale about a crane who transforms herself into a woman. One of the most popular of postwar plays, it has been transformed into both an opera and an adaption using traditional *nô* and *kyôgen* techniques. In

this photograph, Yamamoto Yasue, who created the role, plays the woman. Her husband is Kuwayama Shôichi.

8.46 PHOTOGRAPH FROM "EVENING CRANE"
1969 (January)
© Yamamoto Yasuenokai; in the collection of the Tsubouchi Memorial Theatre Museum, Waseda University

Here Yamamoto Yasue, who continued to perform the role of the woman in "Evening Crane" during her long and successful career, plays opposite Uno Jûkichi, a founding member and leading actor of the People's Theater.

8.47 PHOTOGRAPH FROM "EVENING CRANE"
1954 (November)
© Shochiku Co., Ltd.; in the collection of the Tsubouchi Memorial Theatre Museum, Waseda University

This version of "Evening Crane" used traditional styles of *nô* and *kyôgen* performance. In this photograph, the crane/woman wears the mask, and the *kyôgen* actor plays her husband.

8.48 PHOTOGRAPH FROM "THE CHERRY ORCHARD"
1950 (January)
© Haiyû-za; in the collection of the Tsubouchi Memorial Theatre Museum, Waseda University

Senda Koreya, the head of the Actor's Theater, which he formed at the end of the war, continued to champion great plays from the European repertory. Here is his 1950 production of Chekhov's "The Cherry Orchard."

8.49 PHOTOGRAPH FROM "MOTHER COURAGE"
1966
© Haiyû-za; in the collection of the Tsubouchi Memorial Theatre Museum, Waseda University

Senda's continuing enthusiasm for the plays of Bertolt Brecht (1898-1956) produced a number of celebrated productions of his major plays in postwar Japan. This photograph chronicles Senda's highly successful mounting in 1966 of "Mother Courage."

8.60

8.62

8.50 TAKIZAWA OSAMU, UNO JUKICHI, AND OTHERS
Self-portraits by actors appearing in "The Lower Depths"
1960
Color on paper
37 x 126 cm
Aitani Yoshiko

During the tour of the successful 1960 production of Gorky's "The Lower Depths" by the People's Theater, the cast members drew self-portraits, signed them, and presented the drawing to a bar in Kyoto that was a well-known haunt for *shingeki* performers and artists.

8.51 PHOTOGRAPH FROM "ROKUMEIKAN"
1963 (October)
© Shochiku Co., Ltd.; in the collection of the Tsubouchi Memorial Theatre Museum, Waseda University

The first dramatist to build an international reputation was the novelist and playwright Mishima Yukio. His 1956 melodrama "Rokumeikan" (which might be translated as "Deer Horn Hall") is an elaborate melodrama set in the early Meiji period. The leading role, originally performed by Sumigura Haruko (see her photo as Blanche in "A Streetcar Named Desire") is performed in this photograph of the 1963 revival by the famous *shimpa* actress Mizutani Yaeko.

8.52 PHOTOGRAPH FROM "MADAME DE SADE"
1965 (November)
© NLT; in the collection of the Tsubouchi Memorial Theatre Museum, Waseda University

Mishima's 1965 play, "Madame de Sade," which concerns the wife of the celebrated Marquis, has an all-female cast. It was written as a pastiche of a French rococo

drama. The play, translated into English by Donald Keene, has enjoyed a number of productions in America and Europe, including one by the Royal Dramatic Theatre of Stockholm, directed by Ingmar Bergman, as described in Section I of the exhibition.

8.53 PHOTOGRAPH FROM "LADY AOI"
1956 (July)
© Bungaku-za; in the collection of the Tsubouchi Memorial Theatre Museum, Waseda University

Mishima also adapted several traditional *nô* plays for modern performers. One of them, "Lady Aoi," is a *nô* play adapted from an incident in Lady Murasaki's great 11th-century novel *The Tale of Genji*. Mishima transformed the incident into a modern psychological drama with ample doses of Freudianism. Translated by Donald Keene, this and others of Mishima's modern *nô* plays have received many Western productions.

8.54 POSTER FOR "ZEAMI"
1963
Paper
73 x 51.5 cm
Tsubouchi Memorial Theatre Museum, Waseda University

Yamazaki Masakazu, widely known as a critic, is also highly respected as a dramatist. His early success "Zeami" is loosely based on the life of the great medieval *nô* master. The poster is for the first production.

8.55 PHOTOGRAPH FROM "ZEAMI"
1963 (September)
© Haiyû-za; in the collection of the Tsubouchi Memorial Theatre Museum, Waseda University

Senda Koreya (founder of the Actor's Theater) both directed and played the title role in the original 1963 production of Yamazaki

Masakazu's "Zeami." The play has been translated into English and has been produced abroad.

8.56 PHOTOGRAPH FROM "ZEAMI"
1988 (November, at Ginza Sezan Theater)
© Shochiku Co., Ltd.
Matsumoto Kôshirô Office

Yamazaki's "Zeami" was revived in 1987, this time with the versatile *kabuki* actor Matsumoto Kôshirô IX in the title role. (See photos of him in "King Lear" and "The Subscription List.")

8.57 PHOTOGRAPH FROM "ZEAMI"
1991 (September, at Aoyama Theater)
Matsumoto Kôshirô Office

In 1991, "Zeami" was transformed into a successful musical, again with Matsumoto Kôshirô, now a veteran of "Man of La Mancha," in the leading role.

8.58 PHOTOGRAPH FROM "GREAT DOCTOR YABUHARA"
1973 (July)
© Gogatsu-sha; offered by Theatro; in the collection of the Tsubouchi Memorial Theatre Museum, Waseda University

Inoue Hisashi is an enormously gifted and popular comic novelist and playwright. His 1973 drama, "The Great Doctor Yabuhara" is a black comedy set in the Tokugawa period and concerns a blind man who commits a series of murders in order to attain fame and wealth. The production was later brought to Edinburgh and New York.

8.59 PHOTOGRAPH FROM "MAKEUP"
Photographer: Yakô Masahiko
1982 (November)
© Chijin-kai; in the collection of the Tsubouchi Memorial Theatre Museum, Waseda University

8.59

8.63

8.64

Inoue Hisashi's 1982 drama "Makeup" is a one-woman play about a woman who performs melodramas in a second-class theater company, and is a remarkable tour-de-force for its sole performer, who is from the Chijin-kai troupe. The original production travelled abroad, and an English-language production was mounted in London.

8.60 PHOTOGRAPH FROM "TANGO AT THE END OF WINTER"
1984 (April)
© Mokutô-sha; in the collection of the Tsubouchi Memorial Theatre Museum, Waseda University

Shimizu Kunio, one of the most accomplished of contemporary playwrights, often creates works of metatheater. The central character in his 1984 "Tango at the End of Winter" is an actor attempting to relive his complex past. The production was directed by Shimizu's longtime colleague Ninagawa Yukio (see photo of his "Macbeth" production). Hira Mikijirô (left) and Matsumoto Noriko, the playwright's wife, played the leading roles.

8.61 PHOTOGRAPH FROM "FRIENDS"
1974 (May)
© Abe Kôbô Studio; in the collection of the Tsubouchi Memorial Theatre Museum, Waseda University

Abe Kôbô, who attained international prominence as a novelist, was also well known and respected in Japan as a playwright. His Kafka-like "Friends," first produced in 1967, concerns the demise of a bachelor whose apartment is invaded by a group of strangers claiming to be his family. Abe himself directed the 1974 revival. Nakadai Tetsuya (see his photo as Hamlet) plays the bachelor.

8.62 PHOTOGRAPH FROM "ALICE IN WONDERLAND"
1970 (May)
© Betsuyaku Minoru, Haiyû-shô Theater; in the collection of the Tsubouchi Memorial Theatre Museum, Waseda University
The prolific playwright Betsuyaku Minoru is known for his laconic style and allegorical settings, reminiscent of Beckett and Pinter. The 1970 production of his "Alice in Wonderland" featured the performance of Betsuyaku's wife, Kusunoki Yûko (center), as Alice.

8.63 PHOTOGRAPH FROM "GONE WITH THE WIND"
1977 (August)
© Takarazuka Revue Company; in the collection of the Tsubouchi Memorial Theatre Museum, Waseda University

Musicals have become increasingly popular in Japan over the past few decades, but the all-female Takarazuka Revue Company has been a leader in this field since the 1920s. This 1977 musical version of "Gone with the Wind" used an actress specializing in male roles to play Rhett Butler, complete with moustache.

8.64 PHOTOGRAPH FROM "MY FAIR LADY"
1973 (August)
© Toho Co., Ltd.; in the collection of the Tsubouchi Memorial Theatre Museum, Waseda University

"My Fair Lady" was the first Broadway musical to receive a full-scale Japanese production. Always extremely popular, the musical has been revived several times. In this 1973 revival, the popular ex-Takarazuka Revue star Kozuki Noboru played Eliza.

IX. The Past in the Future
Explosion of the Japanese Avant-Garde

Posters in the 1960s and Early 1970s

Young talented graphic designers, such as Yokoo Tadanori, Uno Akira, and others, often made posters for new, young, ambitious performing groups in the 1960s. Their posters were both fascinating and innovative themselves. They not only drew many young people to the theaters, but also stimulated many subsequent artists who were designing posters for the avant-garde theater.

9.1 Jokyo Gekijo
Koshimaki Osen (Osen in a Petticoat)
1966
Design: Yokoo Tadanori
Silkscreen poster
105.4 x 74.6 cm
The Museum of Modern Art, New York. Gift of the designer. Photograph © 1997 The Museum of Modern Art, New York

9.2 Tenjo Sajiki
Ôyama Debuko no Hanzai (The Crime of Ôyama, the Fat)
1967
Design: Yokoo Tadanori
Poster
107 x 76 cm
Nakajima Hideo

9.3 Tenjo Sajiki
Kegawa no Marie (Marie in Fur)
1967-71
Design: Uno Akira
Poster
Sasame Hiroyuki; The Modern Theatrical Posters Collection Project

9.4 68/71 Black Tent
Ah, Nezumikozo Jirokichi (Ah, The Rat Jack, Jirokichi)
1971
Design: Hirano Kôga
Poster
The Black Tent

9.5 68/71 Black Tent
Kigeki, Abe Sada (The Comedy, Abe Sada)
1973
Design: Hirano Kôga
Poster
The Black Tent

Photographs of Buto Dancers

Bodies of great *butô* dancers are the subjects of works by photographers. The aura of dancers' bodies emitting the essence of *butô*, as conveyed in fine photographs, inspire *shôgekijô* practitioners as well as *butô* artists.

Stage Photographs of Significant Productions in Early Shogekijo Movements

Both Waseda Shôgekijô (now SCOT) and Tenkei Gekijô, disbanded in 1988 but then inherited by the leading playwright and director Ôta Shôgo, have used the Japanese body to explore what is authentically dramatic in our age. This exploration focuses more on physical than on verbal representations. These photographs are of their landmark productions in the avant-garde movement.

9.6 Waseda Shogekijo
Gekitekina-mono o Megutte I/II (On the Dramatic I/II)
1969-70
Scot

9.7A-B Tennkei Gekijo
A) Komachi Fuden (The Legend of Komachi)
1977
B) Mizu no Eki (The Water Station)
1981
Ôta Shôgo

Panel of Photographs of Tent Theaters

Tents were brought in along with the concept of itinerant troupes; they were supposed to change the corners in modern cities, which are usually under strict official control, into liberated, festive spaces. The Red Tent came first in the 1960s, followed by the Black Tent. The Purple Tent was brought in much later, at the end of the 1980s, by a group of young players who had once been members of the Red Tent.

9.8A-C A) Red Tent (Jokyo Gekijo, or the Red Tent)
B) Black Tent (The Black Tent)
C) Purple Tent (Shinjuku Ryozanpaku)

9.1

9.11 A-B

9.20B

Posters and Handbills I

Sets of posters and handbills for productions by some representative groups of the first and second generations. All materials are lent by the groups, except for the two named.

9.9 Ôta Shogo
Sarachi (The Vacant Lot)
1996

9.10 Yume no Yuminsha
Hanshin (One-half God)
1986
Noda Map

9.11 Yume no Yuminsha
Koyubi no Omoide (The Memory of the Little Finger) (Revival)
1986
Noda Map

9.12 Daisan Butai
Relayer III
1996

9.13 a-b Daisan Butai
Parade Ryodan (The Parade Brigade)
1995

9.14 a-b Daisan Erotica
a) ClichÈ
1994
b) Yotsuya Kaidan, Kaibo-shitsu (The Ghost Story at Yotsuya, The Dissection Room)
1995

9.15 a-b On-Theater Jiyu Gekijo
a) Shanghai Vance-King
1981
b) A-Ressha (The A-Train)
1989

9.16 a-b Banyu Inryoku
a) Inu Gami (The Dog God)
1996
b) Kaspar Hauser
1995

Posters and Handbills II

Sets of posters and handbills for productions by some representative groups of the new generation. All materials have been lent by the groups.

9.17 a-b The Gazira
a) The Apres-guerre
1994
b) Yami no Makuraeshi (The Pornographer in the Dark)
1995

9.18 a-b Shinjuku Ryozanpaku
a) Sennen no Kodoku (Millennium Solitude)
1988
b) Ningyo Densetsu (Legend of The Mermaids)
1990

9.19 a-b Rinkogun
a) Kamigami no Kuni no Shuto (Capital of the Country of Gods)
1993
b) Kujira no Bohyo (Grave Markers for Whales)
1994

9.20 a-b Seinendan
a) Minami e (Southward Bound)
1995
b) Tokyo Notes
1994

9.21 a-b Furen Dance
a) Sukarabe
b) Inu Hime (The Dog Princess)

Posters and Handbills III

Sets of posters and handbills for productions by some groups under female leadership. All materials have been lent by the groups.

9.22 a-b Gekidan 300
a) Sinya Tokkyu–Mezamereba Betsu no Kuni (The Midnight Express–Awaken in Another Country)
1997
b) Kaze no Furu Mori (The Wood Where the Wind Blows Downwards)
1995

9.23 a-b Nitosha
a) Papa no Democracy (Papa's Democracy)
1997
b) Toki no Monooki (The Storeroom of Time)
1994

9.24 a-b Jitensha Kinkurito
a) Haitori-Gami (The Flaypaper)
1994
b) Hoou-Cho no Hininyaku (Contraceptive Pills Prepared by the Vatican)
1994

9.25 a-b Noise
a) Nippon Cha! Cha! Cha!
1988
b) Asa, Tsumetai Mizu-de (Morning, with Cold Water)
1994

9.12

9.18 A

9.19 A

9.16A

9.22A

9.22C

9.22B

9.23A

9.26A-B KAMONEGI SHOT
A) FUJIN JAMP 2–KENKOU O IWATTE
(WOMEN'S JAMP 2–TO OUR HEALTH)
1991
B) HADAKA NO KUNI (THE NAKED
COUNTRY)
1995

POSTERS AND HANDBILLS –
THE PUPPET THEATER

Sets of posters and handbills of productions
by Yûki-za, a unique experimental group
associated with the traditional Japanese
marionette theater. The materials are offered
by Yûki-za.

9.27A-C YUKI-ZA
A) PELLÉAS AND MÉLISANDE (THE PLAY BY
MAETERLINK)
1992
B) ANOKO (THAT GIRL)
C) MIZU NO KUNI NO GULLIVER
(GULLIVER IN THE WATER COUNTRY)
1995

POSTERS AND HANDBILLS –
PERFORMANCE

Sets of posters and handbills for productions
by "performance" groups. Dumb Type and
Pappa Tarahumara, in particular, are known
throughout the world for their beautiful
stagings of images, sounds, and movements,
which appeal directly to the senses. The
materials are offered by the groups.

9.28A-B PAPPA TARAHUMARA
A) THE BUSH OF GHOSTS
1994
B) FUNE O MIRU (SHIP IN A VIEW)
1997

9.29A-B DUMB TYPE
A) pH
Design: Takatani Shiro/Dumb Type
1990-3
B) S/N
Design: Minami Takuya
1992-6

9.30 HANDBILLS

It is very usual for theatergoers to be handed
many colorful handbills at the doors of
shôgekijôs.

VIDEO TAPES

YUME NO YUMINSHA
Hanshin (One-Half God; 1986; see no. 9.10)
Koyubi no Omoide (Memory of the Little
Finger; 1986; revival; see no. 9.11)

YUKI-ZA
Anoko (That Girl; 1994; acted by puppets,
actors and slide figures; projected by old-
fashioned Japanese projectors; see no. 9.27B)
Mizu no Kuni no Gulliver (Gulliver in the
Water Country; 1995; see no. 9.27C)

PAPPA TARAHUMARA
The Bush of Ghosts (1994; see no. 9.28A)
Fune o Miru (Ship in a View; 1997; see no.
9.28B)

DUMB TYPE
pH (1990-93; see no. 9.29A)
S/N (1992-96; see no. 9.29B)

IX. THE PAST IN THE FUTURE
THE NAKEDNESS OF LIFE: *Butô*

9.31/1 ROJIN TO UMI (THE OLD MAN AND THE SEA)
1990
Dancer: Ôno Kazuo
Photographer: Helmut Steinhauser
NECO-print on *washi* (Japanese paper) and frame
129 x 111 cm
Helmut Steinhauser, Kyoto

9.31/2 KINKAN (GOLDEN CIRCLE)
1985
Sankai Juku
Photographer: Helmut Steinhauser
NECO-print on canvas and frame
316 x 269 cm
Helmut Steinhauser, Kyoto

9.31/3 HYPER DANCE
1985
Sankai Juku
Dancer: Mizuno Ritsuko
Photographer: Helmut Steinhauser
NECO-print on canvas and frame
151 x 116 cm
Helmut Steinhauser, Kyoto

9.31/4 CRYSTAL PEOPLE
1985
Byakkosha
Photographer: Helmut Steinhauser
Ektachrome
150 x 100 cm
Helmut Steinhauser, Kyoto

9.31/5 OZEN (THE TABLE)
1985
Dancer: Ôno Kazuo
Photographer: Helmut Steinhauser
Ektachrome
150 x 100 cm
Helmut Steinhauser, Kyoto

9.31/6 SLIDES AND VIDEOS, INCLUDING "THE STIFLED SCREAM" (1980)
Lender and maker: Helmut Steinhauser, Kyoto

9.32/1 DANCE EXPERIENCE NO KAI (A GATHERING OF DANCE EXPERIENCE)
1961
Hijikata Tatsumi (1928-1986)
Poster: 73 x 52 cm
Design: Kanô Mitsuo
Hijikata Tatsumi Memorial Archives (Asubesuto-kan)

9.32/2 DANCE EXPERIENCE NO KAI (A GATHERING OF DANCE EXPERIENCE)
1961
Hijikata Tatsumi
Chirashi
Design: Kanô Mitsuo
Hijikata Tatsumi Memorial Archives (Asubesuto-kan)

9.32/3 KIKEN NI TATSU NIKUTAI (BODY ON THE EDGE OF CRISIS)
Book with photographs of dance performances by Hijikata Tatsumi
25.5 x 21 cm; 100 pages
Publisher: Parco Co., Tokyo, 1987
Hijikata Tatsumi Memorial Archives (Asubesuto-kan)

9.32/4 HIJIKATA TATSUMI BUTO DAIKAN (THE HIJIKATA TATSUMI BOOK OF BUTO– THREE DECADES OF BUTO EXPERIMENT)
29.5 x 23 cm; 198 pages
Publisher: Yûshisha, Tokyo, 1993
Hijikata Tatsumi Memorial Archives (Asubesuto-kan)

9.32/5 HIJIKATA TATSUMI: BUTO TO BIJUTSU (HIJIKATA TATSUMI: BUTO AND ART)
Video
Hijikata Tatsumi Memorial Archives (Asubesuto-kan)

9.32/6 BARA IRO DANSU (ROSE-COLORED DANCE)
1965
Hijikata Tatsumi and Ôno Kazuo
Poster: 103 x 73 cm
Design: Yokoô Tadanori
Hijikata Tatsumi Memorial Archives (Asubesuto-kan)

9.32/7 NIKUTAI TO HANRAN–HIJIKATA TATSUMI TO NIHONJIN (REBELLION OF THE BODY–HIJIKATA TATSUMI AND THE JAPANESE)
1968
Poster: 105 x 74.5 cm
Photographer: Hosoe Eiko
Design: Yokoô Tadanori
Hijikata Tatsumi Memorial Archives (Asubesuto-kan)

9.33/1

9.35/5

9.28A

9.28B

9.32/8 SHIKI NO TAME NO NIJUNANABAN (TWENTY-SEVEN NIGHTS FOR FOUR SEASONS)
1972
Poster: 63 x 103.5 cm
Design: Yoshino Akirô
Hijikata Tatsumi Memorial Archives (Asubesuto-kan)

9.32/9 SHIZUKA NO IE (CALM HOUSE)
1973
Poster: 103.5 x 73 cm
Photographer: Yamazaki Hiroshi
Design: Tanaka Ikkô
Hijikata Tatsumi Memorial Archives (Asubesuto-kan)

9.32/10 650 EXPERIENCE NO KAI (650 EXPERIENCE PERFORMANCE)
1960
Chirashi: 30 x 42 cm
Design: Kanô Mitsuo
Hijikata Tatsumi Memorial Archives (Asubesuto-kan)

9.32/11 ANMA (BLIND MASSEUR)
1963
Chirashi: 49 x 49.5 cm
Design: Katsui Mitsuo
Artist: Ikeda Masuo
Hijikata Tatsumi Memorial Archives (Asubesuto-kan)

9.32/12 BARA IRO DANSU (ROSE-COLORED DANCE)
1965
Chirashi: 20 x 41.5 cm
Design: Nakanishi Natsuyuki
Hijikata Tatsumi Memorial Archives (Asubesuto-kan)

9.32/13 SHIKI NO TAME NIJUNANABAN (TWENTY-SEVEN NIGHTS FOR FOUR SEASONS)
1972
Chirashi
Photographer: Fujimori Hideo, et al.
Hijikata Tatsumi Memorial Archives (Asubesuto-kan)

9.33/1-2 TOMOE SHIZUNE & HAKUTOBO IMAGE POSTERS
1990
Location: Tamagawa River
Tomoe Shizune and Hakutôbô

9.33/3 RENYO (FAR FROM THE LOTUS)
1994
Location: New York Joyce Theater
Main Dancer: Akeno
Video
Tomoe Shizune and Hakutôbô

9.33/4 KAZE NO MANAZASHI (EYES OF THE WIND)
1991
Tomoe Shizune and Hakutôbô at Osaka Kirin Plaza
2 videos
Tomoe Shizune and Hakutôbô

9.33/5 TELEPRESENCE
1996
Tokyo-New York Multimedia collaboration of butô, bunraku, music, motion capture, and visual media.
Directed by Akeno
Guitar: Elliott Sharp
Video
Tomoe Shizune and Hakutôbô

9.33/6 KAZE NO MANAZASHI (EYES OF THE WIND)
1996
Location: Edinburgh International Festival
Chirashi
Tomoe Shizune and Hakutôbô

9.33/7 RENYO (FAR FROM THE LOTUS)
1994
Main dancer: Akeno
Location: New York Joyce Theater
Chirashi
Tomoe Shizune and Hakutôbô

9.33/8 SPECIAL CHIRASHI FOR EDINBURGH INTERNATIONAL FESTIVAL
to commemorate participation
1966
Tomoe Shizune and Hakutôbô

9.33/9 RENYO (FAR FROM THE LOTUS)
1994
Location: New York Joyce Theater
Main Dancer: Akeno
Chirashi
Tomoe Shizune and Hakutôbô

9.33/10A-B TOMOE SHIZUNE AND HAKUTOBO IMAGE POSTERS
A) Location: Miura Peninsula
1990
B) Location: Sarugashima Island
1993
Tomoe Shizune and Hakutôbô

9.33/11 SHUMU (THREADS–COSMOS–DREAMS)
1994
Image Poster for performance in Somido Hall, Tokyo
Tomoe Shizune and Hakutôbô

9.36/9B

9.36/10

9.33/12 KAZE NO YORISO ONNA (WOMAN IN THE WIND)
1989
Chirashi
Tomoe Shizune and Hakutôbô

9.33/13 KAZE NO MANAZASHI (EYES OF THE WIND)
1991
Kirin Plaza, Osaka
Chirashi
Tomoe Shizune and Hakutôbô

9.33/14 RENYO (FAR FROM THE LOTUS)
1993
Chirashi
Tokyo FM-Hall
Tomoe Shizune and Hakutôbô

9.33/15 NINGEN TO BUTO (MAN AND BUTO)
1993
Chirashi
Asian Collaboration at Kirin Plaza, Osaka
Tomoe Shizune and Hakutôbô

9.33/16 97 TELEPRESENCE
Tokyo-New York Multimedia Collaboration of *butô*, *bunraku*, music, motion capture, and visual media
Directed by Akeno
Chirashi
Tomoe Shizune and Hakutôbô

9.34 NAMERIKAWA GORO (1950-)
Video

9.35/1 YOBUTSU SHINTAN (TALE OF THE GOD PHALLUS)
1973
Dairakudakan
Poster
Design: Mochitsuki Nobuhito
Video
Dairakudakan

9.35/2 JUNI NO HIKARI SERIES (12 LIGHT SERIES)
1980
Poster
Design: Tamura Seiji
Dairakudakan

9.35/3 KAIDAN–KAIIN NO UMA (GHOST STORY–THE SUPERNATURAL, SEA-DAPPLED HORSE)
1990
Poster
Design: Yokoô Tadanori
Dairakudakan

9.35/4 KAIDAN–KAIIN NO UMA (GHOST STORY–THE SUPERNATURAL, SEA-DAPPLED HORSE)
1995
Poster and Chirashi
Design: Tanaka Noriyuki
Dairakudakan

9.35/5 UGETSU–SHOTEN SURU JIGOKU (RAIN MOON–HELL RISING TO HEAVEN)
1995
2 Posters and Chirashi
Design: Okumura Yukimasa
Dairakudakan

9.35/6 SHISHA NO SHO 96 (BOOK OF THE DEAD)
Dairakudakan
Poster and Chirashi
Design: Okumura Yukimasa
Video
Dairakudakan

9.36/1 GOTEN–SORA WO TOBU (PALACE FLYING IN THE SKY)
1993
3 Posters
1 Video
Ôno Kazuo Butô Kenkyûjo

9.36/2 HANABI NO IE NO IRIGUCHI (ENTRANCE TO THE HOUSE OF FIREWORKS)
1996
Video
Ôno Kazuo Butô Kenkyûjo

9.36/3 ÔNO KAZUO NO SEKAI (THE WORLD OF ÔNO KAZUO)
1996
Video to mark the Students' Entrance Ceremony
at Keio University
Ôno Kazuo Butô Kenkyûjo

9.36/7 ÔNO KAZUO
1997
Performance at Milan
Poster
Ôno Kazuo Butô Kenkyûjo

9.36/8 TENDO CHIDO (HEAVENLY WAYS, EARTHLY WAYS)
1996-97
Performances in Italy
Poster
Ôno Kazuo Butô Kenkyûjo

9.36/9A-C WATASHI NO OKASAN (MY MOTHER)
1981
Ôno Kazuo
2 Posters and 1 Chirashi
Ôno Kazuo Butô Kenkyûjo

9.37/1   9.38/1

9.36/10A-B LA ARGENTINA-SHO
(HOMAGE À LA ARGENTINA)
1994
Ôno Kazuo
Chirashi
Ôno Kazuo Butô Kenkyûjo

9.36/11 SUIREN (WATER LILY)
1994
Ôno Kazuo
2 Posters and 1 Chirashi
Ôno Kazuo Butô Kenkyûjo

9.36/12 KACHO FUGETSU (FLOWERS,
BIRDS, WIND AND MOON)
1996
Ôno Kazuo
2 Posters
Ôno Kazuo Butô Kenkyûjo

9.37/1 JOMON-SHO (HOMAGE TO PRE-
HISTORY)
1982
Sankai Juku
Theatre de la Ville, Paris
Poster
Photographer: Ueda Yoshihiko
Sankai Juku

9.37/2 UNETSU (THE EGG STANDS OUT
OF CURIOSITY)
1986
Sankai Juku
Theatre de la Ville, Paris
Poster
Photographer: Ueda Yoshihiko
Sankai Juku

9.37/3 SHIJIMA (THE DARKNESS CALMS
DOWN IN SPACE)
1988

Sankai Juku
Theatre de la Ville, Paris
Poster
Photographer: Ueda Yoshihiko
Sankai Juku

9.37/4 OMOTE (THE GRAZED SURFACE)
1991
Sankai Juku
Theatre de la Ville, Paris
Poster
Photographer: Ueda Yoshihiko
Sankai Juku

9.37/5 YURAGI (IN A SPACE OF PERPETUAL
MOTION)
1993
Sankai Juku
Theatre de la Ville, Paris
Poster
Photographer: Ueda Yoshihiko
Sankai Juku

BUTO PERFORMANCE ART

9.38/1 ON THE TABLE
1990
Shimoda Seiji
Poster
Video
Shimoda Seiji

9.38/2 WHAT'S NEXT?
1995
Shimoda Seiji
Poster
Video
Shimoda Seiji

9.39A-B DANCE BUTTER TOKIO
Video, Posters, Photographs
Dance Butter Tokio, Berlin

BIBLIOGRAPHY

FROM SHAMANISM TO *BUTO*: Continuity and Innovation in Japanese Theater History

Eliade, Mircea.
1961 "Recent Works on Shamanism: A Review Article," *History of Religions*, 1 (Summer): 142-186.

Fukuda Tsuneari.
1966– *Fukuda Tsuneari Hyôronshû* (Collection of Fukuda Tsuneari's Critical Essays). Tokyo: Shinchôsha.

Gotô Hajime.
1975 *Nôgaku no Kigen* (The Origin of Nôgaku). Tokyo: Mokujisha.

Hisamatsu Senichi.
1963 *The Vocabulary of Japanese Literary Aesthetics*. Tokyo: Center for East Asian Cultural Studies.

Hoff, Frank.
1978 *Song, Dance, Storytelling: Aspects of the Performing Arts in Japan*. Ithaca, N.Y.: Cornell University East Asia Papers, No. 15.

Hori Ichiro.
1983 *Folk Religion in Japan*. Chicago and London: University of Chicago Press, Midway Reprint.

Kirby, Ernest Theodore.
1975 *Ur-drama: The Origins of Theatre*. New York: New York University Press.

Kurihara, Nanako.
1996 "*Butoh*: Hijikata Tatsumi and His Dance," unpublished Ph.D. dissertation. New York University, New York.

Leims, Thomas.
1990 *Die Entstehung des Kabuki: Transkulturation Europa-Japan in 16 und 17 Jahrhundert*. (The Origins of *Kabuki*: Interculturalism Between Japan and Europe in the 16th and 17th Centuries). Leiden/New York: Brill.

Matsumura Takeo.
1954-1958 *Nihon Shinwa no Kenkyû* (Studies of Japanese Myths). 4 vols. Tokyo: Baifûkan.

Miner, Earl.
1958 *The Japanese Tradition in British and American Literature*. Princeton: Princeton University Press.

Nearman, Mark J.
1978 "Zeami's *Kyû-i*: A Pedagogical Guide for Teachers of Acting," *Monumenta Nipponica*, 33, no. 3: 299-332.

_____.
1980 "*Kyakuraika*: Zeami's Final Legacy for the Master Actor," *Monumenta Nipponica*, 35, no. 2: 153-197

_____.
1982 "*Kakyô*: Zeami's Fundamental Principles of Acting," *Monumenta Nipponica*, 38, no. 1: 51-71.

Ortolani, Benito.
1964 *Das Kabukitheater: Kulturgeschichte der Anfänge* (The *Kabuki* Theater: A Cultural History of the Origins). Tokyo: Sophia University Press.

_____.
1971 "Fukuda Tsuneari: Modernization and *Shingeki*." In *Tradition and Modernization in Japanese Culture*. Donald Shively, ed. Princeton, N.J.: Princeton University Press: 463-499.

_____.
1984 "Shamanism in the Origins of the *Nô* Theatre," *Asian Theatre Journal*, 1 (Fall): 166-190.

_____.
1995 *The Japanese Theatre: From Shamanistic Ritual to Contemporary Pluralism*. Rev. ed. Princeton: Princeton University Press.

Philippi, Donald L., trans.
1969 *Kojiki*. Princeton and Tokyo: Princeton University Press and Tokyo University Press.

Pinnington, N. J.
1994 "Strategies of Legitimation: An Approach to the Expository Writings of Komparu Zenchiku," unpublished Ph.D. dissertation, University of Cambridge, Cambridge.

Rimer, Thomas and Masakazu Yamazaki, trans.
1984 *On the Art of the Nô Drama: The Major Treatises of Zeami*. Princeton: Princeton University Press.

Savarese, Nicola.
1992 *Teatro e Spettacolo tra Oriente e Occidente* (Theater and Spectacle in the Orient and Occident). Rome/Bari: Laterza.

Thornbury, Barbara E.
1997 *The Folk Performing Arts: Traditional Culture in Contemporary Japan*. Albany: State University of New York Press.

Thornhill, Arthur H., III.
1993 *Six Circles, One Dewdrop: The Religio-Aesthetic World of Komparu Zenchiku*. Princeton: Princeton University Press.

Umehara Takeshi.
[1972] 1981 *Kakusareta Jûjika: Hôryûjiron* (The Concealed Cross: a Treatise on the Hôryû-ji Temple). Reprint. Tokyo: Shinchôbunko.

Webber, Akemi Horie.
1982 "The Essence of *Kabuki*: A Study of Folk Religious Ritual Elements in the Early *Kabuki* Theatre," unpublished Ph. D. dissertation. University of California, Berkeley.

JAPANESE THEATER IN THE WORLD

Caldwell, Helen.
1977 *Michio Ito: the Dancer and his Dances*. Berkeley and Los Angeles: University of California Press.

Chamberlain, Basil Hall.
1890 *Things Japanese*. Rutland, Vt., and Tokyo: Tuttle.

Chiba, Yoko.
1992 "Sada Yacco and Kawakami: Performers of Japonisme," *Modern Drama*, 35 (March): 35-53.

Claudel, Paul.
1937 *The Satin Slipper*. Translated from the French by Fr. John O'Connor. New York: Sheen and Ward.

1972 *Claudel on the Theater*. Miami: University of Miami Press.

Dickins, Frederick Victor, trans.
1880 *Chiushingura: or the Loyal League*. London: Allen.

Dolby, William.
1976 *A History of Chinese Drama*. New York: Barnes and Noble.

Endô Shûsaku.
1984 *The Samurai*. New York: Random House.

Eppstein, Ury.
1993 "The Stage Observed: Western Attitudes toward Japanese Theater," *Monumenta Nipponica*, 40, no. 2: 147-166.

Oida, Yoshi.
1992 *An Actor Adrift*. London: Methuen.

Richie, Donald and Miyoko Watanabe, trans.
1963 *Six Kabuki Plays*. Tokyo: Hokuseido.

Salz, Jonah.
1993 "Intercultural Pioneers: Otojiro Kawakami and Sada Yacco," Kansai University of Foreign Studies, *The Journal of Intercultural Studies*, No. 20: 25-74.

Sekine, Masaru and Christopher Murray.
1990 *Yeats and the Noh*. New York: Barnes and Noble.

Shionoya Kei.
1986 *Cyrano et les Samurai*. Paris: Publications Orientalistes de France.

Tanenaka Masahiro.
1995 *Jesuit Plays on Japan and English Recusancy*. Tokyo: Renaissance Institute of Sophia University.

Whitman, Walt.
1982 *Walt Whitman: Complete Poetry and Collected Prose*. New York: Library of America.

ANCIENT ROOTS: *Kagura* and *Minzoku Geinô*

Barth, Johannes.
1972 *Japans Schaukunst in Wandel der Zeiten* (Japanese Performing Arts in Changing Times). Wiesbaden: Steiner.

Gotô Hajime.
1987 *Chûsei Kamen no Rekishiteki* (Masks of the Middle Ages: Historic and Ethnologic Studies). Tokyo: Kinseisha.

Hoff, Frank.
1978 *Song, Dance, Storytelling: Aspects of the Performing Arts in Japan*. Ithaca, N.Y.: Cornell University East Papers, No. 15.

Honda Yasuji, Tanaka Yoshihiro, and Mimura Kôichi.
1975 *Kagura Men* (*Kagura* Masks). Tokyo: Tankôsha.

1995– *Nihon no Dentô Geinô* (Japanese Traditional Arts). *Kagura*. Vols. 1-7; *Dengaku*, vols. 8-9; *Furyû*, vols. 10-13. Tokyo: Kinseisha.

Immoos, Thomas.
1968 "Das Tanzritual der Yamabushi" (The Dance Rite of the Yamabushi). In *Mitteilungen der OAG* (Communications of the German Asiatic Society). Vol. L. Tokyo: OAG: 1-25.

_____.
1968 "Ein Ritual der Wideregeburt in den Yamabushi *Kagura*" (A Rite of Rebirth in the Yamabushi *Kagura*). In *Mitteilungen der OAG* (Communications of the German Asiatic Society). Vol. L. Tokyo: OAG. 1-25.
_____, and Fred Mayer.
1975 *Japanisches Theater* (Japanese Theater). Zurich: Orell Füssli.

Kyôto Kokuritsu Hakubutsukan, ed.
1982 *Komen* (Ancient Masks). Tokyo: Iwanami Shôten.

Ortolani, Benito.
1995 *The Japanese Theatre: From Shamanistic Ritual to Contemporary Pluralism*. Rev. ed. Princeton, N.J.: Princeton University Press.

Raz, Jacob. *Audience and Actors: A Study of Their Interaction in the Japanese Traditional Theatre*. Leiden: E. J. Brill, 1983.

Thompson, Fred.
1988 "Archaische Raumordnung im Shintô-Fest (*Matsuri*)" (Archaic Order of Space During Shinto Festivals [*Matsuri*]). In *Das Gold im Wachs* (The Gold in Wax). Elizabeth Gössmann and Günter Zobel, eds. Munich: ludicium: 81-91.

Thornbury, Barbara E.
1997 *Folk Performing Arts: Traditional Culture in Contemporary Japan*. Albany: State University of New York Press.

Zobel, Günter.
1986 "Formen des Ländlichen und Kultischen Volkstheaters in Japan" (Forms of Rural and Ritual Folkloric Performing Art in Japan). In *Nô and Kultisches Volkstheater in Japan*. Tsuruoka and Günter Zobel. Tokyo: OAG: 17-35.

_____.
1988 "Okina und Shishi" (Okina and Lions). In *Das Gold im Wachs* (The Gold in Wax). Elizabeth Gössman and Günter Zobel, eds. Munich: ludicium: 155-173.

GIGAKU AND BUGAKU

Araki, James T.
[1964] 1978 *The Ballad Drama of Medieval Japan*. Berkeley: University of California Press, 1964 Reprint: Rutland,Vt: Tuttle, 1978.

Blau, Hagen.
1966 *Sarugaku und Shushi: Beiträge zur Ausbildung dramatischer Elemente im Weltlichen und Religiösen Volkstheater der Heian-Zeit unter Besonderer Berücksichtigung seiner Sozialen Grundlagen* (Sarugaku and Shushi: Contributions to the Formation of Dramatic Elements in Secular and Religious Popular Theater of the Heian Period). Wiesbaden: Otto Harrassowitz, 1966.

Gabbert, Gunhild.
1972 *Die Masken des Bugaku. Profane Japanische Tanzmasken der Heian und Kamakura-Zeit* (The Masks of *Bugaku*: Secular Japanese Dance Masks of the Heian and Kamakura Periods). 2 vols. Wiesbaden: Otto Harrassowitz, 1972.

Garfias, Robert.
1959 *Gagaku: The Music and Dances of the Imperial Household*. New York: Theatre Arts Books, 1959.

Gotô, Hajime.
1965 *Nômenshi Kenkyû Josetsu* (Introduction to the Study of Nô Mask History). Tokyo: Meizendô Shoten, 1965.

Harich-Schneider, Eta.
1973 *A History of Japanese Music*. London: Oxford University Press, 1973.

Kleinschmidt, Peter.
1966 *Die Masken der Gigaku, der Altesten Theaterform Japans* (The Masks of *Gigaku*, the Oldest Theater Form of Japan). Wiesbaden: Otto Harrassowitz, 1966.

Nelson, Steven G.
1997 *Bugaku Hôe: A Musical Synthesis of Gagaku* (Court Music and Dance) *and Shômyô* (Buddhist Chant). New York: Japan Society, 1997.

Niizeki, Ryôzô.
1964 *Gekibungaku no Hikaku Kenkyû* (Comparative Studies in Dramatic Literature). Tokyo: Tôkyôdô, 1964.

Nishikawa, Kyôtarô.
1978 *Bugaku Masks*. Translated and adapted by Monica Bethe. Tokyo: Kôdansha.

Ortolani, Benito.
1995 *The Japanese Theatre: From Shamanistic Ritual to Contemporary Pluralism*. Rev. ed. Princeton, N.J.: Princeton University Press, 1995.

_____.
1978 *Bugaku: The Traditional Dance of the Japanese Imperial Court*. New York: Performing Arts Programs of the Asia Society. Monographs on Asian Music, Dance, and Theater in Asia, 1978.

Tanabe, Hisao.
1936 *Nihon Ongaku Kôwa* (Conversation on Japanese Music). Tokyo: Iwanami Bunko.

Togi, Masatarô.
1971 *Gagaku: Court Music and Dance*. Tokyo: Walker/Weatherhill, 1971.

Wolz, Carl.
1981 "Bugaku Today." In *Japanese Tradition: Search and Research*. Judith Mitoma Susilo, ed. Los Angeles: University of California Press, 1981: 115-124.

SNOW IN A SILVER BOWL: Nô Theater

Barth, Johannes.
1972 *Japanische Schaukunst im Wandel der Zeit* (Japanese Performing Art in Changing Times). Wiesbaden: Steiner.

Bethe, Monica, and Karen Brazell.
1978 *Nô as Performance: An Analysis of the Kuse Scene of "Yamamba."* Ithaca, N.Y.: Cornell University East Asia Papers, No. 16.

_____.
1982 *Dance in the Nô Theatre*. 3 vols. Ithaca, N.Y.: Cornell University East Asia Papers, No. 29.

Bohner, Herrmann.
1956 Nô: *Die Einzeinen Nô* (Nô: One by One). Tokyo: OAG.

De Porter, Erika.
1986 *Zeami's Talks on Sarugaku: An Annotated Translation of the "Sarugaku Dangi."* Amsterdam: J.C. Gieben.

Gellner, Winfried.
1990 *Die Kostüme des Nô-Theaters*. Vol. 6. Stuttgart: Steiner, Publication of the Asia Department of the Kunsthistorisches Institut der Universität Köln.

Gotô Hajime.
1975 and 1981 *Nôgaku no Kigen* (The Development of Nô Art). 2 vols. Tokyo: Kijisha.

_____.
1964. *Nômen-shi Kenkyû Josetsu* (The History of Nô Masks in Basic Expositions). Tokyo: Meizendô Shoten.
_____ and Hirota Ritsuko, eds.
1991 *Chûgoku Shôsû Minzoku no Kamengeki*. Tokyo: Mokujisha.

Hagemann, Carl.
1921 *Spiele der Völker. Eindrücke und Studien auf einer Weltfahrt nach Afrika und Ostasien* (Drama of the People: Impressions and Studies of a Journey to Africa and East Asia). Berlin: Fischer.

Hare, Thomas Blenham.
1986 *Zeami's Style: The Noh Plays of Zeami Motokiyo*. Stanford, Ca.: Stanford University Press, 1986.

Hoff, Frank, and Willi Flindt, trans.
1973 *The Life Structure of Nô: An English Version of Yokomichi Mario's Analysis of the Structure of Nô*. Tokyo: Concerned Theatre Japan.

Immoos, Thomas.
1986 "Das Nob als Psychodrama" (Nô as Psychodrama). In *Die Sonne Leuchtet um Mitternacht* (The Sun Shines at Midnight). Olten: Walter: 134-57.

_____, and Fred Mayer.
1975 *Japanisches Theater* (Japanese Theater). Zürich: Füssli.

Keene, Donald.
1966 Nô: *The Classical Theatre of Japan*. Tokyo and Palo Alto, Ca.: Kôdansha.

Komparu, Kunio.
1983 *The Noh Theatre: Principles and Perspectives*. New York and Tokyo: Weatherhill/Tankosha.

Nakanishi Tôru.
1985 *Nômen* (Nô Masks). Tokyo: Tamagawa Daigaku Shupanbu.

Niessen, Carl.
1958 *Handbuch der Theater-Wissenschaft*. (Handbook of Theatre Studies). Vol. I, Part 3: *Drama, Mimus und Tänze in Asien* (Drama, Mime, and Dance in Asia). Emsdetten: Lechte.

Nobori Asaji.
1954 *A Philosophy of the Japanese Noh Drama: An Excerpt from My Book*. Tokushima-shi: no publisher given (booklet).

Okano, Moriya.
1988 "Das No-Spiel un die Yushiki-Lehre" (The Nô and the Teachings of Yushiki). In *Das Gold im Wachs* (The Gold in Wax). Elizabeth Gössmann and Günter Zobel, eds. Munich: ludicium: 223-248.

O'Neill, P. G.
1958 *Early Nô Drama: Its Background, Character and Development, 1300-1450.* London: Lund Humphries.

Ortolani, Benito.
1976 *Zenchiku's Aesthetics of the Nô Theatre.* Riverdale Studies, No. 3. New York: Riverdale Center for Religious Research.

_____.
1990 "Nô." In Japan Handbuch. 3d ed. Horst Hammitzsch, ed. Wiesbaden: Steiner: 1862-1872.

Rimer, J. Thomas, and Masakazu Yamazaki, trans.
1984 *On the Art of the Nô Drama: The Major Treatises of Zeami.* Princeton: Princeton University Press.

Tamba, Akira.
1981 *The Musical Structure of Nô.* Translated by Patricia Matoréas. Tokyo: Tokai University Press.

Thornhill, Arthur H., III
1993 *Six Circles, One Dewdrop: The Religio-Aesthetic World of Komparu Zenchiku.* Princeton: Princeton University Press.

Yanagita Kunio.
1975 *Matsuri kara Sairei e/Vom Fest zur Fier* (From Festival to Celebration). Japanese-German ed. Translations and commentary by Toshiharu Nakamura, Kikuo Negishi, and Günter Zobel. Tokyo: Waseda University Press.

Zobel, Günter.
1987 *Nô Theater: Szene und Dramaturgie, Volks und Völkerkunliche Hintergründe.* (Nô Theater: Stage and Dramaturgy, Folkloric and Ethnographic Backgrounds). Tokyo: OAG.

SATIRE, PARODY, AND JOYOUS LAUGHTER: *Kyôgen*

Bakhtin, Mikhail.
1981 *The Dialogic Imagination: Four Essays.* M. Holquist, ed. Translated from the Russian by C. Emerson and M. Holquist. Austin and London: University of Texas Press.

_____.
1984(a) *Problems of Dostoevsky's Poetics.* Translated and adapted from the Russian by C. Emerson. Minneapolis: University of Minnesota Press.

_____.
1984 (b) *Rabelais and his World.* Translated from the Russian by Helene Iswolsky. Bloomington: University of Indiana Press.

Brandon, James R., ed.
1997 *Nô and Kyôgen in the Contemporary World.* Honolulu: University of Hawaii Press.

Brazell, Karen, ed.
1988 *Twelve Plays of the Noh and Kyôgen Theaters.* Ithaca, N.Y.: Cornell University East Asia Papers, No. 50.

Kenny, Don.
1968 *A Guide to Kyôgen.* Tokyo: Hinoki Shoten.

_____, trans.
1989 *The Kyôgen Book.* Tokyo: The Japan Times.

Matsumoto Shinhachirô
1970 "Kyôgen no Hassei" (The Emergence of Kyôgen). In *Kyôgen Nihon no Koten Geinô* (Kyôgen: Japanese Classical Performing Arts). Vol. 4. Geinôshi Kenkyûkai, ed. Tokyo: Heibonsha: 7-26.

McKinnon, Richard, trans.
1968 *Selected Plays of Kyôgen.* Tokyo: Uniprint.

Morley, Carolyn
1993 *Transformation, Miracles, and Mischief: The Mountain Priest Plays of Kyôgen.* Ithaca, N.Y.: Cornell University East Asia Papers, No. 62.

Okura Toraakira.
1973 "Waranbe Gusa" (Grass of Laughter). In *Kodai Chûsei Geijutsu Ron Nihon Shisô Taikei* (Ancient Middle Ages Artistic Discussions: Outline of Japanese Ideas). Tokyo: Iwanami Shoten.

Sakanishi Shio, trans.
1960 *Japanese Folk Plays: The Ink-smeared Lady and Other Kyôgen.* Rutland, Vt., and Tokyo: Tuttle.

Tsuji Zennosuke.
1919 "Azuchi Shûron no Shinsô" (True Account of Azuchi Shûron). In *Nihon Bukkyôshi Kenkyû* (Studies of Japanese Religious History). Vol. 2. Tokyo: Iwanami Shoten: 122-160.

Ueda Makoto.
1964-65 "Toraaki and his Theory of Comedy," *Journal of Aesthetics and Art Criticism,* 24: 19-25

Yoshikoshi Tatsuo and Hata Hisashi.
1982 *Kyôgen.* Translated by Don Kenny. Osaka: Hoikusha.

English-Language Video Documentaries on *Kyôgen*

Shigeyama Akira.
1996 *This is Kyôgen.* Translated by Jonah Salz. Kyoto: Akira Shigeyama International. Projects.

_____.
1996 *Busu* ("Poison Sugar"). Translated by Jonah Salz. Kyoto: Akira Shigeyama International Projects)

MARGINS BETWEEN THE REAL AND UNREAL: *Bunraku*

Adachi, Barbara.
1978 *The Voices and Hands of Bunraku.* Tokyo: Kôdansha.

_____.
1985 *Backstage at Bunraku.* Tokyo: Kôdansha.

Barthes, Roland.
1970 *Empire of Signs.* Translated from the French by Richard Howard. New York: Hill and Wang.

_____.
1977 *Image, Music, Text.* Translated from the French by Stephen Heath. London: Fontana.

Brandon, James R., trans.
1975 *Kabuki: Five Classic Plays.* Cambridge, Ma.: Harvard University Press.

_____, ed.
1982 *Chûshingura: Studies in Kabuki and the Puppet Theatre.* Honolulu: University of Hawaii Press.

Copeland, Rebecca.
1992 *The Sound of the Wind: the Life and Works of Uno Chiyo.* London: Peter Owen.

Dunn, Charles J.
1966 *Early Japanese Puppet Drama.* London: Luzac.

Gerstle, C. Andrew.
1986 *Circles of Fantasy: Convention in the Plays of Chikamatsu.* Cambridge, Ma.: Harvard University Press.

_____.
1995 "Amateurs and the Theater: The So-called Demented Art of *Gidayû*," *Senri Ethnological Studies,* 40: 37-57.

_____.
1996 "Hero as Murderer in Chikamatsu," *Monumenta Nipponica,* 51, no. 3 (Autumn): 317-356.

_____. "Heroic Honor: Chikamatsu and the Samurai Ideal," *Harvard Journal of Asiatic Studies.* (forthcoming)

_____, Kiyoshi Inobe, and William P. Malm.
1990 *Theater as Music: The Bunraku Play, "Mt. Imo and Mt. Se: an Exemplary Tale of Womanly Virtue."* Ann Arbor: Center for Japanese Studies.

Jones, Stanleigh H. Jr., trans.
1985 *Sugawara and the Secrets of Calligraphy.* New York: Columbia University Press.

_____, trans.
1993 *Yoshitsune and the Thousand Cherry Trees.* New York: Columbia University Press.

Keene, Donald, ed.
1956 *Anthology of Japanese Literature: Earliest Era to Mid-nineteenth Century.* Tokyo: Tuttle.

_____, trans.
1961 *Major Plays of Chikamatsu.* New York: Columbia University Press.

_____.
1965 Bunraku: *The Art of the Japanese Puppet Theater.* Tokyo: Kôdansha.

_____, trans.
1971 Chûshingura: *The Treasury of Loyal Retainers.* New York: Columbia University Press.

Kume, Soshichi.
1979 *Ningyôshi Tenguya Kyûkichi Geidan* (Artistic Commentaries of Puppet Master Tenguya Kyûkichi). Tokyo: Soshisha.

Nihon Shomin Bunka Shiryô Shûsei (Collection of Japanese Cultural Resources).
1975 *Ningyô Jôruri.* Vol. 7. Tokyo: San'ichi Shobo.

Shuzui, Kenji.
1959 *Chikamatsu Jôrurishû II* (Collection of Chikamatsu's Works, II). Tokyo: Iwanami Shoten.

Uchida, Sumiko.
1987 *Bunraku Ningyôshi Ôe Minosuke* (Puppet Master Ôe Minosuke) Tokyo: Kindai Bungeisha.

Uno, Chiyo.
1943 *Ningyôshi Tenguya Kyûkichi* (Puppet Master Tenguya Kyûkichi). Tokyo: Buntaisha.

THE ACTOR'S WORLD: *Kabuki*

Araki Chikashi, ed.
1992 *Kabuki Kaigai no Kiroku* (Record of Foreign Tours of Kabuki). Tokyo: Shôchiku Kabushiki-gaisha.

Ariyoshi Sawako.
1994 Kabuki *Dancer: A Novel of the Woman Who Founded Kabuki.* Translated by James R. Brandon. Tokyo: Kôdansha.

Blumner, Holly A., et al., eds.
1995 *101 Years of Kabuki In Hawai'i.* Honolulu: Department of Theatre and Dance, University of Hawaii at Manoa.

Brandon, James R., trans.
1975 Kabuki: *Five Classic Plays*. Cambridge, Ma.: Harvard University Press.

Doi Tadao, Morita Takeshi, and Chonan Minoru, eds. and trans.
1980 *Hoyaku Nippo Jisho* (Japanese-Portuguese Dictionary). Tokyo: Iwanami Shoten.

Dunn, Charles J. and Bunzô Torigoe, trans.
1969 *The Actors' Analects*. Tokyo: Tokyo University Press.

Ernst, Earle.
1974 *The Kabuki Theatre*. 2d ed. Honolulu: University of Hawaii Press.

Gunji Masakatsu.
1970 Kabuki. Translated by John Bester. Palo Alto, Ca.: Kôdansha.

Leiter, Samuel L., tr. and comm.
1979 *The Art of Kabuki: Famous Plays in Performance*. Berkeley: University of California Press.

_____
1991 "'Kumagai's Battle Camp': Form and Tradition in *Kabuki* Acting." *Asian Theatre Journal*, 8 (Spring): 1-34.

_____.
1997 "The Kanamaru-za: Japan's Oldest *Kabuki* Theatre." *Asian Theatre Journal*, 14 (Spring): 56-92.

_____
1997 *New Kabuki Encyclopedia: A Revised Adaptation of "Kabuki Jiten."* Westport, Conn.: Greenwood.

Malm, William P.
1963 Nagauta: *The Heart of Kabuki Music*. Rutland, Vt.: Tuttle

Moriya Takeshi.
1988 *Mura Shibai* (Village Theaters). Tokyo: Heibonsha.

Moriya Takeshi.
1985 *Kinsei Geinô Kôgyôshi no Kenkyû* (Study of Pre-Modern Theatrical Production).Tokyo: Kobundo.

Nakamura Matazô.
1990 Kabuki *Backstage, Onstage: An Actor's Life*. Tokyo: Kôdansha.

Nyûgatei Ganyû (Namiki Shôzô II).
1972 *Sakusha Shikihô Kezairoku* (Rules for Playwriting: Dramatic Gems for the Neophyte). In *Nihon Shiso Taikei 61, Kinsei Geidôron* (Compilation of Japanese Thought 61, Premodern Theories of Art). Nishiyama Matsunosuke, ed. Tokyo: Iwanami Shoten.

Saito Makoto, trans.
1977 *Edo Sanpu Ryôkô Nikki* (Visiting Edo, a Travel Diary). Toyo Bunko 303. Tokyo: Heibonsha.

Shaver, Ruth.
1966 Kabuki *Costumes*. Rutland, Vt.: Tuttle.

Suda Atsuo.
1957 *Nihon Gekijôshi no Kenkyû* (A Study of the History of Japanese Theaters). Tokyo: Sagami Shobô.

Thornbury, Barbara E.
1982 *Sukeroku's Double Identity: The Dramatic Structure of Edo Kabuki*. Ann Arbor: University of Michigan Press.

Tsunoda Ichirô, ed.
1971 *Noson Butai no Sogoteki Kenkyû* (Collective Study of Village Stages). Tokyo: Ofusha.

JAPAN IN THE MODERN WORLD: *Shingeki*

Abe Kobo.
1969 *Friends*. Translated by Donald Keene. New York: Grove

Goodman, David, ed.
1986 *After Apocalypse: Four Japanese Plays of Hiroshima and Nagasaki*. New York: Columbia University Press.
_____, ed.
1989 *Five Plays by Kishida Kunio*. Ithaca, N.Y.: Cornell University East Asia Papers, No. 51.

Kinoshita Junji.
1979 *Between God and Man: A Judgment on War Crimes. A Play in Two Parts by Kinoshita Junji*. Translated by Eric J. Gangloff. Tokyo and Seattle: University of Tokyo Press and University of Washington Press.

Kubo Sakae.
1986 *Land of Volcanic Ash*. Translated by David Goodman. Ithaca, N.Y.: Cornell University East Asia Papers, No. 40.

Masakazu Yamazaki.
1980 *Mask and Sword: Two Plays for the Contemporary Japanese Theater by Yamazaki Masakazu*. Translated by J. Thomas Rimer. New York: Columbia University Press, 1980.

Minamitani Akimasa.
1990 "Hamlet in Japan," *Japan Quarterly*, 32 (April-June): 176-193.

Minoru Fujita and Leonard Pronko, eds.
1997 *Shakespeare East and West*. New York and London: St. Martin's.

Mishima Yukio.
1957 *Five Modern Nô Plays*. Translated by Donald Keene. New York: Alfred A. Knopf.

_____
1967 *Madame de Sade*. Translated by Donald Keene. New York: Grove Press.

Rimer, J. Thomas.
1974 *Toward a Modern Japanese Theatre: Kishida Kunio*. Princeton: Princeton University Press.

Rolf, Robert T., and John K. Gillespie, eds.
1992 *Alternative Japanese Drama: Ten Plays*. Honolulu: University of Hawaii Press.

Senda Akihiko.
1997 *The Voyage of Contemporary Japanese Theatre*. Translated by J. Thomas Rimer. Honolulu: University of Hawaii Press.

Takaya, Ted. T., ed. and trans.
1979 *Modern Japanese Drama: An Anthology*. New York: Columbia University Press.

Ueno, Yoshiko, ed.
1995 *Hamlet and Japan*. New York: AMS Press.

THE PAST IN THE FUTURE: Explosion of the Avant-garde

Gendai Engeki 60s-90s (The Contemporary Theater, 1960s-1990s).
1991 *Taiyô* (The Sun). Special issue (March).

Goodman, David.
1988 *Japanese Drama and Culture in the 1960s: The Return of the Gods*. Armonk. N.Y., and London: M. E. Sharpe.

Kara Gumi, ed.
1982 *Kara Gumi: Jôkyô Gekijô Zen Kiroku* (Kara Gumi: Complete Records of Jôkyô Gekijô). Tokyo: Parco Shuppan.

Kara Jurô.
1984 *Tokkenteki Nikutai Ron* (Essays on the Privileged Body). Tokyo: Hakusuisha.

Kazama Ken.
1984 *Engeki no Kôya kara: Atarashii Engeki no Kishutachi* (From the Wilderness of Theater: New Bearers). Tokyo: Shiritsu Shobô.

Ôta Shôgô.
1975 *Ôta Shôgô Engeki Ronshû: Hishô to Kensui* (Ôta Shôgô's Essays on Theater: Flying and Suspending). Tokyo: Shiritsu Shobô.

Senda Akihiko.
1983 *Gekiteki Renaissance: Gendai Engeki wa Katau* (Dramatic Renaissance: The New Theater Speaks: Interviews). Tokyo: Libroport.

_____.
1997 *The Voyage of Contemporary Japanese Theater*. Translated by J. Thomas Rimer. Honolulu: University of Hawaii Press.

Suzuki Tadashi.
1973 *Suzuki Tadashi Engeki Ronshû: Naikaku no Wa* (Suzuki Tadashi's Essays on Theater: The Sum of the Interior Angles). Tokyo: Shiritsu Shobô.

_____
1986 *The Way of Acting: The Theatre Writings of Tadashi Suzuki*. Translated by J. Thomas Rimer. New York: Theatre Communications Group.

Terayama Shûji.
1971 *Chika Sôzôryoku* (The Underground Imagination). Tokyo: Kôdansha.

Mainichi Graph.
1993 *Terayama Shûji: Hangyaku kara Yôshi e* (Terayama Shûji: From Revolt to Style). Special issue (October).

Waseda Shôgekijô and Kôsakusha, eds.
1977 *Gekiteki Naru Mono wo Megutte* (On Dramatics). Tokyo: Kôsakusha.

THE NAKEDNESS OF LIFE: *Butô*

Asbestos Kan.
1987 *Kiki ni Tatsu Nikutai* (Body on the Edge of Crisis). Introduction by Makoto Ooka. Tokyo: Parco Shuppan.

Amagatsu Ushio and Guy Delahaye.
1994 *Sankai Juku*. Paris: Editeur Actes Sud.

Ekoda Bungaku.
1990 "Hijikata Tatsumi: *Butô*." Special issue, 9, no. 2. (Winter).

Haerdter, Michael and Kawai, Sumie, eds.
1988 Butoh: *Die Rebellion des Körpers. Ein Tanz aus Japan.* (*Butô*: The Rebellion of the Body). 2d ed. Berlin: Alexander Verlag.

Japan Times.
1986 "Interview with Fujimoto Kazuko." July 19.

Kennedy, Gilles.
1995 "Interview with Kazuo Ôno." *Tokyo Journal* (January): 18-21.

Kisselgoff, Anna.
1984 "Japanese Avant-Garde Dance is Darkly Erotic." *New York Times*, July 15: 9-10.

Klein, Susan Blakely.
1988 *Ankoku Butô: The Premodern and Postmodern Influences on the Dance of Utter Darkness.* Ithaca, NY: Cornell University East Asia Papers, No. 49.

Kuniyoshi, Kazuko.
1985 "An Overview of the Contemporary Japanese Dance Scene." *Orientation Seminars on Japan.* No. 19.

Motofuji Akiko.
1990 *Hijikata Tatsumi to Tomo ni* (A Life with Hijikata Tatsumi). Tokyo: Chikuma Shobô.

Myerscough, Marie.
1983 "*Butô*: Bodies Beautiful and Vile." *Tokyo Journal* (October): 10.

Nakanishi, Natsuyuki, Yokoô Tadanori, Hosoe Eikô, et al.
1986 "*Bijutsu to Hijikata*" (Art and Hijikata). *Bijutsu Techô* (Monthly Art Magazine *Bijutsu Techô*). Special issue, 38, No. 561 (May): 25-79.

Oyama, Shigeo.
1985 "Amagatsu Ushio: Avant-garde Choreographer." *Japan Quarterly*, 32 (January-March): 69-72.

Richie, Donald.
"*Abangyardo,* Japan's Off, Off, Off Experimental Theater." *Winds: The Inflight Magazine of Japan Air Lines* (April): 15-17.

Takahashi Chikako.
1986 "Events Scheduled to Honor *Butoh* Originator." *Asahi Evening News*, May 2: 5

Viala, Jean, and Nourit Masson-Sekine.
1988 Butoh: *Shades of Darkness.* Tokyo: Shufunotomo.

Yamada Ippei (Yamada, Bishopp).
1992 *Dansa* (Dancer). Tokyo: Ôta Shuppan.

Yamada Kôsaku.
1992 *Kindai Buyô Hôka* (Beacon of Modern Dance). Tokyo: Ars Shuppan.

INDEX OF ESSAY SECTION

ERRATA

p. 10, line 15, left column
Miwa Susuda entered...

p. 10, line 27, left column
Mie Ishii's present fellowship at The
Metropolitan Museum of Art's Textile
Department has been made possible with
grants from the Matsushita International
Foundation and the Samuel H. Kress
Foundation Fellowship for Art Conservation.

p. 32, illus. 2.31C should be 2.31B

p. 91, entry 1.33A-B, line 11
199 should be 1919

p. 91, entry 1.34, line 1
COSTUME BY MOHRI TOMIO

p. 93, entry no. 2.9, line 5
Wood, lacquer, horsehair

p. 101, entry 2.55, line 1
ERIME; KAGURA-BUTAI-KAZURI

p. 102, illus. 2/3.1 should be 2/3.2

p. 102, entry no. 2/3.3 line 5
Wood, lacquer

p. 105, entry no. 3.16, line 5
ca. 1880

p. 106, entry no. 3.18, line 3
Chinese original

p. 106, entry no. 3.21, line 1
TWO BUGAKU DANCERS OF

p. 110, entry 3.43, after line 10
B) Woodblock print in Shukô Jishû (3.4)

p. 111, entry 3.49, after line 11
B) Woodblock print from Shukô Jishû (3.4)

p. 111, entry 3.51, after line 6
B) Illustration from Shinzei-kogaku-zu (3.1)

p. 112, entry 3.53, after 6
B) Illustration from Shinzei-kogaku-zu (3.1)

p. 117, entry no. 4.32, lines 5 & 6
1. Sculpting and painting (from left to right)
Material: a dry cedar (hinoki) block

p. 120, entry 4.44A-B, line 2
Five wigbands A) For younger women; B) for
elderly women

p. 122, entry 4.73, line 2
An example of a sea water pail...

p. 122, entry 4.74A-B, line 2
Two water pails with wave pattern

p. 126, entry no. 5.3, line 1
KYOGEN KOZU HARIMAZE BYOBU

p. 128, entry 5.14, line 8
white nô/kyôgen dandelion crest suggests
the...

p. 128, entry 5.15, line 1
NUIHAKU (KIMONO) WITH WRITING,
BLINDS, AND PAULOWNIA
DESIGN

p. 129, entry 5.17, line 8
flax

p. 129, entry 5.21A-C, lines 2 & 3
kimono: green with crysanthemum design

p. 129, entry 5.22, line 6
[no happi]

p. 130, entry 5.26, lines 7 & 8
Used in "Koshi Inori" (Praying for a Hip
Cure).

p. 130, entry no. 5.29, lines 3, 7
18th c.
[entry text incorrect; replace with] Used for
demons and characters impersonating
demons

p. 132, illustration numbers
upper left: 5.45A; upper right 5.45B; lower:
5.45C

p. 133, illustration numbers
5.47A-D should be 5.47A; 5.43 should be
5.43C

p. 144, illustrations
7.10 should be 7.14; 7.14 should be 7.13;
7.9 should be 7.10; 7.11 should be 7.9;
7.12 should be 7.11; 7.13 should be 7.12

p. 153, entry no 7.63, line 1
UTAGAWA KUNIYOSHI

p. 153, illus. 7.58 should be 7.77

p. 162, illus. 7.121 should be 7.122; 7.120
should be 7.121

p. 164, illus. 7.133 should be 7.134

p. 164, entry 7.133, line 1
DESIGNER: MOHRI TOMIO

p. 165, illus. 7.137A should be 7.137B

p. 165, entry no. 7.137, line 9
London Coliseum, 1994

p. 171, entry 8.34, line 2
"Ninagawa Macbeth"

p. 172, entry no. 8.42, lines 3 & 4
1983 (February)
© Shochiku Co., Ltd., Matsumoto Kôshirô
Office

p. 173, entry no. 8.43, line 3
Zaizu Ichirô plays the Fool.

p. 174, entry no. 8.51, line 12
performed by Sugimura Haruko

p. 174, entry no. 8.56, line 2
1987 (March)

p. 178, entry 9.28A-B and some of the video
titles
PAPPA TARAFUMARA

Plate 57: 74 should be 7.4

Plate 68: 7.134 should be 1.34

Plate 69: 7.137B should be 7.137A